VICTORIAN LABOUR HISTORY

In *Victorian Labour History: Experience, Identity and the Politics of Representation*, John Host addresses liberal, Marxist and postmodernist historiography on Victorian working people to question the special status of historical knowledge.

The central focus of this study is a debate about mid-Victorian social stability, a condition conventionally equated with popular acceptance of the social order. Host does not join the debate but takes it as his object of analysis, deconstructing the notion of stability and the analyses that purport to explain it. In particular, he takes issue with historical evidence, noting the different possibilities for meaning that it allows and the speculative character of the narratives to which it is adduced.

Host examines an extensive range of archival material to illustrate the ambiguity of the historical field, the rhetorical strategies through which the illusion of its unity is created, and the ultimately fictive quality of historical narrative. He then explores the political contingency of the works he addresses and the political consequences of representing them as true.

John Host is Associate Lecturer in History and Sociology at the Centre for Aboriginal Programmes, The University of Western Australia.

VICTORIAN LABOUR HISTORY

Experience, identity and the politics of representation

John Host

London and New York

First published 1998
by Routledge
11 New Fetter Lane, London EC4P 4EE

Simultaneously published in the USA and Canada
by Routledge
29 West 35th Street, New York, NY 10001

© 1998 John Host

Typeset in Garamond by M Rules
Printed and bound in Great Britain by
Biddles Ltd, Guildford and King's Lynn

British Library Cataloguing in Publication Data
A catalogue record for this book is available from the British Library

Library of Congress Cataloging in Publication Data
Host, John, 1946–
Victorian labour history : experience, identity and the politics of
representation / John Host.
p.   cm.
Includes bibliographical references (p.   ) and index.
ISBN 0–415–18674–9 (hardcover)
1. Working class—Great Britain—Political activity—History—19th century.
2. Labor movement—Great Britain—History—19th century. 3. Representative
government and representation—Great Britain—History—20th century.
4. Chartism—History. 5. Labour Party (Great Britain)—History. I. Title.
HD8395.H67   1998
322' .2' 094209034—dc21   98–15335
CIP
ISBN 0–415–18674–9

CONTENTS

Acknowledgements   vii

Introduction   1

1   Narratives of the past or histories of the present?   8

    Whig Interpretations and the Marxist Challenge   10

    Revisionist Approaches and the New Conservatism   34

2   Social identity and the representation of experience   60

3   Who are 'the people' in mid-Victorian labour history?   92

    Identity and Experience – the 'Standard Sample'   93

    Discordant Voices and Counter-Discourses   119

4   Narrative history and the politics of exclusion   152

    Hayden White and the Politics of Interpretation   153

    The Content of the Form in Labour History   163

    From Thatcher to Blair – Discursive Convergence in British Politics   171

    Labour History and the Politics of Thatcherism   181

    Afterword   185

    Appendix: Evidence of witnesses in the cases of William Pearce
          and James Bristol . . .   187

    Notes   199

    Bibliography   256

    Index   273

v

ACKNOWLEDGEMENTS

Before proceeding, I should like to acknowledge the assistance I have received. For the scholarship that enabled me to undertake this project, I thank the University of Western Australia and the Australian Research Council. For their generous supervision, I thank Iain Brash and Rob Stuart. They do not share my views about historical practice and their task must therefore have been difficult. I am also grateful to Richard Bosworth, who inspired my interest in historiography and found the time to comment on several chapters. Finally, I am indebted to Heather McCallum at Routledge for her editorial support; to Juanita Doorey, Ian Morris and Maureen Perkin for their moral support; and to my friend, Shawn Hollbach, for the stimulating discussions out of which my ideas have developed.

INTRODUCTION

When I began postgraduate study in 1991, I planned to write about economic and political power in nineteenth-century England. I was particularly interested in the mid-Victorian period, partly because it seemed to stand out as something of an aberration, a moment of equipoise marked off by Chartist conflict on one side and socialist agitation on the other; and partly because I was not satisfied with explanations of this postulated condition.[1] It was generally agreed that stability in the post-Chartist decades reflected popular acceptance of the prevailing social order and debate focused substantially on the extent to which this acceptance signified the consolidation of middle-class hegemony.[2] But the subtle processes of ideological conditioning outlined by Gramsci, with reference to whom the concept of hegemony was usually discussed, were not adequately explored. Most historians suggested that capitalist power relations came to be seen as inevitable, yet they pointed paradoxically to the growth of popular independence and the unique character of working-class respectability to suggest that hegemony was successfully resisted. In my view, since most working people remained excluded from the franchise and were reliant on middle-class employers for their livelihoods, their 'independence', if such it could be called, was of doubtful value. By all accounts, moreover, their version of respectability was based on industry, thrift and restraint, the very virtues which their social superiors recommended. The argument that it owed little to middle-class influence was therefore less than convincing. Finally, although the emergence of socialism towards the end of the century was seen further to subvert any notion of ideological incorporation, it was unclear why the demand for justice and equity in which socialist militancy was expressed should have arisen with such urgency, if indeed respectability and independence had become generally attainable in the mid-Victorian period.

These concerns ordered my early research. Because the histories in question were informed by theories of social identity, I began by examining the documents to which they appealed, the memoirs and autobiographies of purportedly representative working-class figures, then enlarged my sample by consulting other subjective accounts of 'experience'. The purpose of my examination was twofold. First, I would seek a clearer understanding of what

1

respectability and independence meant to the writers of these documents, thus to determine whether the documents themselves reflected the social identities which historians had devised. Second, I would explore the extent to which structural/discursive imperatives dictated popular choice by shaping common sense in ways which favoured dominant interests. Reversing a fairly standard formula, according to which too great an emphasis on hegemony obscures the agency of past actors, I reasoned that, if the subtleties of hegemony in the past could be illuminated, the scope for agency in the present might be widened. As my research proceeded, however, my prefigurative assumptions were drawn increasingly into question. I found abundant evidence with which to illustrate my argument and indeed to dispute the conventional problematic of social stability, but the evidence was assimilable to a multiplicity of interpretations. Faced with this ambiguity and aware that there were no independent criteria whereby any particular interpretation could be judged 'objectively' correct, I concluded that whatever meaning the evidence appeared to figure forth was given, effectively, by the narratives to which it was adduced. My conclusion did not prevent me from advancing a consistent argument; I had simply to imitate the practice of the historians with whom I took issue, or to select the data most adaptable to my interpretative framework and then acknowledge the speculative character of my conclusions. Yet the histories which I had considered generated truth effects which seemed to override any admission of their contingency, and to follow this procedure while holding such a dim view of its consequences would, I was convinced, have been to engage in deliberate artifice. I was therefore constrained to rethink my project.

I remained interested in the question of power but turned my attention to the power of description or, more accurately, to the discursive technologies whereby historians produce and authorize particular representations of the past. Because these representations circulate and must make sense in the present, the present has become the terrain on which my inquiry proceeds, and the object of my analysis has become the debate in which formerly I sought to participate.[3] This focus requires some preliminary consideration of 'power', not only to clarify my own usage but also as a way of emphasizing the ambiguity with which the term resonates in the histories I address, where it is employed without definition as though its meaning were transparent and uncontested. My approach follows that of Michel Foucault, whose primary aim is to explore 'modes of objectification which transform human beings into subjects'.[4] To facilitate his inquiry, Foucault outlines a speculative analytics of *power relations,* taking care to explain that it is not a theory about 'phenomena of power', is not designed to deduce origins, and does not implicate him in the kind of *a priori* objectification he seeks to expose.[5]

Power, according to Foucault, is a mode of action or practice which draws disparate elements into particular kinds of relationship.[6] Wherever it occurs it is being exercised, and always in a particular direction, 'guiding the possibility of conduct and putting in order the possible outcome'.[7] It has no substantive reality and can exist only when made operative, yet in any given society it is omnipresent.[8] A society without it 'can only be an abstraction' for power relations 'are rooted deep in the social nexus' and are inseparable from the conditions of social life.[9] 'It is easy to see who lacks power,' he observes, but because it operates indirectly, those who control it are often difficult to identify.[10] Yet power is something more than control or repression and it is accepted, he continues, because 'it traverses and produces things . . . induces pleasure, forms knowledge', generates discourse and is synonymous with truth.[11] Truth, he suggests, 'is linked in a circular relation with systems of power which produce and sustain it'.[12] Every society has its regimes of truth, or discourses accepted and made to function as true which are 'not merely ideological or superstructural but a condition of . . . [social] formation and development'.[13] Hence, 'truth is not outside power', nor can it be emancipated from systems of power for it 'is already power'.[14] Nevertheless, power contains within itself the possibility of resistance. A form of action on the actions of others, it is constituted as a relation in which 'action upon' denotes a degree of 'power over' but the actions 'acted upon' signify the freedom to act and hence the potential to resist. Resistance, according to Foucault, takes various forms but is generally directed to the most obvious and immediate effects of power.[15] To see beyond these effects to the character of the relations within which they are produced, he concludes, we must detach power 'from the forms of social, economic, and cultural hegemony within which it now operates'.[16]

To facilitate this detachment, Foucault plots a strategy which links five points of analysis: systems of differentiation which enable power to be exerted; the types of objective pursued; the means of instituting power relations; the forms those relations take; and the degrees in which they are rationalized. Proceeding, he observes that differentiation reflects economic, linguistic, cultural, intellectual and/or competency distinctions, and is 'determined by law or traditions of status and privilege'. Objectives include 'the maintenance of privileges, the accumulation of profits, [and] the bringing into operation of statutary authority'. Means range from 'the threat of arms' to 'the effects of the word'; forms of institutionalization 'may mix traditional predispositions, legal structures, [and] phenomena relating to custom or to fashion'; and rationalization might vary 'in relation to the effectiveness of the instruments . . . the certainty of the results . . . [and] the possible cost'.[17] Clearly, then, Foucault does not attempt to 'deduce' power or 'to reconstruct its genesis'.[18] Instead, he offers a way of thinking about power relations and the political technologies which function to rationalize and validate them. In doing so, he illuminates questions from which historical truth has been substantially exempted and which suggest that historical practice could function as one of the technologies to which he refers. Hence my emphasis, in what follows, on the power of description, 'the power of the word' and the productive quality of the work I address.

This emphasis is calculated to invalidate hierarchy – the embodiment of 'power to act upon' – and points thus to the political predicates of my own project. It also suggests the limits of what I can hope to achieve; for if, as Foucault indicates, power relations and social relations are coterminous, then any form of social organization will involve some degree of hierarchy. But if power relations cannot be transcended, they can, according to Foucault, be transformed. To this purpose he adduces a dynamic strategy, the effectiveness of which is contingent on its use, and I use it to expose the contingency of the histories with which I engage. Ultimately, I suggest, those histories help to constitute a certain kind of subject by conveying the impression that the hierarchy of capitalist society is immutable, and that acquiescence is the only appropriate response to it. Not only do they define 'identity' in particular ways, they valorize a conception of 'common sense' which dictates conformity to their definitions. This process is not unlike one described in a recent work of fiction by Salman Rushdie. As Rushdie's story unfolds, a central character, arrested as an alien and subjected to sustained brutality, begins to mutate. He subsequently finds himself imprisoned with other mutants, one of whom explains that they have been deliberately transformed by the agents of authority, thus to justify their treatment. In response to the question 'how do they do it', the second mutant replies: 'They describe us . . . that's all. They have the power of description, and we succumb to the pictures they construct.'[19] For 'evidence' of this power he refers to their own experience, which neither discerns is likewise a product of the narrative which they inhabit. In what follows, I will not discuss 'mutants' but I will, as foreshadowed, explore the power of description, the power to constitute experience, and the narrative technologies through which that power is implemented.

The book is divided into four chapters, three of which are further subdivided to make their subject matter more assimilable. Chapter 1 is a detailed historiographical survey in which commentaries on the mid-Victorian labour experience are set in the context of a wider debate about nineteenth-century radicalism. The survey also functions as a political genealogy, relating interpretative shifts in the debate to the political imperatives with which they coincide.[20] In the first of its two sections I pay particular attention to work on Chartism from which the problematic of mid-Victorian labour history, 'relative social harmony', has effectively been derived; in the second, I explore the political contingency of this problematic and of the narratives to which it has given rise. Noting the different ways in which Chartism and its decline have been characterized, I suggest that to describe the subsequent period as harmonious or stable is to exclude other representational possibilities and to predetermine not only the evidence consulted but the meanings with which it will be inscribed. The paradigms which shape this procedure, I argue, are devised in the present and reflect present-centred political concerns. Hence, in the 1950s, 1960s and early 1970s, when socialism appeared to have a future, images of the nineteenth-century working classes locked in revolutionary struggle with their bourgeois oppressors made eminently good sense. By the 1990s, however, when the demise of socialism had become yesterday's news, analyses in which working people conspired with their social betters to create a climate of stability and harmony seemed far more realistic, at least to those telling the story. Earlier conventions were thus displaced, the evidence to which they appealed was reconstructed or discarded and power relations ceased to be discussed. Capitalism became a phenomenon at once immutable and benign while the popular struggle for justice and equity became a commitment to the pursuit of an accessible independence. In the guise of political neutrality, I conclude, the new conservatism transformed the mid-Victorian period into a validating reflection of Thatcher's Britain.

In Chapter 2 I consider the technologies employed in this process. I begin by examining the theories of social identity from which the various narratives proceed and then explore some of the evidence to which they are referred for confirmation. The theories in question are ways of characterizing popular attitudes, motives and behaviour by deducing from structural and discursive analyses the subject positions with which the Victorian populace supposedly identified. In 'class' constructions identity is held to have been shaped decisively by economic imperatives while the 'populist' approach attributes it to discourses which projected a vision of social inclusiveness. The evidence against which these theories are tested consists, as noted above, of memoirs and autobiographies in which various working-class 'representatives' recount their experiences. Adherence to this formula of inference and verification produces a uniform judgement in which the popular pursuit of respectability and independence exemplifies acceptance of the prevailing social order and explains the advent of stability or social harmony. The question of whether acquiescence signified the implementation of middle-class hegemony or the commitment of working people to a broadly shared populist tradition then becomes the object of debate.

In addressing this debate, I criticize both theoretical and empirical aspects of the various contributions. With regard to the former, I argue that contributors employ the terms identity and experience not as discursive categories which they themselves have introduced but as self-evident ontological foundations. To illuminate this problem I describe the processes in which subjectivity and experience are constituted. I suggest that any given society is ordered by a multiplicity of underlying power structures (discourses)[21] which distribute its inhabitants along a range of structural axes. It is therefore likely that the conditioned responses of individual subjects to structural imperatives (agency), and indeed the specific imperatives to which they respond, might differ substantially from one subject to another and from one instant to the next. Treating identity as a product of the tension between structure and agency, I define experience as the moment or site of this tension, and conclude that both (identity and experience) are fluid and ambiguous. I then manipulate the evidence of experience cited in the relevant histories to illustrate this proposition and to cast doubt on the 'representative' historical figure, but also to stress the contingency of truth effects produced by any historical narrative, including my own. This part of my discussion also owes a great deal to Foucault. In its focus on the links between identity and power, and on the mutually validating ways in which notions of identity and representativeness function, it suggests that the subject is always incomplete and undecidable, challenges essentialized constructions of identity, and endorses Foucault's critique of modern ontology.[22]

These emphases are carried over into Chapter 3 where I suggest that the historical field itself is irreducibly ambiguous and that historical information is constituted as evidence by, and acquires its meaning from, the narratives to which it is adduced. In the chapter's first section I explore further the autobiographies referred to above to demonstrate that their authors, although they are treated as 'representatives' and often distinguish themselves as such, persistently define themselves against their 'constituents' and refer to the latter with outspoken contempt. Removed from one context and incorporated in another, comments by these men might indeed indicate that they were exemplary, and that the 'social identities' assigned to them by particular narrative histories therefore had wide currency. But, without exception, the writings from which such comments are drawn are rich in statements which one could inscribe with a range of antithetical meanings while remaining well within the limits of accepted historical practice. Giving special emphasis to such statements, I argue that the difference of their speakers from other workers was established by their very adoption of representative roles, and that it increased as they ascended the social hierarchy, many into important public positions. The extent to which, as a consequence, they ceased to identify with their constituents I then suggest by noting the conformity of their views to those of 'great men', historical figures for whom they expressed admiration and contemporaries with whom they had become intimate.

On the basis of this speculation I elaborate two propositions. The first is that the identities of these men were as fluid as their experiences were diverse. The second is that if, as their memoirs indicate, they were representative in no more than a nominal sense, then the social identities which they are held to have exemplified and which underpin explanations of mid-Victorian stability are drawn into question. I then move to a critique of the problematic with which explanation begins, using the same commentaries to illuminate a perspective from which the prevailing condition was anything but stable and harmonious. The burden of this critique is to depict the object of explanation as a myth or meta-narrative which produces truth effects quite independently of any analysis or debate. Hence, in part two of the chapter, I draw on evidence which the debate excludes to initiate a counter-myth. The evidence consists of statements by people for whom society appears to have had no use. These people describe lives not of harmony, stability and independence but of discord, uncertainty and deprivation. Irrelevant to their own society, I suggest, they are also irrelevant to narratives the function of which is to valorize that society. My point is not to promote a view more truthful or objective than those I criticize. It is rather to stress the mythical quality of my own and other commentaries by demonstrating that the historical field is sufficiently diverse to provide 'evidence' for the most contradictory narratives and that the only means of resolving any such contradiction, or of establishing historical truth, is historical convention. I consider this idea further in Chapter 4, which explores the politics of interpretation.

Chapter 4 is divided into four sections. In the first part I engage at length with the work of Hayden White to develop my emphasis on the mythical or fictive quality of narrative history. I also rely on his scholarship to illuminate the processes and technologies whereby historical practice currently functions to naturalize hierarchy and to justify existing political authority. In the second part, I return to mid-Victorian labour history to demonstrate its conformity to the procedures which White outlines. I give particular attention to what he terms 'explanation by representation', and to how the object of explanation in the work to which I have addressed myself has emerged. What began as political quietude or the demise of Chartist agitation, I note, has been transformed descriptively and gradually into 'reformism', 'equipoise', 'stability' and 'harmony', with each transformation approximating to the political climate in which it was effected. Hence at every stage of its evolution, I propose, the myth has functioned as a validating reflection of the current social and political *status quo*.

To illustrate this claim I note the parallel trajectories of the myth itself and recent political discourse. My argument addresses four themes which are developed in the last two sections of this chapter. The first stage comments on Thatcherism's defeat of socialism and its consolidation as the leading expression of dominant truth. The second plots the Labour Party's rightward shift and the conversion of its discourse from one which spoke in defence of the destitute and powerless to one which excludes them, directing its appeal to 'middle Britain' and embracing the dominant truth of economic rationalism. The third characterizes British socialism as an unwitting instrument of hegemony, a narrative which represented itself as the only possible alternative to capitalism and which thus signified, by its defeat, that capitalism is inevitable. Finally, I describe the reflection of these trends in the recent evolution of labour history, suggesting that the latter portrays capitalism in a way which not only endorses claims that it is equitable, but promotes the view that it is inevitable.

1

NARRATIVES OF THE PAST OR HISTORIES OF THE PRESENT?

Throughout the twentieth century and increasingly in recent decades, the life-expectancy of historiographical conventions has tended to diminish. Empirical research uncovers evidence which modifies or even negates earlier accounts; new theoretical developments, reflecting different epistemological positions, undermine the truth effects of conventional histories; and current events serve to falsify the teleologies of existing narratives, demanding new constructions of the past and demonstrating the extent to which the meaning of the past is determined in the present.[1] Predominantly, though not exclusively, the production of 'new' history has been an enterprise of the Left, an important aspect of whose role has been to challenge dominant truth. And perhaps nowhere more, nor with more intellectual rigour, has the past so consistently been rewritten than in the historiography of the nineteenth-century English working classes.

Chartism serves as a salutary example of this process. In some histories it has been interpreted as a purely working-class phenomenon; in others as a movement linked to and influenced, even compromised, by middle-class radicalism. Research *now* indicates that Chartism exerted a profound effect throughout Britain and Ireland, yet a 1925 publication, in which the 1839 Newport debacle was depicted as Chartism's most memorable event, was sufficiently respected at mid-century to be republished with two additional print-runs.[2] And whereas the movement could once be dismissed as a futile expression of protest against temporary distress, which dissolved when conditions improved, it has since been represented as an important agent of change which foreshadowed and precipitated substantial ameliorative reform.[3]

Class is another site at which the history of Chartism has been subjected to persuasive and authoritative reinterpretation, notably by the proponents of a new populist historiography, but the class character of the movement is a convention which continues to resist displacement. Hence the prevailing consensus is that the Chartist era was a watershed beyond which an older, more spontaneous radicalism based on an appeal to tradition, or customary rights, gave way to organized political agitation which reflected popular acceptance of social and economic change and a growing consciousness among working people of their class identity.[4] Class consciousness is seen as an awareness among workers that their interests were different from, and in tension with, those of the employing and propertied classes. In E.P. Thompson's formulation, it was 'the consciousness of an identity of interests as between . . . diverse groups of working people and as against the interests of other classes'.[5] This consciousness, according to Thompson, was awakened simultaneously among the middle and working classes in a process largely completed by 1830.[6] More recently, however, it has been suggested that workers began to identify in class terms only with (or after) the advent of the 1832 Reform Act, and that they did so less antagonistically than Thompson discerned. But insofar as class consciousness continues to be discussed, it is construed in terms of one class defining itself against another.[7]

If the interpretative importance of class consciousness has diminished in recent decades, it nevertheless remains the most substantial historiographical link between Chartism and mid-Victorian radicalism.[8] It is seen by many commentators to have informed the mid-Victorian fulfilment, albeit in varying degrees and modified forms, of a range of Chartist objectives. Some exception to this construction is taken by the liberal minority among labour historians, who recognize a progressive improvement in the working-class condition but suggest that it was an inevitable development which had little to do with class consciousness.[9] Marxist historiography also resonates with the idea of progress, but renders it in terms of working-class achievement, in an equation to which class consciousness is an indispensable term. In constructions of the later period this equation constitutes a problem, for the evidence appears to indicate that, with the demise of Chartism, politicized workers often sought accommodation with the bourgeoisie, and working-class initiatives were far too narrowly based to constitute class actions. Historians have therefore been constrained to address the question of why the working class has not fulfilled the role of 'revolutionary class actor' in which Marxian theory cast it.

This need has produced a range of explanations, some of which point to the direct and deliberate practice of social control, and others, based on more sophisticated analyses, to the ideological incorporation of the lower classes with the help of a co-opted labour aristocracy. Such explanations have been contested, however, in histories which elaborate the crystallization of a distinctive and independent working-class culture – with indigenous criteria for self-definition, self-respect and respectability – which successfully resisted ruling ideas. Much of the historiography referred to here is, thus, in a sense, counter-factual, for although it seeks explicitly to engage with working-class experience in terms of what people did and why they did it, its implicit concern is to explain why the working classes failed to institute Marx's dictatorship of the proletariat. More importantly, the latter approach seeks to demonstrate that this failure did not reflect false consciousness or a lack of working-class agency or complete acquiescence in bourgeois hegemony. It is mainly with this latter body of scholarship that my analysis will be concerned.

9

At one level, the work in question can be situated within the contours of the general debate about mid-Victorian radicalism. However, because of the implied continuities between the Chartist and mid-Victorian periods, its context is considerably broadened. The first step, therefore, will be to illuminate this context in a survey of the main interpretative positions adopted in Chartist and mid-Victorian radical studies, thus to identify important issues which generally constitute the framework of debate and are therefore omitted from discussion.[10] It will then be possible to delineate certain inconsistencies and interpretative problems in the treatment of experience, consciousness and identity by historians of mid-Victorian radicalism, and to raise questions about the character of the historiography itself. Because of its length, the survey will be divided into two sub-chapters. The first will be concerned with liberal and Marxist interpretations which adhere to positivist epistemology. The second will focus on revisionist approaches, most of which employ 'post-structuralist' concepts and attempt to distance themselves from positivism.[11]

WHIG INTERPRETATIONS AND THE MARXIST CHALLENGE

In the first full-length history of Chartism, published in 1854, R.G. Gammage described the movement as one committed to the elimination of social inequality through the political empowerment of the working classes. Its social vision he outlined as a state in which all shared fairly in the work of production, in which no one evaded 'useful labour' thus to overburden others and to diminish 'the public stock of wealth'.[12] Its political purpose he found encapsulated in the People's Charter, the document from which it took its name. A response both to the 1832 Reform Act, which extended the franchise to £10 householders, effectively excluding most workers, and to a declaration by Lord John Russell that no further extension would be considered, the Charter, he indicated, was a refusal of such limits. The political power implicit in the measures which it proposed – universal male suffrage, annual parliaments, vote by ballot, abolition of the property qualification, payment of Members of Parliament and an equitable electoral redistribution – was in his view such that the working classes, had they obtained it, might have eliminated the social misery by which they were beset.[13] But the opportunity was denied them, Gammage concluded, by a self-serving cadre of Chartist leaders who divided the movement and eventually destroyed it.[14]

Writing in 1894, Sidney and Beatrice Webb also judged Chartism an unmitigated failure, and although they described it as the most important event 'in the working-class annals from 1837 to 1842', they treated it as a minor aberration in the larger scheme of things, writing it off in 4 of the volume's 540-odd pages.[15] They made no reference to Gammage, but like him, they attributed the 'collapse' of Chartism to a flawed leadership which reduced 'Lovett's high ideal of a complete political democracy to an ignoble scramble for the ownership of small plots of land'.[16] They characterized Chartism as revolutionary but found that, as 'the ruder methods of the Class War' gave way to industrial diplomacy, the working-class mind rejected the appeal of revolution for that of a new system of society based on universal agreement.[17] Prominent members of the Fabian Society, the Webbs were exemplars of the kind of socialism which it espoused, condescending from a conspicuous height to the classes which they proposed to transform. They accorded working people no aptitude to control their own affairs and were contemptuous of any attempt to do so. Hence they found that fledgling trade organizations, unserved by 'professional' leaders, were inevitably short-lived, while the New Trade Unionism went from strength to strength under the guidance of 'able and energetic' individuals like the solicitor W.P. Roberts and, implicitly, themselves.[18] They were obviously convinced that power, politics and leadership should be left to those who knew best. And in the best Whig tradition, they made it equally clear that misguided initiatives like Chartism had little hope of seriously affecting society's progress.[19]

Between 1898 and 1920 a series of more specifically Chartist studies emerged in England and abroad.[20] They offered a range of perspectives and gave rise to considerable debate, though always within the limits imposed by positivism and a Whig-like teleology. This framework did not inhibit the repudiation of certain aspects of conventional wisdom. Indeed, in a posthumous 1918 publication, *The Chartist Movement*,[21] which subsequently became and remained for many years the definitive history of Chartism, Mark Hovell effectively overturned the traditional interpretation to pronounce Chartism a qualified success.[22] Nevertheless, though interested in structural developments, he lacked a structural critique. He projected a sense of the uniqueness of the English political system, and on the basis of certain state-instituted reforms whose effects he scarcely analysed, he depicted it as one singularly responsive to popular demands in which 'revolutionary initiatives from below' were rendered irrelevant by the inexorable progress of British democracy.[23]

Hovell defined Chartism as a movement born in revolt 'against intolerable conditions of existence . . . whose immediate object was political reform and whose ultimate purpose was social regeneration'.[24] Unlike Gammage, he found its social programme to be vague and unproductive, 'a protest against what existed' rather than 'a reasoned policy to set up anything concrete in its place'.[25] Nevertheless, he identified the deferred implementation of Chartism's revolutionary political agenda as a measure of the movement's achievement. 'Its restricted platform of political reform', he wrote, 'though denounced as revolutionary at the time, was afterwards substantially adopted by the British state without any conscious revolutionary purpose or perceptible revolutionary effect'. 'Before the Chartist leaders had passed away', he concluded, 'most of the famous Six Points became the law of the land'.[26]

In declaring Chartism a partial success on the basis of these developments, Hovell struck a note of irony, for, as he remarked, implementation of its political programme began well after the movement's demise, and only when the programme was no longer seen as the instrument of social transformation which its architects claimed it would be.[27] In addition, he indicated that the ideals embodied in the Charter had been cherished long and widely in English society and that, as it became possible to enshrine them in law, the state did so, quite independently of any need for revolution.[28] In this formulation, he simultaneously dignified Chartism and rendered it precocious if not superfluous, for he recognized the state, not Chartism, as the real agent of change. And although he acknowledged that much was yet to be done, he was unmistakably impressed with what the state had thus far accomplished.

As it had become practicable, Hovell observed, 'the excessive cruelties of the criminal code' had been abolished, factory reform initiated, religious disabilities dissolved, anti-combination laws repealed and restrictions on free trade removed. If nowadays 'the gulf between classes is bad enough', he continued, 'it is difficult for the present generation to conceive the deeply cut line of division between the governing classes and the labouring masses in the early days of Victoria'.[29] At that time, '[i]t was the duty of the common man to obey his masters and be contented with his miserable lot' but this, he suggested, was no longer the case.[30] As a consequence of the Reform Acts of 1867 and 1884, he wrote, the suffrage had been extended 'to every adult male householder, and to some limited categories beyond that limit'. And, in 1917, Parliament had begun to enfranchise certain classes of women.[31] It was therefore only a matter of time, he confidently predicted, before voting was universal.[32]

Notwithstanding his Chartist focus, Hovell's thesis was a celebration of what he saw as the progress of English democracy, though 'progress' which occurred quite independently of popular influence and democracy narrowly conceived. He may have looked forward to universal suffrage, but he virtually denied the anonymous majority the capacity for independent thought, organization and action in the public sphere. His history was one of leaders, and he cast followers less as actors than as objects acted upon.[33] According to a brief biography, he was strongly sympathetic to ordinary individuals 'distressfully working out their own salvation',[34] implicitly in private. His book suggested that the state was making it progressively easier for them to do so, and should be left, undisturbed, to continue its good work.

Hovell's image of a benign society persisted with few modifications into the interwar years of the twentieth century. It was challenged in 1929 by the proto-Marxist, Theodore Rothstein, but to little effect.[35] Dismissed as inaccurate by G.D.H. Cole, then the doyen of labour historiography, Rothstein's scholarship was effectively buried.[36] By and large, Cole endorsed Hovell's construction although he found that Chartism's ultimate aims were economic rather than social or political. He also opened up debate about divisions within the movement based on occupational, regional, cultural and religious differences.[37] He defined Chartism as an economic movement with a political programme which failed because it was premature and bereft of 'any common constructive principles'.[38] The lack of a unified policy he found reflected in divisions between Chartist leaders. He drew these men in the value-laden terms of his own self-confident liberalism to reproduce a more elaborate version of Hovell's earlier assessment.[39] Because of their disunity, he wrote, they 'led all ways at once',[40] blindly attempting to effect economic transformation through political change at a time which was ripe for neither.[41] An adolescent working-class movement 'still undeveloped, uneducated, unequipped with adequate organisation or leadership of its own', he continued, it 'was bound to go down' before 'a dominant economic power strongly entrenched, ably led, and, above all, full of the self-confidence of actual and prospective achievement'.[42] Only with the forward march of history and the further development both of capitalism and the working class would the struggle between capital and labour 'be waged on equal terms'.[43]

Like Cole, contributors to a collection of local studies edited by Asa Briggs and published in 1959 skirted the issue of working-class empowerment.[44] In each analysis Chartism hovered enigmatically as something external to the immediate concerns of the communities in question. It was characterized as a leadership in search of a cause and a following, which attempted to incorporate local discontents in a national campaign but became irrelevant when distress was ameliorated by improved trade and economic conditions. The general theme of these essays was that, from the 1830s, workers oppressed by economic hardship were alienated by the strict adherence of employers to the new political economy. Hence, when agitators advanced the Charter as a solution to local economic grievances, they won impressive support, not least the extreme and irrational partisans of physical force. However, as the economy revived and the first flush of *laissez-faire* enthusiasm wore off, employers' attitudes softened and workers wisely joined them in a new spirit of co-operation. In one locality after another, need for the reforms which the Charter advocated was obviated and 'intelligent' workers looked elsewhere for their utopias.[45] Chartists were doomed from the start, according to Briggs, because of their 'class attitudes' and 'their unwillingness to draw on outside support'.[46] By the time it had become self-evident that 'revolution by force was quite impracticable in Britain', the movement was in decline.[47] Its spirit lingered on, he concluded, to sustain demand for the 'six points' which Chartism itself failed to secure, but in the mid-Victorian years, as prosperity killed the hope of large-scale reform, 'class language withered away'.[48] Despite its similarities to the scholarship of earlier liberal historians, Briggs's collection reflected a subtle interpretative shift whereby workers were engaged less as objects acted upon than as agents who chose to accept or to reject the overtures of Chartist agitators.[49]

During the 1960s and 1970s, local studies were drawn on by authors of synthetic works for evidence not only of rank-and-file assertiveness, but of the movement's diversity in membership, social background and class attitudes. The more this diversity was emphasized, the more detached from Chartism's political aims and strategies interpretations became. At the same time, clarity of definition faded to the extent that, in 1965, the movement could be depicted by F.C. Mather as 'an emanation from the rising public opinion of the provinces which, fostered by the growth of industry and the improvement in communications, began to snatch the leadership of English radicalism from London in the closing years of the eighteenth century'.[50] Facts continued to emerge in great profusion to suggest that Chartism was strong in industrial centres which were of medium size or decaying, but weak in the countryside;[51] that its popularity waxed and waned; that it attracted the practitioners of some trades but not of others;[52] that the movement was divided between supporters of physical and moral force;[53] and that it was fuelled alternatively by cyclical depression, poor harvests and political conviction, though little if at all by the industrial revolution.[54]

An unfortunate consequence of this diversity, it transpires, was that Chartism lacked unity,[55] and nowhere more than in class attitudes did this disunity reveal itself. Hence, some Chartists were found to have been intensely hostile to the middle classes, while others believed that the aristocracy was the common enemy and sought accommodation with employers, whom they saw as fellow-producers.[56] This division was seen to have been so pronounced that Brian Harrison and Patricia Hollis identified 'two kinds of working-class consciousness: the self-reliance of working men, which led them to emancipate themselves from the fetters of patronage, and the spirit of class warfare'.[57] Such ambiguity became a historiographical commonplace and was perhaps inevitable, for the facts were susceptible of various constructions. The most notable constant across the broad range of new accounts was that the People's Charter remained peripheral. Depicted as the rallying-point on which diverse interests converged, it was then effectively set aside to be recalled in concluding paragraphs rather as an afterthought, to exemplify the movement's short-term failure. Yet even in the short term, failure, it seems, was only partial, for all the while Chartism was cultivating class consciousness and self-help and promoting popular education, political awareness, and independence. It was also training the working classes for eventual participation in democracy.[58] Chartists may have been 'slow to learn that constitutional change could only be brought about by co-operation with middle-class radicals'. But learn they did, gradually winning middle-class support and transforming themselves, in the years after 1848, into a 'force sufficiently united to launch its own political party'.[59]

These analyses and conclusions were synthesized by J.T. Ward in his 1973 publication, *Chartism*. Introducing this volume, Ward suggested that the work of Cole and Briggs was more important than the political and sociological tracts of writers like Rothstein, Gaitskell and Groves, who saw 'Chartism as an ancestor of their own philosophies'.[60] The 'political neutrality' which he imputed to Cole and Briggs with this observation he also claimed implicitly for himself, noting that he neither advanced any 'particular group as the legatee of Chartism', nor saw 'Chartism as part of some amorphous "Working Class Movement"'.[61] Like his liberal predecessors, Ward found that although Chartism languished when the causes of discontent on which it throve were removed, it was not an unmitigated failure. With the exception of annual parliaments, all of its aims were eventually implemented[62] and in addition it illuminated working-class consciousness, thus to create a state of mind conducive to further achievement, as the Fabian, Julius West, had discerned in 1920.[63] Ward denied, however, that class consciousness gave rise to unqualified class antagonism. Chartism was not, as Engels had suggested, 'the compact form of [proletarian] opposition to the bourgeoisie',[64] nor were Marx and Engels to be regarded as reliable 'authorities on the movement because of their own preconceptions and sparsity of contact with working people'.[65] In his closing statement, he asserted that Chartism was a typically British movement, largely unconcerned with the dialectics of continental philosophers. Its nature, he argued, 'is not to be found in word-chopping exercises', but 'in the courage of ordinary, grass-roots supporters'.[66] A range of problems inheres in this summary relating to the character of facts, theory and interpretation, which will presently be explored, along with the status of historical contact with working people and the issue of preconceptions, including Ward's own.[67] At this point, however, I will consider another variant of the liberal view.

Writing in 1982, Edward Royle and James Walvin engaged Chartism as an extension of earlier radicalism, indicating that it was well under way before the Charter was published in 1838 and that, by 1848, it had established the preconditions of democracy.[68] Of particular significance in their account, which remained firmly embedded in the Whig tradition, was the year 1839, for although conditions then prevailed which were conducive to revolution – widespread popular unrest and administrative disorder – they noted a determined reluctance to take such a step and a subsequent decline in popular support for the movement.[69] Nevertheless, Chartism survived the rejection of its 1848 petition (as it had those of 1839 and 1842), and moderate Chartists subsequently united with middle-class radicals behind Joseph Hume's 'Little Charter'. Even the former 'revolutionary', G.J. Harney, was ultimately pleased to observe that the middle and working classes had now joined hands without reserve or dissimulation.[70] 'Despite the sense of failure in 1848 among radicals of all hues', Royle and Walvin concluded, 'the mid-Victorian era was to see the Golden Age of radicalism as a political force both inside and outside the walls of a Parliament increasingly open to the pressures of public opinion'.[71]

In a further study of Chartism published in 1984, Dorothy Thompson drew conclusions less extravagant than, but not incompatible with, those of Royle and Walvin. Marxist to the extent that it was a class analysis,[72] Thompson's thesis was unremittingly positivist in its rationale and liberal in its conclusions, insofar as it suggested the wisdom of working-class radicals who elected to work within the system rather than to oppose it, and the capacity of the system to respond to their needs. In a prefatory defence of empiricism, Thompson suggested that it was time to stand back from 'theoretical preconceptions' to see what the people in question 'actually were demanding, what they were defending, and why they took certain forms of action'.[73] This attempt to separate theory from history, by which Thompson suggested that her interpretation was somehow 'theory-free', was perhaps not altogether disinterested. After all, the discounted theories informed a revisionism which had begun, in the 1980s, to challenge the very utility of class analysis and hence the kind of approach on which the reputations of historians like Thompson were based.[74]

In keeping with her empiricist agenda, Thompson drew on a vast body of contemporary data as well as recently produced books and theses, to elaborate a 'global' view of Chartism, 'at least in some of its aspects', and 'to suggest some possible re-interpretations for consideration by those making further detailed studies'.[75] She defined Chartism as 'the channelling into a series of demands for political rights of a large number of grievances and experiences of oppression felt by the common people in the early decades of the nineteenth century'.[76] Her thesis, it has been suggested, identified Chartist activists, elucidated their social and political attitudes, illuminated relations between leaders and led, and conveyed something of 'the contemporary feel and understanding of the ordinary people who made their contribution to its political life'. It emphasized O'Connor's central importance as a 'unifying force', the significance of the Irish to the movement, the role of Chartist women, and the diversity of interests which coalesced under the Chartist umbrella.[77]

Introducing her study, Thompson wrote that '[f]or a short period, thousands of working people considered that their problems could be solved by a change in the political organization of the country', and that '[t]he political question dominated all others'.[78] But by 1850, she observed, the pursuit of political power had lost its urgency. Repeal of the Corn Laws in 1846 had not resulted in the dire consequences which Chartist leaders had predicted. Trade had 'improved in many sectors of industry', and with the Ten Hours Act, introduced by the middle-class John Fielden in 1847, 'the possibilities of pressuring the existing structures seemed to be demonstrated'.[79] In 1850 Ernest Jones warned workers that 'cooperation is at the mercy of those who hold political power', but by then 'the fundamental importance of the Charter had been undermined'.[80] Long before working people 'became converted to Liberalism', she found, they had 'lost faith in political solutions'.[81]

Insofar as the Charter was concerned, Thompson conceded, the movement was a complete failure. The Chartist 'vision of a Parliament regularly and frequently responsible to the whole people was never achieved.'[82] The 'aim of one man one vote' was not realized until after the Second World War; enfranchisement was slow and piecemeal; and 'as more and more players were allowed onto the field, the rules of the game were being constantly changed'.[83]

Real power was restricted to the privileged few, and the first working men to enter Parliament 'were "safe" men who had already demonstrated their reliability by cooperation with the Liberals in local politics or in industrial negotiations'.[84] Nor did Chartists ever win popular control of education as they had sought to do, and, although some of the worst aspects of the New Poor Law were eventually modified, the workhouse test and 'remnants of the Settlement Acts persisted into' the post-First World War depression.[85] Nevertheless, Thompson insists, 'movements for change rarely ever achieve the specific change they are seeking',[86] and, despite its failures, Chartism made real gains 'in the sphere of independent working-class organizations with limited aims'.[87]

Achievements included 'legal recognition of trade unions, the *de facto* recognition of apprenticeship regulation by the unions, of wage bargaining and the negotiation of other aspects of working class conditions by at least some of the trades'.[88] Indications were, therefore, that 'some successes could be achieved without the suffrage'.[89] Co-operative and friendly societies also 'represented victories', for, although they made 'very little impact on the lives of the very poor', they enabled 'skilled workers and others in regular employment' to provide for their own security.[90] In Thompson's view, the 'unity of the Chartist period' was lost when political organization was abandoned. Moreover, she continued, when the vote was eventually obtained, it was cast in favour of the Liberal Party which was seen to be non-political.[91] But consistently with this belief, a division was accepted 'between "political" and "industrial" activity which Chartism had never recognised' and workers, she concluded, 'advanced in the industrial sector' sufficiently to ensure some share 'in the great industrial expansion of Victorian Britain'.[92]

Like others before her, then, Thompson found that certain Chartist goals were attained in the post-Chartist period, and that on this basis the movement should be seen as a 'qualified' success. She seemed to claim some novelty for this approach and, suggesting that earlier writers were unanimous in their judgement that the movement was a failure, neglected to note that their conclusions were as qualified as her own. Their interpretations were in her view flawed, both by short-term perspectives and the implicitly mistaken assumption that the Chartist political programme could have succeeded.[93] Thompson did not indicate precisely how long an acceptable perspective might be, but in pointing to the 'apolitical independence' of the trade union movement in the post-Chartist years as evidence of working-class achievement, she herself, it can be argued, failed to adopt a sufficiently long view. For, when trade unions flexed more muscle than the establishment was prepared to tolerate – albeit a century further on – Thatcher's administration opposed and effectively defeated them. Moreover, as Thompson concedes, other working-class 'gains' during the mid-Victorian period accrued predominantly to skilled and regularly employed workers. They cannot, therefore, be seen, even in the short term, to have been broadly based working-class achievements.

17

Nor is Thompson's political analysis altogether convincing. Hope that the Chartist political programme would or could be adopted might well have been untimely and, with the defeat of Chartism, the possibility of political empowerment might have seemed remote. But although workers may have found that much could be achieved without the suffrage, they continued to agitate for it, and voted Liberal when it was obtained. Neither of these issues is particularly compatible with the notion that faith in political solutions was lost. Popular electoral influence may indeed have been neutralized by 'constant changes to the rules of the game'. But why workers embraced liberalism and returned only safe working men to Parliament remains an open question. Thompson effectively evaded the issue with which, if the expressed aim of the People's Charter and a great deal of surviving documentary evidence are to be believed, Chartism began: the conquest of political power as a prerequisite to establishing a just and equitable society. She also failed to explain why the fundamental belief, that only with political power could workers have real independence, should have been abandoned. For if that conviction were as firmly held as records of Chartist oratory and journalism indicate, there was every reason for workers to suspect that, without political power, they might not be able to maintain the conditions which, purportedly, they came to enjoy in the 1850s.

Such were the concerns of Marxist historians who, in the 1950s, had begun to challenge liberal conventions with a critique prefigured in 1929 by Theodore Rothstein. Focusing on the relationship between working-class radicalism and expanding capitalism, Rothstein drew conclusions about Chartism and the British state perhaps as antithetical to liberal constructions as a positivist framework would permit. Central to his analysis were the issues of class consciousness and power. During the years prior to the passage of the 1832 Reform Bill, he wrote, bourgeois consciousness was heightened by the prospect of enfranchisement and that of the proletariat was cultivated by astute radicals like Bronterre O'Brien.[94] But only with the introduction of the New Poor Law, protest against which was suppressed by armed force, did workers fully realize their invidious position. Their political aspirations betrayed by the Reform Bill, they were now oppressed by the class legislation of their former allies.[95] Proletarian consciousness was sharpened, and, expressed in a renewed demand for democratic reform, presently gave birth to Chartism.[96]

Rothstein engaged Chartism as the first 'political class movement of the modern proletariat', the first attempt of the working class 'to establish a party of its own for the conquest of political power'.[97] Because the working classes constituted a majority, Chartists believed, and the establishment feared, that universal male suffrage would extend control of that power to working people. Its conquest, in his view, was what Chartists meant by revolution, and they were convinced that it would enable them to end economic exploitation and to eliminate social injustice.[98] The failure of the Chartist challenge he attributed to a combination of inept leadership, the effectiveness of state coercive power, and the unstable character of proletarian consciousness.[99]

18

The besetting inadequacies of Chartist leaders were, in his view, their inability to discern the 'true' nature of capital, their detachment from the movement's rank and file and their failure to seize opportunities as they arose.[100] 'Unable to grasp the dialectical character of the capitalist process,' he wrote, they were repelled by 'the violent and "artificial" character of the stage known as "primitive accumulation"', and 'looked for the economic emancipation of the people not to the further development of capitalism, but to its abolition and to a return to the pre-capitalist order'.[101] This backward focus, he believed, dimmed the class consciousness of workers and the appeal of revolutionary tactics.[102] He also found, however, that when the proletariat was ripe for insurrection, Chartist leaders were unprepared to act.

When the Convention moved to Birmingham in 1839, he wrote, the government determined to destroy it, and instituted a reign of terror.[103] Martial law was declared, irate workers took control of the town and, as news travelled, mass protests erupted throughout the industrial north, invariably ending in bloody confrontation with troops and police.[104] Had the Convention called then and there for insurrection the call would, in Rothstein's view, have been answered.[105] But Chartist leaders failed to read the popular mood and, divided by Lovett's 'moral force' faction, vacillated over the adoption of 'ulterior' measures. Meanwhile, popular revolutionary ardour cooled, the Petition was rejected and the Convention urged ultimately against all but moral protest before dissolving itself.[106] By its timidity, Rothstein found, the Convention 'showed the ruling classes that it need not be taken seriously'.[107] Moreover, in his view, the hesitancy of Chartist leaders and the movement's general lack of cohesion served to encourage the government's ongoing terrorism.[108] The Newport incident, spuriously styled an insurrection, he wrote, served as a pretext for mass repression.[109] Prominent Chartists were arrested, the movement was forced underground and '[r]eaction triumphed all along the way'.[110]

In 1842, Rothstein continued, O'Connor and his colleagues attempted to assume leadership of the Plug Plot and to transform it into a general strike. But their inability to reach and to unify the masses manifested itself yet again. They failed to rally support for the factory operatives from other sections of the workforce, and the strike ended in defeat.[111] After the crisis of 1842, improved economic conditions diverted workers back to trade unionism.[112] Increasingly 'reconciled to the existing order', they sought to improve their condition under it. Like the new consumer-oriented co-operatives and the ten-hour movement which attached important sections of the working classes to the establishment, trade unionism, he wrote, was antagonistic to, rather than an outgrowth of, Chartism – a current which drew the masses away from it.[113] Hence, between 1844 and 1847, Chartism stagnated, even though O'Connor struggled to resuscitate it, first by attempting to link it to the Irish question, and then with the land plan.

In 1848, Rothstein observed, the movement was revived for the last time by revolution abroad and economic crisis at home. Mass meetings occurred throughout the industrial north as did riots and violent encounters with the authorities. Again, the government, assisted by the press, prophesied imminent revolution and with a massive force, assembled under the Duke of Wellington, prepared to put it down.[114] Of profound significance in this enterprise were the organized workers of the factory movement. Now pacified and eager to defend law and order, they enrolled in their thousands as special constables.[115] The government's brutal behaviour in 1848 provoked great hostility throughout the industrial proletariat but Chartist leaders offered little comfort. When they convened to discuss action in May 1848 talk quickly degenerated into the old debate about physical versus moral force.[116] By now, the masses were growing indifferent to the movement and its leaders were deserting to the bourgeois camp with increasing frequency. A Chartist conference held in Manchester in 1852 was so poorly attended that it met no more.[117]

With the decline of Chartism, Rothstein continued, the active working-class pursuit of political power dissolved, and proletarian consciousness, already eroded by government repression and changing conditions, was finally subverted by Christian Socialism. The authors of this doctrine conspired with turncoats like Lovett to persuade the people that 'the Chartists were utopian dreamers', and that their own programmes of class co-operation and self-improvement were more likely to win support and to ensure success.[118] Promising that the worthy would be set free by God himself, they promoted moral self-help and consumer co-operativism as the means to true liberty and happiness. On this basis, they cultivated an opportunist mentality which, in the trade union movement, had already informed the emergence of a self-serving labour aristocracy which collaborated with the bourgeoisie and successfully fostered acquiescence in the *status quo*.[119] Though clearly disappointed by what he saw as the failure of Chartism and the character of subsequent radicalism as it progressed through the Victorian period into the twentieth century, Rothstein applauded the Chartist vision. If the class consciousness of English workers was unequal to the task of resisting the onslaught of opportunism and animating a unified revolutionary force, Chartist strategies anticipated 'all the subsequent developments of the political labour movement'.[120] When Chartism disappeared, along with 'the conditions which had brought it into being', its 'spirit lived on' as an inspirational and creative force, eventually to animate 'militant and glorious Communism'. This, he concluded, was Chartism's historical significance.[121]

Since the publication of Rothstein's book, Chartism has been extensively reinterpreted. In biographies of the movement's eminent personalities, local studies and works of general synthesis, a mass of documentary evidence has emerged and the conclusions of earlier writers have been scrutinized, confirmed, rejected. But few original questions have been posed, those raised have not been adequately explored, and those concerned with the issue of 'power' have only with difficulty been kept on the agenda.[122] Rendered largely irrelevant in biographies which focus on the characters and careers of individuals, and in local studies where Chartism tends to be reduced to a protest against immediate distress, working-class empowerment is transformed in general histories into the self-interested pursuit of a dubious independence; dismissed as a revolutionary ambition which had no hope of succeeding; or equated, after the manner of the Fabian G.D.H. Cole, with obtaining the franchise. Traditional Marxist scholars were less sanguine than their liberal counterparts about the gradual implementation of the Charter and democracy. Nevertheless, indicating that, for various reasons, the issue of working-class empowerment raised by the Charter defied resolution in the Chartist era, they projected it into the future, to be dealt with by historians of mid-Victorian radicalism.

One such writer was E.J. Hobsbawm who agreed with Rothstein about the class character of Chartism; endorsed his conclusions about the Chartist experience; spoke out, like him, against the falsification of history by unscrupulous liberal historians; and developed his ideas about the labour aristocracy.[123] Fundamental to Hobsbawm's thesis was a distinction between working-class and proletarian consciousness. The former, he suggested, emerged between 1815 and 1848 to inform a spirit of collective solidarity such that the labour movement became not merely an expression of self-defence, protest and revolution, but a way of life for the labouring poor.[124] The latter, he found, took longer to develop, and in 1848 remained imperfectly formed because its 'Jacobin' element – the demand for 'respect, recognition, and equality' – had not fully been awakened.[125] Hence he suggested that Chartism was unified by little more than a handful of traditional and radical slogans, a few influential journalists who wrote for publications like the *Northern Star*, and a small group of powerful orators.[126] Its greatest strength inhered in its ability to mobilize vast masses of the incompletely proletarianized, but its leaders could not provide them with a strategy beyond petition and protest. They were unable to utilize the general strike of 1842, largely because the English were unfamiliar with the idea of insurrection, the organization which it required and the transfer of power to which it pointed.[127]

Nor, Hobsbawm indicated, were the circumstances propitious. Echoing Lenin, he argued that, for revolution to succeed, increased hardship and political awareness among the masses must coincide with the emergence of capable working-class leaders and 'a crisis in the affairs of the ruling order'.[128] The ruling élite experienced such a crisis only once, he argued, during the years immediately following the 1832 Reform Act. Then, however, the labour movement – though united by the shared experience of hunger, wretchedness, hatred, hope and desperation – lacked the appropriate consciousness, organization and maturity to make 'their rebellion more than a momentary danger to the social order'.[129] For the mature proletarian consciousness, he looked, unsuccessfully, to the post-1850s period where, in the debate which he generated about the 'labour aristocracy', he explored the question of working-class empowerment at much greater length.

Both the labour aristocracy and Christian Socialism were seen by Rothstein as instruments of ideological control, and just as Hobsbawm developed the former concept, John Saville took up the latter. In doing so, Saville struck a further blow at liberal historical orthodoxy, endorsing Rothstein's view that Christian Socialism, designed to subvert Chartism, also survived it, to exert a powerful anti-radical influence in the Victorian era.[130] More recently and to some extent more controversially, Saville has developed another aspect of Rothstein's thesis to suggest that, in the final analysis, it was state coercive power which broke the back of Chartism. In this connection, he argued that the resurgence of the movement in 1848, and the links it established with left-wing Irish nationalists and French revolutionaries, signalled 'a general escalation of events in central Europe' and a specific challenge to the Whig regime at home.[131] In response to this threat, he continued, Lord John Russell's government mobilized all of the coercive force at its disposal under a tightly articulated administration of national and local authorities.[132]

As repressive measures were instituted, the planned mass presentation of a new petition to Parliament on 10 April was undermined. The crowd was confined on Kennington Common and the presentation, made by a few eminent Chartists, was robbed of much of its impact. Undeterred, Chartists developed 'the embryo of an illegal movement' while, 'on the ground', meetings and demonstrations continued. During summer, however, mass arrests occurred throughout the country and, by September, the entire movement had been crushed.[133] In Ireland dissidents were tried before juries of loyal Protestants, under the hastily passed Crown and Government Security Act, which abolished the death penalty for treason and therefore increased the likelihood of conviction. In England the Home Office resisted appeals from local magistrates for the arrest of Chartist leaders until May, predicting accurately that middle-class jurors would, by then, be alarmed sufficiently by the prospect of revolution to put down 'the social beast of Chartism'.[134] The trials, he wrote, epitomized 'the obliteration of reason by prejudice and the subversion of legal principles by partisanship of a virulent order'.[135] In conclusion Saville observed that 'Chartism was finally broken by the physical force of the state, and having once been broken it was submerged, in the national consciousness, beneath layers of false understanding and denigration'.[136] The stage was thus set for at least partial bourgeois ideological hegemony.[137]

Saville's analysis was firmly embedded in the Marxist tradition. He engaged Chartism as a class movement, albeit one in which not all workers participated. In his view the conditions of its emergence and existence were economically determined, and its initiative in 1848 was a 'class action', a proletarian challenge to the bourgeois state. Ruthless and efficient in its response, the state triumphed. Assisted by the press and other media, it subsequently reduced Chartism to a brief, trivial event, effectively excising it from popular memory. Deprived thus of historical precedent, mid-Victorian radicals were unable to fashion an appropriate anti-capitalist critique and succumbed, to some extent, to ruling ideas. Saville did not regard this process as one of crude social control, nor did he propose the complete ideological incorporation of the working classes. Instead, invoking Gramscian theory and 'what Bottomore call[ed] the weaker version of the dominant ideology thesis', he proposed that a condition of at least partial hegemony was instituted.[138] Bourgeois ideas were inscribed in the structural determinants of popular choice, there 'to inhibit and confuse the formulation of an appropriate counter-ideology'. As a consequence, radicalism was to some extent immobilized, for it adopted a labourist philosophy incompatible, by and large, with the liberal understanding of parliamentarianism, and the sense of the moral rightness of the existing order, which had begun to take root among the working classes.[139]

Most historians, even those who stress the greater significance of continuity,[140] would agree with Saville that the character of working-class radicalism changed in the post-Chartist period. Change has generally been emphasized, however, by the most self-consciously political writers, from the Fabian liberal Webbs, for whom its relation to the progress of society as a whole was uncomplicated, to Marxists such as Rothstein, Saville and Hobsbawm, who have taken a very negative view of it. In the historiography of the mid-Victorian period, Hobsbawm, Royden Harrison and John Foster have been the most consistent defenders of the Marxist position from which Hobsbawm and Saville engaged with Chartism. Accordingly, they construct working-class reformism as a diversion from the revolutionary pursuit of political power rather than as a legitimate alternative to it. From this perspective, change is linked closely to a decline in revolutionary class consciousness, a decline allegedly precipitated by the labour aristocracy. Described as a privileged stratum of skilled workers, the labour aristocracy is held to have served the employing class as subcontractors of exploitation and management and to have assisted in proliferating a bourgeois world view among the working classes. Elaborated by Lenin on the basis of earlier work by Marx and Engels, this thesis has more recently been taken to indicate that the aristocratic stratum was simply bought off and engaged actively to cultivate reformism and chauvinism in the proletariat, thus to subvert its revolutionary potential.[141] Indeed, Harrison described a concerted and to some extent successful bourgeois attempt to incorporate the better class of worker. But although this interpretation has also been imputed to Hobsbawm and Foster, they in fact outlined a far more complex process.[142]

Writing in 1954, Hobsbawm sought to verify empirically the existence of a labour aristocracy and to illuminate the subtleties of its relationship to working-class reformism. He found that it emerged during the 1850s and comprised 'certain distinctive upper strata of the working class, better paid, better treated and generally regarded as more respectable and politically moderate than the mass of the proletariat'.[143] Comprising between 10 and 15 per cent of the labour force, its members, he argued, were predominantly artisanal workers who formed themselves into exclusive societies and unions, recruiting by apprenticeship and limiting entry to their various trades. They thus maintained demand for their services and ensured that those services continued to attract the best possible remuneration.[144] They were defined by 'the level and regularity' of their earnings, their 'prospects for social security', their superior working and living conditions, their 'relations with the social strata above and below' them, and their potential to advance themselves and their children.[145] Most important was the level and regularity of their earnings. Some drew in excess of 40s. a week and none less than 28s. to 30s., considerably more than the unskilled labourer's maximum of 21s.[146]

By contrast to the unskilled, Hobsbawm went on, labour aristocrats also enjoyed fairly regular employment, were able to provide against sickness and loss of work, and were not seriously affected by wage fluctuations.[147] Nevertheless, as the century progressed and industry expanded, certain traditional skills were made redundant and new ones created. As a consequence, many lost their aristocratic status while opportunities arose for formerly semi-skilled workers to become aristocrats.[148] Although the labour aristocracy shaded over into the strata above and below it, it identified by and large with the lower-middle class – shopkeepers, independent masters, foremen and managers.[149] Its members, because they laboured for their livings, defined themselves against the employing classes, but they also saw themselves as something 'other than' and superior to common labourers. This, he emphasized, was also the view of the contemporary Thomas Wright, a skilled metalworker who observed that '[t]he artisan creed with regard to the labourers is that the latter are an inferior class and that they should be made to know and kept in their place'.[150]

According to Hobsbawm, the labour aristocracy was a politically moderate force with little interest in forming 'an independent working-class party'.[151] He conceded, however, that 'certain old-established' aristocrats, having become unsettled in the 1880s by 'the competition of machinery and the threat of down-grading', subsequently affiliated, like the chief new unions, with the Labour Representation Committee.[152] Throughout the second quarter of the century, however, labour élites remained conservative, partly because of their identification with the lower-middle classes, but predominantly for economic reasons. The extent of their conservatism depended on their exclusiveness relative to others in their trades. Cotton aristocrats, he explained, 'defended positions of privilege in an industry in which, under normal circumstances, they would have stood much lower'. Boot and shoe workers, by contrast, 'had carved out an abnormally large group of "middle incomes" from what would otherwise have been a much larger proportion of depressed ones'. Hence the latter were less extreme than the former, which indicated to Hobsbawm that the political and economic positions of the various élites 'reflect[ed] one another with uncanny accuracy'.[153]

The wage differentials which so distinguished skilled from unskilled workers – the labour aristocrat from the plebeian – were transformed by capitalism. Formerly, scales had been determined by custom and comparison – by what had always been considered fair and what others in similar positions earned. Accordingly, the labourer's remuneration was fixed at subsistence and the artisan's at roughly double that of the labourer. Workers 'were slow to learn how to charge "what the traffic would bear"', and capitalist employers engaged even aristocrats for less than they might otherwise have fetched.[154] But skilled workers 'generally enjoyed the power to make their labour artificially scarce'. And although the gap between skilled and unskilled wages narrowed between 1851 and 1911 in certain traditional industries, in most cases it widened. Sometimes it increased by several hundred per cent, especially where unskilled labour was performed predominantly by women and children.[155] Nevertheless, the prospect of rising into the middle classes was remote, even for élite workers. It was the relative superiority of labour aristocrats to the unskilled and their determination to maintain it, Hobsbawm found, which accounted for their conservatism and their suitability for the role of subcontracting exploitation and management.[156]

The structure of early nineteenth-century British industry was, in Hobsbawm's view, such that all grades of workers 'except the lowest labourers contain[ed] men and women who . . . [had] some sort of profit incentive'.[157] To minimize overheads, entrepreneurs subcontracted work to piece-masters and the latter engaged and paid craftsmen as did craftsmen their labourers. Like piece-masters, foremen hired and had 'a financial interest in such labour as did not work on subcontract'. Enabling 'all groups worth humouring' to derive some profit from the productive process, this system was effectively one of co-exploitation insofar as it made aristocrats 'into co-employers of their mates and their unskilled workers'.[158] Noting that many aristocrats regarded the various forms of subcontracting with hostility, he indicated that sweated industries were less likely to be 'those with a strong labour aristocracy'. He found, however, that although co-exploitation was not a determinant of the aristocracy's emergence, it 'reinforced its existing position' and probably strengthened its feeling of qualitative superiority to plebeians and intermediate workers.[159] In the last quarter of the century the practice began to recede as 'more "scientific" methods of payment by results' were instituted. This industrial rationalization often increased the earnings of aristocrats in the short term, but it also served to dissolve the barrier between them and common workers and eventually, from 1914, to undermine the aristocracy itself. Not only did it render many old skilled handicrafts redundant, thereby declassing those who practised them, it also transformed the majority of formerly unskilled workers into semi-skilled machine-operators, thus narrowing the gap between aristocrat and plebeian. Finally, the white-collared managerial stratum, which in the past had been recruited from among élite workers, had begun to reproduce and to interpose itself between labour élites and the employing classes.[160] In this construction, then, the labour aristocracy was not a wilful agent of bourgeois ideology but a product of structural determinants, most specifically economic imperatives which opposed its interests to those of other workers. It did not

25

simply cultivate a reformist mentality among those beneath it but it also, Hobsbawm seems to suggest, embodied the competitive capitalist ethos in its character, thereby legitimizing society's hierarchical structure by its very existence. Hence the mechanisms of subcontracting and co-exploitation, rather than the aristocrats themselves, functioned both to erode worker solidarity and to 'naturalize' capitalist principles and practices.

Royden Harrison joined the debate in 1965 and focused on what he termed the conscious and deliberate aspects of co-optation. Taking issue with the view that the labour aristocracy was a Marxist invention, he argued that 'the story of working-class politics in the third quarter of the century' was predominantly one of the aristocracy's activities and aspirations.[161] Indeed, he went on, the stratum was 'a commonplace of mid-Victorian social and economic literature' and without reference to it '[t]he distinctive institutions of mid-Victorian Labour become unintelligible'.[162] Harrison located the emergence of the labour aristocracy in a process of fundamental change in the labour movement itself and also in the economic, social and political environment between the second and third quarters of the century. In his view, the decline of Chartism left working-class radicalism without a clear ideological basis. Apart from positivism, which failed to inspire more than a handful of workers, 'there was no political philosophy which influenced working men, or won adherents among them by assigning to the working class a distinctive political function or independent role'.[163] Hence, in the 1860s, the 'prophets', 'visionaries' and 'demagogues' who had formerly led labour were displaced by great men of business who, to use Hobsbawm's idiom, courted all those workers 'who mattered', promoting reformism, patriotism and class co-operation as the path to progress.[164] Sensitive to their vulnerability in an environment of increasing polarization 'as far as property ownership was concerned', and to 'the opportunities and responsibilities of the large employer of labour', new model employers discerned the need, in the absence of a peasantry, 'for some alternative basis of mass support for property'.[165] Even before the 1850s, Harrison observed, it was a commonplace that if the artisan class was reduced 'to the level of the labourer . . . the Charter will have been granted'. In the 1860s, he continued, 'large employers turned their sense of the Labour Aristocracy's importance into a coherent policy', attributing to it a vital social role and treating it accordingly.[166] '[T]he class of persons is gradually being diminished,' wrote Thomas Brassey, railway contractor and friend of trade union leaders, 'who without large means, enjoy the advantage of holding a position of independence. Theirs is an order essential in a happily constituted society, as the connecting link between the rich and the poor. They are the defenders of property, while in their modest and frugal households there is nothing which obtrudes itself in painful contrast to the condition of the less independent wage-earners among whom they live.'[167]

The successful cultivation of the labour aristocracy by such entrepreneurs helped, in Harrison's view, to explain the paradox whereby, as the proletariat grew, its revolutionary temper declined.[168] Hence labour leaders now promoted the franchise as a means of rising in the social scale rather than as one of striking property on the head, as Chartists had done,[169] and the labour élites made every effort to maintain their privileged position. They affected to represent ordinary workers but at the same time excluded them from the benefits which they, the aristocrats, had come to enjoy.[170] By the third quarter of the century, 'the Labour Movement had become pre-eminently a movement of the Labour Aristocracy', and under its auspices, co-operativism passed 'from community-building to shop-keeping' – all that was retained of its former identity was its voluntary character, its working-class self-perception and an anti-competitive rhetoric; trade unions became 'less like "schools of war" and more like the workman's equivalent to the public school'; political activity gave way substantially to the promotion of 'social and industrial' movements; and 'the vigorous insistence upon an independent class basis for such activity diminish[ed]'.[171]

Although the working class as a whole improved its standard of living during the years of prosperity between 1848 and 1864, Harrison suggested, 'there was a relative worsening of their position *vis-à-vis* the labour aristocracy'.[172] Domestic production was in decline, the 'unskilled mass' visibly increased and distinctions among workers, which had begun to collapse between 1825 and 1850, were revived. As a consequence, the aristocracy acquired further importance and came to enjoy greater social security than labourers, better prospects for upward mobility and superior treatment by employers. In addition, he observed, they gained some control over the job, though they did not seek to extend it to the entire productive process. Like Hobsbawm, however, he found that their privileged position 'was most evident in the height and regularity of their earnings'.[173]

With illustrations drawn from various levels of contemporary society, he also endorsed Hobsbawm's view that the lower margin of the élite stratum was precise and rigid, and one across which mutual antagonism was often played out. Artisans, remarked one middle-class commentator, 'are as conscious of the superiority of their lot over that of their poorer brethren as is the highest nobleman in the land'.[174] And in the workshop, an anonymous workingman recorded, class distinctions, sharply defined, are if necessary violently maintained: 'Evil would certainly befall any labourer who *acted upon* even a tacit assumption that he was the social equal of the artisan.'[175] Labourers evidently smarted under such contempt, complaining that they were rarely treated 'like as if we was the same flesh and blood as other people'.[176] According to one, bricklayers appeared 'almost as demigods, the way they shouted for mortar or bricks and the difference between their treatment and ours by the boss'.[177] Another was adamant, however, that 'we reckon we'reselves quite as good as what them is for all that'.[178] This indignation was not without its irony in Harrison's account, for he discerned very definite social gradations among unskilled workers themselves. Dockhands condescended to attached labourers while navvies refused to associate with 'Rodneys' or piece-workers and disdained the unemployed.[179] These attitudes were apparently not fixed, however, for several attempts were made between the years of 1850 and 1875 to form general unions.

In the same period, Harrison went on, both the wage differentials and social distance between the labour aristocracy and the rest widened. Elite workers organized to improve their own conditions, but, when their assistants endeavoured to do likewise, they refused to support them. Hence, between 1850 and 1875, the labour movement became dominated by labour aristocrats; and working-class institutions, because of their high subscription costs, were kept beyond the reach of most unskilled workers. The latter were similarly excluded from co-operatives, shares in which were set at £1 when the 'millions' earned less than 15s. a week. Nevertheless, élites presumed to speak for all workers and they were seen to be representative by their social superiors. At the same time, 'big capital' refused to compromise with general unions but made concessions to craft unions, paying their members high wages, submitting to collective bargaining and promoting the resolution of trade disputes by arbitration and conciliation.[180] For Harrison, then, the mid-Victorian period was marked more by change than continuity. The militant confrontation of the Chartist era dissolved into compromise and accommodation. New model employers courted the labour aristocracy in general and labour leaders in particular. And 'weary of apocalyptic forecasts and revolutionary movements', the latter accepted their overtures, preferring, at least temporarily, 'a pedestrian success to an heroic failure'.[181]

Writing in 1974, John Foster also saw the middle years of the century as a period of crucial change in the nature of English capitalism, the structure of English society and the character of working-class consciousness. In the early 1800s, he wrote, economic crisis, precipitated by the French Wars, undermined capitalist authority systems and involved 'a large part of the labour force in economic struggle'. This struggle gave rise to labour consciousness which, with renewed economic crisis in the 1830s and 1840s, was transformed into revolutionary class consciousness.[182] The latter, however, degenerated into sectional consciousness during the 1840s and 1850s when a fundamental modification or liberalization 'of the socio-economic system' produced 'an altogether new pattern of social subdivision within the labour force'.[183] Central to this latter phase was the emergence of a labour aristocracy.

Foster's study focused on Oldham in Lancashire, and made comparative reference to Northampton and South Shields. He sought, however, 'to place Oldham within an overall perspective of capitalist development in England',[184] and in this connection made general observations about the changing character of working-class consciousness. In the early decades of the nineteenth century, he wrote, illegal unionism flourished and the 'bourgeois state', its power eroded along with its resources by the French Wars, lacked the means to repress it. By the late 1830s, civil control had deteriorated to the extent that 30,000 troops had been assigned to permanent garrison duty in England and Wales, but, frustrated by seemingly inert local authorities, they were powerless against entrenched radical opposition. Not only did organized labour seek persistently 'to enforce *long-term* determinants of higher wages'[185] by actions which constituted common law offences even after repeal of the Combination Acts in 1825, but it framed rules, affixed penalties and inflicted punishments, effectively establishing a labour community.[186]

Prior to 1825, Foster observed, the state's diminished strength was exemplified in the almost total absence of prosecution under the Combination Acts. Recovery did not really begin until the 1840s, and in the meantime, in some places, labour made real gains. Its illegal, often intimidating, tactics were proof against military force, a consequence not so much of 'the government's outright military weakness as its loss of control over local administration'. In Oldham this loss arose from the dependency of four-fifths of the electorate on working-class custom. The town's radicals, he wrote, 'were old hands at using food prices for political ends' and at boycotting unsympathetic shopkeepers.[187] 'The army by itself could do nothing', for '[a]s long as the police, the inquest jurors and the Poor Law officials (with their list of inhabitants) refused to co-operate, there would be no arrests, no witnesses and no evidence. The magistrates and army commanders were left to a dangerous game of blind man's buff amid an overwhelmingly hostile population'.[188] The labour consciousness of Oldham workers was demonstrated persuasively for Foster, then, by their extra-legal unionism and industrial bargaining, their ability to influence local government and the response which that influence elicited from the central administration. For over a generation, he observed, it 'insulat[ed] working people from outside control'.[189] During the 1830s and 1840s, he concluded, a unique combination of developments which did not obtain in Northampton and South Shields transformed Oldham's 'labour consciousness' into revolutionary class consciousness.

By 1841, Foster continued, the majority of Oldham's labour force was employed in the cotton industry, three-quarters of them 'in mills with over a hundred workers'. By the late 1840s, while processed output trebled, its value increased by little more than a third. Prices fell by over a half and profit margins narrowed. Unlike the earlier period, when there was only one year of serious depression, there were four such years in the 1830s and five in the 1840s during which, at any given time, 'up to thirty per cent of the labour force would be out of work'.[190] Real wages also declined substantially, especially for cotton spinners, the largest group of adult male mill workers, and their nominal wages were cut by an increase in the employment of cheap female and child labour. Having virtually achieved the status of skilled workers during the 1810–20 period, spinners now saw their trade 'diluted'.[191] As the condition of workers deteriorated, its contrast with the opulence of employers – whose profits continued to rise even though 'the rate of profit was under pressure' – became more marked. The fifty great employing families enjoyed perhaps half of the community's entire income.[192]

The economic downturn also adversely affected Oldham's mining industry. In the 1830s the railways began to flood the Manchester market with cheap coal from south-west Lancashire. The 'still partly protected local market' was subsequently undermined by the crisis in cotton and, as in cotton, child labour was increased and wages fell.[193] To combat declining conditions, working-class radicals took up with new intensity what, since 1816, had been 'the common objective of all Lancashire cotton workers': the pursuit of a short-time factory act. It was the short-time movement, Foster observed, which 'accustomed workers to viewing their industry in overall politico-economic terms' and also showed them the efficacy of political action.[194] As prices continued to fall and the government opposed effective factory legislation, the climate became increasingly conducive to the class rhetoric of labour activists. A rhetoric which pointed to the contradictions inherent in industrial capitalist production, it generated 'a fairly high level of mass understanding'.[195]

Whereas the absence of a unified labour movement in Northampton and a prevailing sectionalism in South Shields impeded the development of class consciousness,[196] in Oldham, according to Foster, 'a vanguard group leading mass struggle and able to use that position to argue for a wider struggle against the system itself' constituted 'the necessary conditions for class formation'.[197] Radicals expressed their aspirations in anti-systemic terms, facilitating 'the overall fight for a wider consciousness' and engendering 'a profound process of mass cultural change'.[198] In this connection, he argued, language played a vital role. The embodiment of 'particular social codes which determine what information is (or is not) acceptable', it (language) articulated key 'social perspectives inherited from everyday industrial' life to the radical agenda.[199] This process was enhanced by 'mass readership of the radical press' which evidently gained 'something near a monopoly in Oldham' during the 1830s.[200] The language of radicalism, he wrote, 'enables us to see the process going on', and, especially in the context of the 'Factory Act experience', it provides 'the most convincing proof that it is class consciousness we are dealing with'.[201]

Ironically, however, the radical project was in Foster's view largely undermined by its own success.[202] Drawing an implicit connection between Oldham and the wider English working-class community, he observed that 'it was sufficiently powerful to bring about a profound modification in the structure of capitalism', but unable 'to maintain its offensive under the impact of these changes' which amounted to a process of 'liberalization'.[203] The radical movement may to some extent have been checked by increasingly efficient agencies of law and order, and its enthusiasm might possibly have been diminished by gradual economic improvement.[204] But it was finally disarmed, Foster believed, by the conciliatory response of a bourgeoisie which, alarmed at the movement's evident power, made a range of concessions designed 'to win back mass allegiance'.[205]

In a process which spanned more than a decade, the bourgeoisie divided and defeated the labour movement by assuming its concerns and co-opting its leaders. Tories lent their support to the Ten-hour Bill in 1846, apparently endorsing 'the working-class case against orthodox political economy', and thereby presenting a choice between accepting a middle-class alliance, which might facilitate the passage of the bill, or rejecting such an alliance and perhaps condemning the bill to failure. The first alternative was adopted, but the decision alienated Nonconformist tradesmen and some old revolutionaries. The latter were won over, some twelve months later, by the Liberals, who had taken up the radical demand for disestablishment and household suffrage. Hence, 'within a year the two major slogans of the working-class movement had been appropriated (or at least undermined) and its leadership split', the new-found bourgeois sympathy for the lower classes being all the more convincing because it was extended 'by two apparently rival factions'.[206] As a consequence, the Chartist remnant was reduced to virtual insignificance.[207]

The middle-class victory was enhanced, Foster continued, by structural changes in the workplace, notably in machine-making and cotton. By 1850, engineering had become Oldham's leading industry. Geared to foreign markets and technologically advanced, it demanded 'not just the creation of a whole new grade of supervisory taskmasters but the simultaneous elimination of an old grouping which has often been mistaken for a labour aristocracy: the highly paid, autonomous craft elite'.[208] Weakened by several years of dilution, artisanal authority in the metal trades was finally undermined, and the artisans themselves reduced to subcontract work, by the defeat of the Amalgamated Society of Engineers in the countrywide lockout of 1851.[209] Henceforth, in Oldham as in the rest of Lancashire, most preparatory work was performed by unskilled juveniles and 'measurable' work 'paid by the piece'. Under this system, the skilled engineer hired and paid the boys who assisted him, becoming 'actively involved – as pacemaker and technical supervisor – in the work of management'.[210]

A similar development occurred in cotton, Foster found, where the automatic mule transformed the adult male spinner into a pacemaker for female and juvenile piecers. Now paid by result, spinners withdrew their support from the short-time movement, thereby distancing themselves from the time-rate piecers whom they 'employed on subcontract'.[211] Although he was unable to detect a clearly defined aristocracy in Oldham's mining industry, he suggested that the 1860 Mines Act, which gave workers the right to elect their own pithead observers, subject to employer approval, served to institute a new authority structure similar to that in engineering and cotton.[212] Hence, by the 1860s, some one-third of the workforce 'were acting as pacemakers and taskmasters over the rest; and in doing so made a decisive break with all previous traditions of skilled activity'.[213] For, '[w]hile the self-imposed work routine of the craft worker served to insulate him from employer control, that imposed by the technological demands of the new industry equally firmly identified the skilled worker with management'.[214] The outcome of this novel authority structure was a broad social polarization in the wider community. Aristocrats linked themselves to employers through religious, educational, temperance and co-operative institutions while unskilled workers ridiculed their work-time taskmasters as bosses' men, rejecting the discipline, subservience and abstinence associated with them. They evolved a culture centred on the public house and, protected by the dialect which the aristocrat was forced, by his new social allegiance, to abandon, they required 'no formal institutions beyond the friendly society to handle the most unavoidable contacts with the authorities'.[215]

Like Hobsbawm, Foster saw the labour aristocracy as a product of complex structural developments. He stated frankly his conviction that 'politically the bourgeoisie have been attempting to split, bribe and hoodwink labour leaders ever since capitalist society first developed';[216] and he clearly saw labour aristocrats as 'collaborators'; but he did not, as has been insinuated, portray them as passive victims of crude bourgeois manipulation.[217] He suggested instead that structural change shaped their choices in a subtle process which rendered certain alternatives more meaningful than others, so that their common interest appeared to be with the employing class rather than with their unskilled fellow-workers. As a result, in the post-Chartist period, the former integrity of the labour movement was undermined, revolutionary class consciousness eroded and the working-class bid for control of political power contained.

In their emphasis on the decline of revolutionary class consciousness, labour's diversion from the pursuit of political power and the need to resume that pursuit, proponents of the labour aristocracy thesis betrayed a strong sense of political purpose. They also exemplified the 'traditional' Marxist opposition to capitalist political economy and thus effectively acknowledged the political predicates of their project. In doing so they oriented other histories politically, suggesting that those which did not oppose capitalism endorsed it, actively or passively. Hence they indicated the political character of all historical writing. Traditional Marxists like Hobsbawm, Harrison and Foster also pointed to the presentism of historical practice by elaborating radical revisions which rendered older constructions compatible with current political reality. When Hobsbawm produced his original analysis in 1954, an earlier optimism, born of his belief that capitalism was 'on its last legs' and that Soviet Russia was pointing the way to 'a new world', had given way to the sobering recognition that British reformism showed no sign of weakening.[218] He was struck, he confessed, by 'the failure of a communist party or of the semi-Marxist left to make decisive headway, rather than [by] the change in the political spirit of the movement as a whole'.[219] Deepening with time, this pessimism, poignantly expressed in the title of his 1978 essay, 'Labour's Forward March Halted?',[220] gradually gave rise to a new teleology which, rather than plotting the inexorable 'progress' of labour, was linked to the question of 'why it had taken the path that it had'.[221] Reflected in subsequent observations by Harrison and Foster, this teleology ordered a concerted effort to keep the issue of working-class empowerment on the historiographical agenda.[222]

Given this assessment and my failure thus far to take issue with what I have characterized as traditional Marxist analyses,[223] it might be assumed that I accept those analyses uncritically. Such an assumption would be wrong, for I find them to be as inconsistent as others to which I have addressed myself. Although they helped to illuminate the political presentism of historical practice, their contingency was never acknowledged. Like liberal and conservative historians, their authors maintained the pose of objectivity, even as they revised and reconstructed. In turn, their revisions were displaced, along with their politics, by a new breed of Marxists who shared with them little more than the tacit and undemonstrable conviction that the further the past recedes, the clearer its truth becomes.[224] Reduced by degrees to contrived expressions of an outmoded socialism, traditional Marxist analyses were ultimately silenced by the most final kind of critique: they were ignored. By representing them without further comment, I do not suggest that they are above criticism, nor do I impute to them any 'objective' relevance. My purpose is simply to provide a contrast in which their political character illuminates that of current narratives and re-illuminates the question of contingency. In this connection, they offer a description of capitalist power relations which in my view speaks powerfully to the present, not in any absolute sense, but as a defensible alternative to prevailing conventions which valorize capitalism and have been substantially underwritten by the new generation of Marxist historians.[225]

As the political pendulum moved to the right during the 1970s and 1980s, this new generation tempered its Marxism with cultural theory, adopted 'broader analytical frameworks' and dismissed the work of its predecessors as narrow and reductive.[226] The labour aristocracy thesis became the focus of a vigorous debate and all of its variants were challenged.[227] The existence of the stratum was never decisively refuted and the thesis continued intermittently to be invoked.[228] It was seriously discredited, however, by writers like Musson and Stedman Jones, who argued that élites of skilled workers, serving as subcontractors and pacemakers, were not a uniquely mid-Victorian phenomenon but had, in one form or another, long existed.[229] On this basis, the aristocracy's explanatory utility was denied and the thesis itself became a somewhat 'outdated theory of class'.[230] Between 1978 and 1984, Hobsbawm moderated but did not substantially change his earlier position. Appealing to a substantial body of evidence which confirmed to his satisfaction both the stratum's reality and its importance to contemporaries, he took issue with the view that it was no more than a theoretical construction.[231] As late as 1985, Royden Harrison reasserted his conviction that, without reference to the transformative role of the labour aristocracy, mid-Victorian reformism is inexplicable.[232] But such arguments were now challenged as both empirically and logically deficient. In a new revisionist historiography, according to which the character of working-class radicalism had been persistently liberal throughout the century, the class-conscious and revolutionary character of Chartism was disputed.[233] The revisionist project emphasized continuity rather than change and a gradual accommodation of radical demands. As a consequence, it was suggested, the working classes were enabled to pursue a respectable independence within the prevailing system and the *status quo* was broadly accepted.

REVISIONIST APPROACHES AND
THE NEW CONSERVATISM

Post-Marxist approaches to labour history vary considerably and indeed some remain tacitly Marxist insofar as they represent modified forms of 'class' analysis. Others dismiss class concepts as anachronistic, and identify the nineteenth-century lower-class mentality as 'populist'. All, however, are revisionist in that they repudiate much of traditional Marxism as crude and reductive, employ novel theories of culture and language as an alternative to the Marxian dialectic, and affect to distance themselves, in most cases, from the positivism of earlier writers.[234] Beyond its cultural and/or linguistic foundations, the historiography to which I refer is distinguished by its emphasis on continuity. Change, it suggests, was less profound and significant than formerly supposed. Conservative in its political implications, the new revisionism coincided with the decline of East European socialist regimes and the re-ascendency of liberal conservatism in the west.

One of the earliest exponents of the new revisionism was Gareth Stedman Jones who, with several impressive analyses of the nineteenth-century labour movement during the 1970s, established himself as one of the decade's most important social historians.[235] In 1982–3, he renounced the social history project, abandoned his Marxist methodology and adopted a linguistic approach.[236] His departure was linked, however, to a prior interest in what he described as the conservatism of the late nineteenth-century working classes. Formerly, from a social-historical perspective which effectively assumed the ontological reality of class, he had sought to explain the absence of class antagonism and the lack of revolutionary spirit. The theoretical framework within which that analysis was developed pointed to ideological incorporation and hence to false consciousness, for in terms of Marx's class-struggle paradigm, political conservatism was inimical to working-class interests. Resisting the reductive implications of false consciousness, he had suggested instead that what appeared to be popular conservatism was in fact a condition of political anomie induced by the defeat of Chartism.[237]

By 1982, the reality of working-class conservatism, apparently illustrated by popular enthusiasm for Thatcher's social vision, could no longer be denied.[238]

Nor could it adequately be explained, in Stedman Jones's view, by a methodology which reduced the political to a function of the social.[239] His former approach, he now concluded, had obscured the essentially political character of Chartism, a character of which Chartists themselves were acutely aware.[240] Historians from Hovell onward, he wrote, had engaged Chartism as the political consequence of economic distress. '[W]hether liberal, social democratic or Marxist,' he continued, they saw it 'as axiomatic that economic power is the cause, political power the effect'.[241] But noting Gammage's observation that 'exclusion from political power is the cause of our social anomalies', he stressed that it was the monopoly of political power by an opulent few that was seen by Chartists to underpin the misery of the 'masses'.[242] He set out to correct this reversal in an analysis of Chartist political ideology which began with what Chartists said and wrote. The analysis would necessarily preclude the treatment 'of Chartist language as a more or less immediate rendition of experience into words', because this would simply 'resolve problems posed by the form of Chartism into problems of its supposed content'. Instead it would analyse language and politics independently of 'a priori social inferences', thus to establish 'a far closer and more precise relationship between ideology and activity than is conveyed in the standard picture of the movement'.[243]

On the basis of this methodology, Stedman Jones found that Chartist vocabulary was, above all else, one of political exclusion, 'whatever the social character of those excluded'. It could never, therefore, 'be the ideology of a specific class'.[244] The Chartist critique of the middle classes, he argued, focused on their manipulation of political power, not their monopoly of the means of production. Many were vilified as corrupt idlers, who sought to enhance their profits by lowering wages, but hardworking masters and sympathetic industrialists, whose practices were fair, were highly respected.[245] Critiques of capitalism were, of course, elaborated, but all tended to reinforce hostility to landlords, money lords and middlemen. All contrasted reasonable and excessive profit; none situated economic exploitation in productive relations.[246] The distinction drawn by Chartists was not primarily, therefore, 'between ruling and exploited classes in an economic sense', but between the 'beneficiaries and victims' of political monopoly and corruption.[247]

A series of developments in the 1830s, Stedman Jones observed, served to polarize the middle and working classes, but they cannot be seen to have given rise to a class-based critique. The 1832 Reform Act, the New Poor Law, mounting cyclical and structural unemployment – all exacerbated the hostility of workers to 'tyrannical' employers. As the demands of the former became more insolent and trade union action more frequent, the hostility was reciprocated.[248] However, the belief that the 'millocrat' and 'cotton lord' 'had now displaced the old aristocracy did not', he insisted, weaken conviction that the origin and determination of oppression was political.[249] And it was precisely because of this conviction, according to Stedman Jones, that when oppression diminished, Chartism declined. During the 1840s, he continued, the state instituted a range of reforms whereby the condition of the working classes visibly improved. 'Peel's reduction of taxes on consumption', continued by Gladstone; the Mines Act and the Budget in 1842; the Joint Stock Company Act, the Bank Charter Act and repeal of the Corn Laws – all indicated that adequate reform was possible within the existing system and radical ideology began 'to lose purchase over large parts of its mass following'.[250] After 1842, Chartist rhetoric became increasingly stale, anachronistic, irrelevant and unable, therefore, to sustain the movement's temporary revival in 1847–8. The rise and fall of Chartism, Stedman Jones concluded, was related in the first instance not to economic fluctuations, internal divisions or immature class consciousness, 'but to the changing character and policies of the State – the principal enemy upon whose actions radicals had always found that their credibility depended'.[251]

Similar conclusions were drawn a year earlier by Craig Calhoun, albeit in a variant of the approach which Stedman Jones rejected. Taking issue in the first instance with E.P. Thompson's thesis, Calhoun sought to demonstrate that 'the social' was ultimately determinative. At a time when traditional modes of production and social existence were threatened and revolution was most likely, he wrote, a community-based artisanate, the backbone of popular radicalism, pursued a transparently reactionary politics. A populist rather than a class movement, its members held traditional values and opposed change, hence their agenda was designed to subvert the consolidation of new social relations and to defend the traditional way of life. The emergence of a class-based radicalism, informed by labour theories of value and nationally organized, he wrote, did not occur until late in the Chartist period, when any tendency to revolution was undermined by the possibility of ameliorative reform within the system.[252]

Predictably, these views gave rise to a spirited defence of class, although Calhoun's analysis was substantially eclipsed as historians closed ranks against Stedman Jones's provocative linguistic approach. According to Neville Kirk, the latter 'amount[ed] to little more than a highly formalized, literal and narrow interpretation of words and ideas rather than to an investigation of . . . the ways in which social *meaning* is constructed, and the role of language in that construction'.[253] Insufficiently sensitive 'to context and complexity of meaning', Kirk suggested, it was not 'a post-structuralist reading of *language* at all', but rather an analysis of radicalism from the standpoint of 'conventional intellectual history'.[254] John Foster expressed similar reservations, observing that Stedman Jones ignored 'the crucial nexus of social practice, language and consciousness', failed adequately to appreciate the historical specificity of language, and never therefore recognized the complexity and fluidity of meaning.[255] These emphases were subsequently taken up in a belated polemic by Bryan Palmer.[256] According to Palmer, Stedman Jones's literalism completed a backward analytical step in which the language of political radicalism was reduced to a published vocabulary, then elevated arbitrarily above class and material context as the proper object of analysis.[257] Remiss in his handling of sources, Stedman Jones was also 'theoretically lazy'. Refusing 'to enter the labyrinth where language and theory intersect', he 'fail[ed] to interrogate the language of radicalism as a produced discourse'.[258] As a result, he effected a kind of 'interpretative containment' in which words that seemed to suggest 'class antagonism and an emerging consciousness of the potency of class power' were stripped of their suggestive connotations.[259] Thus characterized, these procedures signified to Palmer an ominous descent into discourse whereby class was discarded and at considerable cost. In an estimate of this cost, he found that everything 'new and class-based in [Chartist] discourse' was suppressed, class antagonism was ignored, and the coercive/repressive aspects of liberal reform were concealed beneath a benevolent gloss. '[T]his linguistically ordered reinterpretation', he concluded, though designed to overcome the reductive deficiencies of class analysis, culminated in nothing more than 'unconvincing idealism'.[260]

To lend weight to his assessment, Palmer referred to a number of other writers, including Joan Scott, but although Scott described similar conceptual problems, she saw them less as fatal flaws than as objects to be overcome in a work of great potential. Stedman Jones, she wrote, correctly discerned that 'there is no social reality outside or prior to language' and thus introduced labour historians to exciting new possibilities.[261] But because he did not fully apprehend the theories he employed, his project failed to achieve its radical promise. Engaging with Chartism as a political language and attending carefully to its terms and propositions, he revealed the radical lineage of Chartist thought and thus restored 'politics to its proper place' in Chartist studies. But he did so, she added, 'only in the most literal way'.[262] His mistake, Scott continued, was to conflate two definitions of politics, one containing the non-referential conception of language with which he began, the other descriptive and close to the approach of conventional intellectual history. Diverted by the latter when he intended to use the former, he subsequently treated meaning as language and the latter 'as a vehicle for communicating ideas rather than a system of meaning or a process of signification'. In doing so he reverted 'to the notion that "language" reflects a "reality" external to it, rather than being constitutive of that reality'.[263] Hence, noting similarities between Chartist discourse and other radical languages like Owenism, trade unionism and Ricardian socialism, all of which identified 'the state as the ultimate source of oppression', he found that state policies rather than relations of production determined the composition and goals of Chartism. On this basis he concluded that Chartism was a political movement and class a political concept, not so much because they were 'formulated in a particular (discursive) conflict' but because they referred to or reflected objective political conditions, problems or practices.[264] '[I]t would have been more useful', Scott observed, 'to acknowledge "class"', to 'locate its origins in political rhetoric', and to examine the multidimensional relationships through which words acquire their meanings.[265] Such an examination might have shown that politics, class and gender are implicated in one another and cannot be analysed separately. It might also have shown how gender has been used historically to articulate and naturalize difference.[266]

Labour historians subsequently adopted the language of Stedman Jones and his critics, but they were as reluctant to acknowledge its relativist consequences as they were to consider Scott's recommendations.[267] Nevertheless, new categories became commonplace and older ones were revised. A casualty of this revision was the labour aristocracy, which came increasingly to be seen as a historical 'construct'.[268] Few commentators were prepared to deny its historical existence, but most agreed that it was as fragmented and as vulnerable to circumstances as the rest of the labouring population. As its privileged status and its special relationship to the middle classes were questioned, so too was its 'mechanical' mediation of dominant ideas.[269] Class consciousness, it was now suggested, survived the demise of Chartism but it was less revolutionary than formerly supposed. Victorian workers did not succumb to ideological incorporation; instead, the dynamic of their quest for self-determination changed. Convinced by the developments of earlier decades that the conquest of political power was not possible, they eschewed political solutions to carve out a distinctive, independent culture within the system itself, pursuing a respectable independence which crystallized around a negotiated version of consensus values. The proponents of this view agreed that the labour aristocracy contributed to social stabilization during the third quarter of the century, but rejected the notion that it functioned as an instrument of bourgeois control, thereby divesting it of any real explanatory significance.[270]

One such commentator was Geoffrey Crossick, who focused on labour élites in the Kentish London towns of Deptford, Greenwich and Woolwich to explain what he termed the relative stability of the mid-Victorian period. Crossick characterized stability as the narrowing of conflict between all classes rather than 'some absolute calm', and he argued that the labour aristocracy was a major element in bringing this condition about.[271] Stabilization, he observed, 'was not simply the outcome of one class's victory over another, but the result of a process of continuing struggle in which the features of a class society determined the outcome in only the most generalized sense'.[272] The struggle, he continued, took place in the context of economic expansion, but the process itself 'could only be interpreted within the wider framework of social relationships and ideological forces . . . [which] determined the consequences of economic developments, in specific places, at specific points in time'.[273] Hence, he proposed to illuminate the labour aristocracy's contribution to social stability by exploring its 'relation to the society in which it lived'.[274]

In Kentish London, he suggested, the labour aristocracy was not merely an economic élite but a distinctive social stratum which emerged in response to mid-Victorian economic and industrial developments. It was not related to the area's traditional crafts – tailoring, shoemaking, leather and wood working – which declined with the onset of industrialization;[275] nor was it linked to an emergent factory proletariat. Its members were employed predominantly in government works which spanned the new metal, engineering and shipbuilding industries. It therefore enjoyed a unique relationship to the local bourgeoisie and professional élite, a relationship conducted at the community level rather than the economic. The industrial structure, however, comprised a second layer of lesser, unstable firms controlled by small masters commonly recruited from the ranks of the employed. As a consequence, 'the path out of a dependence on wage employment [did not] appear totally closed', and the area remained relatively free of the economic and social tensions which arose elsewhere.[276]

Unlike Hobsbawm, Harrison and Foster, for whom the labour aristocracy was the product of structural developments, Crossick suggested that, in the Kentish London context, the stratum invented itself, achieving its position 'through struggle and conflict'.[277] Its struggle, he indicated, was conducted on two fronts. On one, it was concerned with distinguishing itself from the unskilled, on the other, with winning the endorsement, approval and acceptance of right-minded people, the local social élites.[278] In an area where Chartism had never established deep roots and radicalism had retained a more traditional critique of privilege and monopoly, 'the need for external recognition', he explained, 'dovetailed into political liberalism'.[279] Concerned less specifically, then, with its class position than its status in the local community, the labour aristocracy identified with the middle classes in terms of values which it felt it shared with them; and distinguished itself from other workers on the basis of 'wages, skill, work situation, economic opportunity, prestige, craft control [and] education'.[280]

The promise of this formulation notwithstanding, Crossick went on to focus rather narrowly on the labour aristocracy's relationship to the middle classes. Although he proposed to illuminate the stratum's emergence and position in the context of society at large and to address working-class 'experience' more broadly, his unskilled, semi-skilled and irregular workers remained shadowy figures who made little apparent social impact.[281] He adduced evidence of their meagre incomes, the instability of their employment, their exploitation on the job by skilled workers, their exclusion from co-operatives and friendly societies, and their frustrated attempts to form unions.[282] He also noted that labour aristocrats disdained them as 'inferior, ignorant and generally immoral' but viewed them with sympathy, rejecting the middle-class myth that poverty was caused by personal inadequacy and recognizing the 'impossibility of respectability on twelve shillings a week'.[283] In their shiftless alterity, they thus became a counterpoint to the aristocrat's respectability and a negative measure of élite status. But Crossick never consulted their views, nor did he explore their 'relationship' to the labour aristocracy. As historical actors, they were altogether excluded from his analysis.

Not so the middle class, in the respectable and independent image of which Crossick's labour aristocrats sought to mould themselves. To such men, Crossick explained, '[i]ndependence was not just the negative freedom from charity and want', but the self-confidence and capacity to choose the voluntary associations one would join, the district one lived in and the accoutrements of respectability one wished to display.[284] It was nevertheless compatible with wage labour,[285] for it was defined in terms of control in the workplace, security of employment and a wage consistent with the aristocrat's superior position. In short, independence was immunity from 'the will and dictates of others'.[286] It included the rejection of patronage from above and also of middle-class individualist tendencies, for it was nothing if not mutualist in character.[287] The will to seek independence and the qualities required to attain it constituted a moral imperative which lay at the very heart of respectability.[288] Respectability represented values which the labour aristocracy held in common with the middle classes and on the basis of which middle-class approval was sought. Those values included industry, thrift, regularity, sobriety, providence, restraint, self-help, good breeding and, of course, independence.[289] There, were, however, qualifications. Sobriety and restraint, for example, were assimilated to a drinking culture which aristocrats refused to relinquish. They rejected the middle-class notion that drink was 'an impossible temptation for working men', proclaimed its medicinal efficacy and were compelled, 'in a sense', to continue drinking to demonstrate their capacity for moderation.[290] Industry required regular employment, the maintenance of which, along with 'respectable' remuneration, was enforced by collective trade union organization and exclusive practices.[291] It was manifested in craft pride and an assertion of the dignity of manual work, which superior classes often disdained.[292] Thrift and providence were pursued in the context of friendly societies and co-operatives and were therefore divested, Crossick argued, of their middle-class individualist connotations.[293] Good breeding was not an inherent virtue but the ability to overcome 'the most basic problems of poverty, intemperance and lack of industry', to demonstrate one's value and respectability.[294]

These qualities were exhibited in a range of ways which included the purchase of houses with 'flourishes of architectural respectability' in status-defined localities;[295] the rejection of privilege and patronage, which was expressed in the abandonment of improvement societies where middle-class influence came to predominate;[296] shopping only at co-operative stores, effectively stating one's independence of the need both for credit and for the adulterated goods which credit purchase often entailed;[297] and membership of voluntary institutions, sometimes of several, which not only distinguished the 'aristocrat' from the generally ineligible lesser ranks, but improved their material position, consolidated their values and culture, and testified to their independence, respectability and moral rectitude.[298] These values and practices added up to self-respect, but they had often to be fought for, notably in the context of trade unionism, to which the middle classes were cool if not hostile. Nevertheless, they were the essence of respectability and the basis on which middle-class approval was courted.[299]

Here, however, Crossick introduced an important caveat. '[I]deas and values are illusory things whose content can change subtly but meaningfully between actor and observer'.[300] Emphasizing 'the constructive and normative character of "aristocrat" consciousness' and speculating on the subjective need of labour aristocrats 'to feel superior', he suggested that 'meaning-systems are relative to the values of those who construct and participate in them'.[301] Hence, he argued, shared values, implicitly derived from a common tradition, took on a different significance among labour aristocrats for whom they could only produce results in the context of a co-operative, mutualist ethos.[302] Moreover, he found that the aristocrat's value system, embedded in a range of institutions and practices, came to constitute an ideology which raised it from an economic élite into a social stratum for whom respectability 'provided an alternative to wealth as a criterion for social judgement' and became 'a means of living with inequality'.[303] Having negotiated both a degree of independence and the meaning of respectability, the labour aristocracy, in Crossick's view, successfully resisted the full implementation of bourgeois hegemony.[304] His account, however, is far from satisfactory.

First, it can be argued that if the labour aristocracy endeavoured, as Crossick indicated, to maintain a superior position in an unequal society, then it accepted the social hierarchy and submitted to the logic of bourgeois hegemony.[305] In this connection, the 'mutualism' to which he referred with apparent admiration seems more like a capitalist tactic than a practice opposed to competitivism. A form of 'internal' co-operation which functioned to exclude other workers from the benefits enjoyed by labour aristocrats, it is scarcely distinguishable, under Crossick's description, from the combinations whereby capital monopolizes markets, thus to protect individual interests. Second, although Crossick purported to explain a prevailing social condition, he never looked beyond the perspective of a social élite. Having declared unskilled and semi-skilled workers peripheral to his focus,[306] he subsequently excluded them from his analysis. Perhaps such figures shared the world view which he imputed to labour aristocrats, or perhaps they lacked the power to influence the social order he described. But because he never consulted them, these possibilities were not explored and his argument remained curiously incomplete.

A further problem was illuminated inadvertently by Gregor McLennan. Although Crossick proposed an explanatory framework based on the argument that the labour aristocracy's ideology and behaviour were determined structurally, by 'particular forces', he went on, as McLennan observed, to assert that the meaning of aristocratic values and practices derived from their own life experience. 'The economic and social system of industrializing Britain was not seen by the workers within it as a totality', Crossick insisted, 'but only as they themselves experienced it'.[307] According to McLennan, this claim was incompatible with the 'concept of ideology and determination required by . . . the Marxist tradition', and suggested not a causal account but a phenomenological method whereby 'the aristocrat's reformist tendencies cease[d] altogether to be a problem of any kind'.[308] McLennan's critique was basically political in that it was advanced not to invalidate phenomenology but to challenge Crossick's Marxist credentials. But it also raised an important question of theoretical consistency. On the one hand, Crossick's argument relied substantially on the notion that the labour aristocracy participated in a collective experience. Yet in the above formulation he suggested the particularity both of behaviour and experience (behaviour was determined structurally by 'particular forces'; British workers saw the prevailing system 'only as they themselves experienced it'). In doing so he appeared to strike a balance between determination and agency (at least for labour aristocrats), but he also contradicted the collective experience on which his explanatory generalizations were based.

Another analysis to which the labour aristocracy was central was R.Q. Gray's 1976 account of Victorian Edinburgh. Gray defined his project as an attempt to explain 'the nature of class domination' in nineteenth-century society and he represented the labour aristocracy as an agent of middle-class hegemony.[309] Borrowing a great deal from Foster, he emphasized the stratum's historical specificity and its stabilizing function. He also stressed authority in the workplace as one of its most fundamental defining features.[310] But he questioned Foster's emphasis on the '"aristocracy's" . . . directly "collaborationist" nature' and deplored the vulgarization both of the labour aristocracy thesis and Marxist methodology by other writers who have treated cultural and ideological differences as passive reflections of economic structures.[311] In this sense he approached Crossick's concerns, emphasizing the need to explore 'the cultural mediation of different economic experiences'.[312] His analysis also resembled Crossick's in that his élite, although it comprised the practitioners of many traditional crafts as well as engineers, metal and transport workers, had generally amicable relations but little direct economic contact with the middle classes.[313] However, unlike Crossick, Gray was less ambiguous about the centrality of the labour aristocracy to the hegemonic process and assimilated a lucid elaboration of Gramscian theory to a fairly conventional Marxist analysis.[314]

Gray's precise aims were 'to establish the reality of class hegemony, the limits it imposed on the articulation of working-class consciousness, and the dynamic and problematic nature of the relationships involved'.[315] He engaged hegemony not as 'a particular set of beliefs' but as a 'mode of organizing beliefs', at once a structured practice and 'a dynamic and shifting relationship of social subordination'. Within this complex, he suggested, value-systems became modified in a 'two-way' process, as subaltern classes adapted dominant values to diverse conditions of existence, while dominant ideological structures incorporated and transformed dissident values and practices, thereby preventing the full working through of their implications and containing potential class conflict. Hence, the formation of the labour aristocracy was 'the outcome of differential socio-economic experience . . . handled through the available ideologies, and actively interpreted in terms of lifestyle and social imagery'. Of particular importance in this connection was the ability of the ruling class to confine working-class struggle 'within the existing fundamental structures' by diffusing socio-cultural imperatives through private institutions or organisms such as voluntary organizations and facilities for leisure, thrift and adult education.[316] It was at the level of such institutions, which were largely controlled by the labour aristocracy, that values and practices were negotiated.

On most substantive issues, Gray's analysis paralleled Crossick's. Consensus values in Edinburgh reflected those in Kentish London and were assimilated to the mutualist traditions of labour aristocrats in similar ways. As in Kentish London, Edinburgh's aristocrats enjoyed relative prosperity but their social position 'had to be fought for, and maintained against the pressure to cut living standards'.[317] They were 'not precisely deferential' and they resisted 'the more direct forms of patronage'. They nevertheless sought middle-class approval, solicited middle-class dignitaries to preside over their functions and expressed their aspirations and norms in middle-class language.[318] Like Crossick's aristocrats, Gray's sought independence, shunned credit, patronized the more exclusive friendly societies and preferred to segregate themselves residentially.[319] Politically their orientation was Liberal and their political critique was directed largely at 'the old radical demonology: monarchy, aristocracy, church, militarism'.[320] Although the spokesmen of their institutions often invoked 'middle-class social imagery' in terms like decency, sobriety and respectability, such values co-existed with alternative and divergent modes of conduct, notably trade unionism.[321] 'The deep-rooted habits of solidarity and mutual aid' which developed in response to the exigencies of working-class existence 'were never completely obliterated by the rhetoric of self-help',[322] and although aspirations to respectability were expressed in the language of the dominant ideology, they retained 'a dimension of class-conscious assertion'. Hence, as an alternative to wealth, dirty hands, which signified hard work, could serve as a measure of prestige.[323] Similarly, '[t]he ritual of certain friendly society lodges gave membership a meaning beyond its purely economic functions'.[324]

The skilled worker's claim to respectability was, in Gray's view, a corporate claim to status recognition which 'must be set in the context of a strong sense of working-class pride'.[325] It was this corporate character which denoted 'the cultural and political formation of a separate stratum'.[326] Nevertheless, he concluded, although artisans disdained patronage and proclaimed their independence, their aspirations were 'expressed in a language "adopted" from the dominant class so that the[ir] institutions and modes of behaviour . . . were contained within a larger local society dominated by the "hegemonic" bourgeoisie'.[327] Their institutions mediated values like respectability, thrift and independence, translating and adapting them to the conditions of working-class life. Labour leaders also played an important mediatory role, with reference to which Gray made an important connection between the *embour-geoisement* thesis and the theory of hegemony, describing the embeddedness of the former in the wider processes of the latter.[328] The ongoing struggle of aristocrats to maintain their social and economic position led to a broadening of the trade union base, the dissolution of craft divisions and the emergence, in the third quarter of the century, of 'relatively autonomous working-class industrial and political movement'.[329] And towards the end of the century structural changes and the advent of socialism may also have drawn skilled and unskilled workers closer together.[330] But the working-class movement lacked an adequate social critique, and although, at the formal ideological level, it cherished the utopian 'hope for emancipation from competitive capitalism', at the experiential level, it seemed to accept 'that there can be no embracing freedom apart from substantial equality in social condition'.[331] Hence, in a complex process, the democratic aspirations of the labour movement 'were, after 1867, effectively contained – despite certain important tensions – within a Liberal movement dominated nationally by middle-class and aristocratic élites'.[332]

By 1980 Gray had distanced himself from the labour aristocracy thesis. Reflecting concerns then current, he suggested that it 'pointed to a series of problems', notably the neglect of gender issues and age divisions within the workforce, 'rather than offer[ing] an explanation'.[333] Apparently, however, he remained satisfied that his analysis of what certain values and practices meant to contemporaries was adequate. Yet meaning has different levels, as he acknowledged. On some, its content may be relatively fixed, while on others it will remain as fluid as the agents who produce it, and the subjects it produces, are diverse. If one accepts this view, then accounts of meaning must at best be speculative. In the histories under review, however, speculation assumes the status of truth, speculative categories become foundations and speculative conclusions are extrapolated to broad sections of the community. This problem is exemplified in the treatment of consciousness by two American liberal historians, T.W. Laqueur and Trygve Tholfsen who, in 1976, made substantial contributions to the debates about respectability and bourgeois hegemony.[334] Laqueur and Tholfsen differed somewhat as to the origin and character of respectability, but agreed that it was a unifying phenomenon, an area of working-class consent to bourgeois hegemony and an important agent, therefore, of social stability. Both have been criticized for their idealism – they made no attempt to relate their concerns to economic developments – and both implied that there was no necessary link between ideology and economic structure. They have nevertheless exerted considerable influence, not least by helping to displace an earlier emphasis on class conflict with a vision of popular support for the existing social order.

Although Laqueur concentrated on the years between 1780 and 1850, his work is not irrelevant to mid-Victorian concerns. For if, in this earlier period, a moral consensus crystallized around respectability as he suggested, why did this consensus not enhance social stability then, as it purportedly did in the third quarter of the century?[335] A survey of his thesis is therefore apposite. Laqueur's aim was twofold: to explore the connections between the Sunday school movement and working-class respectability, and to demonstrate that the movement was not an instrument of bourgeois hegemony. He argued that although Sunday schools were initiated by the superior classes in the late eighteenth century, they were gradually surrendered to working-class control. Staffed, financed and taught by working people, the schools extended their influence to 'nearly every working-class child' outside the metropolis, and became a focal point of community life.[336] Even those few schools 'whose managers were of a higher social standing . . . operated in a remarkably democratic fashion'.[337]

The movement's ethos was imbued with the puritan ethic: hard work, thrift, self-help, self-improvement and time-consciousness, along with cleanliness, orderliness, diligence, piety and obedience. The essence of respectability, these values were in no way imposed. They derived from a shared moral tradition which was firmly embedded in Protestant Christianity and revitalized during the late eighteenth-century evangelical revival.[338] In the Sunday school context, they enhanced the pursuit of literacy, 'a component of the psychological revolution which accompanied and made possible the industrial revolution'.[339] The schools themselves 'were the product of a new, more humane, more tolerant, indeed more optimistic view of childhood'.[340] An outgrowth of Arminian theology, which gradually displaced Calvinist predestinarianism and the allied belief that children were inherently wicked, this view was adopted, apparently spontaneously, both by genteel philanthropists and substantial numbers of their inferiors.[341] Linked to a growing conviction that 'the Bible [should] be accessible to the lower orders', it also reflected a new sensitivity among working people to the benefits of rational education. Hence, literate working people undertook to teach the children of their neighbours to read and write, approaching their mission as one of 'moral rescue'.[342] 'It would [therefore] be a mistake,' Laqueur warned, to conflate the precepts or ideals of respectability 'into a distinct bourgeois ideology,' for they found vehement working-class supporters.[343] Proclaimed by successful working men, themselves almost invariably the products of Sunday school education, they were instilled in working-class children by working-class teachers. He found this unremarkable: 'the personality traits of the successful business man are, after all, not very different from those of the successful political leader, journalist, or trade union leader', and a 'congruence between the fundamental values of the middle class and "respectable" working classes is thus natural and not difficult to understand'.[344]

In Laqueur's view, the Sunday school movement was a significant cultural achievement which exemplified the moral and intellectual independence of working people. It also demonstrated the depth of their religious conviction, and in this connection he took particular issue with E.P. Thompson's judgement that their religion amounted to a chiliasm of despair, an anodyne alternative to the social justice and political equality which eluded them in the material world. 'A religion which places great emphasis on the promise of an afterlife', Laqueur insisted, 'is not just the chiliasm of the defeated and the hopeless, the solace of failed revolution. It is also the religion of those for whom death from consumption, smallpox, cholera, fever or accident is an ever-present oppressive reality.'[345] But religion was far more than a source of comfort to the bereaved. It was a spur to the pursuit of literacy and justified instruction;[346] it strengthened the determination of working people, so assiduously cultivated in the Sunday school, to transform their condition through self-help, self-improvement and moral excellence; and it armed those exceptional men who went forth from the schools to lead the working-class struggle in the public sphere.[347] The demand for literacy may have had an economic aspect, Laqueur conceded, but it was far more intimately related to the Evangelical revival, to the spirit of which the printed word was so vital.[348] The definitive expression of this thirst for literacy and religion was the Sunday school which '[i]n large part', he found, 'originated as an expression of that faith in the efficacy of education and the malleability of human nature which is still dominant today'.[349]

During the nineteenth century, Laqueur conceded, bourgeois hegemony indeed came to prevail and its definitive expression was respectability. But it was extended with the consent of working people. Although its form was distinctively middle class, it was acceptable because its essence was the same religious and moral tradition which flourished in the Sunday school and the community-at-large.[350] According to Laqueur, that tradition had serious implications for popular radicalism, for it was inimical to the development of revolutionary consciousness. It nourished working-class political ideology and informed its contempt for injustice and inequality, but it contained no metaphor for a more fundamental social critique.[351] Moreover, 'religion absorbed the psychological energies born of frustrated revolution' and 'contained the political fervor of the poor by providing it with a readily available alternative focus'. Nevertheless, in a curious reversal, Laqueur went on to suggest that a revolutionary ideology did not emerge because there was no revolution: 'working-class politics lacked . . . a rhetoric of 1789 less because of religious education than because England did not experience a 1789'.[352] This fortuitous absence, he concluded, was 'due to the stability of English society and the cohesion of its ruling class'.[353]

Many aspects of Laqueur's thesis have been criticized: his conclusions were often inconsistent with his evidence;[354] he underestimated sectarian differences;[355] his account of school personnel and finance was inconclusive.[356] His argument for the economic independence of Sunday schools was 'tendentious'; he exaggerated the connection between working-class notables and the Sunday school movement; and, in his dossier of pupils and teachers who subsequently won fame in the working-class movement, he made serious errors.[357] He did not distinguish between the radical advocacy of political advancement 'through collective help and democratic control' and the Sunday school ethos, which promoted individual competition and achievement 'while making failure as conspicuous and painful as possible'.[358] To this list can be added his almost total disregard for economic, social and political context. He depicted the Sunday school movement as a world apart, an oasis of peace and calm in which infinitely inventive working men and women deeply rooted in the 'ethic of education, religion and respectability' fashioned 'a culture of discipline, self-respect and improvement'.[359] Ideology hovered detached from this world, a nebulous essence which frustrated would-be revolutionaries because it was not amenable to change but which, in the Sunday school context, was mere 'window-dressing on a reality determined by the nature of the institution'. The significance of economic imperatives was likewise discounted.[360]

It did not occur to Laqueur that the middle classes may not have practised the values and virtues which they promoted, apparently with resounding success, among the lower orders. Nor did he ever define, let alone problematize, words like ideology, class and consciousness. Instead he invoked them as immutable foundations, the meanings of which were fixed and self-evident. Similarly, observing that Sunday school tracts were intended for no other reason than to counter the influence of corrupt parents and to promote 'the public good',[361] he attempted neither to define the public nor to question the judgement that parents were corrupt. He did not even explore the possibility that the public good may have been perceived differently by people of different socio-economic backgrounds. With transparent approval he noted contemporary faith in the efficacy of education, but not the extent to which the quality, content, kind, and availability of education varied from one status group to the next. Overall, he presented an idealized working class, eminently satisfied with the *status quo*, whose virtues and ambitions were well worth imitating in 1976.[362] Conspicuous by their absence from Laqueur's moral utopia were the severely disadvantaged and disaffected. Unemployment, starvation, anti-Poor Law demonstrations and the Factory Reform movement might hardly have existed, while Chartism and its radical agenda for social and political change were reduced to virtual insignificance. In a climate where the prevailing social order was beyond criticism, and the moral and material improvement of the lower orders proceeded apace, demands for social justice and political equality, faintly heard, seemed scarcely necessary. Paradoxically, although the respectability which Laqueur depicted was of an order substantially different from that supposedly prized in later decades, his very oversights made his construction compatible with the mid-Victorian respectability thesis. For, in addition to celebrating working-class independence, the proponents of that thesis, in line with the conservative revisionism which began its ascendancy in the 1970s, were also concerned to divest the century's social and political protest of its revolutionary connotations, and to demonstrate that the working classes had neither the capacity nor the desire to change the *status quo*.

47

Such was the character of Tholfsen's interpretation. 'Looking back from the 1970s', Tholfsen undertook to explain the swift transition from early-Victorian working-class militancy to the 'relative quiescence of the age of equipoise'.[363] The basic premise of his argument was that the moral and social values which predominated in nineteenth-century England were not the specific attribute or product of any one class, but an inheritance forged from Enlightenment rationalism, evangelicalism and romanticism, in which all of society shared.[364] Conflict arose as working people opposed their own egalitarian formulations of this inheritance to the narrow, self-interested bourgeois version. But working-class radicalism, because of its own 'reformist, non-revolutionary orientation', was unable to provide 'a genuine alternative to liberal reformism', and gradually accepted middle-class predominance. Nevertheless, radicalism 'did not merely dissolve into middle-class ideology, but persisted in a different form, continuing to resist propaganda from above and to foster a spirit of independence and pride among workmen'.[365] Consensus did not mean capitulation.

Tholfsen advanced an argument of great subtlety. The cynical efforts of bourgeois ideologues to maintain the lower classes in respectful subordination were never far from his relentless gaze, and his admiration for Chartist leaders and their intellectual independence was transparent. The latter may not have been revolutionary or socialist, but nor were they simply 'the passive creatures of forces that determined their being'.[366] In addition to the hungry handloom weavers of textbook accounts, Chartism comprised profound thinkers who 'voiced a trenchant critique of the political and social order' and explicitly rejected 'the ideology that an aggressive bourgeoisie was trying to impose'.[367] Their goals may have been ill-defined, even utopian,[368] but they 'gathered up the ideas and aspirations of the early-Victorian Left into a single mass movement that demanded the enactment of the Charter'.[369] Above all, they were committed to 'the intellectual and moral improvement of the individual', a commitment which survived their militancy to become 'the basis of mid-Victorian consensus and equilibrium', and also of a distinctive, independent working-class culture.[370] In the latter phase, there were indeed those who accepted the role which bourgeois society extended to them, thus to generate a 'cult of respectability'. '[C]onditioned to defer to their superiors, emulate their behaviour and manners, and look to them for approval', such individuals sought nothing more than 'to work hard, please their boss, accept gratefully the wages offered, and perhaps strive for slightly better jobs for themselves and their children'.[371] But the real heroes of Tholfsen's story were the mid-Victorian radicals who, having assessed the objective possibilities of their situation, evolved a distinctive subculture within which to pursue a respectable independence. Alert to the sham of middle-class morality, they devised an account of consensus values which began with the dignity of work.[372] They asserted their manhood against middle-class condescension and insult; sought not to change the system but 'to participate responsibly and rationally in the processes of government'; maintained their commitment to the 'democratic and egalitarian principles that still embody the best aspirations of western culture'; and accepted their subaltern role.[373] Implicitly, in Tholfsen's view, these were wise choices, for so long as workingmen shared so many liberal values and assumptions, they were, in effect, the only choices.

Like Laqueur's thesis, which in some ways it resembles, Tholfsen's account has attracted substantial criticism, notably in relation to its explanatory deficiencies. How did 'one version of liberalism change . . . into another' and why did one form develop 'to the exclusion of another at any given moment?'[374] Why was the working-class commitment to fundamental political and social change abandoned?[375] Beyond suggesting that Chartism bequeathed a legacy of improvement to future generations,[376] Tholfsen never dealt with the movement's demise. It simply faded, at a certain point, from his analysis. Some commentators have suggested that these problems arise because of his failure to utilize the insights of economic and social historians, a failure which they link to an animus against Marxism, so clearly implied in the preface and opening chapter of his book.[377] A further problem was his imprecise usage of various terms, notably class and culture.[378] He gave no clear indication of who belonged to the different classes referred to in his discussion, and he employed culture variously to mean values, ideas, ideologies and institutions.[379] His use of hegemony as an analytical tool was equally problematical. Adopting Gramsci's formulation of the concept, he proposed to divest it of its Marxist implications, thus to take 'note of the hegemonic impulses of the middle class, but without treating liberalism as essentially an instrument of class domination'.[380] As one writer has argued, however, he seemed forced, 'at many points throughout the book', to treat liberalism in precisely that way.[381] Another has pointed out that he employed the notion of hegemony 'as a catchword outside Gramsci's theoretical framework'.[382]

Though unsympathetic to Marx, Tholfsen found Durkheim eminently useful. He employed the latter's theory of the 'conscience collective' to analyse a sample of social gatherings arranged by a Mechanic's Institution and some half-dozen co-operatives. All of these affairs were attended or presided over by middle-class dignitaries who found much to commend in the institutions and their members.[383] The air on each occasion was heavy with 'consensus values' and the meetings amounted, according to Tholfsen, to 'religious events celebrating a common secular faith'.[384] He found this religious atmosphere particularly pronounced at the Mechanics' function where, in a presentation to Sir George Grey, who had just laid the Institution's foundation stone, the speaker intoned: 'We thank you for the courtesy you have shown us this day, and at the same time respectfully congratulate you, sir, as one in authority, and for ourselves gratefully acknowledge the prosperity and peace and goodwill among men, which, under Divine Providence, at present reign not only in this district but throughout our common country.'[385] Such rituals, in Tholfsen's opinion, reflected Durkheim's conception of 'liberalism as the secular religion that provides the social cohesion of modern industrial society'.[386] On the basis of the brief survey just cited, he concluded that, although 'overdrawn' in some respects, Durkheim's 'account of the religion of humanity' corresponded closely 'to the consensus liberalism of the mid-Victorian cities'.[387] How representative Tholfsen's mechanics and co-operators were of mid-Victorian humanity might be considered in the light of a further example of his lack of definition. Throughout his thesis he used the terms equality and egalitarianism to characterize the radical ethos, apparently assuming that their meanings are self-evident. Yet they might well be considered meaningless in the context of the exclusive institutions which his respectable working-'men' inhabited, institutions which evidently denied lesser men and women entry,[388] just as Tholfsen denied them representation in his history. Perhaps the radical commitment 'to democratic and egalitarian principles' only went so far. And perhaps an account designed to celebrate what working people achieved 'within the system' would be compromised by any acknowledgement of the less fortunate, those excluded from any share in economic and political power but who, perhaps, paid most dearly for working-class achievement.

Nor were such people more than a peripheral consideration in an interpretation advanced by F.M.L. Thompson in 1988. Unreceptive to conventional notions of class, Thompson portrayed Victorian society as a multi-layered organism, the strength of which lay in the opacity of its lines of division.[389] A great deal of social mobility occurred between these layers and, as a consequence, 'stark polarization into the battle lines of class' did not occur.[390] Respectability, the cement which held society together, took many forms which were specific to the lifestyles and living standards of the diverse groups and subgroups who embraced it. Its various codes 'had no single taproot'. They were not 'imitative or imposed from outside or above', but represented 'a bundle of self-generated habits and values derived from past customs and present responses to living and working conditions'.[391] Nevertheless, they came implicitly under the influence of evangelical ideology whose 'grip on the language of public discourse on manners and morals' during the 1840s and 1850s 'became nearly total'.[392] With the advent of the New Poor Law, minimum standards of respectability were promoted even among the lowest ranks. Initially, it was the evil reputation of the workhouse which discouraged applications for relief. But by the later nineteenth century, remaining independent 'had become a matter of avoiding social disgrace: avoiding not merely the moral disapproval and criticism of the middle classes, but avoiding above all disparagement and humiliation in front of friends and neighbours'.[393] Equally degrading was the pauper burial, and the ability to provide for a decent funeral was further evidence of respectability, so coveted, apparently, that by 1900 all but the 'residuum', the bottom 10 per cent, 'were drawn into the basic respectability net'.[394]

Thompson's respectable workingman, a key Victorian figure 'on whose good sense hopes of social harmony were based', had no desire to undermine the 'system which provided the job'.[395] He was 'conspicuously indifferent to fighting the class war',[396] and, if a labour aristocrat, he did not involve himself with the employing class in anti-revolutionary conspiracy.[397] He was a creature of the job, and social tranquillity was largely a matter of industrial maturity, as 'work, working practices, and workers all changed together to produce a restyled factory culture'.[398] Respectable workers were largely apolitical. They pursued their independence within their communities and, as far as possible, away from authority. Other than the agreeable postman, few ever saw, or wanted contact with, officialdom.[399] In fact, labour leaders who sought to mobilize political support for parliamentary campaigns to improve 'the lot of the masses' met with widespread indifference.[400] 'Many of the working classes perceived the state as simply a source of mischief, or at best as an irrelevance in their lives, and saw little point or attraction in political activity'.[401] Instead, they joined work excursions to the seaside or went to the music hall, for '[t]he thinking work-ingman quite rationally preferred enjoyment in music-hall comfort to the discomfort of attending political meetings about remote and pointless causes'.[402]

Like the respectable poor, women also appeared in Thompson's narrative, but although they were not confined precisely to an optional chapter, nor were they permitted to speak. Hence, the conventional patriarchal view of Victorian society was not compromised.[403] In fact, like the rest of the working class, women and the poor were consigned to orderly apolitical roles in which they seemed happy to be left alone. Described appropriately as a 'Thatcherite history book',[404] Thompson's volume conveys the unmistakable message that, although Victorian society was imperfect, and bequeathed structural, identity and authority problems to the twentieth century,[405] the respectable values which purportedly rendered the great majority of its workers independent – that is to say, which ensured that they would make no claim on the public purse – were well worth emulating in the 1980s. So, too, he implied, was a carefully drawn popular apoliticism. From the 1840s, when Chartists were suddenly no longer able to generate mass support because people doubted 'the wisdom of resorting to physical force',[406] to the early 1900s, when the state's irrelevance to the concerns of ordinary people was made manifest in the indif-ference of the latter to the overtures of politically ambitious labour leaders,[407] political apathy went hand in hand with, and enhanced, independent respectability. An older construction, in which the disenfranchised masses struggled persistently for social justice and political equality, was thus con-signed to history's dustbin. Whereas writers like Crossick, Gray and Tholfsen chose to discuss prevailing power relations in terms of a negotiated consensus between dominant and subaltern parties, Thompson did not engage with the issue. His account of popular political apathy suggested that the working classes were satisfied with a subordinate role. He thus effectively justified the status quo.

Equally validating is Patrick Joyce's culturalist approach, according to which working people did not merely acquiesce in 'the social regime of capi-talist industry' but were emotionally committed to it.[408] Apparently passive in their reception of social identity and meaning from discursive structures, they recognized a community of interest with their employers whose religious and political orientations they readily adopted.[409] The primary focus of Joyce's analysis, though one from which he often generalizes, is post-1850 Lancashire where, he argues, mechanization in the cotton industry engendered social stability by drawing employer and operative together in a mutually satisfying relationship of paternalism and deference. By contrast, where technological change was implemented at a slower pace – notably in Lancashire's fine-spinning and weaving centres and Yorkshire's woollen and worsted towns – social and political unrest persisted.[410] Joyce characterizes his approach as 'post-structuralist',[411] but it is in many ways anchored in the empiricism of his earlier work, a survey of which is therefore apposite.

The analytical framework of his original monograph has been described as broadly Marxist, but although he engaged with Marxist categories, his purpose was to dispense with or radically to revise them.[412] He subsumed the economic under an amorphous cultural rubric, thereby diminishing its explanatory utility, and reduced the political to a manifestation of the social, dissolving power relations and conflict into a vision of class co-operation and social harmony. Questioning the historical importance of class struggle, he suggested that historians emphasized it unduly and accorded too little attention to 'the mechanics of stability and class domination'.[413] With regard to the labour aristocracy thesis, he found that '[a] concentration on what is taken to be an élite in the working class not only diverts attention from the majority, but fails to discern that what working people had in common is more important for an understanding of class relationships than that which is held to have divided them'.[414] In both cotton and engineering, he argued, grade distinctions were conspicuously absent and voting was sufficiently uniform to belie 'any notion of a political and cultural divide in the working class'.[415] Where radicalism persisted, labour aristocrats were among the most prominent agitators. Far from being the agents of bourgeois ideological hegemony, they staunchly defended traditional work practices with Chartist-like political activism.[416] Nor was this remarkable, for Chartism had been precisely the 'pre-mechanical ideology' of artisans threatened with loss of control over the labour process, 'the most characteristic expression of the ferment preceding the consolidation of mechanisation'.[417] Finally, Joyce rejected the theory of ideological hegemony, concluding that it did 'not begin to explain the inwardness that characterised the accommodation of so many northern factory workers in the social system of modern, factory production'.[418]

The controlling assumption of Joyce's original contribution was that technological innovation wrought fundamental cultural change. In the unmechanized sector, textile workers retained a high degree of craft control and old cultural patterns persisted. When custom was threatened, customary political methods were brought to its defence.[419] Mechanization, however, served to transfer control of production to the employer. Debasing traditional skills, it subordinated workers to the wage system and factory discipline.[420] But it also incorporated the working-class family as the basic work unit, restoring to it the integrity which industrialization had initially shattered by reconstituting its economy within the factory system. Because employment, recruitment and training were family functions, they extended into the work-place the authority exerted by the head of the household over other family members.[421] Hence, although the substance of artisanal status was lost, its form was retained, 'subsumed in and contained by the family dimension at work'.[422] The family authority structure served to validate industrial hier-archy,[423] and paternalist manufacturers seized the initiative to transform the operative's subordination and dependency into deference.

Deference was secured both by inducement and coercion. If employers pro-vided housing, they also used the threat of eviction to enforce workplace policy.[424] If they established churches and Sunday schools, they linked job security and advancement to attendance.[425] Workers were chosen and pro-moted for their political biases while employers seeking political office promised 'to sell out and go' if their operatives did not support them.[426] Yet religious participation, though mandatory, fostered a climate of 'partnership and community' in which manufacturers, through justice and benevolence, won the respect and commitment of their operatives.[427] Continuous work, good conditions and fair treatment ensured 'popularity and a stable work-force'[428] while generosity earned frequent testimonials.[429] Celebrated as 'the big man of the locality', the kindly employer served to link the 'factory regime' to 'the spirit of the neighbourhood', a spirit which came to 'permeat[e] the recesses of the instincts'.[430] Because the employer was seen as 'the provider for all', the industrial authority structure was accepted and workplace loyalty translated into stubborn political partisanship. All grades of operatives came to identify 'with the mill at which' they worked and, as the franchise was extended, 'pro-employer voting' became a matter of convention.[431] For the rural immigrants who flooded into this increasingly harmonious environment between 1840 and 1860, the transition was one 'of coherence and stability',[432] and their offspring became 'tabula rasa on which the factory impressed its mighty stamp from childhood on'.[433] Only when socialism intruded itself as a 'disruptive outside influence' in the 1880s was the base of labour activism substantially broadened and even then, in Lancashire and parts of Yorkshire, the old patriarchal status quo remained stable.[434]

Critics commended Joyce for raising important issues but also observed that his arguments were often asserted rather than demonstrated, that his conclusions resisted the implications of his own evidence[435] and that his reduc-tion of the labour force to artisans and proletarians failed to account for workers who were neither.[436] It was also noted that, having identified the family as the crucial link 'between the individual and society' and 'the everyday experience of work' as the key to understanding factory culture, his attention to the dynamics of family and factory life was cursory, as was his treatment of women's roles, even though the workforce in the towns of his study was predominantly female.[437] His view that pro-employer voting resulted less from intimidation than from genuine deference was disputed, and his account of accommodative politics was found to resist his own and other evidence.[438] It was further suggested that his account of Chartism, mid-Victorian radicalism and socialism was one-sided and reductive, that he conveyed little sense of popular agency and that his working people tended 'to be shadowy and anonymous figures . . . like villagers in an ethnographic monograph'.[439] Joyce later speculated that deference may have been a function 'of inter-dependence rather than dependence alone'[440] and that it was less ingrained and more calculating than he had formerly thought.[441] But as critiques of his more recent work indicate, he never adequately addressed the problems adverted to above.[442] Instead, maintaining resolutely that Victorian social relations reflected a commitment to inclusiveness and harmony rather than exclusion and conflict, he sought to validate his thesis by filtering it through a different paradigm, a procedure suggestive of predetermined conclusions.

Writing in 1991 as a post-structuralist dealing with the plurality of identity, Joyce asserted that the 'hopelessly idealized categories' of class, revolutionary and labour consciousness had 'become superannuated' by 'theories of language and ideology'.[443] Reducing class analysis to its most economistic form and class consciousness to a language of expropriation which was scarcely ever spoken, he concluded that class position in Victorian society was sufficiently 'fractured and ambiguous' to draw the very notion of class into question.[444] Noting the contemporary currency of class rhetoric, he accorded it a place among other culturally constructed languages[445] but declared attempts to reconstruct the nineteenth-century labour experience 'based on the idea of class interest' to be 'feeble in the extreme'.[446] Citing 'new considerations' of post-1850 workplace relationships,[447] he insisted that workers maintained 'a stake in the ownership and control of production', that employers needed to secure their consent, and that both workers and employers therefore had a vested interest in co-operation.[448] Hence, 'the inter-dependence of capital and labour' rather than 'an overmastering, trans-historical tendency towards conflict' was the prevailing reality.[449] The undue emphasis on class, he wrote, had caused other visions of the social order to be suppressed. He undertook to explore those visions and suggested populism as a 'more important and colourful alternative'.[450]

Proceeding from the assumption that experience is 'actively constituted by language',[451] Joyce set out to demonstrate that contemporary discourse generated a range of 'social identities' through which experience was negotiated. The discourses with which he concerned himself ranged from formal public 'bodies of utterances' about politics, morality and work to symbolic codes, often assumed and unspoken, which related to custom and the imaginary constitution of the social order.[452] '[E]xtra-economic in character and inclusive and universalizing in their social remit,' he wrote, these discourses and the identities which they produced were unmistakably populist.[453] The clearest exposition of his argument emerged in his discussion of popular politics. Political languages were to 'be understood as actively creating both political appeals and . . . the political constituency itself . . . [R]esonating with the preoccupations of those who received them', they elaborated 'unifying identities' which 'overlaid differences' and made 'sense of people's conditions and outlook'.[454] They appealed to non-electors, 'the excluded heirs to constitutional liberties', as 'truly political person[s]' in terms which stressed fair play, independence, freedom, honour, manliness and democracy. But the democracy which they described co-existed with a vision of 'society as a system of interdependent functions, often of a hierarchic or at least not a levelling character'.[455]

Populist vocabulary might periodically have taken on 'class' connotations but 'class' terminology was 'unfixed and provisional'. It could at times be '"economic" and conflictual', but it more often projected an understanding of society 'to which conflict was foreign', which retained a 'decidedly moralistic and universalistic set of meanings', and which often accented fraternity and conciliation.[456] Populist language and associations prevailed in earlier decades because they 'ma[de] sense to people . . . in their daily and political lives', and liberalism succeeded largely 'by feeding off this radical past'.[457] Both radicalism and popular liberalism turned on an 'appeal to collectivities other than class, for class rule, the rule of the aristocracy, 'had been tried and had failed'. Its end would be assured by '[b]ringing "the rich" into communication with the people'.[458] This communion was foreshadowed by popular political leaders like Feargus O'Connor and Ernest Jones, who had 'forsaken their own kind, paradoxically, to affirm the underlying unity of all people'.[459] 'The gentleman leader represented transcendance of class – the high became low to show that all people were one,'[460] and in 1868, this unity was consolidated when Gladstone, 'the people's William', gave 'the working classes a stake in the nation'.[461]

No less than the political universe, the world of work was articulated to a populist outlook. Experience and identity were constituted by narratives of community, co-operation and social inclusiveness – the 'moral discourses of labour' – which predominated over economic categories until the early twentieth century.[462] The paternalism, deference and social harmony which formerly Joyce had attributed to mechanization he now explained in terms of these discourses.[463] Accordingly, he found that a language of mutuality delineated the productive sphere as one in which capital and labour were drawn together by shared interests.[464] Grounded in customary notions of the trade, this language spoke of reciprocal rights and obligations, fair profit, just employment and proper trade practices. It defined labour as 'the fundamental source of value' and the worker's 'skill' as 'property' which conferred 'a vested interest in the trade' and 'underpinned much of what it meant to be a man'.[465] Exploitation was 'seen as extrinsic to production' and 'located in moral' rather than 'economic realms'.[466] Convinced that popular movements of earlier decades 'were not of a production-based class sort',[467] he concluded that 'mid-century social reconciliation' was less remarkable than had formerly been thought.[468]

As control of production was consolidated and the permanence of capitalism acknowledged, new trade unions were constituted from 'the old organisational and discursive resources of the trade'.[469] The unions 'gave voice to both the new and the old sentiments of labour, reformulating the old in terms of new demands and opportunities'.[470] Adopting the view that the system, though 'natural . . . could and should be subject to human intervention', they undertook to civilize capital and to moralize the market to which their activities were now confined.[471] Union discourse became 'a means of organisation', though belief in the shared interests of employers and workers persisted and, along with the moral categories of custom, a populist outlook predominated.[472] Union leaders had often to deal with 'recalcitrant material', but they 'worked with the grain of their members' values and expectations' and, in Joyce's view, achieved remarkable success, not only with skilled workers, but with 'the unskilled majority, including women'.[473] Elaborating a discourse which stressed unselfishness, the importance of collective rather than individual interests, and the reciprocal responsibilities of capital and labour, they shaped values 'by reflecting them in a creative way'.[474]

From the 'discourses' of politics and work, Joyce proceeded to a consideration of popular culture – art, literature, dialect and 'the imaginary constitution of the social order' – all 'codes', he explained, which 'people use[d] to confer meaning and order on the world'.[475] The key to these codes was custom, which, because it regulated, reflected and shaped values and outlooks, provided access to 'assumed, often unspoken knowledge'. By exploring 'custom in both its conscious and unconscious aspects', he wrote, he would transcend 'boundary and category' to gain insight into contemporary thought, even that of 'the less articulate'.[476] He subsequently claimed to identify 'a utopian current which celebrated the fellowship of all people'. Generated by the need for dignity and respect, popular utopianism was expressed in 'a rage for order' and gave rise to 'a culture of control', central to which was 'a claim to justice' but also a 'desire for human fraternity and reconciliation which sprang from . . . recognition of a basic human equality'.[477] One of the most striking features of this culture was stoicism, a determined 'putting up with things'[478] that was made possible, according to Joyce, by the literature of Burns, Shakespeare, Milton and especially Byron, who supposedly 'taught the poor workingman to *feel*, [thus] liberating him from the mental and physical confines of poverty'.[479]

In Joyce's view conceptions of culture and language – sayings, stories and the ritualized repetition of popular wisdom – fixed what was known and understood. They were at once 'the mechanism of transmission and the content of the transmitted form', a code 'which define[d] the contours of dream and reality' and which, in its symbolic as much as in its literal significations, 'lay very close to the creation of social and personal identity'.[480] Oral culture

provided 'history's master narrative', a discourse rooted 'in the local and particular' which told 'against the larger solidarities of class' and informed a
utopian desire to transcend social differences.[481] Dialect generated 'meaning
with which to manage daily life';[482] popular literature 'dissolve[d] the bound-
aries between the actual and the potential, offering a vision of the possible,
the future, the ideal';[483] popular ballads glorified 'the ordinary man pitched
against the odds, conquering himself and the incompetence of his superiors'.[484] The most famous twentieth-century exponent of the ballad and 'the
most powerful of all contemporary icons of social identity', Gracie Fields,
'represent[ed] the nation to itself'. In her songs and subsequently her films,
she symbolized patriotism, social reconciliation and national unity.[485] A mill
girl who became a 'theatrical grande dame', she embodied both the possibility of success[486] and a tradition of popular art which empowered the powerless
across the decades in a way 'that was real, not imaginary; or, more properly,
real *because* it was imaginary'. That tradition, according to Joyce, endowed
knowledge and afforded a vision of hope as real as 'the deformations of
poverty'.[487]

Some critics have received *Visions of the People* as an imaginative reconceptu-
alization of nineteenth-century labour history but others have been less
sympathetic.[488] The most consistent criticisms have been that it is linguistically reductive – its organizing assumption that experience is constituted by
discourse fails adequately to account for agency – and that, both substantively
and theoretically, its argument is asserted rather than demonstrated.[489] It has
also been suggested that, notwithstanding Joyce's ostensible post-structuralist
orientation, his thesis is resolutely empiricist.[490] This charge draws the value
of his work into question, for, as an empiricist analysis, it scarcely stands up.
His evidence, though voluminous, is narrowly selected[491] and his substantive
argument is undermined, according to one writer, by his deconstructive
method.[492] Nor does his thesis conform to the most fundamental postulates of
the post-structuralist project. The 'discourses' with which he concerns himself
are oral and printed statements which he submits to a positivist rationale
whereby their meanings appear self-evident and uncontested.[493] Engaging
with neither his own subjectivity nor that of contemporaries, he objectifies
experience by reducing agency to the 'use' of a limited range of discursively
constructed social identities.[494] Yet all recognizably post-structuralist paradigms are informed by an epistemology which assumes the subjective character
of interpretation and which renders meaning fluid, elusive and variable. Joyce
advances no theory of ideology, draws no connection between ideology and language, and fails to recognize that language is a site of conflict.[495] Instead, he
portrays a docile and contented workforce 'relaxing warmly in the glow of
[uncontested] populist discourse'.[496] His history, virtually devoid of struggle,
is one in which power appears to hover, unrelated and undefined, as a kind of
spiritual energy from which all might draw. A vision in which the system is
immutable, hierarchy natural and acquiescence desirable, it is remarkably like

one described by Thatcher in the 1980s. As a percipient reviewer from another discipline has observed, 'from the End of History', Joyce's portrait of 'nineteenth-century Britain looks a lot like the New World Order'.[497]

Joyce's approach reflects a thinly disguised political conservatism which, during the past several decades, has come to predominate in nineteenth-century labour historiography.[498] Central to the new orthodoxy is an affected apoliticism whereby the inevitability and legitimacy of capitalist power relations are assumed and the nineteenth-century political *status quo* is treated as given. The working classes of the time are held to have accepted the prevailing legal-political system, commentary is confined to their supposed perceptions and experiences, and the system itself is excluded from critique. An intensely political act, this exclusionist procedure, which persistently evades censure, is exemplified in the introduction to a 1991 volume of essays edited by Eugenio Biagini and Alastair Reid. After 1850, Biagini and Reid argued, '"New Model" unionists . . . realised that their success depended on their ability to use and modify the law, rather than to challenge and subvert it.'[499] 'Historians of a wide range of views', they proceeded, 'now generally agree that since the eighteenth century, the British legal system had been developing firmly in the direction of equal rights for all citizens, and was thus able to play an increasingly important role in mediating conflicts between (and within) social groups.'[500] In one sense, this narrative seems perfectly disinterested. It neither attacks nor defends the legal-political system but simply suggests that, in the view both of contemporaries and historians, it was adequate. In another sense, however, exclusion of the system itself from analysis denies the narrative's 'objectivity' and the implied apoliticism of its authors. For the question of whether equality before the law was real and of whether, for example, material considerations deprived the poor and disorganized of access to the legal mechanisms by which the rich defended their rights, is never addressed. Though its endorsement of the *status quo* is subtle, the new conservatism is no more neutral than the overtly political Marxism of writers like Saville, Hobsbawm, Foster and Royden Harrison. Yet many younger 'Marxists' have been more inclined to join the retreat from class than to attack the apolitical pretensions of the New Right.[501] Their analyses have become progressively more moderate and their relations with conservative counterparts have mellowed to the extent that, in 1978, Robert Gray could be congratulated because his book employed Marxist methodology not, 'as is so often the case, as a propaganda weapon, but as a powerful historical tool'.[502] 'Propaganda' in this context seems clearly to mean criticism of the *status quo*, which, in a capitalist society, one might have thought was a Marxist's job.

My purpose here is not to defend class analysis or to accord it special authority. Indeed, I propose to question some of its most fundamental assumptions and categories. I simply emphasize that its pre-eminence has been challenged by a new conservative historiography, and that discussion of power relations has been displaced in the process. Hence, British labour history has gradually been rewritten as a celebration of working-class achievement, to which the social and political agitations of radical minorities were largely irrelevant. The 'real' gains were made by 'consensus', in a benign system which implicitly permitted a respectable independence to all. The most disadvantaged social strata, the human consequences of a system which demands their existence as a spur to the competition on which its operation depends, are never addressed. With the decline of class analysis, class struggle has virtually disappeared and the 'independent workingman' has become a metaphor for the lower classes. By valorizing the system and discarding the losers, the new history deprives today's 'detritus' of precedent and legitimacy.[503] It implies that they are unique, not only in their condition, but in their failure to rectify it.

What emerges most suggestively from the above survey is the extent to which the meaning of the past is formulated in the present.[504] When historical convention is superseded, it is reinvented. Facts are reordered and perhaps added to, while those not currently required are omitted, all to render the past meaningful in terms of the present. Apparent also is the political/ideological character of history production. All of the works surveyed conform to a logic consistent with the prevailing truths of economic rationalism and seem thereby to suggest that dominant ideas determine historical orthodoxy. Hence, although Rothstein's analysis reflected political developments with which its production coincided, even the Fabian Socialist Cole could dismiss it as flawed, inaccurate and meaningless, for political power in Britain was then controlled by the Right and conservatism ruled in the academy.[505] In the 1960s and 1970s, however, the political Left had a more substantial presence. The Labour Party governed for much of the period (though with little confidence or direction in the 1970s), socialism had not yet been discredited, and the welfare state remained intact. Under such conditions, Marxist histories, although they differed from Rothstein's only in the most superficial detail, enjoyed considerable authority. But as the Labour government floundered between 1974 and 1979, the Right increasingly set the terms of political debate. Conservative verities began to acquire a new legitimacy and Marxist scholarship, as I read it, began to reflect a vision exhaustively elaborated by Thatcher during a four-year campaign which was to culminate in the 1979 Conservative triumph.

The above emphasis on present-centredness is linked to two distinct kinds of criticism. One relates to the historical evidence and the generalizations to which it gives rise, the other to epistemological questions about the nature of truth and meaning. In the next chapter I will address these problems, suggesting various ways in which both class and populist analyses fail to meet their own criteria and draw conclusions which their evidence cannot sustain. In particular, I will focus on the treatment of consciousness, identity and experience in representations of the mid-Victorian working classes.

2

SOCIAL IDENTITY AND THE REPRESENTATION OF EXPERIENCE

As I have indicated in the above survey, historians of Chartism generally agree that support for the movement's confrontational strategies did not endure beyond 1850. In narratives about the mid-Victorian labour experience the decline of Chartist activism becomes popular acceptance of the prevailing social order and debate focuses on the changing character of popular mentalité. Consistently with this focus, contributors to the debate base their discussions on theories of identity and consciousness which in various ways indicate the interpellation of individuals as subjects, or their assimilation to structurally determined subject positions in which they see themselves reflected. Some analysts imply that interpellation is irresistible. They look to structures and discourses for their answers and do not concern themselves with the views of the people/subjects whose experience they purport to illuminate. Most commentators, however, treat agency as an important variable and refer to more or less extensive autobiographical samples to confirm their theories empirically.[1] Yet the very idea of confirmation implies foregone conclusions which might possibly predetermine the results of empirical research. In this chapter I will explore this possibility. I will suggest that the theories to which I have referred shape empirical practice, dictating the selection of evidence, imposing narrative unity on historical ambiguity, and concealing the contingency of meanings thus produced.

There are basically two categories of identity to which historians consign Victorian working people: 'class' and 'populist'.[2] Class identity is seen to have been generated by industrial capitalism and both Marxist and liberal analyses are articulated to class terminology.[3] Class analysis postulates two fundamental social identities – bourgeois and proletarian (or capitalist and worker) – each of which is constituted by its objective relation to the means of production.[4] Capital is held to control the means of production to which labour is in turn subordinated; hence, bourgeois and proletarian identities exist in a state of tension and each is defined against the other. It is in their accounts of how this tension was resolved, and in their treatment of class 'consciousness', that Marxist and liberal historians differ. Traditional Marxists argue that, during the Chartist era, working people were aroused to class consciousness and to an understanding that the prevailing system, predicated on political inequality, was inimical to social justice. They conclude, however, either that the worker's revolutionary spirit was crushed along with the Chartist movement itself by state coercive power or that class consciousness gradually succumbed to ideological corruption. Liberal historians reject notions of state coercion and ideological manipulation. They propose instead that, as the century wore on, the social and political order became more flexible and capital and labour more tractable. An older hostility gave way to compromise, a more conciliatory approach was taken to the resolution of class tensions, and working people resigned themselves to the pursuit of a respectable independence within the existing system. The liberal approach is scarcely distinguishable from a number of nominally Marxist accounts according to which popular acquiescence in the *status quo* derived partly from the extension of bourgeois cultural hegemony and partly from the recognition that revolution was not a realistic alternative. By contrast, conservative and revisionist historians insist that the prevailing social identity was populist, although the populism which they describe bears little resemblance to that of conventional definitions.[5] Patrick Joyce, for example, describes a populist identity shaped by broadly shared moral and cultural traditions which was untroubled by social distinctions. Its touchstone was a vision of 'the people' which embraced all social ranks in harmonious co-existence and which was largely realized during the mid-Victorian period.[6] Such constructions either deny that class was an issue among contemporary workers or insist that it was of little importance.

These theories are all firmly grounded in extensive empirical research, yet, although they are in many ways irreconcilable, they all aspire to historical authenticity. It is therefore apposite to pose several questions: what is the 'truth' value of evidence if indeed it can mean so many different things? Could it be that some 'facts' relate to certain highly specific groups or circumstances but not to others? Have historians therefore generalized unacceptably from the 'facts' available to them or from those which they have chosen to privilege? Or have they failed to account adequately for the fluidity and 'constructedness' of identity and consciousness? Could the speakers in the documents cited, and indeed all contemporaries, have been one thing on one occasion and something else on another? Could they, at certain times in their lives, have been preoccupied with the importance of 'class', in one or some of the term's various definitions, and at other times, in response to different combinations of structural or linguistic imperatives, have defined their reality in populist or alternative terms?

To address these questions, it is appropriate to begin with the very notion of 'social identity' and with the literature on which accounts of such identities are based. After all, unless and until the postulated identities are shown to have been abroad in society, they remain no more than empty 'objective' categories. The kinds of class analysis which began to dominate labour history in the

1960s were mostly structural. Identity, according to these narratives, was determined by economic imperatives which defined the available ways of being and seeing, constituting working people as a distinctive economic class regardless of whether they were 'class conscious'. Although some of these works referred to Thomas Wright, the 'journeyman engineer', and a handful of others as token representatives of 'the working-class perspective', they relied substantially on statistical data, official documents and the views of middle-class observers to illustrate the class identity of working people. It was in the broader field of 'social history' that writers like E.P. Thompson, John Burnett and David Vincent sought to 'initiate a dialogue' with the working classes, recovering their writings, exploring their subjectivity, according them agency and suggesting the one-dimensional poverty of structuralist theory.[7] Some historians, notably John Foster and Gareth Stedman Jones,[8] eschewed this kind of engagement, but by the late 1970s most were illustrating their accounts of identity with statements by working people.

In linking the issue of social identity to that of popular agency, labour historians have acknowledged, explicitly or implicitly, the capacity of 'ordinary people' to influence the course of events. This recognition does not simply apply to collective agency, for individuals are also singled out. The most notable of these exemplars are labour leaders, charismatic figures who purportedly persuaded large groups of people to adopt particular goals and strategies with important economic and political implications. Because some of these figures are depicted as more persuasive than others or as more convincing at some times than at others, it can be held to follow that the masses whom they exhorted must have chosen, as individuals, either to support or not to support them.[9] To draw this conclusion is not to deny the extent to which choice might be affected by group dynamics or to which agency is structured and limited by a whole range of moral, cultural, economic and political imperatives. But because societies are ordered by a multiplicity of underlying structures, it seems unreasonable to assume that every individual is influenced by the same structures, or the same combination of structural influences, at the same time; that every individual interprets structural imperatives in the same way; that every individual accords every structural imperative equal importance; or that, in ranking the imperatives which they consider important, all individuals accord the same degree of importance to the same imperatives. I suggest, in other words, that because the structural/discursive fields in which subjects are constituted are diverse, individuals are constituted differently and their identities are fluid: the more diverse the field, the less predictable their responses to given imperatives. Moreover, to the extent that they are compelled to respond, they are also compelled to make choices which will impact on the field (society) as a whole.

Hence, whether free will is held to be 'real' though limited or simply an illusion, agency is an important consideration, for the capacity to choose is also the capacity to influence society in unpredictable ways. In the nineteenth century, for example, skilled workers may have elected individually to act collectively and thus have exerted economic and political effects. 'The poor' doubtless helped as individuals to bring the hated workhouse under public scrutiny by perpetuating images which ranged from the mandatory separation of sheltered families to the bestial scenes associated with Andover.[10] The 'criminal classes' may effectively have been legislated into existence, but the very process of criminalization implied that agency was unpredictable, that subjects could not be trusted to act in prescribed ways, and that their impact, *as individuals,* could be profound. At every level of society, it seems, people had the potential to make choices and to influence events. It also seems that, at different times, different people thought and acted in different ways, that a multiplicity of 'social perceptions' may have been current, that consciousness and identity may have differed from the articulate and 'respectable' workers, so prominent in historical narrative, to the historically silent and perhaps disreputable masses. 'Appearances' suggest the possibility that identity and consciousness are, after all, fluid, ambiguous and elusive. How adequately, then, have historians addressed this possibility?

As noted above, I assume that commentators who acknowledge the importance of popular agency also recognize that it was an attribute of all social groups and individuals. To accord it only to prominent figures or politically active workers, in the absence of any qualifying variable, would be arbitrary and inconsistent. Moreover, enterprising researchers have recovered a substantial body of literature in which nineteenth-century working people describe not only their subjective perceptions[11] but active choices which they have made.[12] Such people may have been 'powerless' insofar as they were unable directly to influence the economic and political mechanisms which shaped their existence. Yet by choosing to act in certain ways they produced effects – such as public enquiries which enabled them to register their views 'historically' – and although the reasons behind their choices may be debatable, their agency, or their ability to make those choices, is not. In the broadest possible critical survey their commentaries might be seen to provide some indication of the extent to which the 'objective' social identities postulated by 'class' and 'populist' historians were reflected in the wider contemporary society. Remarkably, however, little of this material has been cited either by labour historians generally or, more specifically, by those writers purportedly concerned with what 'ordinary people' thought. In Dorothy Thompson's class analysis of Chartism, for example, other historians are urged to attend more carefully to what 'the people actually' demanded and defended – to what they did and *why*[13] – and Thompson herself consults the views of labour leaders, but 'the people', by and large, remain silent. Even in a chapter entitled 'Leaders and Followers', the followers never appear. The discussion is devoted almost exclusively to the reflections of prominent leaders on the influence of Feargus O'Connor, the instability of Bronterre O'Brien and the potentially destabilizing effect of leadership rivalry.[14] Thompson observes that '[a] handful of autobiographies provide valuable historical sources', yet, without any further explanation, she concludes that they have 'distorted the picture by their very existence'.[15] Presumably the picture to which she refers is the 'true' picture as she sees it. But can contemporary perceptions be any less valid because they disagree with her own? And how adequate is a hermeneutics which seeks to address the question of *why* people acted as they did and to establish the identity of a 'class', but privileges the observations of some members and rules out those of others?[16]

Like 'the people', women are invariably spoken for in Thompson's analysis by husbands, sons and radical journalists.[17] Many, she writes, were active Chartists, and some even addressed meetings or wrote letters to the press.[18] But for the substance of what they said she relies on the testimonies of their men. One woman, a Bradford power-loom weaver named Miss Ruthwell, 'did', she observes, 'leave some account of her life, as well as a strong impression of her personality'.[19] The account to which Thompson refers tells of how Ruthwell, on being dismissed from her job for attending an earlier meeting, ceased to be an 'unreflecting slave of the power-loom'. Unconcerned that the middle and upper classes might regard her as 'a bold and forward girl', she warned employers that power-loom weavers would soon 'rise above their thraldom', that she would continue to 'strive for the emancipation of her class' and that, 'ere long . . . the female workers in Bradford would be a *powerful auxiliary* in the onward march to "a fair day's wage for a fair day's work"'.[20] Although Thompson treats these words uncritically as Ruthwell's own, her source is not Ruthwell's speech but a report of it in the male-operated *Northern Star.*[21] Most working women may, as Thompson suggests, have failed to leave records. But even were one to accept that the thoughts of past actors are accessible, can any account of their subjectivity – their identity and consciousness – be adequate or reliable without such records?[22] Is it perhaps predictable that, in a portrait constructed almost entirely from the observations of men, Chartist women should appear to support the 'class' struggle but show little concern for 'gender' issues; that they should advocate the rights of man but remain 'philosophical' about their own 'auxiliary' role? And even were it demonstrated that Ruthwell's address was accurately reported, can it be assumed that her 'personality' was encapsulated in this brief historical moment or that she spoke for other women?[23] The practice of adding the occasional woman into narratives ordered by male concerns and perspectives has been roundly criticized by Jutta Schwarzkopf in her 1991 publication, *Women in the Chartist Movement.*[24]

Schwarzkopf introduces this volume as an inquiry into 'the impact of Chartism on the construction of gender and on gender relations as an integral part of the working class'.[25] As her narrative proceeds, she consults the views of various contemporary women to suggest that they deplored their inferior status and embraced opportunities which arose with Chartism to pursue political equality.[26] They did not seek to abandon their role as mothers and wives;

indeed, they invoked it to justify their political aspirations but they did not, according to Schwarzkopf, fall for 'the myth of the maternal instinct'.[27] Nevertheless, when the decline of Chartism robbed them of the forum in which their activism throve, she concludes, they gradually succumbed to an ideology of domesticity which was fostered vigorously by men of all classes, not least their own.[28] This study undoubtedly helps to correct the under-representation of women in the historiography of Chartism, yet the author's attempt to problematize gender is ultimately defeated by her failure to discern the instability of other categories. She recognizes that identity is a function of class as well as gender, but while she explores the contingency of the latter she treats the former, and other categories like consciousness and ideology, as foundations. Hence 'male ideology' becomes a one-dimensional, ahistorical attitude; working women become an undifferentiated 'class'; and consciousness is reduced to the momentary perceptions of certain very erudite exemplars who convey the impression that they are anything but ordinary working women.

Nor is Schwarzkopf sufficiently sensitive to the ambiguity of language. She employs illustrative evidence as though it were transparent and does not seem to suspect that the meaning of abstracted statements might be shaped by her own narrative. Curiously, moreover, having judged 'traditional' histories to be flawed, she often relies on them to corroborate her own views.[29] Finally, although she writes authoritatively about 'laws of textual production', she seems to imagine that historical texts are exempt from them. 'In a work of fiction', she writes,

> an author creates a world governed by coherence, a world in which each action and each incident make sense through being related to each other and to the whole of the plot. This 'world' of fiction is not a mirror image of the real world, but an ideological entity that has been created out of certain literary devices that the author has selected for the formation of a particular subject matter. Even though a literary text about Chartism may maintain empirical historical accuracy, the treatment remains fictive in that historical data operate according to the laws of textual production. Through this process, the work of fiction becomes an expression of its author's perception of social reality.[30]

A useful description of literary production, this passage has important implications for historical writing. For if, as Schwarzkopf insists, literature remains fictive even when it is empirically accurate, then empirical accuracy cannot be invoked to distinguish history from literature. Moreover, historical works, like works of fiction, are textual, and must surely therefore obey the same 'laws of textual production'. Since Schwarzkopf does not clarify these matters, it seems fair to conclude that her commentary reflects her own 'perception of social reality' rather than the views of ordinary Chartist men and women.

In a 1991 exposition of the populist approach, Eugenio Biagini and Alastair Reid also proclaim the importance of the thoughts, demands and actions of 'ordinary people'.[31] And like other contributors to their volume, they delineate the 'populist' mentality which they impute to such people with illustrations from the writings of certain working-class individuals.[32] Biagini, for example, cites Thomas Paine, Joseph Arch, J. Hawker and J.B. Leno to demonstrate a tradition of working-class opposition to the Corn Laws. He then argues that the 'repeal' movement reflected 'popular' rather than merely middle-class concerns,[33] and that the political attitudes of late nineteenth-century labour leaders reflected neither 'class' nor 'trade union' consciousness but a populist outlook which 'belong[ed] to a long-standing tradition of popular radicalism'. His portrait is drawn predominantly from the observations of Robert Knight who, between 1871 and 1898, served as general secretary to the United Society of Boilermakers and Iron and Steel Shipbuilders.[34] John Shepherd enhances the populist image with a vignette of Henry Broadhurst who, as he mourned the passing of Gladstone, reflected with satisfaction on his own career, a career during which he rose from humble stonemason to 'a place of honour' in the House of Commons.[35] Scattered throughout the remaining essays are brief references to a further twenty-odd memoirs, some by Nonconformist clergymen and some by distinguished members of the working classes, whose apparent conviction that popular discontents could be reconciled constitutionally within the existing legal and political system is regarded as additional evidence of a populist mentality. The roots of this mentality, it is claimed, can be traced back to the seventeenth century,[36] and Chartism is seen implicitly to have been an aberration.[37]

In their introduction Biagini and Reid suggest that, by restoring to 'their own political context' the 'Liberal and Labour activists' with whom they and their contributors are concerned, it will be possible to demonstrate 'enough continuity in popular radicalism . . . to make the search for social explanations of major changes unnecessary'.[38] Hence they argue that popular radicalism survived 1848 to become a major political force which impacted both on Gladstonian Liberalism and on the Labour Party, and achieved not only most of the reforms sought 'in vain by previous generations' but others 'which were of greater practical significance to the industrial working classes than anything asked for by the Chartists'.[39] Until 'well into the twentieth century', they find, the most persistent popular political goals – 'open government and the rule of law', 'individual liberty and community-centred democracy', '"anti-corruption" and "fair play"' – were scarcely distinguishable from those of radical liberalism.[40] There was some disagreement among activists 'over how far government ought to be *by* the people, but demand for the extension of the franchise was one of the most outstanding continuities in the mainstream, and radicalism in general was democratic in its commitment to government *for* the people and with their consent, and to the prevention of tyranny through the separation of powers'.[41] Throughout the period, Biagini and Reid conclude, popular radicalism was characteristically pragmatic 'in its acceptance both of constitutional methods and of the already existing aspirations of the people'.[42]

How popular aspirations are discerned, however, remains unclear, for although Biagini, Reid and their contributors generalize frequently to the community-at-large, they never really look beyond the views of *extra*-ordinary individuals. And despite the introductory claim that '[w]hat ordinary people thought . . . matters and ought to be taken seriously', it is only the 'the politically active among them' whose demands, according to the editors, must be assessed in the context of their 'own needs, desires, and capacities'.[43] Hence 'the people' are reduced to 'the politically active', even though the careers of those referred to – trade union officials and MPs – might well have removed them from the routine experiences of their constituents and have rendered them less than representative. From their elevated positions, some luminaries of the labour movement might indeed have doubted the wisdom of extending the franchise indiscriminately and have claimed for themselves the responsibility of drawing all social ranks harmoniously together. But is it reasonable to assume that the unenfranchised shared such views and passively accepted the role to which, according to the populist approach, they were consigned? If the thoughts of less ambiguously 'ordinary' people were consulted, would a different picture emerge?

Similar questions are raised by contributions to a debate about the mid-Victorian labour experience where popular autobiography informs the discussion of working-class respectability. Respectability is characterized in various ways which indicate that it implied different things to different people (or that it means different things to different historians). 'Class' analysts consider the extent to which its pursuit by working people signified capitulation to middle-class hegemony, corruption of their class consciousness and loss of class identity. The 'populist' approach suggests that respectability and 'social identity' were mutually reinforcing. In John Foster's view, respectability evolved as a middle-class set of ideals which, adopted by labour aristocrats in the 1850s and promoted among those beneath them, served effectively as an instrument of social control.[44] According to T.W. Laqueur, it grew out of a shared moral and cultural tradition which preceded and transcended class differences.[45] Alternatively, Neville Kirk defines it as an indigenous institution which arose 'in the determining context of the material conditions of working-class existence',[46] while F.M.L. Thompson insists that it derived from 'a bundle of self-generated habits and values' which were not class-specific but 'derived from past customs and present responses to living and working conditions'.[47] For Trygve Tholfsen, R.Q. Gray and Geoffrey Crossick, respectability was far more ambiguous. Bound up with the assertion of 'independence', the dignity of manual labour and 'class pride', it also implied the acceptance of a moral and cultural universe in which the middle-class ideals of industry, thrift, sobriety and self-help predominated, thus uniting the respectable elements of all social ranks to the exclusion of the disreputable.[48] From the 'populist' perspective,

Patrick Joyce finds that respectability sprang from 'the values and social imagery of the workers' own culture'; that it was not engineered by a treacherous labour aristocracy; that it meant different things in different contexts; and that it shared sufficient common ground with middle-class definitions to invite 'widespread class cooperation'. It did not preclude class pride but it demanded deference, for the latter was embedded in a 'caste system [which] stood "natural, complete and inviolate"', answering to popular needs and expressing 'not the class struggle but the battle of life itself'.[49]

Clearly, each of these analyses offers a different account of social identity, for a community subordinated to a set of ideals not its own would scarcely identify with society-at-large in the same way as one consciously committed to a tradition which it shared with that society, or as one which generated its own values and prized its independence. Yet, although the notion of 'social identity' implies conformity, the analyses themselves, and the accounts of 'experience' to which most appeal, suggest diversity. Diversity is also indicated *within* particular works which are cited as supporting evidence for both 'class' and 'populist' claims. What does this diversity mean? Does it undermine the utility of 'social identity' and 'experience' as objective analytical categories? The problem to which these questions point is explored by other writers in other contexts[50] but it is set out with particular clarity by Joan Scott in her 1991 essay, 'The Evidence of Experience'.[51] Engaging with a number of contributions to the history of difference, Scott argues that in their emphasis on making visible the experiences of groups conventionally excluded from history, they disregard the discursive processes by which subjects are constituted/positioned and experiences produced. As a consequence, she suggests, 'experience' is essentialized: it becomes a pre-discursive, ontological foundation to which, as it were, history speaks.[52] Hence, whether it is defined as accumulated knowledge, a distinctive kind of consciousness, a set of external forces to which individuals react, or a synthesis of external influences and subjective feelings, 'the existence of individuals [is taken] for granted' and questions about 'how conceptions of selves (of subjects and their identities) are produced' remain unasked.[53]

This procedure, Scott continues, occurs within an ideological framework which makes 'individuals the starting point of all knowledge' and naturalizes certain analytical categories 'by treating them as given characteristics of individuals'.[54] 'Preclud[ing] inquiry into the processes of subject construction . . . the relationships between discourse, cognition, and reality', the relevance of any given subject's position (including that of the investigator) to the knowledge produced, and 'the effect of difference on knowledge', it functions to constitute subjects as fixed, autonomous and 'reliable sources of knowledge' whose experience gives access to reality. The separation of experience from the discourses in which identities are constituted and contested may appear to rescue agency from structural determination and may also remove 'historians from critical scrutiny as active producers of knowledge'.[55]

But it also 'establishes a realm outside of discourse' and independent of historical forces in which '[t]he evidence of experience works as a foundation providing both a starting point and a conclusive kind of explanation'.[56]

Beyond these provisions, she observes, few questions are asked or seem necessary, 'yet it is precisely the questions precluded – questions about discourse, difference, and subjectivity, as well as about what counts as experience and who gets to make that determination – that would enable us to historicize experience, and to reflect critically on the history we write about it, rather than to premise our history on it'.[57] In this formulation, Scott emphasizes 'the productive quality of discourse'. She refuses any separation between experience, 'a subject's history', and language, 'the site of history's enactment', and describes the former as a linguistic event in which agency is discursively conferred and limited by the conditions of the subject's constitution. She also notes, however, that 'there are conflicts among discursive systems, contradictions within any one of them, [and] multiple meanings possible for the concepts they deploy'.[58] Hence, she suggests, although experience occurs within established meanings, it is not 'confined to a fixed order of meaning'; and although it is collective as well as individual, 'since discourse is by definition shared', there is no reason to assume that it will be understood by everyone in the same way. On the basis of this discussion, Scott urges historians to abandon 'belief in the unmediated relationship between words and things' whereby experience is naturalized and the evidence of experience taken to be straightforward, transparent and reliable.[59] Instead, she recommends that all categories of analysis be treated as contextual, contingent, contested and political. A focus on these categories, she concludes, would historicize the relationship between 'the power of the historian's analytic frame' and events taken as the object of study. 'Denying the fixity and transcendence of anything that appears to operate as a foundation', it would become a 'history of foundationalist concepts themselves'. It would also become 'the evidence by which "experience" can be grasped and by which the historian's relationship to the past he or she writes about can be articulated'.[60]

The works presently under consideration embody precisely the practices with which Scott takes issue. In each case, the historian's relationship to the past remains obscure and experience is treated as an essence which can be discerned by analysing various kinds of documents. Identity is problematized sufficiently to accord it a collective character but otherwise remains, like consciousness and experience, an intrinsic human quality which can be understood if properly described. Proper description includes reference to various contemporaries, whose representative status is prefigured by theories of collective identity and whose autobiographies then become manifestations of collective experience. Yet the historian's role in constituting the experience represented is never addressed. Hence, in what follows, I will examine in detail not only the autobiographical literature adduced but the categories to which it is subordinated, thus to consider the connections identified by Scott.[61] As my discussion develops, the assumption that certain figures were representative will be challenged. I will argue that, in various ways, not least by bequeathing their 'histories' to posterity, they distinguished themselves from the popular majority. My narrative will be no more truthful or objective than those I criticize, nor will it provide deeper insights into authorial subjectivity. It will simply suggest that the identities and consciousness of the autobiographers were as fluid, ambiguous and elusive as their experiences were diverse; that such diversity cannot be reduced to a single definable experience; and that any attempt to do so, by subordinating past actors to a unified and anachronistically devised 'social identity', is productive of no more than an elaborate fiction.

As indicated, John Foster is largely unconcerned with subjective material. He defines class identity in structural terms and infers consciousness not from personal accounts of what people thought but from putatively objective evidence of what they did. Hence he finds that, in the Chartist era, working people sought to take control of the labour process and, in doing so, exhibited revolutionary class consciousness. Endorsing the judgement of earlier historians like the Webbs and G.D.H. Cole, however, he concludes by suggesting that bourgeois hegemony was successfully implemented during the mid-Victorian period when popular revolutionary consciousness was subverted by middle-class notions of respectability. F.M.L. Thompson, by contrast, denies that respectability was in any way imposed and has no use for the notion of bourgeois hegemony. He speculates on popular thoughts and motivations but, although he may have consulted contemporary popular writings, he provides no documentation. Moreover, his brief bibliography indicates that his thesis is based almost entirely on secondary sources. The remainder of the historians considered above inform their work with a great deal of contemporary documentation. They also use autobiographical writings more or less extensively, though in ways which do little to illuminate their accounts of popular identity, even when they consider, as Laqueur sometimes does, authorial reflection on subjective experience.

As noted in Chapter 1, Laqueur attempts to demonstrate two basic propositions: the first is that popular respectability was an outgrowth of moral and cultural traditions shared by all social classes and not a bourgeois imposition; the second is that the Sunday school movement was a working-class institution and a substantial working-class achievement.[62] To illustrate his thesis, he supplements voluminous 'objective' documentation with frequent references to autobiographical material.[63] From the schoolmaster James Hillock he infers that 'feeling towards children' softened during the nineteenth century and from the minister F.W. MacDonald that most Sunday schools were independently funded.[64] Samuel Bamford, Thomas Whittaker, Joseph Livesey and Adam Rushton comment on the efficacy of Sunday school instruction,[65] and Thomas Wright notes that parents preferred Sunday schools to British Foreign and National schools.[66] Joseph Barker, George Edwards and Tom Mann inform him that, because they were unable to afford time or money for school, 'Sunday school was . . . [their] only resource';[67] while Benjamin Brierley observes that Sunday schools emphasized secular instruction, ranked students according to ability and, in some instances, further enhanced the possibility of self-improvement by providing evening classes on topics ranging from classical literature and languages to chemistry and electricity.[68] Marianne Farningham recalls her disappointment at being withdrawn from school to help in the home. Another self-improver, however, she completed her education at Sunday School and 'went on to become [the eminently respectable] editor of several Dissenting journals'.[69]

Others who were introduced by the Sunday school to 'the culture of self-improvement', often with the encouragement of their parents, were Thomas Burt, John Wilson, Thomas Carter, Thomas Cooper, William Lovett, George Holyoake and Ben Tillett.[70] Lovett's mother banned all but religious books on Sundays, permitted no walking except to Chapel, and took great pains to keep him 'scrupulously clean and respectable'.[71] Edwards's mother stayed up late on Saturday nights cleaning and preparing his clothes for Sunday school; Carter's mother was obsessive about cleanliness; and Brierley feared that 'boys who had been left motherless [would go] . . . to rags both in clothing and morals'.[72] Burt's father, evidently a seasoned Bible scholar, insisted on selecting Burt's recitation piece for an annual Sunday school sermon, rejecting the teacher's choice as inappropriate.[73] Wilson conquered drink by becoming a Sunday school teacher, then experienced a religious awakening and pursued a life of politics, preaching and self-education.[74] Cobbett reminded young men that 'the right to live was associated with the obligation to work';[75] Cooper urged those who claimed to have no time for learning to make time by sleeping less;[76] and, in Barker's view, the poor had 'every station of life open to them'.[77]

Clearly the authors in Laqueur's sample reflect on a number of subjective concerns – their reverence for literacy, their commitment to respectability and their perception of the Sunday school as a formative and profitable institution. But their commentaries do not illustrate the class identity which Laqueur imputes to them, and through them to virtually all working people.[78] Neither do they demonstrate the claim that respectability was not a middle-class imposition. Nor, as it happens, are these matters illuminated by Laqueur's 'objective' evidence. Indeed, he never problematizes class identity but simply assumes it, and his discussion of hegemony and consent, elaborated in a brief concluding chapter, amounts to little more than speculation and assertion. Summarizing his analysis, he observes that the Sunday school embodied a distinctive working-class culture firmly rooted in the ethic of education, religion and respectability. Though founded by middle-class philanthropists, the institution was surrendered within two decades to working-class control.[79] The chief agency of popular literacy, it was also intimately connected 'by personnel and spirit' to the world of political radicalism and did less, ultimately, to instil 'counter-revolutionary virtues' than to create readers of 'seditious and corrupting' radical books and newspapers.[80] If working-class politics failed to generate a revolutionary ideology, literacy and Sunday school instruction were not to blame, for Protestant Christianity is intrinsically neither revolutionary nor oppressive. Social stability was maintained, he insists, because a cohesive ruling class ensured that 'England did not experience a "1789"'.[81] Nevertheless, he proceeds, literacy contributed extensively to a psychological revolution which accompanied and enabled the industrial revolution. It underpinned working-class radicalism but at the same time altered the personality structure 'in ways congruent with the requirements of industrial society'.[82] Hence, Laqueur concludes, a bourgeois world view triumphed in the nineteenth century with popular consent. It did not subvert the class identity of working people, whose culture of discipline, self-help and improvement fortified them, though they lived 'under conditions that degrade[d] the mind', in their ongoing battle for social justice and political equality.[83]

As an account of identity and hegemony, this commentary is naïve and unconvincing. First, it reduces class identity to the intrinsic quality of those whose given lot was to toil away 'under conditions that degrade[d] the mind'. Laqueur does not ask why workers should have accepted this view of themselves, if indeed they did. Nor does he explain why, when consigned to such a condition, they should have still bothered with self-discipline and self-improvement. He considers neither the contingency nor the political ramifications of the categories he employs; hence discipline, along with self-help and respectability, join identity as intrinsic attributes, influenced and even transformed by literacy and the Sunday school, but intrinsic nevertheless. The same superficiality allows him to suggest that the populace was transformed 'in ways congruent with the requirements of industrial society' and that 'a bourgeois world-view' subsequently triumphed, but that 'class identity' was not compromised for hegemony was implemented with popular consent. How consent may have been engineered, if indeed it was given in the way he suggests, is another question left out of his equation.

Equally unsatisfactory is his account of popular consciousness – of what working people thought and why they thought it. Affecting little interest in the material conditions of popular existence, he fails to recognize the extent to which the identity and consciousness of his modestly successful and supposedly representative working-class figures might have been shaped by exceptional opportunities. Some, for example, tell of finding their way into apprenticeships under the patronage of male relatives or their mothers' employers. They also emphasize the clean, orderly environments in which they were raised, their early exposure to respectable values and the encouragement they received from their parents. Such advantages might well have helped to constitute them differently from others, endowing them with a degree of self-esteem and self-confidence which others lacked. Unrelated to such variables, consciousness becomes another essence, albeit one nurtured by and within a hermetic world of Sunday school, religion and respectability. Although Laqueur suggests that this world was linked to the larger economic, social and political universe, the connection is never elaborated. His portrait is one in which material imperatives influenced neither action nor thought. Hence, when he refers to the working-class battle against injustice and inequality, it is unclear whether he means the organized struggle of radical activists to effect economic, social and political change, or simply the efforts of self-improving individuals to advance themselves towards equality with those above them. If the former, why should such a battle have been deemed necessary when, by his own reckoning, it was widely held that responsibility for improvement resided in the individual? If the latter, what, precisely, did working people consider to be unjust if they were convinced that they could and should advance themselves by personal initiative?

Literacy is likewise detached by Laqueur from any material consideration, and it becomes one more foundation the meaning of which is assumed to be self-evident and uncontested. Its transformative effects are then described, but questions about how people responded to what they read and how their responses were conditioned remain unasked. Doubtless, literacy enhances the capacity to see more and to see differently. But if, as Laqueur suggests, people became more favourably disposed to industrial society upon acquiring it, their disposition was surely as much a consequence of the way(s) in which they responded to the kind of knowledge into which literacy initiated them, and to the material conditions in which that knowledge, like their experience, was embedded, as of literacy itself. After all, there are many historical instances of literate individuals and groups who were trenchantly opposed to industrial society. Because he does not acknowledge the categorical status of literacy, he does not realize that its meaning will depend on how it is used. Finally, his conviction that behaviour was predicated on intrinsic attributes and a preexisting ideology is reversed when he suggests that radicalism did not generate a revolutionary ideology because England did not experience social revolution![84] Treating identity and consciousness as given quantities, he leaves no room for agency or choice, and his undemonstrated assertion that bourgeois hegemony was extended with popular consent is meaningless, for consent *implies* choice. Moreover, his exemplars are ultimately irrelevant to the class identity he postulates, for they are permitted to speak only about values and virtues which might have been perfectly compatible with many other determinants of identity, and prized regardless of whether a middle-class world view was accepted. Beyond this superficial treatment, he never addresses the constitution of working people as subjects.

Tholfsen, Crossick, Gray and Neville Kirk also assume class identity and use examples from popular autobiography to illustrate analyses which dispute the equation of respectability with an erosion of class consciousness and a capitulation to bourgeois hegemony. They define respectability in terms of class pride, independence and literacy, and link the decline of confrontational politics to the growing ability of workers to attain to a respectable independence within the existing system. In each analysis, independence is a key explanatory term which denotes both intellectual and economic self-reliance. Intellectually, it implies the capacity to resist bourgeois accounts of socially appropriate behaviour and to elaborate a distinctively working-class version of moral and cultural values. Economically, it refers to self-reliance underpinned by a measure of control over the labour process and exemplified in the establishment and maintenance of self-help institutions such as co-operatives and friendly societies. Accordingly, Crossick, Gray and Kirk stress the importance of material imperatives. Tholfsen, however, advances an essentially idealist analysis which, like Laqueur's, gives only the most marginal consideration to the links between 'mentality' and the material conditions of existence. He shows greater sensitivity than Laqueur to the elusive character of subjective experience but, because he fails adequately to consider the extent to which material circumstances might impinge on consciousness and identity, his conclusions tend to strain against his subjective evidence.

Like Laqueur's working-class representatives, Tholfsen's are often cited for their objective perceptions of contemporary society. Robert Owen, he writes, denounced both individualism and political economy and thereby influenced working-class scepticism of middle-class propaganda.[85] Joseph Livesey, a middle-class cheese merchant who began his working life as a humble weaver, found that plain-speaking teetotal artisans were very effective in advancing the temperance cause.[86] William Lovett characterized the New Poor Law as an instrument of class oppression and urged working people to resist it.[87] Thomas Cooper remarked, in what Tholfsen describes as 'stark class terms', that the middle classes sought to keep Chartists 'at arm's length'.[88] Clearly these examples indicate the currency of 'class' language, but they do not explain what that language meant to the contemporaries who used it, and they scarcely suggest that class identity predominated. Nor do more subjective reflections easily sustain the arguments to which they are adduced. Thomas Whittaker, for example, observes that he began working in a cotton mill when he was six years old; that Methodism introduced him to the temperance movement where he found God and salvation; and that signing the pledge provided him with 'an earnest purpose' which lived with him thereafter.[89] But it is difficult to see any direct correspondence between these observations and class identity, despite Tholfsen's assertions to the contrary.[90] By contrast, when he discusses what he delineates as a 'cult of respectability', his evidence is far less ambiguous. As notable participants in this cult, he identifies certain members of the temperance movement who desired middle-class status, conformed to a middle-class account of how respectable workers should behave, and sought to distance themselves from their working-class background. One such individual, addressing a Newcastle demonstration in 1847, was cheered by his companions upon remarking that 'he thought they were all middle class men'. Another, though 'not ashamed of being called a working man', aspired 'to higher and greater things' and urged his auditors to do likewise.[91]

Against this survey should be set Tholfsen's treatment of William Aitken and G.J. Holyoake, whose personal careers he explores in more detail. Aitken, a cotton-piecer at eleven years old, subsequently became an activist in the short-time movement, a schoolteacher, a Chartist and finally a high-ranking Oddfellow. An 'eloquent spokesman for radical values', he opposed 'political economy and the gospel of success', promoted better education for working people and spoke out against low wages and the excessive demands made on labourers. Although, 'in occupational and economic terms, he may be said to have moved out of the working-class', writes Tholfsen, 'he displayed few signs of "embourgeoisement"'.[92] Clearly, from this description, Aitken exhibited the attitudes and values of Tholfsen's respectable, class-conscious worker. He demonstrated neither the deference nor the aspirations to middle-class status exhibited by the temperancers, nor, apparently, did he cease to encourage the 'independence' of workingmen and to defend their dignity, even after he himself had advanced, 'in occupational and economic terms', into the middle classes. But perhaps Tholfsen's criteria are inadequate; perhaps certain questions remain to be asked. How, for example, did the sympathetic interest which Aitken evidently maintained in working people, after his 'class' status had changed, differ from that of other kindly disposed middle-class individuals who nevertheless, as Tholfsen indicates, did not wish to dissolve class distinctions?[93] And regardless of Aitken's expressed sympathies, could his identity and consciousness have been unaffected by changes in his material condition? Can it be assumed that, when he came to enjoy comparative material security, which possibly he felt he had earned and probably wished to preserve, his motivations continued to reflect those of working people struggling to make ends meet or unable even to find work, and with no material security to defend?[94] Is it possible that such people might often have been more preoccupied with the material exigencies of daily existence than with elaborating their own account of consensus values and resisting middle-class versions, or with contemplating the dignity of work? Have Tholfsen and other idealists who disregard or minimize the significance of material imperatives to identity and consciousness and to explanations of *why* people acted as they did ever themselves experienced economic disadvantage? Is it because they have not that they attribute so little importance to economic considerations, and to the extent to which working people might be preoccupied with the problem of making ends meet? As an 'independent workingman', Aitken is at best a paradox. As a representative of working-class mentality, he is less than convincing. Then what of Holyoake?

Holyoake, Tholfsen suggests, was acutely class conscious and defined his class identity in terms very similar, in a number of ways, to those employed by Marx. He endorsed the view that the prevailing system 'must be changed and not the Rulers alone', denounced class distinctions and described 'all social inequalities' as 'monster evils'. He also characterized several journals which he edited as socially communistic, morally utilitarian, politically republican, and devoted to destroying religion, class rule and private property. He did not discern the mechanics of surplus value extraction as Marx would do, but he suggested the commoditization and brutalization of labour and indicted the capitalist who span 'humanity up in his mills, w[ove] into his calico the hopes, affections, and aspirations of the poor, . . . move[d] heaven and earth for new markets to sell them in', and grew rich 'out of' the worker's misery. Tholfsen notes that Holyoake's views mellowed with time, though not that his changing attitude may have reflected a fundamental change of consciousness. Hence he writes that, in 1842, Holyoake distinguished the working classes as 'the source of all wealth', insisted that the middle classes could not be trusted, and regarded the notion of genuine co-operation between the middle and working classes as a dangerous chimaera.[95] Yet by 1854 he was sufficiently reconciled to the middle classes to publish a defence of Richard Cobden's 'claim to be considered a Radical'. A contemporary, the London shoemaker Charles Murray, subsequently advanced a critique of Cobden in which he dwelt on middle-class treachery and denounced Holyoake for currying middle-class favour, preferring their patronage and becoming a 'servile defender of their fraudulent and destructive system of society'.[96] Tholfsen dismisses Murray's critique as 'charming', sentimental and idealistic, explaining that, in attacking the middle classes, he appealed to the very values which they recommended to working people in their 'most saccharine' propaganda.[97] He does not comment on Murray's perception of Holyoake, though he does indicate that, by 1866, the latter was prepared to confer honorary working-class status on anyone who worked hard enough.[98] Perhaps an appropriate comment would be that Holyoake made this concession at least partly because, having acquired, like Aitken, a degree of material security to defend, he now identified more closely with other such individuals than with workers whose only property, by and large, was their labour.[99]

The apparent modification of Holyoake's attitudes to what some historians would characterize as 'socially inclusive' and populist, Tholfsen attributes to the tendency of prevailing cultural patterns 'to assimilate and [to] deradicalize the principles of the early-Victorian Left'.[100] He does not relate it to a shift in identity as Murray did, even though such a shift could be inferred from his account of Holyoake's changing circumstances.[101] By 1866 Holyoake's position, status and income were possibly closer to those of the classes which he had formerly criticized than to those of the common workers who were once his equals and whom he now sought to guide in less radical paths.[102] Tholfsen insists that '[h]is ideological development is central to an understanding of working-class radicalism both in its early- and mid-Victorian phases'.[103] But it is far from clear why he, or for that matter Aitken, should be seen as representative figures. Nor is it clear, if Holyoake's 'left-wing' principles were 'assimilated and deradicalized' by dominant cultural tendencies, why he should not be equated with the temperance advocates who purportedly adopted a middle-class account of respectability. He may not, like the latter, have proclaimed an aspiration to middle-class status but he evidently rose to such a status, in material terms, to a degree which many temperancers might have envied. It is not intended here to suggest that Holyoake was 'bought off', as certain critics of the labour aristocracy thesis might charge, but rather to question the notion of an identity and consciousness unaffected by the material conditions of its bearer's existence. With regard to Aitken, Holyoake and others in his sample, Tholfsen leaves a great many questions unasked. His analysis therefore fails to explain the inability of Chartism to sustain its struggle against political powerlessness and socio-economic inequality into the mid-Victorian period, for although it consults and comments on a handful of exceptional individuals, it reveals nothing about the subjective experience – the consciousness, identity, aims and motivations – of most contemporary working people.

Unlike Laqueur and Tholfsen, Crossick and Gray relate the pursuit of respectability far more closely to the material conditions of working-class experience. For Crossick, respectability 'stemmed from the need to cope with inequality, hardship and insecurity in an economic and social system that increasingly seemed permanent'.[104] Gray emphasizes the importance of thrift to the respectable artisan, any account of whose culture, he writes, 'must consider the extent to which he attempted to solve the pressing problems of economic survival by the individual exercise of thrift, restraint, [and] economic prudence in personal and family decision making'.[105] Each writer delineates respectability as the expression of a negotiated consensus, on certain moral and cultural values, between working people and the middle classes.[106] Both, however, focus on the labour aristocracy and it is the consciousness and identity of labour aristocrats with which they are primarily concerned. Yet, although they consider at length the material circumstances which might have influenced the thoughts and actions of such individuals, their attention to subjective experience is as cursory as Laqueur's and Tholfsen's.

Most of Crossick's information about the 'experience' of his 'aristocrats' is derived from the accounts of two middle-class women, Ellen Chase and Jane Connolly, whose social status he never reveals beyond noting that they were 'visitors',[107] and from two anonymous workingmen, one of whom can be identified as the stonemason James Turnbull, and another whose working-class 'credentials' cannot be verified. Chase wrote approvingly of a man taken on at the Woolwich Arsenal, whose steady habits 'practically' assured him of permanent work, thereby affording his family a measure of comfort and security.[108] She also noted, though with some bewilderment, that, to escape disreputable neighbours and middle-class patronage, some of her respectable unskilled workers fled to jerry-built artisan cottages.[109] In the Woolwich dockyards, according to Connolly, poverty was unknown, the sons of men employed there were favoured with apprenticeships, and the fluctuations which occurred in the unskilled labour force 'did not touch the good, established workmen'.[110] The latter, she observed, 'were steady and thrifty, paying into building societies until they own[ed] their own homes, educating their children well, and giving them the benefit of good home influence'.[111] Wisely, she implied, few joined temperance lodges where subscriptions were high, benefits low and activity 'weak and fragmented, often descending to that sectarian squabbling that thrives on failure'.[112] So resoundingly Thatcherite in retrospect, Connolly's tone might have made Crossick suspicious, yet he seems to accept her views and those of Chase uncritically.[113]

Equally sanctimonious was the anonymous author of *Working Men and Women* who remarked that '[h]e of the better type is a man of provident inclinings, a man who . . . attempts to provide against the proverbial rainy day. He is usually a much-clubbed man, a member of a trade, a benefit, a yard and slate club . . . while more likely than not he has a few pounds invested in the Post Office Savings Bank or in some building society.'[114] This commentator also dwelt on 'workshop etiquette' whereby mechanics condescended to labourers;[115] on the dire consequences invited by 'any labourer who tried to assume equality with the artisan';[116] on the nature of 'contemporary opinion', according to which the trade union and the friendly society were 'the marks of the labour aristocrat';[117] and on the refusal of unions to require their skilled workers to seek jobs which would undermine their dignity.[118] If, indeed, this anonymous writer was the workingman he claimed to be,[119] his narrative, insofar as it has been deployed by Crossick, reveals as little about his own motivations as do the accounts advanced by outsiders like Chase and Connolly about the subjective experiences of their clients.

No less 'objective' are the comments of Thomas Frost on O'Connor's Land Company;[120] of George Howell on the 1866 Liberal Representation of the People Bill;[121] and of Thomas Wright on female employment in Deptford, on the absence of thrift among the unskilled, on the custom whereby artisan organizations met at public houses, and on the tendency of 'intelligent artisans' who sought to rise out of the working classes to contribute nothing to the social life of the trade unions and friendly societies from which they benefited.[122] In a more self-reflective moment, Wright expressed irritation that circumstances had at one time compelled him, a first-class mechanic, to live in a poor working-class area.[123] Also sensitive to status were C.E. Buckley, who gave his address as New Cross rather than Deptford because he thought the former was more dignified,[124] and Harry Gosling, who explained that the wives of lightermen, stevedores and shipwrights regarded each other as equals but would not be seen shopping with labourers' wives, whom they held to be inferior.[125] In further moments of self-reflection, Gosling noted that he would 'never buy anything unless he could pay ready money for it',[126] and James Turnbull expressed his resentment towards bricklayers who behaved like demigods and criticized the sectionalism and exclusiveness of trade unions.[127] Even the most 'subjective' of the above observations do very little to illustrate 'class' identity, nor do they describe negotiations in which working people and the middle classes strove for consensus on the meaning of moral and cultural imperatives. And regardless of Crossick's conviction that Chartism exerted at best a moderate influence in Kentish London,[128] they do not speak to the most fundamental concern of nineteenth-century labour historiography: the question of why the mid-Victorian working classes apparently withdrew their support from the Chartist movement which sought to empower them, and acquiesced in the *status quo*.

What Crossick's subjective sources point to most suggestively, when he considers the self-reflection of their authors, is a preoccupation with status and a degree of social fragmentation rather than the conformity of workers to a unifying class identity. A similar impression is conveyed in Gray's work, where Alexander Somerville is cited to the effect that masons, jealous of their trade privileges, would not allow those privileges to be discussed by other men, even 'labourers who might be subject to the injustice of those privileges'.[129] The exclusive self-interest of skilled workers is also suggested by a Scottish tailor who recognized the prevalence of 'sweating' in clothing manufacture but noted with apparent relief that the upper end of the trade was not affected.[130] A similar theme was pursued by Thomas Wright who implied that those in favourable employment concerned themselves with the 'tail' of the trade only to the extent that, through illness or some other misfortune, they might fall into it.[131] By contrast, Wright felt that the intelligent artisan who looked to the improvement of his class was commoner in working-class institutions than the educated workingman who strove to climb out of it and that, when on the tramp, it was better to be 'had' sometimes than, from over-suspicion, to refuse a request for help from a fellow-tradesman.[132] Less prepared, apparently, to be generous to the superior classes, he remarked: 'I am a working man – what a gentleman wanting my vote (if I had one) at election time, or the chairman at a prize-distribution meeting of an industrial exhibition, would probably call "an intelligent artisan".'[133] In addition, Gray consults an octogenarian printer named Fleming, who reflected on how, in the past, Edinburgh workers turned out in their craft regalia on special occasions like the royal visit in 1822 and the Reform demonstration in 1832;[134] Somerville and Hugh Miller on the blurred distinction between work and leisure time;[135] J.S. Blackie on 'evening entertainments called soirees';[136] and William Paterson on the progress of his career through various white-collar jobs to an apprenticeship in his father's joinery, then general secretary of the joiners' union and finally fire master in Glasgow.[137]

In the context of Gray's analysis, the above examples might well indicate the negotiation of consensus values. They might also imply that class was an important determinant of identity. In their original contexts, however, they lend themselves to a range of interpretations and favour no particular one. The memoirs themselves do not address the negotiation of values to which Gray refers, and although they sometimes suggest consciousness of class, they give no

indication that it was an abiding preoccupation. Nor do they permit any conclusive judgement about the extent to which class was implicated in the
constitution of their authors as subjects. Restored to the passages from which
they have been drawn, the conversational remarks of Somerville, Miller and
Blackie lose the significance they acquire in Gray's narrative, and only Wright
reflects on his own thoughts and motivations. The rest of the chosen commentators, as noted above, can be seen to point like Wright to social fragmentation
rather than class unity, though it would be presumptuous to conclude either
way from a sample too narrow to exemplify the identity of a class, or even that
of a social stratum. Indeed, the very notion of class consciousness seems inappropriate in a discussion which focuses almost exclusively on a collectivity the
members of which, according to the representatives consulted, resisted identification with the mass of workers, diminishing if not denying their importance
as Gray himself does by refusing to engage with them.

Neville Kirk appears to differ from the historians thus far consulted in that
he defines popular respectability as an indigenous institution which grew out
of the material conditions of working-class existence. Effectively, however, he
replicates the fundamental assumptions of the 'negotiated consensus theory',[138]
according to which the working classes developed a distinctive version of
shared values. Although Kirk has been applauded for problematizing the
ethnic and religious dimensions of popular experience,[139] his treatise is largely
a synthesis of earlier analyses. And although he recognizes gender as an important consideration, he regrets, albeit in a footnote, that he has not carried out
a 'detailed search for information on female activists'.[140] He does not speculate
on how the results of such an inquiry might be used, but his demonstrable failure to problematize the categories he employs suggests that he would adduce
them as further illustrations of a unified (and foundational) experience. This
judgement seems justified by his treatment of a contemporary who represents
himself as his wife's creator and the object of her worship.[141] Preoccupied
with the respectable working *man*'s conception of the ideal family, Kirk
scarcely comments on how the wife may have regarded such an arrangement.
Nor does he consider the possibility, so well delineated in the words of his
exemplar, that gender functioned to articulate and naturalize difference. He
does not suspect, therefore, that gender may have been implicated in the dif-
ferentiations through which class identity was created and understood.[142] He
simply asserts that working women 'did not have the time to keep a record of
their thoughts and actions' and that it is thus difficult 'to know how Marcroft's
wife and other women experienced and viewed their changing role' (not
roles).[143] He nevertheless writes confidently about the experience of working
women, constructing it, like that of working men, from selected comments by
mostly male 'representatives' marginally more numerous than those cited by
other authors, but arguably no less exceptional.

Kirk refers to a substantial body of biographical and autobiographical literature including the writings of Ben Wilson, C. Rowley, Thomas Cooper,

George Howell, W.H. Chadwick, Benjamin Grime and Thomas Wright. Wilson, cited to the effect that his Halifax co-operative increased its capital and turnover between 1849 and the 1880s, also tells of how, by example, he encouraged working men to improve their condition by investing in a co-operative the money which otherwise they would have spent on drink.[144] Chadwick remembers Chartism and Liberalism as 'natural allies', and Rowley recalls the fine lectures on Milton and Constantine the Great which he and fellow-Chartists had attended.[145] Rowley also reflects on the glee evenings at the Stockport United Free Gardeners; the religious, cultural and recreational attractions of St Paul's, Ancoats, which had conspired with good home influence to save local youth from the streets; and his subsequent career as a town councillor, 'an honourable career', he insists, which was 'not to be despised or avoided by our best men and women'.[146] Cooper expresses contempt for the workingmen of 1887 who, preoccupied with their greyhounds, 'Co-ops' and building societies do not interest themselves as did the poorer though more intelligent men of the Chartist era, in 'the great doctrine of political justice';[147] Howell notes that the language of success was spoken chiefly by labour leaders;[148] and Grime equates success with self-help and education, which could occasionally lead to municipal office.[149] Wright regrets that thousands of workingmen have been driven to ruin by slovenly wives; and that 'crushers' – unenterprising individuals who blamed the system for their condition – held back the industrious, literate and intelligent workers who sought to elevate themselves. But he also reminisces about the joy of returning home from work to glistening furniture, a well-cooked meal, a presentable wife and clean, tidy children.[150]

Beyond these comments, Kirk's evidence of working-class experience is drawn largely from the writings of William Marcroft and Benjamin Brierley. He describes Marcroft as an exemplary workingman who began life in dire poverty and ended it one of the wealthiest individuals in his leadership sample. Through hard work, self-education and self-help he acquired considerable property, including an eight-bedroom family residence, and on his death 'left an estate valued at the sum of £14,753'. After the decline of Chartism he became a founding member of the Sun Mill Corporation and apparently a 'leading influence in the re-direction of working-class energies into co-operation'.[151] Other co-operators regarded him as a model husband, admiring his clean, tidy house, his sober, industrious family and his well-domesticated wife, who, according to Marcroft, made home her 'heaven' and her husband 'the altar of her worship'.[152] It was in the home, Marcroft insisted, that children must be taught politeness, economy, industry, sobriety and reasoned thought. Hence he advised young men contemplating marriage to ascertain the prospective bride's background, thus to ensure that she came from thrifty, industrious, courteous, healthy stock.[153]

Like many of his peers, Kirk observes, Marcroft believed 'that workers were in the process of securing a place in the system' and, as evidence that this belief was justified, he cites the *Co-operative News*, according to which a 'vast number' of 'people who had started life as "the poorest of the poor"' were now 'comfortably situated'.[154] Clearly convinced by such evidence, Kirk proceeds to argue that, precisely because respectable independence had become widely accessible, the mid-Victorian working classes acquiesced in the *status quo*. But he does not address the possibility that Marcroft may have lacked the ability to 'speak the minds' of 'ordinary' working people, that he neither saw their condition as they saw it nor understood their reasons for acting as they did. He treats John Foster's claim that Marcroft was contemptuous of unskilled workers as an irrelevancy,[155] though, implicitly, it is because of Marcroft's supposed 'identification' with working people that Kirk elevates his observations to the status of 'insights'. Yet not only can Marcroft's writings be seen to express the contempt discerned by Foster; they indicate that, for most of his adult life, his affinities were not with working people but with management and the middle classes.

Marcroft may have been admired by certain co-operators, but his projected plan for a co-operative village, which outlines a 'partnership' between labour and capital, favours the latter in every detail. To promote the earnestness and hard work which in his view would keep prices low and demand high, employees would be required to purchase a minimum number of shares which the company would redeem at 'cost' when employment was terminated. Workers were to be multi-skilled so that as few as possible would be needed; their wages were to be adjusted to the rate of profit; and they were to share profits *after* 'capital ha[d] been paid for its use'. Because they were mere children, who required oversight and direction, they were to defer to the superior wisdom their capitalist fathers.[156] The latter knew best how to manage their skills which consisted mainly in brute strength and energy. They were to be engaged and discharged at the discretion of the board, on which they were also to be represented 'by men of their own condition'. But when decisions about employment and policy were disputed, it was to be the right of the largest investors to demand a ballot in which one vote could be cast for every four shares held.[157] Investors rather than workers were therefore to be the chief beneficiaries of the enterprise and control was to be invested in the largest shareholders among whom the architect seems clearly to have counted himself. He may have been a pillar of the co-operative movement but his version of co-operation, which identifies a need to create dependencies and presupposes winners and losers, assigns working people an unremittingly subordinate role and suggests that he may have been remote from their concerns.

Elsewhere, Marcroft writes that as a young man in the metal trades his industry won him the favour of more seasoned men who, because he 'was so much of a scholar', also made him 'secretary of the trades' society'. He also notes, however, that to amass capital of £1,000, thus to become 'independent', he made various compromises which alienated him from other workers. By one such compromise, he renounced his Chartist and trade union connections to secure and ultimately to advance his position in a machine manufactory, becoming, as he puts it, a 'master's man'.[158] Disliked, he writes, because he refused to waste his money on drinking sprees, he in turn disdained the tradesmen for their dishonesty, and compiled a 'secret account' of 'discrepancies between the piece[work] book and the time book'. Suspecting a conspiracy to have him replaced, he presented this account to his employer and was rewarded with promotion to a management position.[159] Several men lost their jobs as a consequence and vowed that if they found Marcroft they would 'kill him'. Though he does not appear to have received any further death threats, he refers often to the animosity with which, because of their low moral character, his underlings regarded him.[160]

Having nominated himself 'a master's man', Marcroft observes that it is 'the master's interest he should ever be looking after'.[161] While 'a mere workman . . . may in justice claim exemption from interference [outside working hours]', one employed as a foreman or manager and paid accordingly 'ought to devote the whole of his time and attention to promote his master's interests, and, in justice, not engage in any other occupation except with the knowledge and consent of the person . . . that pay[s] him his wages'.[162] He thus explains his abandonment of trade unionism which he proceeds to declare obstructive and, since the passing of the 1856 Joint Stock Companies Act, no longer necessary.[163] An instrument used by irresponsible workers to persecute their employers, the union was an institution of 'cowardly' men who sought others 'to do for them what is within their power to do for themselves'.[164] If operatives are unable to negotiate agreeable conditions, Marcroft concludes, they should seek alternative employment.[165] No less than Kirk's account, this portrait of Marcroft could be criticized for being overdrawn and one-dimensional. But it is not offered as a more 'valid' representation. It is meant rather to emphasize that Marcroft's identity was fluid and as subject to change as his circumstances and affinities. Indeed, he reflects that such a process is inevitable when one 'passes from a workman's condition to the position of an employer'.[166] As one who, by his own admission, ceased long ago to be a member of the working classes, he is a most dubious 'exemplar' of 'working-class identity', and there seems no compelling reason to assume that his 'insight' into popular thoughts, motivations and predispositions is any greater than that of other detached middle-class observers.

Also doubtful as a representative figure is the dialect poet, Benjamin Brierley. For Brierley and his companions, Kirk observes, life after Chartism was devoted to intellectual pursuits. Abjuring the frivolities of youth, they did not frequent the public house but cultivated the nobler ambition of mutual improvement. At the Failsworth Improvement Society, where billiards, cards and smoking were all banned, they read and marvelled at Shakespeare, Wordsworth, Byron, Burns, Locke and Bentham.[167] They occasionally attended a dance and enjoyed a good hearty flinging up of heels, but they observed the strict morality of respectable workers and did not indulge in hugging. Nor would they abide 'ratting' or dog and horse racing which they regarded as immoral and inimical to serious thought.[168] According to Kirk, Brierley's commitment to respectability exemplified a dominant trend among workers in the post-Chartist decades, but the mutual practices through which it was cultivated served merely as a means. Its essence was competitive individualism and the doctrine of success, which seriously compromised mid-Victorian 'class solidarity'.[169] Yet the 'consciousness' and 'identity' implied by 'class solidarity' is never problematized and the extent to which Brierley depicts himself as part of an exceptional minority is never acknowledged.

By his own account, the one brief period during which, as a Chartist and a participant in the 'Plug Plot', he supported what might be termed a 'popular' initiative, Brierley recalls as a youthful aberration. With retrospect he implies that such measures were unwarranted, observing that his own earnings would have been higher had he not been held back by fellow workers and that his father, a moral force man, was compelled to grind pikes for fear of 'being [judged] a traitor' by the less circumspect. It was a time, he concludes, when 'the English Statute Books [were] confronted by mob law'. But drawing away from 'the mob' he surpassed other boys and also teachers in literacy, and attached himself to a young book-keeper who read superior literature and was 'looked upon as being of a higher class'. Emphasizing the importance of good connections he notes how they facilitated his own upward mobility and also eased his brother's entry into the Oldham Police Force. With what could be interpreted as self-importance, he observes that he has dined with 'the highest in the land', that he took an extended trip to America (something which most contemporaries might only have dreamed about) to revive his flagging creativity, and that just '[for] a change I allowed myself to be pitchforked into the Manchester City Council, which position I held for a period of six years'. Like Marcroft, Brierley characterizes himself as one who has moved decisively beyond his working-class origins. It seems likely, therefore, that distance might possibly have compromised his 'insight' into the subjective experiences of those beneath him, the 'unexceptional'. But, once again, this possibility is not investigated.

Kirk describes his focus as mid-Victorian England and it is to the mid-Victorian decades that his autobiographical sample refers. Nevertheless, declaring an interest in 'process', 'change' and 'contradiction', he describes the Chartist era as one of class solidarity and the subsequent period as one in which class identity was fragmented. Only at the turn of the century, he suggests, was the 'sense of class unity' renewed.[170] Hence, although he finds that, from 1850, the values implied by working-class respectability were increasingly assimilated to the bourgeois ethos of competitive individualism and 'success', he locates this development in the 'process' which, in his view, eventually restored working-class integrity. He therefore seems to resist the notion that bourgeois hegemony was successfully implemented. Abstracted from their original contexts and assimilated to his narrative, Kirk's examples seem unambiguously to indicate that their authors were preoccupied with 'serious' literature, puritanical morality and the economic virtues, and that they embraced co-operativism enthusiastically, as a means to individual self-improvement. His sources also appear to suggest the absence of class solidarity which, according to Kirk, distinguished the mid-Victorian decades, and to support the view that individuals were held increasingly responsible for their own condition. But the unified class identity which he seems convinced obtained both in the Chartist years and at the turn of the century – even though he asserts ambiguously that the working class does not share 'a single, common consciousness' – remains undemonstrated. Nor does he explain adequately why a sample which, as he acknowledges, is made up of exceptional individuals, should be seen as broadly representative.[171] Although, like other historians in the survey, he defines his subject as the working classes, he never attempts to engage with the mass of working people.[172] It is unclear, therefore, whether he assumes that the latter chose actively to adopt the attitudes of their leaders or that they accepted passively the roles to which they were assigned. Either way, he seems convinced that their thoughts and motivations are irrelevant to his purposes.

Kirk's ambiguous challenge to the notion of a single, common working-class consciousness is extended by Patrick Joyce to include social identity. In Joyce's view class had its place as one 'among a range of possible social and political identities available to and used by the labouring populations'.[173] He defines these identities as 'classical', 'liberal', 'conservative' and 'radical', observing that the 'radical strain' predominated but that, as 'a family of populisms' which fostered, articulated and validated a vision of social inclusiveness, all were closely related. It is to the demonstration of this populist vision that he adduces his evidence, yet his treatment of that material suggests that he is more interested in constructing experience himself than exploring the diverse predicates of its construction in the past. He asserts that experience is constituted by language and proceeds to interpret the meaning of certain contemporary discourses – formal, colloquial and symbolic – regarding them as a semiology of the social order.[174] Apparently, however, he is not alert to the possibility that contemporaries who engaged with the discourses to which he addresses himself may have inferred a multiplicity of meanings quite unlike those discerned by him. Accordingly, his autobiographical references are offered as objective confirmation of his own views.

Joyce does not engage extensively with theories of discourse. Instead, although his documentation is often imprecise, he attempts to illustrate his theoretical speculation with a reading of nineteenth-century and retrospective literature from which he selects, orders and describes 'facts'. Hence, as evidence of the widespread belief that employers created work and that the processes of capital were 'magical', he refers to a 1924 volume by J.R. Clynes.[175] From Brierley, Stephen Reynolds and a backward-looking Robert Roberts he infers that social distinctions were seen as 'natural' and broadly respected.[176] Brierley also comments on north–south rivalry among working people and the ambivalence of popular attitudes to advancing industrialization and urbanization.[177] J. Wilson is consulted on the powerful currency of witchcraft beliefs;[178] Lovett on appeals to the Bible to sanction notions of evil spirits;[179] Burt on the tendency of religion itself to become a source of superstition;[180] Wright and Ben Turner on the popularity and influence of the penny ballad.[181] All of these observations might be assimilated with little difficulty to class, populist or other interpretations.

With two exceptions, the remainder of Joyce's autobiographical references, though they occur in a discussion of what certain discourses meant to nineteenth-century working people, are unaccompanied by examples. Hence, when he claims that a renewed interest in class language in the 1840s reflected concern over 'divisions *within* as much as *between* classes', and suggests that the work of Thomas Wright confirms this claim, his reference is to a secondary work and it is difficult to know what aspects of Wright's 'language' he is interpreting.[182] Elsewhere, suggesting that '[t]he struggle for liberty in the 1860s and 70s' was seen by workingmen 'as part of a centuries-old history . . . marked by the progress of reason', he asserts that '[t]he autobiographies of Liberal, ex-Chartist, workingmen activists bear witness to this sense of the seamlessness of the old cause'. But he neither illustrates his argument nor asks how the autobiographies in question perform the function imputed to them. Nor does he explain why the views which he attributes to his activists must necessarily have reflected those of other working people. These issues are not illuminated by his documentation which consists of nothing more than two book titles.[183] Also undocumented is a speech attributed to Lloyd George which, Joyce observes, 'call[ed] for justice' not between 'rich and poor' but between 'man and man', since 'men were all born the same way'. For Stephen Reynolds, he continues, the speech perfectly expressed contemporary 'working-class political loyalties and aspirations'. Hence, he concludes, Lloyd George exemplified 'the continuing potency of the underlying populism of the radical tradition'. Possibly Reynolds and Lloyd George did entertain the same view of working-class attitudes. But beyond asserting that the prevailing social identity was populist, Joyce never demonstrates that popular loyalties and aspirations conformed to that view.[184]

From twenty-odd autobiographical references Joyce includes only two substantive quotations and considers neither as commentary on its author. Instead, he treats them as objective evidence of broad working-class attitudes. Hence, from a lengthy observation by Aitken encouraging the union of labour and capital and noting the blessings bestowed on society by public-spirited capitalists, Joyce extrapolates conceptions of mutual interest to the community-at-large.[185] Traditional notions of 'the trade', he writes, 'pick[ed] up on new ideas of industrial partnership and progress, in part employing the discourse of the economic market, yet still serving as the matrix of the new in attempting the moral regulation of capital, the moralising of the market'.[186] Articulated to the customary values of 'the trade', he suggests, was a novel emphasis on industrial progress and 'reproductive employment', and the trade subsequently came to mean industry at large, not only for skilled men 'but also for the unskilled majority, including women workers'.[187]

The only evidence offered for this series of claims is Aitken's quotation. Yet Aitken makes no reference to 'moral matrices', 'the old and the new' or the 'interests of the trade'. His emphasis is material rather than ideal or moral, and his tone could well be interpreted as that of one seeking earnestly to persuade his reader rather than of one preaching to the converted. If Joyce succeeds in illustrating anything at all it is an imprecise correspondence between Aitken's terminology and that of some union and reform literature referred to in preceding paragraphs.[188] He does not, however, explain why the meanings which he imputes to that literature and to Aitken's text should be accepted as definitive, even for Aitken. And beyond his regularly repeated but never theorized assertion that language constitutes experience, he never demonstrates the currency, in the broader community, of the attitudes which he describes. With a casual nod to 'plurality', he notes that 'the trade' came to be suggestive of two meanings which he then delineates as 'the craft', which had traditional connotations, and 'industry at large, in its various manifestations at the level of town, region, nation, and even the immediate locality'.[189] But if meaning can be plural, why not multiple and why, therefore, should his interpretation be recognized as the 'correct' one? Why should it be assumed, even were one to accept the linguistic constitution of experience, that the masses, skilled, unskilled, males and females, were constituted in the way which he suggests?

No less imaginative is Joyce's treatment of a lengthy quotation from Benjamin Grime.[190] Proceeding from the unobjectionable claim that rhymes and ballads generated by and among working people were exceedingly popular, Joyce elaborates a narrative in which the ballad acquires a range of determinative functions. Not only 'a means of handling the workaday vicissitudes of city life, arming the unwary in their transactions with landlords', publicans and others, it was also a mechanism for handling more intimate arrangements like courtship and marriage, 'a literature of advice, warning and admonition', 'a moral commentary on the life of the people', and an integral part of the political 'loyalties bred by partisanship'. Enabling the people to 'sing their aspirations', the ballad was defined by popular expectation and the conventions of the ballad form but the latter, in turn, set limits to what could be expressed and, despite its flexibility, 'privileged certain views of the world and denied others'.[191] As proof of these claims, he cites Grime's 'objective' assessment of the ballad as an accurate reflection of the sympathies, antipathies, proclivities, emotions, hopes and aspirations of 'the great untaught'.[192] But he accepts Grime's commentary uncritically and, perhaps predictably, does not speculate on what it might say about Grime himself. Instead, he proceeds to an analysis of the dialect idiom.

In this discussion, he refers to the writings of Allen Clarke, a union journalist, and Ben Brierley, the dialect poet, interpreting them as conclusive
evidence of a prevailing populist identity.[193] Clarke, he explains, 'was a child
of the moral and emotional world of the nineteenth century' whose work, like
that of Brierley, emphasized 'the humanity of all folks', not least the monarchy.[194] He elaborated a 'universalistic conception . . . of the social order' in
which the ideal employer and the proper relationship between master and
worker were clearly delineated; in which revolt was 'far removed from the class
war'; and in which democracy was defined neither as class rule nor the rule of
the working class, but as that 'of the nation, embracing all and tempering different social elements one with another'.[195] In this vision, democracy was 'but
Christianity applied' and socialism 'was about the reconciliation of all God's
children in a commonwealth of the people'.[196] This characterization reflects
another in which, according to Joyce, '[h]ome and family relations' were
depicted by dialect writers in such a way that 'barriers of gender seem to have
been as little marked as those of status within the working classes'.[197]

In each of these instances, however, the words are Joyce's own. He does not
illustrate his comments on gender and the family, nor does he refer them to any
particular nineteenth-century source. As evidence of Clarke's views, he offers
a book title, a list of journals and a prose-poem by Brierley.[198] The narrator of
Brierley's poem is a workingman who describes the gentleman as 'a sponge',
the aristocrat as a 'useless hanger-on' and the magistrate as a lackey of the rich.
His 'feyther', he continues, 'passed sentence on me when I're fourteen, an'
comdemned me, for th' crime o' coming into th' world, to six days a week hard
labour'. Finally, on the question of 'freedom', he observes that 'A mon'll say
"Rule Britannia" . . . when at th' same time he takken a hoss's place in th'
shafts of a carriage, an' happen his dowter's working sixteen heurs a day wi' her
needle, for just a bare livin'. An' this is a *free country*.'[199] As difficult as it is to
find any hint in these words of harmony and social inclusiveness, Joyce seems
convinced that they corroborate his 'populist' vision. He also seems convinced
that the poem 'articulated the preconceptions' of its readers, and that dialect
was a medium which described and prescribed popular identity, speaking to
the condition of the people in their own language.[200] Hence, in Joyce's formulation, 'the medium was the message'.[201] The trouble with this metaphor
is that it fails to address the possibility that Brierley's work, and dialect literature in general, may have meant different things to different readers.
Subscribers may have made sense of it in a variety of ways, precisely as the contrast between Joyce's interpretation and my own suggests. Moreover, however
one might choose to define the poet's 'social vision', other aspects of his writings which have been explored above indicate that he defined himself as
someone distinct and different from 'the people' whose 'populist identity' his
writings supposedly illuminate.

Brierley's literature may have been produced for a popular market but the
characters in his autobiography are most often exceptional people – those who

contributed to his own advancement and self-improving boyhood friends who subsequently carved out impressive careers. Common people – those one might think of as an economically and politically powerless majority – are at best peripheral to his discussion. When he refers to them, it is usually to assert that their younger cohorts enjoy better conditions but are less respectful than in his own day, or to emphasize the timeless and all 'too common frivolities of youth' which he and his adolescent friends avoided. He may have regarded himself as a worker but he also defined himself against other workers and claimed affinity with more élite circles. He may have been exercised by the issues which, according to Joyce, were central to his poetry and to the 'universalistic' social vision which it purportedly articulated. But he does not reflect on them in his autobiography where, beyond an implicit endorsement of the *status quo*, his self-construction seems remote from the world view supposedly embedded in his literature. If the 'vision' which Joyce describes had little apparent influence on the identity of its purported architect, there seems little reason to assume that it interpellated anyone else, moulding their identities with an uncontestable set of meanings, simply because Brierley's literature was 'popular'.

The premises of Joyce's discussion might well be characterized as the condescension of posterity and an implicit endorsement of élite theory. On the one hand, Joyce invests himself and superior individuals like Aitken, Grime and Brierley with sufficient agency and intellectual complexity to enable their objective detachment, and hence a capacity to see through simple folk to their thoughts, expectations and aspirations. On the other hand, the simple folk themselves are portrayed as so thoroughly structured and their world view so thoroughly defined and limited, notably by the ballad form, that their identities and thoughts are transparent and their motivations, therefore, perfectly visible. Yet, once again, other than asserting that language constitutes experience, Joyce never explains the remarkable gift of insight into the consciousness of the mid-Victorian populace which he claims for himself and certain mid-Victorian commentators. Nor, because of his inadequate illustration and documentation, can his conclusions easily be evaluated. He never consults the people whose identity he presumes to define, nor, because he fails to address his own role in constructing their experience, does he consider the extent to which his narrative may be shaped by his own concerns.

Beyond his engagement with Aitken and Grime, Joyce's autobiographical material escapes the 'close analysis' which, in his introduction, he promises will illuminate his commentary.[202] He scarcely speculates on what these works might reveal about the thoughts, attitudes and motivations of their authors and it is also very difficult to assess his treatment of them. Because he provides few illustrations and his documentation is imprecise – generally a series of page/chapter numbers for each reference and often only a title – one can never be sure what part of any particular text is being interpreted. Had Joyce focused predominantly on the diverse categories implicated in the constitution of identity and experience, these oversights might have been of less consequence. But his approach is essentially descriptive. He sometimes suggests that meaning is multiple but in practice treats it as uncontested and self-evident, and his 'constitutive' discourses become just one more way of representing experience. Having established that experience to his own satisfaction, he suggests its wide currency among contemporaries with a series of general references to autobiographical material. But because he does not give adequate access to his sources, it is difficult to speculate on whether experience was constituted as he suggests even for his exemplars.

Although Joyce claims to have adopted a post-structuralist orientation, his epistemology conveys little sense of post-structuralist relativism. Nor does his emphasis on the constructedness of experience prevent him from treating it as an ontological foundation which can be accurately described. Without explaining why, he treats identity not as a conditioned and conditioning process of being or becoming, but as something which people 'use', a doubtful procedure which enables him simultaneously to assert the 'plurality' of identity and to ignore the ramifications of his assertion. Accordingly, he postulates a finite range of linguistically determined subject positions by which people were in his view interpellated and which he represents as populist. He then delineates those positions in unremittingly positivistic terms, as though their meaning were intrinsic and fixed. Yet the fluidity and ambiguity of identity and meaning suggest themselves repeatedly in the writings of the very individuals whom he enlists as exemplars of populist mentality, for, almost without exception, these individuals betray to other historians all of the hallmarks of class identity. Moreover, the writings at issue, as the above commentary indicates, can also be seen to suggest division and fragmentation rather than the unity, integrity and social cohesion implied, albeit in different ways, both by class and populist definitions and analyses.

No less than the other historians surveyed, Joyce endeavours to confirm the currency of the social identity which he postulates through a very problematical and inadequate form of hermeneutics. To a greater or lesser extent, all interpret the writings of a virtually 'standard' body of working-class exemplars, thus to 'penetrate' their thoughts and to attribute to them particular ways of seeing, then generalize their conclusions to the community-at-large. Yet this group of workingmen can well be viewed as singularly unrepresentative. They describe supportive parents who encouraged their early development, education and self-confidence, initiating them, as it were, into the mysteries of the prevailing social system. Some acknowledge patronage which enabled them in their youth to gain apprenticeships in more or less lucrative trades, or in later life to establish themselves as editors or even publishers. Others indicate that literacy and skilled status facilitated their advancement in the labour movement and their subsequent entry into local office or parliamentary careers. Without even speculating on what these advantages may have 'meant' to them, it is possible to suggest that, in the nineteenth as in the late twentieth century, the majority of working people were not male (although most of those who received wages may have been); did not enjoy any significant patronage; did not have the opportunity to learn lucrative skills; did not become proprietors in the publishing field or in any other; and did not become labour leaders, local officials or Members of Parliament. It is also likely that an individual like Aitken, for example, whose father was a sergeant-major in the army and retired after thirty years' service 'with a competency for life', was subjected to formative influences quite unlike those which shaped the identities of people whose parentage was less exalted, even if he did begin work as a cotton piecer at eleven.[203] It might also be assumed that, if contemporary experiences were so diverse, so too were perceptions of reality and the identities which those perceptions informed.

The above conclusions suggest at least two possibilities. The first is that, to establish whether identity can be reduced to a 'class' or 'populist' definition, a wider sample must be introduced. Perhaps if a substantial number of 'subjective' sources are examined not only for their social commentary but for their self-reflective implications, a prevailing social identity might reasonably be postulated. The second possibility, if nothing conclusive can be inferred from such an examination, is that the meaning of the material from which identity is inferred is generated not by the material itself but by some other source. These alternatives will be explored in the following chapter.

3

WHO ARE 'THE PEOPLE' IN MID-VICTORIAN LABOUR HISTORY?

In Chapter 2 I argued that the social identities on which historians base their accounts of mid-Victorian consensus and stability are theoretical categories, the historicity of which is not adequately examined or acknowledged. Those categories, I suggested, operate as *a priori* foundations which naturalize and validate particular conceptions of the past, subserving a practice in which representation stands for explanation. I then considered some of the literature which historians have adduced to demonstrate the contemporary currency of the proposed identities, stressing the ambiguity of the literature itself – its capacity to sustain a range of meanings – and the manipulative processes through which it is transformed into evidence. My discussion embodied two kinds of criticism. One spoke to the narrative strategies employed in history writing and will be resumed in Chapter 4. The other addressed the works under review on their own terms, engaging with their explanatory categories on the ontological level to which they are raised and evaluating their treatment of 'evidence', content and context. With reference to a small autobiographical sample, I speculated that the social identities to which explanations of stability are articulated are not (and perhaps cannot be) convincingly illustrated. I also disputed the representative status of the autobiographers themselves, noting their apparent predisposition to take hierarchy for granted, to prize individual success, to disdain less competitive types, and to define themselves against the mass of ordinary workers. In short, I described attitudes which tell against the cohesive, integrated social visions of class and populist constructions.

My critique of the representative figure has prompted me to ask further questions. Was the respectable independence which purportedly underpinned the advent of conciliatory politics in the mid-Victorian period, and to which the sample group seems to have attained, accessible to the majority? Did the apparent acquiescence of certain individuals in the *status quo* signify that society had become generally more equitable, or merely that the individuals themselves had been able to improve their material condition? Did many workers fail to become 'independent' and, if so, can it be assumed that *they* regarded the system as just and equitable? Might their 'acquiescence' have simply reflected a conviction that they were impotent to do otherwise and must find alternative ways of supplying their needs? Finally, if the identities devised by historians cannot be shown to have had general currency, do they lose their explanatory significance?[1] These questions will shape my discussion in this chapter, which situates the inquiry initiated above in a wider context. The chapter is divided into two parts. In the first I consider accounts of identity and experience against a more extensive sample of the autobiographies from which their corroborative evidence has been drawn. In the second I test them against the observations of less exalted contemporaries who describe experiences sufficiently diverse to cast doubt on the notion that popular identity can be reduced to fixed, reified subject positions. As the context of my inquiry broadens, this ambiguity increases, suggesting that it is from interpretative rather than historical contexts that historical data acquire their meanings, and that the selection of material for interpretation is itself prefigured by questions which are historical, contingent and political.

IDENTITY AND EXPERIENCE –
THE 'STANDARD SAMPLE'

The questions raised above and on which my analysis is based reflect the economic character of the theories with which I am concerned. Each theory shapes a narrative more or less different from the others, but all emphasize the extent to which identity was ordered by the pursuit of respectability and to which respectability was defined by the economic virtues.[2] And all suggest that the more assiduously these virtues were practised, the greater the 'independence' likely to result. Commentators often applaud the industry, thrift, self-reliance and self-denial with which the 'success' of their exemplars was bought, and it is with success stories that they persistently concern themselves.[3] Hence, although they agree that respectability meant discernibly different things to different people, its significance to those it eluded, whose industry, self-denial and efforts to obtain work went unrewarded, is never addressed. Nor is the extent to which Victorian society was predicated on inequality, structured to deny opportunity to the majority, and calculated to maintain the dependency of the most exploited. Informed by present-centred political concerns, these objections and my introductory questions function, like the theories devised by other writers, to shape the construction of a particular past. In effect, they determine the selection of evidence and the meanings with which it will be inscribed. But they raise the possibility that what has been described retrospectively as active acceptance of the contemporary social hierarchy may for some have been silent resistance or reluctant submission. They also suggest that justice, equity and real independence for working people may be incompatible with the capitalist system. Most importantly, they challenge the theories of social identity which inform and

93

underpin histories of mid-Victorian social harmony by indicating that the 'evidence' adduced to support them is susceptible to inscription with different and disparate meanings. The use of that evidence will now be explored, along with the meanings ascribed to it.

At various points in their respective narratives, all of the autobiographers thus far consulted make statements which are amenable to class and populist constructions. When refracted through class paradigms, these statements can be manipulated to suggest that working people shared a common class identity, that they held social classes to exist in objective relation to the means of production, or that their class identity remained intact despite their apparent acceptance, in the mid-Victorian period, of a bourgeois world view. Other observations, assimilated to so-called populist models, seem to indicate a commitment to social harmony based on widespread respect for the dignity of labour, popular satisfaction with the political system and general acceptance of social stratification as natural and desirable. When such statements are considered independently, however, attributed meanings and connotations slip away, and when they are returned to the texts from which they have been abstracted, other interpretative possibilities become available. Those possibilities can be enhanced or limited by what might be called contextual fabrication – a kind of meta-narrative closure which determines the contemporary discourses against which the texts will be considered – and by the questions which order the new interpretation. In the context which I have devised and in response to my interrogation, the memoirs examined thus far indicate that their authors were substantially detached from any 'common condition'. I have therefore disputed the capacity of those individuals to represent a common identity and experience. In Chapter 2 I noted that four such individuals, William Marcroft, Benjamin Brierley, William Aitken and G.J. Holyoake, seem to have identified increasingly with higher strata as their careers led them out of the working classes.

Other supposed representatives, although they often emphasize their commitment to hard work, also describe circumstances that were in various ways remote from those of most working people. Hugh Miller, for example, writes that his father's untimely death at sea caused his family considerable hardship, and that his subsequent apprenticeship in stonemasonry was a time of intermittent poverty. But he also observes that his father had owned land, as well as the boat with which he earned his living; that two paternal uncles, both businessmen, assisted his distressed mother who was unable immediately to claim her deceased husband's insurance; and that although his uncles wished to further his education, he *chose* to leave school and to become a tradesman.[4] He maintained his family connections, however, eventually 'taking leave of the lower classes' to become a bank accountant, then the 'manager of a metropolitan newspaper'.[5] He confesses that he has had no direct experience of industrial society but he does not equivocate about the form it should take. Hence he insists that industrial strikes cannot be justified and that their instigators, 'stump orators and Chartist lecturers', are made of very inferior 'stuff'.[6] Proceeding, he consigns working people to a range of categories, assessing them against his own intellectual and moral attributes. To a greater or lesser degree he finds that skilled workers approach his personal standards but that the unskilled masses are degenerate – indolent rogues and halfwits[7] – especially their female numbers who have declined 'to the condition of negroes'.[8] Typical are his tenants, more of 'the profligate poor', who frequently fail to pay their rent.[9] Indeed, Miller wonders 'how this class – constitutionally degraded, and with the moral sense, in most instances, utterly undeveloped and blind – are ever to be reclaimed'.[10] It might be argued that this characterization is of no relevance to his treatment by Robert Gray who, as noted in the preceding chapter, cites him simply to confirm that the contemporary distinction between work and leisure time was blurred.[11] But Miller is also treated as a working-class spokesperson and his comment is assimilated to a context in which mid-Victorian working people are constructed in a particular way, in this instance as collaborators in a moral consensus with the middle classes. Consulted as a representative figure, he ceases to be an 'objective' commentator and becomes a subjective participant. He thus acquires an authority which helps to validate Gray's metaphor for 'working-class experience' and his 'objectification' of working-class identity. By a similar process, the equally unlikely Benjamin Grime has also been enlisted as a reliable commentator on popular identity and experience.

Grime, as noted above, has been cited to illustrate both class and populist constructions,[12] yet this 'prim and disapproving Gladstonian Liberal', to quote Joyce, evidently regarded himself as in no way typical or representative of the common worker.[13] Another newspaperman, whose *Memory Sketches* were first serialized in the *Oldham Weekly Chronicle*, Grime confesses that he sympathized as a youth with certain radical initiatives.[14] In retrospect, however, he distances himself from all popular radical measures. Even 'exclusive dealing' he finds 'detestable'[15] and Chartists he recalls as predominantly 'rabid', lawless men who 'indulged in most violent language, carried arms about with them, incited to violence, and committed [various] outrages'.[16] Elsewhere, he observes that self-help, self-education and a 'longing for distinction' enabled certain workingmen, 'by perseverance in self-acquisition, to raise themselves to the highest level in the municipality'.[17] In the context of Neville Kirk's analysis this remark becomes an illustration of class consciousness.[18] Paradoxically, however, it can be seen quite straightforwardly to point to ambitious individualism rather than strong working-class identification. In a further comment, Grime asserts that dialect literature reflects popular attitudes, aspirations and identity. Having already declared the 'dialect idiom' populist in character, Joyce invokes this comment as evidence of a prevailing populist identity.[19] Yet Grime speaks as an 'objective' and detached observer, not as an 'insider' describing a subjective experience. He seems never to have consulted 'the people' themselves about their predispositions, and in a further passage expresses frank bewilderment at their actions, suggesting that his views on those whom he characterizes as 'the great untaught' are more speculative than insightful.[20] As the analysis proceeds, it will become evident that all contemporaries chosen by historians as 'representative' figures can be regarded as exceptional and to a greater or lesser degree different from the classes they supposedly represented. It might nevertheless be claimed that many are 'reliable' commentators because, as 'labour leaders', they maintained close ties with 'the masses'. Such individuals will therefore constitute the main focus of the present discussion although others, notably those held to be exemplars of class identity because of their Sunday school connections, will also be considered in detail.

In his account of the Sunday school movement, Laqueur implies a conventional definition of class, assumes the contemporary currency of that definition and portrays the Sunday school as a distinctively working-class institution, the ethos of which reflected and reinforced working-class attitudes and values. Framed by this construction, enthusiasm for the Sunday school movement might be seen as a persuasive indicator of class identity, and Laqueur's exemplars certainly stress their admiration for, and debt to, the institution, describing its invaluable contribution not only to their education and respectability, but to their independence and success. Yet their writings, when considered more carefully, suggest conceptions of class quite at odds with Laqueur's construction and indeed with any existing definition of class identity. If anything conclusive can be inferred from the commentaries in question, it is that class meant different things to different people. Some writers scarcely refer to it; others, as suggested in Chapter 2, use it as a descriptive term to distinguish one social or occupational group from another. Yet others employ it as a political category, opposing the 'productive' middle and working classes to the leisured aristocracy and attributing social ills to the aristocratic monopoly of political power.[21] Even *within* individual accounts this varied usage sometimes occurs. The only notable consistency from one narrative to the next is a general lack of emphasis on the *economic* aspects of class and the absence of any indication that class was a pre-eminent factor in the constitution of identity.

Among the autobiographers surveyed, those for whom class does not, in any definition, seem to have had particular relevance – Thomas Carter, James Hillock, Thomas Whittaker, Marianne Farningham and Adam Rushton – appear in Laqueur's sample. Although Laqueur is concerned with the period between 1780 and 1850, all of these authors have direct significance for subsequent decades: Carter because mid-Victorian workers supposedly inherited their class consciousness from the period of which he writes; the remainder because they refer extensively to their mid-Victorian experiences. By Laqueur's reckoning, Thomas Carter's concern for order and cleanliness was a distinctive working-class trait and a sign of his class identity. Yet, throughout his narrative, Carter repeatedly emphasizes that his values alienated him from workmates, the vast majority of whom he regards with open contempt.

'[C]hoosing companions from among my fellow-workers', he observes in one instance, 'was wholly out of the question . . . Their habits, language, and modes of thinking were alike incongenial [sic] with my own.'[22] Elsewhere he denounces the ignorance and the dissolute habits of his colleagues,[23] the lack of 'good housewifery' in their homes,[24] their 'degrading actions' and again their 'disgusting language'.[25] He expresses sympathy for the 'genuinely poor' who do not obtrude themselves on public notice, but those who make their condition visible he dismisses as a 'class of sturdy and clamorous mendicants whose well-conditioned although ragged and dirty persons g[i]ve the lie to all their melancholy tales of impending starvation'.[26] Nor, noting that the improvident and intemperate workers of his acquaintance 'work best if half-starved', does he overlook the 'positive' side of deprivation.[27] Out of forty workfellows, in another situation, he found and befriended one who was not altogether reprobate but who could nevertheless 'descend quite as low as any around him both in language and demeanour'.[28]

Proceeding, Carter reflects that the behaviour of working people on election days would 'have reflected dishonour upon a horde of savages'[29] and implies that self-styled working-class representatives like Hunt and Cobbett were little better than rabble-rousers.[30] A popular demonstration which he describes as a riot perpetrated by Hunt's partisans inspired in him, he reflects, a 'real horror' of popular government ('mob' government in his formulation); and he applauds the use of military force to disperse the crowd, regretting only that most of the 'delinquents' evaded the 'smart blows' which some received 'from the broad-sides of the soldiers' swords'.[31] Carter refers to an 'orderly and decent class of poor people'[32] but never seems to have made their acquaintance. His respect and admiration seem to have been reserved for those to whose condition he could not attain[33] and, by his own account, he 'was a solitary being'.[34] His usage of the term 'class' is infrequent and suggestive of nothing more than 'classification'. He seems quite deliberately to have defined his identity and interests *against* those of other workers and writes of how readily, when he was younger, the latter took advantage of his diligence on the job, forcing him to do their work as well as his own.[35] Insofar as he stresses his commitment to the economic virtues[36] he might be equated with others in the sample, but he affects distaste bordering on hostility for the wider community of working people. And regardless of whether his admiration for cleanliness and order was a distinctive trait of respectable workers, his writings vigorously resist any notion that he was interpellated by a unifying social identity – class – populist or otherwise.

James Hillocks, like Carter, makes much of his devotion to industry, self-education and improvement but conveys little if any sense of 'class' consciousness. His fond recollection of Sunday school might, inserted into Laqueur's interpretative framework, seem to reflect the concern for children which Laqueur equates with working-class respectability. Yet the broader context of Hillocks's writings suggests a harsher reality, one in which Sabbath schooldays were a moment of respite in a world of exploitation, oppression and grinding poverty from which children were not exempted. Deploring what he calls a 'great national suffering', he attributes it to the cynical abuse of political power. Because of 'existing errors in upper quarters', 'misgovernment' and 'the wickedness of the strong', he observes, 'the poor are assailed and robbed' on 'every side',[37] and authority has become the 'stronghold of all that is base and degrading – a terror to sufferers and a protection to the treacherous'.[38] To combat these conditions, he embraced Chartism and soon became a branch secretary of the National Charter Association, whereafter he was blacklisted by local employers. So convinced was he that the problem was political, he would, he declared, have 'unseat[ed] every Member of both Houses of Parliament' had it been possible.[39] But he also believed that Corn Law Repeal would supply pressing need in the short term and that Repealers and Chartists should cooperate rather than 'foolishly contending with each other while the common foe', the monopolizers of political power, laughed 'fiendishly . . . at their insane folly'.[40]

Hillocks's self-improving pursuits proceeded apace with his 'social critique' and began to pay dividends. Recounting his achievements as a journalist, schoolmaster, medical practitioner, preacher, writer, publisher and lecturer – and supporting his commentary with testimonials from various notables – he describes the personal effort with which those achievements were invested and is apparently very proud to have succeeded where others failed.[41] Publication of his prize autobiography in 1860 resulted in job offers from influential people and earned him the patronage of three professors, one of whom facilitated his entry to a congregational ministry.[42] At this stage in his career his own attitude to 'upper quarters' evidently 'softened', notably towards the Queen and the Prince Consort, who won his admiration not, he is adamant, because of their 'elevated positions' but rather because of their 'personal virtues and moral greatness'.[43] He acknowledges, however, that the Queen received his autobiography warmly and that the press therefore promoted it, making him something of a celebrity. Possibly these developments and a Civil List Pension – £75 per annum to subsidize his literary earnings[44] – predisposed him, in later work, to recognize a more vicious side of poverty and to forget the inequality of opportunity to which formerly he had been sensitive.[45] They might also have informed the reflection that his earlier claims about the abuse of power were 'in large measure' wrong and that there had never, in any case, been anything in his heart 'that could be called malice towards an individual'.[46]

The privileged group which in Hillocks's view monopolized political power was constituted by the aristocracy and perhaps larger manufacturers. He distinguishes this group from the politically impotent poor among whom he counts workers and most employers. On the basis of this distinction he might be seen to hold some conception of politically defined 'classes', but not of class as an economic category. Nor does he express himself in class language. He appears from his narratives to have had a well-developed social conscience, though one susceptible of modification when he perceived the need to resolve contradictory ideas. Hence, in later life, when he began to identify with those whose patronage he has come to enjoy and who occupied strata where political power resided, he resiled from an earlier critique which attributed mass poverty to political corruption. Asserting that the powerful could, after all, be paragons of virtue and morality, he now implied that the poor might in some instances be vicious, and responsible for their own condition. To speculate in this way is not to pass moral judgement on Hillocks but to illustrate the various meanings to which his writings are assimilable. Laqueur's questions (and assumptions) serve to invest him with a class identity; those outlined above produce the impression that his identity was fluid and contradictory, that it changed according to the influences which impinged on it, and that it did not conform to the criteria set out in class or populist paradigms. The same can be said of Thomas Whittaker, Marianne Farningham and Adam Rushton.

Transplanted, as it were, into Laqueur's narrative, statements by these individuals about the importance of the Sunday school in their lives and their commitment to the values which it promoted seem to confirm their class identity. But their memoirs, when interpreted differently, yield different observations which indicate that they lacked attributes whereby their identities might be designated class, or for that matter populist. Whittaker, for example, distinguishes himself primarily as a temperancer and, like Thomas Carter, defines his identity and interests very much *against* those of other workers. The latter, he observes, 'looked upon me as their enemy, and they taunted me as such. They secretly spoiled my work . . . damaged my machinery . . . and misrepresented me to my employers.'[47] In one situation, he continues, they also refused to work with him because he would not be paid, like them, in the pub. Hence, for the sake of industrial peace, he was dismissed, even though he was a 'model worker'.[48] Reflecting on his childhood, he recalls that his father was reduced to poverty by 'the oppression of power and the inequity of the law', yet the poverty of others, he insists, is a consequence of their intemperate habits.[49] Having noted that his own abstinence enfranchised him by enabling him to rent a house at £12 a year, he observes that 'the country is studded with men' whose success has been hard won, and he contends that 'there is no law in heaven, nor in this land, to keep . . . down' those who would emulate them.[50] He scoffs at the notion that the poor are 'driven to the public house because of the wretchedness of the[ir] homes'[51] and is convinced that they could, in the vast majority of cases, resolve their own plight simply by renouncing drink and using the money thus saved to rent more agreeable habitations. But until they were prepared to elevate themselves, any effort to assist them would be wasted: 'Put a pig into a palace', he explains, 'and the palace becomes a pigsty.'[52] It is difficult to recognize in Whittaker's self-portrait any traits which might delineate his identity as class or populist. Indeed, he seems, by his uncompromising individualism and his transparent distaste for the majority of working people, to have alienated himself from all but fellow teetotallers. He is evidently proud of his achievements and tells of how, after working from 1837 to 1849 as an agent of the British and Foreign Temperance Society, he continued to serve the temperance cause, though as 'an independent man', travelling extensively in Britain and the United States.[53] Yet, considering his expressed contempt for most workers, he seems to have admired success more than the dignity of labour and to have measured his own respectability and independence by the extent to which they set him above the common condition.

Scarcely less exclusive is the social vision elaborated by Adam Rushton. Commencing work at the age of five, Rushton soon graduated to mill-work. After twenty-five years as a 'factory slave' he managed, by industry and thrift, to acquire a share in a silk manufactory.[54] Throughout this period he enjoyed an intimate connection with the Sunday school and gradually developed a religious vocation.[55] Hence, in 1854, he began formal preparation for the Unitarian ministry into which he was ordained five years later at an annual salary of £100.[56] According to Rushton, the Sunday school facilitated his pursuit of useful knowledge and predisposed him to the temperance cause.[57] It also gave him access to 'the best families of working people' and strength to endure the daily demands of the outside world.[58] But his portrait of the institution bears little resemblance to that drawn by Laqueur. Rather than a focus of working-class life in general, he depicts an enclave of respectability with which only a minority identified. By contrast, in the world-at-large disreputables are suggested to have prevailed in a variety of forms: 'rough' lads who trespassed on his father's farm to steal fruit;[59] bad debtors who threatened the stability of his business; worthless staff who wasted his raw materials 'in the most shocking manner'; and a particular employee who robbed him of a sovereign.[60] He refused to concede that such people were oppressed by anything more than their own depravity and, in public debate, defended the view that poverty was a consequence of vice, corruption and drunkenness.[61]

A brief flirtation with Chartism might have alerted him to the possibility that the poor were not altogether responsible for their condition, for he writes that rhetoric about 'dear bread, low wages and long hours of labour' spoke to sufferings which his family had endured and which moved him deeply.[62] He explains, however, that his interest was temporary, induced by a utopian visionary who addressed local meetings. He also reflects that the movement failed, at least in part, because the very people whose condition it sought to improve lacked commitment to its strategies.[63] Apparently convinced that such people were incorrigible, he turned his attention to their children, recommending that all who were dull, degraded, vicious and unteachable 'be forced into reformator[ies]' where specially trained teachers might 'draw out the best possible results obtainable from such unruly natures'.[64] If, as Rushton indicates, the Sunday school was an important influence in his life, it seems never to have tempered his disdain for common people. His long attachment to the institution might, in the context of Laqueur's narrative, be seen to illustrate his 'class' identity, as might certain abstracted statements about his Chartist sympathies and factory slavery. In response to my questions, however, his autobiography represents neither a 'class-conscious' working person nor one who identified in populist terms but rather a condescending individualist who favoured social justice for the respectable minority and rough justice for the rest.

Like Rushton, Marianne Farningham writes of the need for appropriate educational facilities, though she envisages them as part of a larger programme to improve the lot of children in general rather than as a disciplinary measure for delinquents.[65] Far less ambiguously than Hillocks, she seems to suggest the novel concern for the young postulated by Laqueur, declaring herself thankful for 'a wonderful growth of respect for the child' and noting that statesmen as well as philanthropists were 'bestirring themselves' to accelerate the trend.[66] She also expresses views which, appropriately deployed, can be used to illustrate either the class identity imputed to her by Laqueur or one which appears to conform to populist criteria. The former might be inferred from the title of her autobiography, *A Working Woman's Life*, or from her claim to be in some ways a socialist.[67] Also suggestive of a class affinity is her hope that future workers would be paid a living wage, enjoy better conditions, and 'take their share . . . in the higher pleasures and pursuits which have for so long a time been the exclusive privileges of the favoured few'.[68] By contrast, her orientation to a Joycean kind of populism could be deduced from her insistence that she is '[o]ne of the people'; from her promotion of respect for the dignity of work and the worker; or from an appeal for social harmony in which she urges all political parties 'to work together for the common good'.[69]

To assign Farningham to a clearly defined 'subject position' on the basis of such statements would, however, be peremptory, for, conversely, she indicates that she is apolitical,[70] a liberal, a friend of reform and 'progress',[71] and an enemy of revolution.[72] Similarly inconsistent is her 'social vision' which in some instances seems to embrace the entire community and in others to be highly selective. Excluded, for example, are the 'roughs' of her childhood and Londoners who intruded seasonally on the local hop-gardens, driving down wages and making the environment 'uncomfortable with dirt and bad language'.[73] No more welcome are 'the lazy good-for-nothings who are too frequently in evidence' and with whom new laws will hopefully deal less leniently.[74] She does not countenance the possibility that what she saw as laziness might simply have been resignation to the reality of insufficient work or reluctance to accept employment for what, as she recognizes, could be less than a living wage.[75] Insofar as these views sometimes conflict with each other, they reflect contradictions discernible in the attitudes and consciousness of many people; for example, those who promote justice and equity yet seize the opportunity to be more competitive in an inherently unequal society.

It might be rationalized, of course, that the greater one's competitiveness, the greater one's power to effect change, and Farningham suggests as much, describing achievements which were both impressive and uncommon. Having acquired education and a high level of articulateness under considerable difficulty, she was able subsequently to obtain work as a schoolteacher, a journalist and an editor.[76] She produced monographs on a range of topics, all of which were well received, and eventually mounted the lecture platform, earning enough from the lecture circuit to purchase a house and to travel extensively in Europe.[77] She undoubtedly worked hard to become independent in what was very much a man's world and perhaps, therefore, believed that the prevailing system would, with a few adjustments, permit everyone to achieve as much. And perhaps it is to be expected that one who worked so hard would emphasize her efforts rather than her opportunities. Inadvertently, however, she describes opportunities – material comforts, encouragement and support – which many other working people appear thoroughly to have lacked.[78] Such people will presently be highlighted to illuminate this contrast, people who suggest that they did not accept the *status quo* but resisted it mutely or resigned themselves to a condition which they felt powerless to change; people who felt powerless because they had been so individualized and divided that any notion of their interpellation by a unifying social identity seems meaningless.[79]

The remainder of Laqueur's representatives sometimes employ 'class' vocabulary, as do those in the wider sample, but their usage is too ambiguous to justify the class identity imputed to them. Moreover, although his sample is the most extensive, it is scarcely sufficient to illustrate the world view of such individuals or to illuminate the thoughts behind their words. Regardless of the frequency with which these contemporaries declare their reverence for the Sunday school, their commitment to the imperatives of respectability or their endorsement of the *status quo*, they invariably express sentiments and attitudes, affinities and antipathies which are contradictory, and for every perception which might be adduced to delineate their identity in a certain way, another can be abstracted to characterize them differently. Alexander Somerville, for example, observes in 1848 that 'the amount of money contributed by the working classes, for various purposes' but especially to establish strike funds, 'afford[ed] proof . . . that working men, by associating together for the attainment of practical objects, have the power' to raise themselves socially, morally and politically.[80] He also notes that unions sought 'to regulate wages by the rate of profits derived from Capital'.[81] A working man himself, Somerville might, on the basis of such views, be held to have identified in class terms.

Conversely, his account of the political crisis which attended the passage of the 1832 Reform Bill could be enlisted as evidence of his populism. In this instance, he places 'the lords and the crown' in opposition to 'the people', 'the nation', 'the national will' and 'the popular branch' (the House of Commons), and deplores the former's attempt to defeat the 'popular principle' with 'the power of the army'.[82] A further construction, however, is equally supportable.

Various observations which distinguish the population as benighted, in dire need of moral and intellectual elevation, unheedful of intelligent, reflective men and ever susceptible to the manipulations of mob orators, indicate Somerville's sense of detachment from the majority of working people and an animus against most of those who presumed to lead them.[83] When, in 1834, he was invited to join a deputation to Whitehall with a petition for the release of 'the Dorsetshire convicts', he suspected that those who approached him were conspiring to overthrow the government. Moved by fear for the safety of the royal family, the ministry and 'the nation', he explains, he 'wrote private letters' to the press and to Lord Melbourne warning of impending revolution.[84] Though he does not substantiate his charge of 'conspiracy', he invites his reader to judge his contribution to the welfare of the country and its rulers,[85] and although he asserts his empathy with 'the masses' and 'the millions' he seems, at least on this occasion, to have identified less with those who declared themselves no longer able to endure the tyranny of the powerful, than with those whose tyranny he elsewhere condemns.[86]

Samuel Bamford seems also to have been detached and condescending. He agrees with a reviewer of his work that he provides greater insight into 'the mind'[87] of 'operatives in the manufacturing districts' than is likely to be obtained from other sources, yet he repeatedly implies that the latter were mindless insofar as they lacked the capacity to think for themselves. They were, by his account, either converted to rational pursuits by right-thinking individuals, including workingmen like himself whose exceptional talents had been nurtured at Sunday school, or seduced by unscrupulous demagogues. Hence, he observes that when the 1815 Corn Bill drove up the price of bread, precipitating riot and destruction, he and like-minded individuals established Hampden clubs which diverted the masses from their recklessness. Inspired by William Cobbett, they saw that popular suffering was a consequence of mis-government, urged parliamentary reform[88] and, asserting the superiority of 'moral force', persuaded the labourers to abandon their riotous ways and to become 'deliberate and systematic in their proceedings'.[89] Acknowledging that in his day 'folly' often accompanied his 'good intentions', Bamford nevertheless emphasizes the accomplishments of the earlier generation and proceeds to draw Chartists into an unfavourable contrast, asserting that they neither avoided a single 'evil which we encountered, nor produced one additional good'.[90] Instead, he writes, they misled workingmen with 'dark counsels and criminal instigations', then abandoned them to wreak 'terror and confusion'.[91] Pleading with the multitudes thus deluded to '[t]urn from those who have hallood you on to havoc',[92] he nevertheless concludes sadly that as yet only 'rare minds' have responded to the voice of reason, whose language is 'too pure, too unassuming, too disinterested, for any human crowds that have yet appeared'.[93] Unlike Carter and Rushton, Bamford does not express contempt for all workers. If the tone of his narrative is condescending, it is also sympathetic. Nevertheless, it is not axiomatic that to sympathize with a group of people is to 'identify' as one of them and Bamford's writings, when considered apart from class and populist assumptions, do not indicate any such identification. They suggest instead not only that he set himself at a great moral and intellectual distance from the mass of workers, but that the latter were, in his view, united by no more than an incapacity to be rational and reasonable.

Similar sentiments can be inferred from the writings of Joseph Barker who, with five citations, is one of Laqueur's main exemplars. Barker clearly indicates that he began life as one of the poor, though not that he identified with them in any broad or persistent way. Moreover, the substantial body of literature which he produced suggests one whose identity was indeed fluid and ambiguous and whose self-portrait was crafted differently for different purposes. In several addresses delivered in 1848 which related to his trial for conspiracy and sedition, he presents himself as a friend of democracy whose pre-eminent concern is the happiness of all the oppressed, using language which could be characterized both as class and populist.[94] He describes the current government as 'a *class* government';[95] condemns laws 'that have consumed the health . . . devoured the wealth . . . sucked the blood . . . stinted the comfort, and destroyed the lives of so many millions of the English and Irish people'; and demands that the House of Commons be reconstituted as 'an assembly of men [sic] chosen from among the common people'.[96] He also acknowledges popular contributions to his legal costs and to a fund established for the support of his family should he be convicted.[97] In a further document he writes that the charge against him was a pretext designed to prevent him from contesting a Bolton election, although he was subsequently acquitted and returned on a ticket of democracy and Chartist principles, a triumph, in his view, for the people.[98] His 'class' vocabulary notwithstanding, Barker's delineation of two 'classes' in these documents – the aristocracy which controls legal and political power and 'other men' who are 'excluded by law from all direct participation in power'[99] – seems to deny him a conventionally defined class consciousness, though it might seem consistent with a 'populist' identity. Repeated expressions of affinity with 'the humbler classes', the victims of an oppressive government, are also susceptible of a populist construction.[100]

In his *History*, however, which first appeared in 1846 and which he saw fit to republish in subsequent decades, Barker expresses views far less sympathetic to many of those to whom, in the above addresses, he is so solicitous.[101] Indeed, he implies that the deserving poor were in a distinct minority and makes no pretence at delicacy when expressing his opinion of the undeserving masses. His father, he writes, enjoyed modest prosperity as a cloth manufacturer until his business was destroyed by falling prices after the French Wars. The family, he proceeds, was subsequently forced to labour 'for other people at a time when work was exceedingly scarce'.[102] Barker himself was sometimes reduced to begging, for his father, a virtuous but foolish man, gave to others at the expense of the family, not least to contemptible preachers who demanded money from the impoverished and indebted.[103] Also contemptible, in Barker's view, were the Poor Law Guardians and those they favoured. The Guardians, he observes, 'seemed to think that those who never *had* applied for relief never *ought* to apply', yet relieved 'those who had received town pay for years . . . as a matter of course'.[104] Recalling the humiliation to which his mother was subjected on the one occasion when she sought assistance, he expresses the conviction that the Poor Law 'did little else but mischief', oppressing 'the honest, industrious, deserving poor', and encouraging vice in the rest.[105] In his experience, he insists, the chief part of the poor rates 'were spent on illegitimate children and their mothers, on old worn out thieves, poachers, gamblers, cock-fighters, dog-breeders, and drunken, profligate, idle folk, that could not support themselves and their families by honest labour when they might, but who could succeed either by importunities or threats, in extorting money from the town authorities'.[106]

Interestingly, Barker's suggestion that the dissolute who are unable or unwilling to do 'honest' work should be denied 'official aid' has resurfaced with considerable urgency in the 1990s, but its underlying assumptions are as dubious now as they appear to have been then. After all, if those who subsist by occupations deemed vicious or criminal are declared unfit for 'legitimate' vocations but are also denied some form of assistance, then they must either perish or persist with their vicious and criminal practices. Implicit though unstated in such demands is an expectation that they choose the former, though invariably they seem predisposed to the latter, perhaps because they regard oppressive legal and moral conventions to be of less consequence than their attachment to life. Regardless of this speculation, it seems patently clear that 'the people' with whom Barker identified were constituted differently for different purposes, broadly when necessary and at other times narrowly. It seems also, however, that when constrained to classify the 'undeserving', those *against* whom he defined himself, he pointed to a group extremely numerous and diverse. Unless it is assumed that this mass of people was filled with self-loathing, and despised the practices by which they lived, then it is difficult to see how Barker can have shared with them a common outlook and identity, whether 'class' or 'populist'.

Yet another understanding of class is suggested by the writings of William Lovett. Describing a career shaped decisively by his commitment to popular radicalism, Lovett refers to aristocratic, middle and working classes and treats them as social categories characterized by economic differences which arise from political inequities. He deplores the general condition of working people and is convinced that if it is to be ameliorated, political power must be won, but he insists that enfranchisement will be of little value unless accompanied by moral and intellectual improvement. The social vision which he elaborates is of a harmonious society in which moral and material improvement is accessible to all, and his narrative has thus been enlisted to illustrate populist as well as class constructions.[107] His views, however, are susceptible of another interpretation which casts him as an uncompromising individualist in the bourgeois liberal mould. If he distinguishes himself as a worker, he also distinguishes himself *from* the mass of workers, affecting an intellectual and moral superiority to which the latter must rise if they wish to empower themselves politically and to use that power wisely.

Writing in 1876, Lovett finds the prevailing level of ignorance to be such that 'vast numbers of our fellow men' are 'content with mere animal indulgences' and 'thousands of our women are deficient of every moral requisite to fit them for wives and mothers'.[108] Reform, he observes, is persistently frustrated by the 'thoughtless and weak-minded' who imitate the vices of the aristocracy and, 'by vote or voice', choose representatives and rulers 'who have neither interest nor sympathy with them'. To advance reform and 'the great cause of human progress', he insists, 'the most intelligent of our brethren' must make 'every intellectual and moral effort' to divert the masses from their ignorance and to promote representatives from within their own and other classes who share their commitment to 'the removal of social and political evils'. Real improvement, he concludes, is impossible until all people unite in 'a system of co-operation for the production of wealth, founded on the mutual interests of capital and labour, and such distributed according to each person's industry, capacity, and intelligence'.[109]

Though Lovett expresses the conviction that all landownership is conditional and subject to the fulfilment of certain obligations,[110] he nevertheless insists that all property, 'honestly acquired', is 'sacred and inviolable'.[111] With similar enthusiasm he promotes individualism, acknowledging the merit of co-operative production but declaring systems of communally held property 'unjust, unnatural and despotic in . . . tendency'.[112] Because humanity is imperfect, he continues, any communal system must discourage personal effort and sacrifice 'the intellectual energies and moral virtues of the few, to the indolence, ignorance and despotism of the many'.[113] He attributes the marvellous inventions of the industrial age to the spirit of individualism and suggests that the fruits of outstanding achievement, now generally applied, enable 'the millions' to enjoy benefits compared to which the wealth accrued to industrialists and the inventors themselves is trifling.[114] Whatever these benefits may have been, and Lovett is never specific about them, he seems to have remained dissatisfied with the common condition, holding both that working people must ultimately elevate themselves and that they had thus far proven themselves unequal to the effort.

When in 1836 he helped to form the London Working Men's Association[115] it was decided, he writes, that membership should be restricted to 'the *intelligent* and *influential* portions of the working classes' for the rest 'had not hitherto evinced that discrimination of independent spirit in the management of their political affairs which we were desirous to see'.[116] It was planned, however, that the latter should be educated morally and politically, delivered from the 'unprincipled candidates for power' who bribed and deceived them, and reclaimed from 'the fumes of the tap-room', where they 'croak[ed] over their grievances with maudlin brains'.[117] Forty years later he regretted that '[t]he working classes are still to a vast extent following blind guides, and trusting to leaders and orators, outside their own ranks, to achieve that for them which their own efforts, self-sacrifices, and organization can alone effect. They still, unhappily, undervalue *mental and moral effort* for raising their class and advancing the welfare of their country.'[118]

If Lovett was as alienated from the people he sought to lead as these judgements imply, it might well have been because he had little in common with them. A Londoner, '[a] skilled craftsman and member of an ancient and exclusive trade union', he was not, according to one commentator, a part of the new industrialism which he so detested, and he had 'no first-hand knowledge of industrial England, with its turbulent population of miners and cotton-operatives, swept together, without traditions or organization, in towns which were little better than mining camps'.[119] As he advanced to higher occupations – lecturer, journalist, schoolteacher, publisher, orator and author of various radical manifestos – his distance from working people seems only to have increased. Doubtless he had to maintain 'contact' with them – indirectly they were his bread and butter! But he made no apparent effort to understand *their* morality or the ways in which *they* may have perceived their needs. Instead, he urged on them his own morality which may not have spoken to their condition, and, when they resisted it, implied that his faith in their moral and intellectual capacities had been shaken. By contrast, those he singled out for praise and with whom he seems increasingly to have identified were 'great men' of popular politics, working-class notables like himself and sympathetic middle-class radicals into whose orbit he had been decisively drawn.[120] He seems clearly to have defined himself *against* the mass of working people and to have been a stranger, by and large, to their experiences. He may have been linked to them insofar as they were the 'object' of his efforts and made meaningful his role as 'leader' or 'representative'. But his closest affinity seems to have been with moral and intellectual paragons, *individuals* whom he regarded as equals or to whose condition he aspired. If, indeed, there prevailed at the time a cohesive 'class' or 'populist' consciousness, it is not illuminated by Lovett, whose reflections suggest little about the 'identity' of common workers other than that they lacked the moral and intellectual endowments which shaped his own.

Similar conclusions can be drawn about Thomas Cooper, another admirer of 'great men' who seems quite clearly to have practised the 'individualism' which Lovett preached. Cooper recalls in great detail a life of hard work, first as an operative in various trades, then as a schoolteacher, preacher, lecturer and radical functionary.[121] He also emphasizes his commitment to the elevation of the masses, distinguishing himself as one who has 'partaken of . . . [their] oppressions'.[122] Imbued with the spirit of radicalism in early youth he was later drawn to Chartism, he explains, because it was on 'the side of the poor and suffering'.[123] He fought to improve the condition of stockingers ground down by 'middle-men',[124] represented oppressed workhouse inmates at court[125] and in 1842, as a consequence of his radical convictions, was sentenced to two years' gaol for conspiracy and sedition.[126] Credentials such as these convince some historians of Cooper's class identity.[127] On his release from gaol, however, he seems to have adopted a far more moderate approach, elaborating a vision of co-operation among and between the various social ranks and validating it with an appeal to England's glorious history of 'great' men and institutions.[128] Hence, in a recent commentary, he has been depicted as one whose writings and speeches linked 'ideas of the people' to 'the nation', an entity which in nineteenth-century England, according to the writer in question, 'provided history's master-narrative'. In this construction, Cooper becomes a 'mediat[or] between "high" and "low" culture', a promoter of social inclusiveness and an exemplar of populist identity.[129]

Though both characterizations – class and populist – are nicely illustrated, they are problematical in that Cooper demonstrates a singular incapacity for co-operation and compromise, indicating that he did not identify more than temporarily with any group or individual. He recalls many disputes and disappointments but seems never to have attempted to resolve them. By his own account, he dealt with them by moving on, and he implies retrospectively that in most if not all instances he had been victimized and alienated by ignorant, immoral or unscrupulous elements. Hence, when he discusses a division in Leicester Chartism in 1841, which seems to have been precipitated by rivalry between himself and the nominal local leader, he does not recall any desire to address the problem. Instead, he holds the opposing faction responsible, implying that its members resented his popularity, and concludes with apparent satisfaction that he reconstituted his own following as a new organization, the Shakesperean Association of Leicester Chartists.[130] Similarly, prior to his imprisonment, he approved of Feargus O'Connor and supported him against 'all who opposed . . . or refused to act with him'.[131] On his release, however, he heard that O'Connor had denounced him, 'resolved never to speak to him again' and 'kept aloof from Chartists and Chartism'.[132] A brief reconciliation was followed by renewed hostility when Cooper rejected O'Connor's land scheme,[133] whereafter he determined never again to be drawn into Chartist 'plots and plans'.[134] Estranged from O'Connor, he abandoned the movement whose subsequent history he dismissed as one 'of violence and failure'.[135]

In other pursuits his unwillingness to compromise – or, as he implies, the unwillingness of others to recognize his wisdom – seems to have been equally marked. When in 1828 he set up as a schoolmaster, he recalls, stupid, listless parents hindered his efforts and would not permit him 'to follow . . . [his] own plans in the tuition of the children'.[136] This problem was exacerbated by the local Methodist superintendent who shirked his duties. By now also a preacher, Cooper felt compelled to do his superior's rounds to the neglect of his school, which soon declined.[137] Disputes with those in authority subsequently drove him from Methodism and he joined a newly established Mechanic's Institute

in Lincoln, where he also became secretary of a choral society.[138] In the latter
capacity he writes, 'I had to put down the authority of the imperfect, and put
the authoritative perfect in its place'. But despite his commitment to 'perfec-
tion', he came to be regarded as a tyrant, was 'called to account' and 'advised
to resign'.[139] He then commenced a career as a journalist but left one situation
after another because of disagreements with his employers.[140] Cooper's individualism and his inability to compromise seem in many ways to have put him
at odds with his fellow-radicals and indeed with the community-at-large. If his
ideas and methods were challenged, he felt slighted and removed himself; if he
could not persuade others to adopt his strategies, he rejected their initiatives
and cut them off. His 'vision' may have been 'socially inclusive' and it may
genuinely have been informed by a desire to elevate the working classes, but
he was evidently unwilling to share it except on his terms. Moreover, his
recurring complaint that others failed to measure up to his idiosyncratic views
on morality, justice and equity indicates that they found his terms largely
unacceptable. If he was as detached from 'the masses' as his writings suggest,
and unable to find common cause even with his fellow-radicals, the notion that
he exemplified some popularly shared social identity seems dubious in the
extreme.

Equally detached from the masses, though a workingman himself and evidently hostile to most so-called labour leaders, was the 'journeyman engineer',
Thomas Wright.[141] A skilled tradesman who subsequently became a school
inspector and the author of three lengthy books, Wright constructs himself as
part of an intellectual, moral and politically aware minority.[142] Also in a
minority, he suggests, are the idle poor, dependent and disreputable creatures
who are prone to 'drunkenness, ignorance, violence and venality'.[143] Between
these two extremes he situates the majority of working people, assigning them
primarily to gender roles. Males he characterizes as predominantly intelligent
and 'political', though he finds that their intelligence is of the common-sense
variety and undermined by lack of education while their politics, uninformed
by any knowledge of political economy, are impulsive rather than committed,
and serve to subordinate them to the influence of 'crushers', professional agitators and unscrupulous demagogues.[144] Misled by these 'political quacks',
they believe that, as the sole producers of wealth, they are exploited by other
classes, the members of which are devoid of human feeling; seek utopian
remedies for their perceived disadvantages; insist 'that all political beliefs
save . . . [their] own are wrong in themselves and dishonestly held'; and react
with hostility to anyone who challenges their views.[145] He concludes, however,
that they possess positive political potential which appropriate instruction
has already begun to unlock in younger men.[146]

By contrast, he depicts working women as essentially apolitical creatures
who require a different kind of education, one which fits them to serve their
husbands. He does not consider them in their own right but accords them a
derivative identity, observing that the working woman is not simply her

husband's wife but 'also his housekeeper, cook, and several other single domestics rolled into one'.[147] Like her husband, she has various faults. Of some she is unaware, Wright observes, while others arise from 'the pernicious idea . . . that the performance of housework is degrading'. For want of technical education she is not what 'it is desirable she should be, and could easily be made'.[148] Most working men, he continues, are forced to choose their partners from a narrow range, at one end of which is the domestic servant and at the other milliners and dressmakers, all of whom are ill-equipped for the role of homemaker. The former has usually been either a slavey to one of 'the let-us-be-genteel-or-die-class' and remains a disorganized muddler, or has been trained in a superior establishment to a single speciality which is of little use in a workingman's house.[149] Worse still are the latter who imagine that they are genteel 'young ladies', try 'to ape their betters', regard domestic servants with contempt and 'go about their housework in a mincing, muddling manner'.[150] But while some become slovenly trollops who make their homes 'miserable and uncomfortable', most are good, virtuous girls who, like their menfolk, are not altogether responsible for their condition.[151]

Curiously, given that Wright is one of the most quoted of all mid-Victorian workingmen, the sharp contrast which he draws between himself and those he so confidently characterizes has never really been problematized. Instead, historians quote him on matters consistent with the meanings they wish to convey. But by removing particular statements to carefully crafted interpretative contexts, they divest them of some connotations and inscribe them with others, exemplifying the practices I have been at pains to describe. Hence, to illustrate the view that mid-Victorian working people were interpellated by a social identity the substance of which was reflected in dialect literature, Patrick Joyce adduces a comment by Wright to the effect that 'formal "penny readings" at which dialect was performed' were highly successful, and that their popularity 'was matched by their freedom from oppressive patronage'.[152] Yet Wright seems quite untouched by the socially inclusive vision to which Joyce's 'populist identity' is articulated, and by 'popular' he seems to mean no more than a condition of being liked or enjoyed. Hence he observes that penny readings were popular because they were cheap but he goes on to note, *contra* Joyce, that they were of minor importance, a welcome though small part of the programmes in which they were included. Moreover, the comment construed by Joyce to signify 'freedom from oppressive patronage' is simply one about the refusal of entrepreneurs to provide 'Reserved Seats' because patronage fell away when they did so.[153] What Wright seems to have been most eager to emphasize was that such programmes increased the exposure of intelligent artisans to great authors and classical literature.[154] But if Joyce is given to interpretative excess, Neville Kirk's imagination also seems to get the better of him. Elaborating the view that in the mid-Victorian period, workingmen who sought accommodation with the classes above them began to outnumber those who remained antagonistic, Kirk includes a comment by

Wright according to which intelligent and energetic workers adopted the principle that they must be the architects of their own elevation.[155] Yet the context in which the cited statement occurs indicates that, in Wright's view, truly intelligent workers were a small minority. Moreover, Wright repeatedly advances the view that the working classes, by and large, remained 'a house divided against itself', debilitated by want of coherence and 'incapable of united action even for a common object'.[156] Evidently convinced that a shared and unifying identity had never prevailed and that the divided majority failed to appreciate the wisdom whereby the intelligent few sought 'accommodation', he seems to refute the two main premises of Kirk's argument.

In each of his major works Wright stresses that others who presumed to speak for the working classes did not share their experiences, did not understand them, did not consult 'their views upon questions in which they were intimately concerned', but instead fathered on them 'views which they did not hold'.[157] He also insists that workingmen exist 'in such infinite variety, that any one man embodying the distinguishing characteristics of the various types . . . would be a monster of inconsistency'.[158] He recognizes no inconsistency, however, in his own claim that, because he too is a 'workingman', he can succeed where others have failed. Nor does he simply 'describe' the working classes; he consigns them to clearly defined categories and also 'fathers' on them a range of views, attitudes and motivations. The possibility that their ways of seeing and their idiosyncratic responses to the imperatives by which their circumstances were ordered might differ from *his* construction seems to escape him – and also the historians who cite him. In the case of the latter, this oversight exemplifies a practice of selective quotation and literal interpretation whereby the 'successful' independent worker is made a metaphor for all working people so that real disadvantage and discontent seem not to have existed.

The extent to which the meaning of historical commentary is shaped by the historian's interpretative context is further illustrated by Geoffrey Crossick. In some ways pre-empting Neville Kirk's thesis, Crossick argues that, in the mid-Victorian period, working-class identity was undermined by stratification and sectionalism, then reconstituted as labour consciousness in later decades. Reconstitution was facilitated, according to Crossick, by 'a process of accommodation to structured inequality'[159] fostered largely, if ironically, by the very élites of skilled workers whom exclusiveness benefited most.[160] To illustrate attitudes which in his view reflected mid-Victorian trade exclusiveness, he adduces several comments by the stonemason, James Turnbull. One such comment, which is made to suggest that bricklayers and their labourers were not treated equally by the boss, and that the former shouted instructions at the latter with such contempt that they seemed like demi-gods, is regarded by Crossick as convincing evidence of stratification. Another, where Turnbull recalls how members of diverse trades entertained him at mealtimes by 'telling tales at the expense of [one another]', serves to exemplify sectionalism.[161] Yet the stonemason conveys little sense that his attitudes and identity were ever informed decisively by consciousness of class or trade status. And when the comments abstracted by Crossick are considered in their original context, they do not easily sustain the meanings imputed to them.

Turnbull certainly observes that bricklayers first impressed him as contemptuous demi-gods to whom employers gave preferential treatment. But he also indicates that this was only the initial impression of a young man new to the city and the trade. He soon found out, he continues, that 'there were no men on the job, only "blokes"', 'jolly good fellows' who extended fatherly advice so that he would not be disadvantaged by his unfamiliarity with London customs.[162] Similarly, when he remarks that tradesmen joked at one another's expense, he proceeds to note that they were all 'fine jolly fellows . . . [who] told their tales with effect . . . [while] the work went full swing all the time'.[163] Nowhere does he refer to hostility bred of sectionalism and exclusiveness, and he seems to have regarded different occupations simply as different ways of being a 'workingman'. His expressed commitment to industry, thrift, sobriety, self-help and self-education seem to suggest his 'respectability', and his claim that the dignity of work is compromised by skilled tradesmen who aspire to higher status might be seen to signify his 'class' identity.[164] Alternatively, 'labour consciousness' could be inferred from his assertion that mining workers had gained many advantages because of their capacity for organization.[165] Yet what he appears most persistently to emphasize is his 'individualism'. Placed in a 'home' at five years old by his widowed mother, he writes, 'I first became conscious that I was one of the many separate existences in this world and that I must think and act for myself'.[166] Taken in, thereafter, by relatives who in his view exploited him, he was further encouraged, he reflects, 'to keep my own counsel and stand entirely on my own two feet'.[167]

Continuing, Turnbull attributes his ability to stay afloat 'in the struggle for existence' to personal competitiveness and the support of an industrious wife, though he is not unsympathetic to the less fortunate. Hence, discussing the inmates of a gaol, he speculates that they prefer prison life to freedom, but only because of an inability 'to earn their living in the fierce competition outside'.[168] Frequently unemployed himself during the depressed 1870s, he recalls, he suffered the scorn of neighbours who judged him a malingerer and urged his wife to leave him. But he 'let it all slide', he writes, secure in the knowledge that he had never avoided work.[169] Evidently unconcerned for respectability which depended on uninformed opinion, he also seems to have lacked what Crossick calls 'labour consciousness'. A moderate drinker though not a teetotaller, he was often overlooked for employment in his own trade, he observes, because a 'workman who was sober, attentive and . . . [studious] was regarded as a possible rival by the foreman . . . [and even] as a possible competitor by the builder himself'.[170] He therefore took work where he could find it, on one occasion in a factory, on others doing odd jobs or devising various 'schemes and dodges' to make a few shillings, and finally determining to take on the paltry tasks 'unnoticed by the man who has a regular job'.[171] Presenting himself as a 'workingman' rather than as part of a trade élite or working class, he 'think[s] a skilled mechanic as good as a Methodist preacher', though he implies that it is up to the individual to prove himself.[172] Radical ideas like socialism do not, he is convinced, 'come under the head of practical politics' but tend largely to exercise overpaid single men who have consumed too much whisky.[173] Nor, although Crossick asserts that his trade was the most exclusive and best organized, does he appear to have considered union intervention when problems arose,[174] and when his employer criticized the standard of his son's work, he dealt with what he evidently regarded as a personal affront by finding the boy another job.[175]

Without suggesting that Turnbull was in any way 'typical', it is possible to conclude that he presents himself as the most 'ordinary' member of the standard sample. Like many of those already surveyed, he travelled to America, though not, as they did, in an official capacity or to enjoy a vacation. He went, he explains, in the hope that he might improve his condition, paying his own fare and returning poorer than when he embarked.[176] Born in 1845, he belonged to a generation of working people in which a high level of literacy was perhaps no longer so unusual, though a workingman who published his memoirs surely was.[177] Often out of work in his prime, he seems to have found secure employment in later life, but he did not become a journalist, publisher or politician, nor, he suggests, did he wish even to be a foreman or manager.[178] It might be imagined, therefore, that historians seeking confirmation for their theories of social identity would regard him as more or less 'average' and a useful commentator. Yet he not only seems to have been the least 'successful' member of the sample, but the least cited.

More widely consulted is a group of labour leaders – Thomas Burt, George Edwards, Harry Gosling, Ben Tillett, Ben Turner and John Wilson – who published their memoirs after winning parliamentary office around the turn of the century. Burt and Wilson served as Liberals, the rest as Lib-Labs or, after 1906, as Labour members, but all describe themselves as workingmen, emphasizing the poverty and hardship of early life, the sacrifices which they made to obtain education, their commitment to self-improvement and their subsequent efforts to better the condition of their class. Born between 1837 and 1863, all entered the labour movement in the second half of the century, all used language indicative of 'class consciousness' and all have been treated as exemplars of working-class identity.[179] Burt, Turner and Wilson have also been enlisted to illustrate Joyce's populist interpretation. Returned by popular franchise, such individuals might indeed be thought to have been 'representative', to have articulated the attitudes and aspirations of those who elected them. Yet their memoirs indicate that, to a substantial degree, they defined themselves against their constituents, condescending to them, criticizing their behaviour and prescribing rather than reflecting their views.

Thomas Burt, for example, writes of a sixty-year connection with the Northumberland Miners Union of which he became secretary in 1865, but he refers to the union as 'their' (the mineworkers') rather than 'our' organization.[180] As kindred spirits he singles out other 'educated' workingmen like Alexander Macdonald who, with Burt, was elected to Parliament in 1874;[181] John Nixon, his wise, intelligent, moderate and conciliatory assistant secretary;[182] and Joseph Fairbairn, autodidact, trade unionist and subsequently colliery owner in America. Courageous and outspoken, Fairbairn 'cared little whether the majority agreed or disagreed with him' and, Burt reflects, exerted a 'formative influence . . . on my character'.[183] Delineating himself as one whose ambition never extended beyond the desire to work hard in the service of humanity, Burt observes that success came to him unsolicited, yet he repeatedly implies that he is exceptional, contrasting his own hard-won intellectual acumen with the inferior capacities of the untaught.[184] Hence he recalls that monthly hiring was dubbed the monthly monster 'with that love of jingling alliteration which is so attractive to the untrained mind', then proceeds, in elevated language, to discuss the intricacies of political economy.[185] Expanding on this theme, he explains that supply, demand and competition 'cannot be abolished' and that strikes are therefore 'irrational [and] wasteful'. Workmen who oppose them, he continues, are 'thoughtful, experienced, and intelligent' while those who support them are irresponsible younger men, 'carried away by their feelings'. The latter, he fears, resort to 'terrorism and coercion' to implicate the rest.[186]

In earlier decades, Burt goes on, both employers and operatives failed to recognize the wisdom of consultation in industrial disputes, but employers had since become extremely reasonable.[187] So, too, had most mining workers who accepted a system of sliding wage-scales, though sometimes reluctantly, and who took advantage of other mechanisms which Burt helped to establish to resolve their differences. These mechanisms, a Joint Committee and a Conciliation Board, were in Burt's view the epitome of fairness, served as they were by 'eminent, capable [and implicitly impartial] men, including Mr (afterwards Sir Rupert) Kettle, Dr Lyon Playfair, M.P., and Sir Farrar Herschell, afterwards Lord Chancellor'.[188] Henceforth, he recalls, when in 'isolated' incidents colliery workers refused to be guided by the Joint Committee, 'they were dealt with patiently, but firmly, and, if necessary, very sternly'.[189] Burt's language and tone are more suggestive of the long-suffering parent attempting to discipline recalcitrant children than of the spokesperson seeking to represent the concerns of his fellows, and his efforts seem to have been geared less to empowering common working people than to subordinating them to the superior wisdom of their betters.

Equally prescriptive is John Wilson, another self-improver who rose from the condition of mining worker to become a prominent figure in co-operativism and trade unionism, a Gladstonian Liberal and eventually a Member of Parliament. Wilson portrays himself as a paragon of courage and persistence who, even as a lad, stood firm against injustice, 'seize[d] the skirts of happy chances' and 'ma[de] up for a weak body' with 'self-will and determination'.[190] A teacher and preacher before entering the political arena, he seems to have combined these capacities with that of labour leader, seeking, like Burt, to instruct and 'to construct' the represented rather than to consult and reflect their wishes. Convinced that if one seeks 'first the Kingdom of God and its righteousness . . . all things else will be added thereto', he accepted with humility the various positions of authority to which he was called and never with any thought of personal gain.[191] Using the influence thus acquired, he then helped to establish a number of co-operative stores and to weld a few scattered individuals into the Durham Miners Association. The latter overcame 'the opposition of employers' and 'the lethargy of workmen', just as other initiatives which he directed held firm against opportunists who sought to turn them to their own advantage and mischief-makers prepared to serve 'any vile purpose' for 'a good place in the pit, and beer *ad libitum*'.[192] Wilson never considers that such people may have been more than spoilers, nor that their convictions may have been as firm as his own. He simply anathematizes and dismisses them.

As hesitantly as he entered public life, Wilson observes, he agreed to write his autobiography, not with 'self-praise in mind' but 'to influence character formation', to promote 'the betterment and progress of the people' and 'to inspire others to follow the way of right and useful living'.[193] To this end, presumably, he reminds his readers of their 'attachment . . . to the throne, the institutions, and the laws under which they live'. He also asserts that what they have failed to achieve for themselves, through trade unionism and co-operation, Gladstone has achieved for them by extending the franchise, enshrining justice and equality and ensuring the prevalence of 'right' over 'might' both in Britain and throughout the empire.[194] Working people have never asked for more than 'a fair field of competition', he insists, and if 'we as a class are still willing to remain behind, then let the shame and loss be ours'.[195] The 'mental culture' for which he and his compeers sacrificed so much was now freely available to all, and ignorance, in his day a misfortune, was now 'a crime'.[196] The 'mental calibre' which he sees 'in many cases wasted or devoted to what is low, vicious, and destructive' must therefore be cultivated, not just to obtain wealth but to acquire the wisdom whereby the places occupied by the likes of himself might be filled even 'more ably than they are now'.[197]

Evidently, in Wilson's political scheme of things, 'equality and justice' had to co-exist with hierarchy, just as it did in his family. The latter he characterizes as a 'Republic' of which he is 'Prime Minister' and his wife the 'chancellor of the exchequer'. In her assigned capacity Mrs Wilson suggests various economies and offers much good advice, but she is often overruled and forced to yield to her husband in whom ultimate power resides.[198] Similarly, it is Wilson's 'liberal' account of justice and equality which workers must accept. His use of 'we' and other inclusive pronouns might seem to signify his working-class identity and therefore his 'representativeness'. Yet he repeatedly stresses his 'difference', prescribing co-operation for others but emphasizing his own individuality, either as an outspoken leader in industrial disputes who suffers disproportionately, or as one who sacrifices his own well-being for that of fellow-workers.[199] When he discusses his contribution to the establishment of homes for aged miners, the latter seem almost an irrelevancy. He is more concerned to emphasize that he has not been afflicted by 'the sorrow which comes from penury' and that he has achieved intimacy with other officials of the project.[200] Hence, even were the 'meaning' of Wilson's discourse regarded as self-evident, there seems no reason to assume that his views were broadly representative. He appears rarely if ever to have consulted those to whom he dictated and prescribed; his own perceptions must surely have been influenced by a condition which he acknowledges was superior; and by his own admission his affinities were with other social strata.

By contrast to the Liberals Burt and Wilson, the later generation of Labour men in the sample stress the ongoing importance of collective organization and the need for increased government intervention in economic and social life. The former write of moderating union activity, participating in voluntary initiatives to relieve instances of distress, and working to effect political change whereby the majority could prosper as responsible individuals in a climate of equal opportunity. The latter suggest that popular political power is tenuous and that it must be consolidated. To this end they promote the amalgamation of unions under centralized control. Some also reflect on their efforts to bring about the nationalization of land, railways, mines and resources, others on their support for some form of old age pension. Edwards, originally 'a most ardent liberal', stood as Liberal/Labour candidate in the 1892 general county council election but the Liberals, in his view, failed to support him and turned the election into a 'class contest'. He subsequently lost faith in them and committed himself to Labour.[201] Turner displays no such ambivalence. A committed 'socialist', he remembers defending his philosophy against no less a luminary than Gladstone and insists that its teaching, preaching and development is '[t]he prime function of the labour party'.[202] Another socialist, by his own reckoning 'the first declared' one in Parliament, is Tillett, who claims to have performed the 'priestly function' of joining together the trade union and socialist movements.[203]

Notwithstanding these differences, the Labour 'representatives' resemble their opposite political numbers in a variety of ways, not least in the degree to which they distinguish themselves from common folk. They admire and identify with upper-class patrons of Labour initiatives, other parliamentarians and working-class notables like themselves;[204] and they depict the majority of workers very much like children whom they attempt to instruct and to guide at great personal sacrifice but who, as often as not, are unheedful and ungrateful. Writing of how he 'blazed the trail of Trades Unionism' for dock-workers, Tillett reflects on the great effort required 'to awaken and fortify

116

social conscience' and to overcome the resistance of skilled men to the organization of general labourers, who, he claims, were thought to be 'outside the
pale'.[205] Edwards notes the difficulty of moving men's thoughts beyond 'the
mere raising of wages' and recalls how various attempts to unionize agricultural labourers were defeated by the apathy of the agricultural workers
themselves.[206] By 1896, he despaired 'that his class would ever be manly
enough to emancipate themselves' and, with a speech in which he stated
frankly that the latter had failed him, determined to retire from public life.[207]
In 1902, however, he was persuaded to establish a new union and, as recruitment proceeded, he found that men were now 'more thoughtful'.[208]
Nevertheless, as late as 1907, he was to insist that workers were still imbued
with a 'spirit of apathy and childlike dependence [which] must cease'.[209]

Similar sentiments are expressed by Harry Gosling who, prior to entering
Parliament in 1924, served as secretary to the Amalgamated Society of
Watermen and Lightermen, a delegate to the Trades Union Congress and a
London County Councillor.[210] In these capacities he quickly learned that
change could not be hurried and that councillors must be paid high salaries
then left 'to do things in their own way' to ensure that the public service
received 'the help of the best brains'.[211] But the members of his union were not
so easily taught. Lacking education and training, they were slow to accept that
changes which 'took from them certain of their rights also bore them forward',
and they did not understand that 'there must be less progress in some places,
because there is greater in others'.[212] Often, therefore, they resorted to self-
defeating, unofficial action, and vilified their leaders as traitors, unable to
realize that the latter were 'going as fast as the great machine . . . [would] let
them'.[213] Nevertheless, he suggests that if TUC officials were to acquire
greater power, momentum might be increased. Indeed, in his view, the 1926
general strike failed precisely because the general council 'lacked supreme
control over its constituents'.[214] Leadership, he writes, is a 'gift', and it requires
that one's lead be 'accepted unquestionably'.[215]

Ben Turner, who first rose to prominence in the textile industry, affects a
more tolerant attitude than Gosling towards rebelliousness in the ranks,
though not to what he characterizes as 'wrongdoing', and not to unfair and dishonest practices like working overtime 'when there are thousands of
industrious men out of employment'.[216] Never, he writes, has he criticized
men for striking against his advice, though they invariably suspected, abused
and blamed him and other officials when disputes were not settled satisfactorily, and were quite as despicable in other instances.[217] During his first election
campaign, for example, one 'dirty-minded creature' made the shameful allegation that his [Turner's] wife had been forced 'to weave for him when he was
working in the mill' and another that his 'mother was in the workhouse'.[218]
He endured many such attempts to 'blacken' his name, he observes, not least
from the left-wing element after he had been elected to Parliament.[219] In his
1908 election address, Turner warned that with nearly a million people out of

work, 'the Poverty Problem' could only be solved by 'Collective Ownership of the means of production, distribution and exchange'. A vote for him, he promised, was a vote for 'the downtrodden and oppressed . . . the hungry children in our schools and . . . the Disinherited Old People'.[220] Yet, when he reflects on past industrial disputes, his sympathy for the lower classes is less pronounced than his admiration for 'altruistic' employers who relieved the distress of strikers and the fair-minded 'eminent men' who adjudicated the disputes.[221] Strikers, he regrets, 'were not always just' in their condemnation of their opponents, and blacklegs he holds in unequivocal contempt, though he is reluctant to criticize the employers who brought them in by the 'trainload'.[222] Like the historians who cite him, Turner fails to address the possibility that blacklegs were no less victims of the system which produced them than were the wretches they replaced.

Simple logic dictates that the act of becoming a 'representative', of becoming what the majority are not, creates its own particular kind of 'otherness'.[223] And the surveyed writings, when appropriately interrogated, indicate that their authors were aware and proud of their 'difference'. They sometimes stress that leaders should maintain a degree of intimacy with their followers,[224] as when Turner observes that the man who does not 'learn something about his members' trade and calling' is not 'worth his place in the movement'.[225] Yet all indicate that, because of administrative and official duties including extensive international travel, they were substantially detached from the rank and file. They also express surprise that goals characterized as 'working-class' but about which workers themselves seem never to have been consulted often failed to attract support.[226] They then cite popular indifference and unforeseen institutional obstacles to explain why certain of their pre-election promises have not been implemented.[227] Perhaps in expiation of their personal success, frequent travel, visits to Buckingham Palace and OBEs, some also insist, as politicians often do, that their material reward has been far less than it might have been had they chosen to serve themselves in other fields.[228] All, nevertheless, express the conviction that the common condition has been substantially improved. Hence Turner 'rationalizes' that although 'there is great unemployment, a bigger body of men and women pleading for work than ever known in British history . . . [and] hundreds of thousands of folks homeless, hungry and ill-clad . . . [l]ife in the mass was never as good as it is now'.[229]

It is important to note that the views expressed by Wilson, Burt, Edwards, Tillett, Gosling and Turner are not the views of mid-Victorian working-class radicals but the reflections of men who, between 1874 and 1924, became distinguished parliamentarians. The extent to which their reconstructions of lived experience during the mid-Victorian period were shaped by intervening events and by their perspectives on the world at the time of writing must remain a matter of conjecture. Their narratives indicate, however, that their identities were fluid and ambiguous, contradictory at any given moment and subject to change over time. And like their counterparts in earlier decades, they seem clearly to define themselves against the mass of working people, claiming superior intellect, education and morality as qualities which set them apart as leaders. They also distinguish themselves by stressing that many instances of conflict – protracted industrial disputes, strikes and lockouts – might have been averted had their wisdom only been shared by their constituents. Moreover, their regular references to conflict, to popular dissatisfaction with the pace of change and to lack of popular confidence in their leadership raise serious questions about what 'relative social harmony' in the mid-Victorian period might mean.

Evidently these figures endorsed the existing system, a system which has remained by and large intact, and were convinced that common folk could and should pursue a 'respectable independence' within it. But they also indicate that they were not representative in any 'reflective' sense, that they did not exemplify a prevailing 'social identity' from which popular attitudes and motivations might be inferred, and that there was abroad in the community considerable dissatisfaction with prevailing social realities. Hence, even were it accepted that the writings of these 'exemplars' contain some fixed, intrinsic and recoverable meaning, there would be no logical reason to assume that such views were held by the majority of mid-Victorian workers. Because the prevailing system remained intact, popular acquiescence might be assumed, but acquiescence, as I have noted, is a problematical idea. Did the populace-at-large actively accept the *status quo*? Did some people only appear to, maintaining a façade of respectability but disregarding social mores in their struggle for survival? Did others surrender to their condition because they felt powerless to do otherwise? These questions will now be put to another body of material; not, it should again be emphasized, to seek definitive answers, but to explore further the ways in which meaning is produced in historical discourse.

DISCORDANT VOICES AND COUNTER-DISCOURSES

It has been argued thus far that evidence adduced to illustrate various histories of the mid-Victorian labour experience can sustain a range of interpretations; that its meaning is determined substantially by the questions to which it is submitted;[230] and that the formulation of such questions constitutes a present-centred, political practice.[231] Shaped by a selective process in which 'facts' amenable to inscription with particular meanings are privileged to the exclusion of others, this practice serves to limit the possible ways in which the past can be rendered,[232] and the narratives which result are, in effect, myths which derive their meaning from, and are designed to make sense in, the present.[233] In terms of the evidence which they incorporate, these narratives are convincing. Collectively, they appear to confirm that, by contrast to the turbulent Chartist era, the mid-Victorian period was one of social and political quietude, consensus and harmony. Individually, with reference to the writings of contemporaries deemed representative of popular attitudes and aspirations, they seem to demonstrate that the social identities to which explanations of social stability are articulated were shared by the wider lower-class community. These impressions are reinforced by the language in which the various histories are couched. Terms like 'social harmony' and 'consensus' imply not only the absence of conflict and discord but a prevailing social condition, a consistent, orderly arrangement distinguished by concord, unity, mutual understanding and friendship.[234] It seems clear from the works cited to validate theories of social identity, moreover, that their authors took pride in their achievements, endorsed the system which made those achievements possible and sought to foster social harmony by procuring the acquiescence of their constituents. But it is not so clear that their expressed attitudes were broadly representative. As the above reading of their memoirs suggests, they defined themselves quite emphatically against the common working people whose outlook they supposedly reflected and it is possible, therefore, that the latter did not necessarily share their views. Hence it is appropriate now to consider the 'evidence' of some of their 'constituents', thus to speculate on the identities which they project, on the attitudes and aspirations which they appear to have entertained, and on how their statements speak to notions of harmony and consensus.

The evidence in question serves to convey a very different impression of popular attitudes to the *status quo*. It consists predominantly though not entirely of Select Committee reports in which commissioners interview applicants for various kinds of assistance. Like the autobiographies surveyed above, these interviews can be seen to indicate 'acquiescence' in the prevailing system, but they contain little which could be construed literally as approval or active support. Respondents might in various ways be seen to identify in class or populist terms and thus to lend weight to the historical myths which theories of class and populist identity inform. But their statements contain little to suggest any sense of inclusion in a socially harmonious whole, and less to indicate belief in the possibility of attaining to a 'respectable independence'. The interviews lend themselves instead to an alternative myth, to a story in which substantial numbers of people, either working under intolerable conditions or without work and scarcely able to sustain themselves, struggle to assert their humanity in a society which seeks persistently to deny it. In assigning this and other commentaries as stories or myths, I do not accord them to inferior status.[235] I simply suggest the historical contingency of the meanings which they bear and the political/ideological character of the 'narrative' form in which they are elaborated, ideas which will be explored in depth in Chapter 4.[236] Hence, the purpose of the proposed story is not to render an account of the past which is somehow objectively more truthful but simply to stress that, when the political content of the interpretative paradigm and the narrative form is changed, other stories are precipitated.

Like all narratives, historical commentaries are subject to 'closure', or confined between a beginning and an end, and this one begins with an 1841 pamphlet on general distress in Bolton. The pamphlet, which refers to three specific individuals, two of whom were previously determined by inquest to have died of starvation, serves as a useful point of departure for two reasons. First, because of its brevity, it can be reproduced in its entirety thus to illustrate its capacity, both as a historical text in its own right and as a context which incorporates other 'texts' or commentaries, to sustain a range of meanings.[237] Second, its ambiguity notwithstanding, it speaks to a state of social crisis with which statements of distress in subsequent decades can be compared, distress which helps by its very oversight to define the problematic of the historiography surveyed above; for whether that problematic is called stability, harmony or consensus, its meaning is shaped by the systematic exclusion of 'contradictory' evidence. Compiled by W. Naisby, a member of the Anti-Corn Law League and a former Poor Law guardian, the Bolton pamphlet reflects its author's interest in the condition of two men, James Bristol and William Pearce, immediately before their deaths.[238] At one level, it can be read as an account of Naisby's work on behalf of the Bolton poor, whose plight he had addressed previously in public speeches and formal representations to the House of Commons. Citing a range of corroborative evidence, Naisby suggests that as a consequence of his efforts, distress in Bolton is no longer 'so great'.[239] At another level, it might be interpreted as a direct political attack on a Poor Law commissioner named Mott, whom he indicts with deceiving Parliament by stating that the town's inhabitants enjoy a 'comfortable living'.[240] Alternatively, the document can be considered at the level of its 'sub-texts', incorporated testimonies which point beyond the dispute between Naisby and Mott. In this connection, the widows of the deceased are of particular significance, one because of her self-characterization, the other, who is scarcely permitted to speak, because of the way she is represented.

At the time of James Bristol's death, recalls his widow, Ann,

> I was lame myself . . . and could not walk[.] My child was blind at the time, having the St. Anthony's Fire; she was then nearly sixteen years of age. I had another daughter, very ill also, aged about thirteen years. I had four other children besides, the eldest of which was nearly eighteen years of age, the next nine years of age, the next seven years of age, and the other four years old: altogether I had six children. For three weeks previous to my husband's death we had nothing but three shillings per week coming in; and we had to live sometimes on potatoes, sometimes on porridge; but had only one meal a day, which we generally made about four o'clock in the afternoon. I think it was for a fortnight that we had to confine ourselves

to one meal a day, sometimes having porridge and sometimes potatoes. When Mr. Naisby found us in this state, we got more food,
otherwise I believe I should have lost more children, for we had got
as far distressed as we well could to be alive. About five months previous to my husband's death I had a child sucking, which died; and
I feel sure that its death was occasioned by my not being able to give
it suck, for want of sustenance. I had no bed, bedding, or anything
whereon to lay, when Mr. Naisby visited us. I had only a stool
whereon to sit, for myself. I had no shop where I could get provisions
at: they all refused to give me credit. My husband wished for a bit of
cheese and bread, the day before he died, but I was unable to procure
him any.[241]

It cannot be assumed with any certainty that the words contained in this
statement are precisely Bristol's own. Affixed to the statement is a 'mark'
rather than a signature and it is conceivable, therefore, that she was not sufficiently literate to express herself with such clarity. And even were this caveat
waived, it cannot be assumed that she said exactly what she meant or meant
exactly what she said. She might, for example, have rendered her testimony in
terms calculated to further her own interests. Finally, her brief narrative cannot
have spoken to her experience in all of its complexity. Nevertheless, it seems
reasonable to infer from a literal or 'surface' reading of her commentary that she
was grateful for Naisby's intervention and that, despite her distress, she was
not predisposed to challenge the social order which made her condition possible and perhaps necessary. It might also be inferred that she did not recognize
any connection between her plight and prevailing social/structural imperatives.
To this extent, she could be said to have accepted the *status quo*.[242] But what
did her acceptance mean?

Possibly the text of Bristol's statement could be assimilated to the theories
of social identity with which I have taken issue. But it does not indicate in any
literal sense that she was satisfied with her position in a recognized social hierarchy, as she should have been according to Joyce's populist construction, or
that she entertained any hope of acquiring a modicum of the independence
which, in the class analyses consulted above, made identity meaningful. She
seems instead to have defined herself substantially by familial ties and to have
been in the process of 'losing definition', for not only was her husband dead of
starvation and her infant of malnutrition, but the lives of her surviving children were threatened by sickness and want. Nor is it likely that respectability
in any definition seemed accessible to one in her state of degradation.
Describing that state, Betty Brown, a neighbour who helped to dress James
Bristol's corpse, observes that the deceased

had lain [in the same clothes] for many weeks, having nothing besides
to keep him warm; when I cut his trowsers [sic] legs and stocking legs

122

open, there were large quantities of creeping filth, which had eaten quite into the flesh, and his legs were nothing but putrid flesh and scabs. He had nothing but straw to lie upon, which was spread on the floor. One of her children had the Saint Anthony's Fire, and the rest were all more or less sickly and bad. They all slept together in one room, and the wife of Bristol had a great hole in her leg, and could not walk or assist her husband.[243]

This assessment is effectively endorsed by another witness, Mary Ann Grimshaw.[244]

Just as Naisby's document shapes the meaning of commentaries adduced to it, it must in turn be shaped by the way in which it is interrogated, or by the interpretative context into which it is placed. Hence, when 'questioned' about how Bristol might have characterized her own condition, it suggests that, to sustain her life and those of her remaining children, she was utterly dependent on the goodwill of people like Naisby. Evidently she was too ill to work; destitute of the wherewithal to be thrifty beyond rationing a scant supply of potatoes and porridge; and unable to introduce a measure of cleanliness into her mean accommodation. She also lacked the most elementary attributes of respectability, as labour historians define the term. Presumably, therefore, she lacked the moral collateral whereby she might have obtained 'credit' and with it 'a bit of cheese and bread' for her starving husband. Moreover, even should her own health have improved, she might well have failed to find work, for the lack of it had apparently forced another woman, Ann Kirkman, into a house of 'four yards square' with fifteen other able-bodied people who were also unable to find jobs.[245] Like Bristol's testimony, Kirkman's account conveys a sense of her powerlessness to affect the circumstances in which she finds herself. 'Respectable independence' seems remote from the experiences and the hopes of these women, and although they are not openly hostile to the system which oppresses them, neither do they indicate that they in any way endorse it.[246]

Although Naisby's exposé serves graphically to illustrate a vision of extreme degradation, he concerns himself neither with underlying social and political causes nor with Poor Law administration as such. His critique seems to be directed specifically at one man: Mott. Perhaps it is no coincidence, therefore, that he characterizes the second widow, Ellen Pearce, whom Mott cites in defence of his own actions, as unreliable.[247] Hence, rather than interviewing Pearce, Naisby refers to other witnesses who depict the Pearce dwelling with even more extreme images of filth and depravity than those invoked in the Bristol case, and also insist that Pearce and her children are mentally deranged. A relieving officer, Thomas Bradshaw, for example, deposes that Ellen Pearce 'is very weak in intellect', that 'any statements she might make, is [sic] not fit to be taken as evidence', and that 'her daughters are the same'. He concludes 'that a dullness of intellect afflicts the whole family'.[248] James Webster, a town missionary, extends this judgement, observing that Pearce and her two daughters are 'of such very weak intellect that it approximates very closely to insanity, and that they are totally incapable of giving evidence that could be depended upon'.[249] A neighbour, Nancy Beswick, adds that she has 'known the family for four years, and . . . [has] always considered them not to be right in their minds'.[250] And William Coop, a local comb-maker, claims that the entire family, which had fed on rotten potatoes salvaged from the midden, is 'to a great degree insane, and quite incompetent to give evidence'. Although he has known Mrs Pearce 'to be in the most abject state of poverty', he continues, she has 'often stated she wants for nothing, and is fearful she will be sent to the Workhouse if she complains . . . Her aversion to going into the Workhouse, I am certain, would make her say and do anything to avoid going there.'[251]

According to Mott, Mrs Pearce informed him that her husband 'had been ailing eighteen weeks' before his death but 'had worked occasionally during that time'; that 'he was a steady, sober man, and had always brought his wages home'; that 'they had two looms at home, on which she and her daughter worked'; that her daughter also had outside work; and that 'she and her daughter earned about 9s.6d. per week'.[252] She 'indignantly denied William Coop's story about the potatoes' and insisted on several occasions that the family was 'comfortable' and 'never wanted food'.[253] In response to this testimony, Naisby accuses Mott of concentrating solely on 'the old woman [Pearce], although he knows she is little better than an idiot', implicitly to justify his failure to deal adequately with the prevailing crisis.[254] The welfare of Ellen Pearce is secondary, if not irrelevant, in this dispute, and her ultimate fate is never established, for Naisby's primary concern is to discredit Mott. To this end he insists that Pearce's testimony is unreliable because she is mentally deficient. Yet the only 'evidence' of her deficiency consists in observations about the wretched state in which she lives and the suggestion that her aversion to the workhouse is irrational. By such criteria, virtually anyone who could not afford respectable accommodation or who shared a commonplace hatred of the workhouse might be held to have been incompetent. Alternatively, it is possible that, distracted by poverty and her husband's death, Pearce chose what to her was the lesser of two evils, avoiding 'the house' and whatever comfort it offered to avert the threat of being separated from her children. Indeed, on the basis of her purported statements to Mott, she appears to have defined herself less as an individual than as part of a family. If such were the case, her assertion of economic independence could be judged an appropriate response to forces which threatened to dissolve her family and with it her identity, rather than a symptom of insanity, or, as another interpretative context might suggest, a compelling indication of 'class' or 'populist' identity.

Although Naisby indicates that, in Bolton alone, 2,656 people were receiving relief in late 1841,[255] it could be argued that Bristol and Pearce represented an exceptional minority, or that the pamphlet is a product of the 'hungry forties' and of no significance to the mid-Victorian period. The present narrative, however, is less concerned with the question of whether the likes of Bristol and Pearce were sufficiently numerous to be of any importance than with that of the authority on which any group is excluded from historical commentary and implied effectively to be irrelevant, simply because of its minority status. Moreover, to distinguish such women as a minority would be to disregard other sites of identification, other larger categories like class and gender in terms of which they may have defined themselves, other levels at which they could be said to have been oppressed. Pearce, for example, is denied the right to speak for herself on grounds of alleged insanity, a construction designed precisely, according to one body of scholarship, to disable women deemed troublesome or objectionable.[256] By speculating in this way I do not suggest that for women like Bristol and Pearce, gender, rather than class, 'the people' or the family, was the primary site of identification. My purpose is rather to emphasize that identity (and oppression) can be multi-dimensional; that the various axes of identification are bent or inflected by a range of power differentials; that individuals might be part of a minority (and feel oppressed as such) on one axis of identification but not on another; that identity is a process in which a range of discursively constructed categories are negotiated; and that to privilege one such category over others is effectively to deny identity its fluidity and ambiguity by reducing it to a fixed attribute.

To characterize Bristol and Pearce as 'victims of gender discrimination' might be deemed anachronistic on the basis that it renders their experiences in 'modern' terms which they could not possibly have understood, that effectively, because they had no language to describe such a condition, the condition did not exist for them. But although the terminology might be inappropriate, another woman of the period, Elizabeth Storie, describes a lifetime of 'victimization' which she attributes as much to gender inequality as to her low socio-economic status. Without suggesting that her views should be regarded as 'representative' it can be assumed that she was not unique in recognizing that she was disadvantaged by her sex. Unlike Bristol and Pearce, who seem resigned to their wretchedness, Storie seems to have resisted hers with singular purpose. According to her memoir, she engaged with the institutions which in her view oppressed her and refused to be intimidated by their eminent representatives. Hence, though badly disabled in early childhood and lacking 'even an ordinary education', this 'poor but respectable' woman, who supported herself with millinery and dressmaking, eventually addressed herself to the highest court in the land.[257] Storie's narrative is one of persistent hardship which began in 1822 when, at four years old, she contracted nettle-rash, a minor childhood complaint, and 'fell victim', as she puts it, 'to the unskilled treatment' of a young surgeon named Falconer.[258] The treatment, she observes, consisted in large doses of mercury which caused her face to blacken and her gums to 'mortify', and agonizing injections of aquafortis (nitric acid), after which she lost her teeth, part of her jawbone and part of her tongue.

Falconer then prescribed a powder which Storie's father did not administer but instead had analysed by another doctor. It was found, she continues, to contain 'as much arsenic as would kill seven persons'.[259] Falconer was subsequently sued and Storie, judged to have been made 'an object for life', was awarded £1,000 compensation. But Falconer absconded.[260] Storie's father pursued the claim until his death, then she began to act in her own behalf, seeking comfort in the church and justice in the courts though ultimately failing, she indicates, to find either.

Her first attempt to enforce settlement was made in 1836 when, after one of many operations to restore mobility to her jaws, she was so reduced in strength that she feared she would no longer be able to earn her living. She engaged a man named Niven to act for her but her original administrator, a Mr Kerr, refused to give Niven 'any information . . . about the previous process'. Her efforts were defeated, her means exhausted, and she was unable to proceed.[261] In 1848, on learning that Falconer planned to emigrate to America, she sought to prevent him from leaving and requested Kerr 'to obtain the original process'. Falconer was duly detained but the process could not be found. Illegally and without her knowledge, Kerr, she continues, instituted a new action which made it appear that she had relinquished the sum awarded in 1823.[262] She refused to proceed but, in 1849, Kerr proposed a further action, convincing her against her better judgement that she must pursue it. '[V]ery probably', he assured her, the old process 'would turn up during these proceedings.'[263] She then set about locating as many as possible of the original witnesses.[264] But at the hearing, Kerr 'allow[ed] into the proof the evidence of [no] more than ten'. The case was lost and Storie was held liable for expenses.[265] She then moved against Kerr for misleading her and against the Glasgow Town Clerks for recovery of the original process. In the former instance she was successful and Kerr was instructed to contribute to her support until the process was found.[266] In the latter she failed. Even though it transpired that the documents had been signed out in 1823 to Andrew Cross, Falconer's agent, and never recovered, the Lord Provost and Magistrates would not prosecute their Town Clerks.[267] By saving her allowance from Kerr, Storie was able to initiate further proceedings but again her action failed. The earlier judgement against Kerr was also overturned and costs were awarded against her. She appealed the decision before the Inner House of the Court of Session and subsequently before the Supreme Court, but it was decided, she observes, that 'after such a lapse of time I am not entitled to redress'.[268] The Supreme Court also awarded costs against her but the defendants declined to claim them, effectively preventing further litigation and forcing her, she concludes, to accept defeat.[269]

By her own account, Storie fared little better in her dealings with the church. In 1853, frustrated in her efforts to recover the lost process, she sought help from the Kirk Session of St Matthews, where she had been a member for some ten years. The Act of Sederunt, she indicates, 'affords a parishioner aid in a just cause' by enabling the ministry and elders 'to enforce a case . . . for litigation'.[270] Not only, however, did the minister, Archibald Watson, refuse to read her petition to the Session meeting, claiming that it contained 'matter with which the Session cannot interfere', but he also struck her from the communion roll soon afterwards.[271] In the presence of witnesses, Storie requested an explanation but Watson refused to be drawn, insisting that she 'was in a state of perfect insanity'.[272] She pursued the matter in letters to Watson and church elders but her correspondence was ignored.[273] On the advice of the Presbytery, she returned 'in all meekness' to the Kirk Session but Watson again rejected her, this time, she claims, quite violently. Finally, she 'took instruments, protested, and appealed to the Synod', after which, as mysteriously as she had been excommunicated, she was reinstated. In a curious letter, Watson 'accepted Miss Storie's explanation', though according to Storie an explanation had been neither solicited nor given.[274] Moreover, when she requested compensation from Watson for the cost of her proceedings against him, 'an officiating elder' threw her petition 'out on the street after [her]'.[275] Finally, she sought extracts of the Session minutes 'to defend herself by publishing them'. Though Watson was unco-operative she finally obtained one at a charge of 10s.6d. but could afford neither the 1s.6d. per page demanded for the remainder, nor, since a woman would not be heard by the Synod, the cost of employing 'an able, honest man' to obtain approval for their release.[276] 'I felt defenceless and unable to continue this unequal struggle', she concludes, and '[m]y appeal to the Synod was thus forced to fall [sic]'.[277]

'[F]rom a healthy child', she speculates, 'I have been doomed to a life time of misery by a young medical practitioner, whose object may have been to gain fame by experimental discovery.'[278] Then, with no regard for the illness, poverty and legal ignorance which so inhibited the progress of her action against this man, the Supreme Court rejected her claim, not because it was unjustified, she insists, but *because I have been unable to make it sooner*'.[279] Finally, she notes, '[i]n seeking consolation from the ordinances of religion, I have been denied and deprived of them'.[280] Hence, she represents herself as 'a victim to the three learned professions' and, with equal emphasis, suggests that low social status and gender are the bases of her oppression. By birth 'the daughter of a tradesman', she writes, 'a barrier seems to have been placed before me and my formidable opponents'.[281] She is convinced that her lawsuits would have been received more sympathetically and perhaps have resulted in a different decision '[h]ad I had the good fortune to have the prefix of "Countess" or "Lady" to my name, or had my opponents been as poor and unimportant as myself'.[282] And her book, she stresses, has been written under 'a strong impression that injustice is often done to the poor, and more especially to the women of that class, who are more defenceless both from their sex, and from the greater difficulty which poverty combined with it exposes them to'.[283] On the basis of these comments it could be argued that Storie had no real sense of gender oppression and that, in confining it implicitly to women of the poorer classes, she effectively reduced it to a function of class or status discrimination. Alternatively, she might be said to exhibit a subtle understanding of how gender and class inequality condition each other. Regardless, however, of any retrospective judgement on the adequacy of her conceptual apparatus, she indicates not only that her identity is shaped by an awareness of gender and class (or social status), but that these 'affinities' failed to mitigate her profound feeling of alienation.

Like any historical document, Storie's narrative raises more questions than it answers. And just as its meaning will be changed by emphases and omissions in any retelling – in this instance my own – her intended meaning was doubt-less shaped by information which *she* excluded. To what extent, for example, was her recollection of infancy modified by the events of her subsequent devel-opment? To what extent did she recall 'given' accounts of her infantile experience rather than the experience itself? And how distorted/distorting might any such accounts have been? Moreover, precisely because it is a narra-tive, her memoir suggests further questions about the way in which its content is shaped by the information which has been excluded. Hence, although she purports to have lacked 'even an ordinary education',[284] she produces a very erudite commentary. How is this possible? Did she have help which she fails to report? It might also be asked how one as poor and powerless as she claims to have been could negotiate the difficulties of publication or, for that matter, the intricacies and costs of some thirty years of litigation. Apart from the tem-porary payment of ten shillings a month by Kerr and a brief period on the Poor Roll, she acknowledges no financial assistance and appears to have enjoyed little moral support. Instead she casts herself as one alone against the world, engaged 'in a desperate struggle between might and right, affluence and poverty, self-importance and insignificance, with no other backing than per-severence, and years of toil and trouble'.[285] Subjected to 'the contumely of the thoughtless, wanton, inconsiderate, and unfeeling', she reflects, she has also been betrayed by the authorities and most of her representatives.[286]

There seems little reason to doubt Storie's sincerity, for she adduces a great deal of legal correspondence as supporting evidence, and would presumably have made every effort to avoid compromising herself in a document intended for publication. Others who shared or observed her experiences might, of course, have construed them differently, but it is not the 'objective truth' of her commentary which is of interest here. Her account might well be thought to demonstrate that contemporary working people could be brutalized with impunity by unscrupulous medical practitioners, disadvantaged by inequity before the law and denied the comfort of religion on the whim of a petulant clergyman; or she might be regarded as an exemplary victim of the practice, purportedly perfected in the nineteenth century and canvassed above, of equating women with 'the irrational' and controlling, trivializing or dis-missing their troublesome numbers by declaring them 'insane'.[287] It might also be argued that the working person and especially the working woman who pursued a grievance to the Supreme Court was a very rare type, although it could scarcely be said, on the basis of such an argument, that grievance itself was rare. Many may simply have lived with their discontent because they believed that redress was virtually impossible to obtain. This much is insinuated in Storie's commentary, which records that her hard-won legal victory was not enforced but nullified, thus challenging the very logic of seeking justice at law. The judiciary, she indicates, functioned in complicity with the church, the medical profession and all those who ridiculed and despised her to consolidate the alienation by which, most persistently and emphatically, she seems to define herself.

Alienation does not, of course, preclude consciousness of class and, in addition to describing herself as poor and the poor as a class, Storie proclaims her respectability, a compelling sign of working-class identity according to some historians.[288] Moreover, her evident conviction that established institutions should have vindicated her and validated her place in society suggests that she may, at the very least, have entertained a vision or an ideal of social inclusiveness reminiscent of Joyce's populist construction. Yet she does not explicitly relate her respectability to 'class identity' and never explains her understanding of the term 'class' which, in her usage, signifies no more than a way of delineating a group of people distinguished by what she apprehends as poverty. Similarly, her recourse to established institutions implies no more than the use of every available means to pursue what to her were her just deserts. She elaborates no 'social vision' and appears to include common folk and social paragons alike among her oppressors. Nor does she ever use the words 'alienation' or 'social exclusion'. None of these meanings is necessarily given by her text; if they are imputed they must originate elsewhere; and it is only in abstraction from her text that certain of her comments will appear to valorize a particular construction. But because the selective process in which abstraction occurs is a function of historical interpretation, meaning and its authenticity must derive from the interpretative framework to which particular comments are assimilated and which, in delineating the object of historical enquiry, also shapes the explanation. The meaning of the present narrative is shaped by questions designed to suggest that such practices generate stories which serve, in the guise of objective historical truth, to underwrite particular political purposes in the present. Because they are articulated to a problematic of consensus and harmony, it is argued, these stories exclude discordant voices and thereby deprive their late twentieth-century counterparts of a validating precedent. By elaborating a counter-myth from material which other historians have excluded, I invite speculation on the contingency of historical truth and its implication in the maintenance of power. In doing so, I offer those who currently find themselves oppressed and powerless a way of repudiating truths which naturalize their condition. Storie's memoir lends coherence to these aims.

At one level, Storie appears to have had little in common with the next group of people to be considered. These people are English rather than Scottish, the only authorities with whom most have dealt have been clergymen or Poor Law officials and all, unlike her, have at one time or another been unable to support themselves.[289] At a deeper level, however, they resemble not only Storie but Ann Bristol and Ellen Pearce, for all describe intolerable circumstances which they are powerless to change, and all can be said to convey the same sense of defeat. Summoned to speak of their condition before various select committees, the people in question appear in some instances as workers protesting against unconscionable imposts on their meagre wages; in others, as the unemployed, the sick or the aged. But although their 'appearance' may change, they speak persistently of the same disadvantage. Evidently resigned to their dependency, they suggest that their energies have been consumed in resisting or appealing against the most oppressive aspects of their condition. They seem never to have heard of the success myth elaborated by contemporary labour leaders, the purported exemplars of their world view, and their commentaries mock historiographical conventions about 'social harmony' and its predicates.

The reports to be examined contain statements which could indeed be used to corroborate class and populist interpretations. In the minutes of a select committee inquiry conducted between 1854 and 1855 to investigate the stoppage of wages in hosiery manufacture, for example, Isaac Abbott, a framework-knitter from Earl Shilton in Leicester, testifies that he 'had nothing to complain of in shortness of employment during the time' he worked for a manufacturer named Everard. He adds that he served a Mr Wileman, for 'perhaps eight or ten years' and that, when trade was bad, he sought and found farmwork.[290] He also refers to farmers 'who are favourable to the spread of temperance, and for the encouragement of their men they give them 1s. a week to go without drink if they choose to do so'.[291] Another witness, Joseph Elliott, describes an alternative system of employment to that under consideration and which, he is convinced, 'has given the greatest satisfaction both to the employer and the workpeople'.[292] These statements might be adduced variously to indicate a popular commitment to industry, sobriety, respectability, independence and co-operation between masters and men, or 'consensus' between the middle and working classes. But they are also assimilable, like the immediate contexts from which they have been drawn, to a construction in which the speakers, regardless of whether they exhibit 'class' or 'populist' attributes, seem most persistently to identify in terms of their oppressive condition and the alienation which it engenders.

Indeed, the cited statements point not to the customary order of things, but to notable exceptions in a story about the dependency of operatives forced by economic reality to submit to imposed constraints and intolerable conditions. Hence, when Abbott testifies that he has found alternative work on the farm of a certain Lady Byron and a commissioner enquires about the 'likelihood of [other] persons getting such work', he replies that 'only occasionally . . . [do]

we have a chance of getting employment under Lady Byron; she is the only person that we have a chance of getting employment under', for other 'farmers are not willing to take stocking-makers as labourers; they believe they are not able to do the work'.[293] It also emerges that temperance advocates who increased the wages of abstainers were but 'one or two', and that Abbott's 'steady employment' was confined to periods when trade was brisk. He had been hired by Everard only during the previous autumn and by Wileman intermittently, having 'worked to [sic] him and left him, and went to him again, for several years; perhaps eight or ten altogether'.[294] Moreover, Everard and Wileman are not numbered among the exceptions who have adopted the alternative system of payment under which operatives actually receive their net wages. They are included with the majority who purportedly persist in reducing average wages, by various deductions, from 10–12s. a week to 5–6s.[295]

Workers called to give evidence often note that their incomes have declined by as much as half – some say over the past fifty years, others over the past ten.[296] But they do not request a return to earlier rates for, as the stockinger John Ginns observes, 'we are well aware that machinery is operating strongly against us'.[297] Nor, states John Sketchley of Hinckley, do 'we ask for any law which shall give us permanent employment'.[298] Instead they seek the abolition of imposts which reduce and sometimes halve their current wages such that, according to Sketchley, 'we are almost at starvation point'.[299] Hence they appeal for 'legislative protection against these stoppages, because as wages diminish while the stoppages remain as they are at present, those stoppages bear more heavily every year upon the workman'.[300] Although there is some objection to winding, seaming and other finishing fees and to the illegal enforcement of 'truck', the main grievance is a rental charge on knitting frames which workers must pay regardless of whether the frame is in use.[301]

According to witnesses, frames were obtained either directly from manufacturers or from 'middlemen' who acted as manufacturers' agents, supplying and overseeing operatives. These agents derived their income from frame rental and therefore sought to maintain the maximum number of units in circulation, irrespective of the quantity of work available. Yet because alternative work was extremely difficult to find, available frames were quickly taken up and retained at full fee, even during periods of illness or when the market was saturated and materials withheld, lest, with improving trade, another frame could not be found.[302] Isaac Abbott explains that operatives, when faced with such deductions, must 'submit or lose their' jobs and be driven into the workhouse.[303] Hence, on one occasion, his wife was forced to wait until mid-week for a minimal amount of work which, on completion, fetched only 2s.4½d. But after charges of 1s. for a full week's rental and 3½d. for seaming she was left with a net wage of 13d.[304] He describes a further instance in which a woman was incapacitated for six weeks, for two of which her frame was in the shop for repairs. On the seventh week she produced work to the value of 4s.2d. but the entire amount was stopped for rental and she was forced to pay a further 4½d. from her pocket.[305] When questioned about the illegal truck system, Abbott speculates that it is more extensively practised than ten years ago. If workers refuse to take provisions in lieu of wages or report any such system, he continues, they will lose their jobs and have 'difficulty in getting employment again', since most employers are truck masters.[306]

With variations in emphasis, virtually all witnesses tell the same story. Some, especially those who claim to speak in a representative capacity, accompany their evidence with written statements and indicate that their constituents are also willing to testify.[307] According to one such 'delegate', Joseph Elliott, the prevailing view in the towns and countryside of Leicester is that workers 'must either submit to what their employer chooses to stop, or starve'.[308] Referring to a petition against current practices which he submitted to the House of Commons, he notes that the document was endorsed by 12,000 to 13,000 people, including some 1,100 'respectable ratepayers'. He suggests, however, that many more workers may have withheld their signatures on pain of dismissal.[309] He also cites specific cases in which the entire value of work had been stopped for frame rental and further payment demanded.[310] Evidently satisfied with his veracity, Sir Joshua Walmsley,[311] a member of the committee, characterizes prevailing rental practices as extortion. In doing so, he reflects the view of a fellow commissioner who, on learning from Sketchley that even workers who owned knitting frames must 'pay something' and often 'the full rent' in order to be employed, observes that rental practices constitute nothing less than the sale of jobs.[312]

There are several levels at which these testimonies can be interpreted, allowing that the questions put to them are present-centred and political; that the views expressed to the commission are understood to reflect subjective perceptions rather than objective truths; and that the meanings attributed to them are not necessarily those intended by the witnesses themselves. This narrative will address two such levels: identity, and expressed attitudes to the social order. Hence, the texts will be considered for what working people say about their own experiences and the society in which they find themselves. It is, of course, possible that the identities and attitudes of these witnesses may have been influenced by individuals, groups and/or circumstances other than those to which they refer. It is also possible that, in different situations, the people at issue may have represented themselves and their views differently. They are constructed as particular kinds of subjects in the text under discussion, but other contemporary discourses may have constituted them differently. Nevertheless, in their statements to the commission, they are distinguished unambiguously as 'economic' creatures. They do not, like members of the 'leadership sample', identify in cultural and moral terms, declaring or implying a disinterested commitment to the service of humanity and affecting disdain for personal wealth and power. Instead, persistently emphasizing that the material basis of their existence is at stake, they define themselves in relation to their material need.

The pre-eminent concern raised before the commission is regulation of an industry which is claimed effectively to hold its workforce to ransom. Preoccupied with declining incomes and unrestrained imposts, witnesses affirm that they would gladly take alternative situations if only alternatives existed. Acknowledging that they are powerless, they plead for intervention, not, as noted, to restore earlier levels of remuneration but simply to prevent additional stoppages on the diminished wages to which they have agreed. Each witness speaks to each concern, and in ways which suggest a plight of such magnitude that 'consciousness' was occupied with little else. Hence, Isaac Abbott confides that he has 'not been fully employed the last 12 months' and that his wife must surrender almost half the value of the little work she receives or lose her job. Despite declining wages, he must remain in the industry for there is 'nothing else to take to'. Abolition of 'rents and charges' might at least, he speculates, exclude those who enter the trade as middlemen and further diminish wages by employing 'the slowest of hands . . . merely for the sake of the rents which they get from the machines'. The present state of affairs, he concludes, is 'decidedly [worse]' than that which obtained during the 'great depression' which beset the trade a decade earlier.[313]

Elliott also reports stoppages which have reduced wages to nil or a few pence, and recalls approaching employers in 'the glove branch' to request that frame-rent be adjusted to 'the number of days the men' worked. Few, he observes, would even 'entertain the question'. A strike ensued but the men could not hold out.[314] These conditions, he explains, are further exacerbated by the absence of any law 'to restrain . . . stoppages', for the middleman 'is at liberty to take what he pleases, without any responsibility whatsoever'. Such a law, he suggests, might protect 'the helpless workmen and also the better-disposed employer'.[315] At present, he proceeds, operatives are forced to live in wretched tenements: 'it is almost out of their idea for a stocking-maker to have a house of his own'. And even this mean accommodation is not secure, for there are many cases in which the tenant, unable to pay the rent because of sickness, 'has either been compelled by his landlord to go out of the room, or his goods have been sold to pay the rent'.[316] John Sketchley, John Ginns and Thomas Newstead speak to the same problems, as does William Richmond, who has since found work under the net system.[317] Each objects to the freedom of employers to charge as they wish; each cites cases in which wages have been reduced to a pittance or withheld altogether and additional payment demanded; and each indicates that workers are powerless to resist.[318]

According to Sketchley, operatives ask only that agreed wages be paid, but their incomes are persistently reduced by employers who give out short work and deduct what they please. These practices, he observes, excite great indignation but little surprise: 'we proposed arbitration but employers would not even listen'.[319] Hence, he continues, we take other occupations 'as fast as we can', and many workmen say that 'if they could only get a start selling lucifer matches, or any thing of that sort, they would gladly do so'. But there are few other jobs to be had and a workman is often 'compelled to stay with his employer', for if he 'gives up his frame he cannot go to the parish', and if he turns in his frame to take another he might 'lose, perhaps, a full week's work'. As a consequence, Sketchley concludes, 'we are almost at starvation point' and 'entirely helpless'.[320] Ginns is equally distressed by the absence of alternative employment and does not, like the eminent William Lovett, believe that workers have been blessed by the marvellous inventions of the industrial age.[321] '[M]achinery is operating strongly against us', he finds, and 'the lower our wages get the more they [the masters] impose upon us by the rent . . . because the men are more dependent on them'. Employers 'have got the money in their possession', he points out, 'and while we hold the frames they claim the rent, and keep it out of our earnings'. Convinced that the trade is in decline, he does not expect wages to be raised. He hopes only for an act of Parliament which will put an end to the stoppages.[322] Newstead, with a particular animus against middlemen, observes that if they took more 'in charges there would be nothing left', and that operatives cannot object because they have no other work to turn to. Their condition is so low, he insists, 'that they must either do what little work there is or go to the parish'.[323] And Richmond, comparing those who work under the charges system with workers like himself who receive net-payment, finds the former 'almost horrible to contemplate', their 'haggard appearance . . . bespeak[ing] the lowness of their wages'. Reflecting on his experience as one of them, he deplores the withholding of work and the imposition of stoppages. Under the charges system, he explains, 'the workman has no power'. He cannot supply his needs for he cannot 'force the master to give him work', and his necessity compels his compliance.[324]

These stockingers might be held to have had faith in the prevailing system and to have supported it with something more than reluctant resignation insofar as they address their request for ameliorative change to its appointed representatives. Yet they also complain that the system favours the manufacturer's interests over their own and resist arguments which defend this imbalance, questioning both the impartiality and the logic of committee members who advance them.[325] Hence, they concede that employers must seek to maximize their returns just as operatives do their wages, but object when commissioners uphold the 'natural' predisposition to pursue profit, and simultaneously invoke moral considerations to urge restraint of the worker's 'natural propensity'. Nor do they accept that, by taking work which they know is subject to stoppages, they surrender the right to object to those stoppages; and they deny the implication that the responsibility would be their own should massive unemployment coincide with the termination of rents and charges.[326] Commissioners agree that excessive imposts are unfair, but they concern themselves predominantly with legalities, and the law favours the employer. The workmen recognize their disadvantage, acknowledge that they are powerless and appeal to the committee, their last resort, to amend the law. The committee was subsequently to recommend that their requests be implemented and the men in question may, as a consequence, have improved their condition.[327] But similar complaints in subsequent decades suggest that many did not achieve this.

Acutely conscious of their subordination, these witnesses seem unmistakably to define themselves against the powerful, whether employers who exploit them or appointed representatives of the state who remind them that they have no 'legal' cause for complaint. They might, on this basis, be said to convey some sense of class, but hardly of class consciousness as it has been characterized by labour historians.[328] They cite the family, not a larger collectivity like class or the people, as their only reliable source of support, and it is as family members that they seem primarily to identify. Isaac Abbott, for example, observes that it is the likelihood of losing their rented accommodations which in many instances induces families to 'live on half rations . . . [rather] than go into the [work]house and have full rations'.[329] And Joseph Elliott notes the extent to which tenement rentals, often as high as 3s. a week, are a family responsibility. '[W]here the father of a family has been sick', he explains, 'other [family] members have been working at some other employment, so as to enable the father to meet his expenses.'[330] Exhibiting a similar sense of commitment, Mary Stevens appears to accept without question the necessity of returning from Stony Staunton, her own place of work, to help settle accounts with her deceased mother's Leicester employer.[331] And William Richmond suggests that, under the principle of rents and charges, families cling 'everlastingly . . . together', to their own economic disadvantage. A net system, he proceeds, 'would ultimately give to many heads of families the means of putting their children to other trades'.[332] Pursuing another possibility, Thomas Newstead suggests that the economic advantages of a net system would enable parents 'to send their children to school, instead of putting them to the wheel; and a man would put his wife to keep the children cleanly, instead of doing part of the work'.[333] Such people, it seems, defined their very existence by material need so acute that the family, the only reliable source of practical support, constituted the pre-eminent focus of identity. They may indeed have shared 'class' or 'populist' affinities but they do not invoke them in their need, nor do they specifically acknowledge them.

Beyond the family, the only people with whom these workers appear to sustain any sense of solidarity are experienced, able-bodied stockingers like themselves. Skilled workers, they insist, suffer idleness under present conditions for profit is derived from frame-rental and employers therefore favour slow, inefficient operatives. Were costs and charges abolished, they would have sufficient work because it would no longer profit manufacturers to engage women, the young, the old and the feeble, all of whom, they argue, are less productive. But although they express sympathy for these groups, they regard them as rivals who should be found other work or consigned to the parish. Some, like Thomas Newstead and William Richmond, speculate that the latter alternative would not be necessary. Newstead observes that the able-bodied workman, fully employed, would be able to keep his wife at home and his children at school,[334] while Richmond suggests that a net system would serve to dissolve the dull apathy which currently prevails and 'induce parties having families to seek other occupations for their children prior to their arriving at a certain age'.[335] The possibility that the people they seek to exclude, not least old and feeble operatives, might object to their proposed arrangement seems irrelevant to them, for they are concerned only with the interests of the skilled, adult, male stockingers.

Joseph Elliott and John Sketchley share this concern but they also acknowledge the likely consequences of a net system. Elliott admits that many might lose their jobs and become dependent on relief should such a system be introduced, but he 'think[s] that if there be no other resource than parochial assistance, it would be far better to throw . . . [a certain portion of the weak hands] upon the rate-payers than to throw the able-bodied . . . out of work'. Proceeding, he asserts that 'there are at this time a great number of these weaker vessels who earn a less amount of wages than able-bodied men could earn, while able-bodied men are in the streets having nothing to do'.[336] Similarly, when a commissioner suggests that any change might deprive some 10,000 people, and especially the aged, of their jobs, Sketchley does not demur.[337] In his estimation, it is presently in 'the interest of an employer to give out as much work as will enable him to take the rent . . . [and] to employ old people in preference to young and active people'.[338] Hence, 'in times of depression young and active men, with small families, will have to go to the union workhouse, while old people who can earn 3s. or 4s. a week only will be kept at work'.[339] Under a net system, he continues, 'the more work the workman could do the better it would be for the employer, because the better his machinery would pay him'.[340] To the suggestion that implementation of his proposal must necessarily put the inexperienced out of work, he replies, indicating that the aged may not always have enjoyed a very secure place in family arrangements, that '[i]t would be preferable that old people should be thrown out of employment rather than the young and active men with families'.[341]

To note the close affinity which these men express for family and other skilled stockingers is not to suggest that they defined themselves exclusively by these orientations. Presumably they identified differently as their circumstances changed and they imply as much, indicating that, when demand was greater and work more plentiful, they were less disposed to contrast themselves to the inexperienced operatives whom they currently distinguished as intruders. But it is the family and fellow-tradesmen, rather than broader social categories like 'class' or 'the people', which they invoke most persistently in response to other determining influences. Hence, to address their immediate circumstances, they seek change whereby manufacturers will be disposed to favour them over the unskilled and they, with more work, will be better able to provide for their families. Expressing no concern for working people *per se* and accepting that the proposed legislation might function to deprive their less efficient rivals of employment, they attempt, it might be argued, to enhance their own status by diminishing that of others, and appealing to those above them to ratify their priorities. Permitted to speak for themselves before the commission, they are prepared to turn the less skilled out of work unheard, and to dictate how their wives and children should be occupied in the event of change.

Although these men imply the co-operative character of family life, their comments about redeploying wives and children and their offhand attitude to the aged seem to reflect a hierarchically ordered outlook which possibly concealed from them the extent to which their condition was structurally determined. For although they describe existing social arrangements as oppressive and suggest that their condition might be improved by 'internal' structural adjustments, they betray no suspicion that the maintenance of their condition might be necessary to that of the existing social order and no desire for fundamental systemic change. Alternatively, it could be argued that even had they fully recognized the structural predicates of their situation, they were powerless to do more than address its symptoms and to seek a measure of protection for themselves, their families and the fellow-tradesmen to whose interests they linked their own. Either way, their statements could be said to reflect neither 'class consciousness' nor a 'populist' commitment to social inclusiveness. Their negotiations are over rents and charges, not 'consensus values' and they seem scarcely to contemplate acquiring a meaningful 'independence'. Their aim, they suggest, is simply to address the worst aspects of their subordination so that they might subsist in a declining trade. If, as Sketchley observes, they were alert to any opportunity, the able-bodied may in some instances have found different work, and it is likely that many of their aged and feeble numbers died off with their frames, as the stockinger Joseph Elliott predicted they would.[342] Doubtless many more were forced to seek assistance from the parish, although, as the minutes of an 1861 select committee inquiry indicate, to ask was not necessarily to receive.

The 1861 inquiry is concerned with Poor Law administration and several of its sessions are devoted to West Ham Union where, it had been claimed in a recent contribution to *The Times*, the poor 'are in urgent want, and numbers of women approaching childbirth are almost without food'.[343] The claim is hotly disputed by the West Ham guardians, one of whom insists that its author, the Reverend Herman Douglas, 'being desirous of raising money to build a church, a parsonage, schools, and other edifices, found that the readiest way of obtaining the necessary funds was to put forth an exaggerated and highly colourful description of the destitute and forlorn condition of the labouring poor, and then to appeal to the public for sympathy and relief'.[344] Another member of the board fears that Douglas has been misled and that his 'kindness has been imposed upon', while yet another insists that 'labour is in greater demand . . . [and] better paid' locally than elsewhere.[345] All are adamant that they deal expeditiously with every request for assistance, providing outdoor relief to the incapacitated and offering the house to the able-bodied.[346] Douglas responds by asserting that regular work is less abundant than the guardians imagine and that 'his poor' are highly respectable, possessed of a 'spirit of independence' such that 'the majority prefer selling their last shirt rather than to apply to the parish'.[347] Clearly Douglas's comments could be adduced to illustrate the popular 'respectability' to which class historians have accorded so much importance, and those of the guardians to indicate an environment in which a 'populist' commitment to social inclusiveness might be meaningful. But the wider context of the inquiry also lends itself to another story in which the poor are held repeatedly by their examiners to be untrustworthy and their purported self-reliance seems a brief respite from parish assistance, a respite financed by the pawn-shop, extended by private charity and divorced from any likelihood of self-sufficiency. Interpreted literally, or in terms of what currently prevails as educated common sense, the language in which the witnesses express themselves is more assimilable to an account of alienation and powerlessness than to one of buoyancy and confidence consistent with the 'independence' of class and populist constructions. The speakers scarcely mention 'respectability' and their 'independence' seems limited to remaining at large rather than accepting the dubious shelter of the workhouse.

Although the inquiry speaks to the condition of such people, it is primarily concerned with the parish authorities whom Douglas, it is held, has accused of refusing to relieve genuine need. Douglas does not, he explains, wish to indict the guardians but simply to point out that they lack adequate resources. Hence, he alleges, applicants have been directed to him by the relieving officer and have been told, at least in some instances, that they 'might starve or go to Mr. Douglas'.[348] The guardians stress that, when out-relief is inappropriate, the house is always offered, and on this basis they and the relieving officer are judged to have acted responsibly. Douglas suggests that, were all able-bodied applicants to accept the house, they could not be accommodated, but the commissioners do not address this possibility, perhaps because they are concerned only to ascertain that applicants have not been denied their legal entitlements.[349] Such legalities seem irrelevant to the applicants themselves who will not accept the house while they are free to choose. But they acknowledge that they have been forced to rely on Douglas for their economic survival and seem, therefore, to refute any notion of their 'independence'. Moreover, although their statements sometimes imply self-respect, 'respectability' could be deemed inconsistent with their acknowledged dependency and their inferior status before the commission. Repeatedly, in illustration of the latter, they are reduced by their examiners to objects of contempt. Bound by oath and directed to respond without qualification to ambiguous questions, they are then held to contradict themselves and warned against perjury. By contrast, their interlocutors are unsworn, at liberty to challenge and accuse them, assumed to be honest, and deemed simply to be mistaken when they misinterpret sworn statements.[350]

Hence, when John Grimditch is asked to recall the last time he applied for relief and answers uncertainly, '[s]ome four years ago, I think', the chairman, Sir John Walsham, responds curtly: 'I do not want any thinks; I ask for the truth.'[351] In another instance, under examination by Mr Tonge, whose connection to the inquiry is unclear, Grimditch insists that he sought help from Douglas only when he could not find work. Tonge dismisses his explanation, suggesting that he has deceived Douglas and declaring his suspicion of any 'man [who] makes very loud professions'.[352] Alternatively, when two gentlemen, Messrs White and Scully, interrupt the interrogation of Henry Laws to impugn his character, they are heard patiently, as unsworn witnesses, even though Walsham has indicated that their charges have no bearing on the present proceedings.[353] White asserts that Laws threatened Scully with violence should he 'speak against Mr. Douglas' and Scully volunteers to be sworn, 'if necessary', to corroborate the charge. By Laws's account, however, it is Scully who was provocative, calling him a cripple and offering him 'a good chastising'. Only then, Laws proceeds, did he invite Scully into the street, promising that '[i]f you did I would put this here [leg] against your body'. But his defence appears to be ignored. As though his criminality has been proven, another gentleman deplores his disdain for the law, and White, observing that '[w]e are assailed . . . threatened to be eternally smashed, and everything else', insists that Laws 'is one of our assailants'.[354] The treatment of Grimditch and Laws is not exceptional for all witnesses are in various ways thus challenged. The witnesses themselves defend their integrity, although predominantly, it seems, to be of use to Douglas, for they acknowledge that by choosing to reject the house they have foregone parish assistance. They relate this choice to a conviction that, while they remain abroad, they might keep their families together and exercise a measure of control over their lives, control which would be terminated should they enter the house. Thus interpreted, their statements accord with those of the Leicester stockingers and the Bolton poor with whom this narrative began.

The statements in question serve effectively to break a doubly imposed historical silence, for most of the West Ham witnesses are both poor and female. In an attempt to address this gender imbalance or asymmetry, I will focus predominantly on the women, but the men are of initial interest, partly because the guardians contend that any need which the women have endured has arisen 'from the neglect of the husbands', and partly because the women subsequently speak to this charge.[355] Of the seven men subpoenaed, one evidently refused to attend;[356] a second, suspected of perjury, is quickly disposed of;[357] and a third, who readily admits that to reject the house is to forego relief, is also dismissed after a brief examination.[358] The remainder are questioned at

139

varying length about their families, employment and history of relief. Although their examiners objectify them as a 'responsibility' which must be dealt with as the need arises, their statements seem to indicate that they are active subjects who consider their possibilities and order their priorities with care and purpose. Each man expresses a determination to keep his family intact despite poverty so abject that they are often without staple foods, and most acknowledge that they have received limited outdoor relief, either for themselves or their wives. Most have also rejected offers of 'indoor' relief and all have been assisted by Douglas. Without recourse to the latter they might possibly have been more compliant, but all seem adamant that they will not be put away.

Having been refused outdoor assistance and referred by the relieving officer to Douglas, John Grimditch expresses particular hatred for the workhouse, observing that a 'man of spirit would never go near it'.[359] '[R]ather than drag my [starving] children to the union,' he observes to the committee, 'I would sooner have gone round the neighbourhood [begging].'[360] Assuming the status of a pariah, Grimditch seems to cherish no illusion that he is 'respectable' but he does affect a perverse 'independence', opting for help to which no conditions are attached. He also refuses to be intimidated by his 'betters'. When it is suggested that he has had more work than he admits, he replies coolly: 'I am not always at work when I am out seeking work.' To more facile questions he responds with transparent sarcasm. Hence, when asked if he is sure that he has seven children, he replies, 'I did not look at the list this morning . . . I forgot to look at the list.'[361] Grimditch and his examiners finally reach an impasse: the latter are satisfied that relief has been offered; the former spurns the bondage on which official relief depends. As the interview draws to a close, one commissioner suggests that Mrs Grimditch might have been helped during her confinement had she or her husband reapplied. 'It amounts to this,' the gentleman concludes: 'some of the people expect we are to hunt them up, because they are too proud to ask.'[362] Both the language and sentiment of this statement convey a sense of profound contempt, from the phrase 'hunt them up', which serves to reduce them to the status of animals, to the claim that 'they are too proud', which implies not only that they should continue to seek relief and to court the indignity of further refusals, as though they were bereft of human feelings, but that pride is something to which they are not entitled. This and other examples of contempt seem to suggest division and hostility rather than consensus and harmony. They may not disprove the currency of the latter, but they serve to raise serious questions about what labour historians mean by such terms.

The sense of antagonism conveyed by Grimditch's interview is reflected in that of Henry Laws who, as indicated above, also duplicates Grimditch's spirited resistance to intimidation. Crippled and in poor general health, Laws earns 12s.6d. a week as a journeyman tailor, scarcely a fortune when bread costs between 5d. and 8d. a loaf.[363] Presumably because of his disability, his wife has been relieved during her confinement without any suggestion that they enter the house.[364] Beyond this 'privilege', he is treated with what seems to be customary disdain. His interview is of particular interest, however, because it allows speculation on the vulnerability of the poor under a system supposedly designed to assist them. A substantial part of Laws's interrogation consists of a dispute about two shillings' worth of goods said to have been advanced to him but which he denies receiving. The relieving officer tenders a ticket signed by one of the guardians as evidence that relief was granted and Sir John Walsham produces a signed certificate from the grocer on whom the order was made, to verify that it was filled.[365] Hence, everyone involved in the transaction except the designated recipient has been protected by certification. Because Laws's receipt has not been required, he has no way of proving that the goods were not supplied. It is quite possible that the grocer defrauded him or that he engaged in such fraud regularly, perhaps in collusion with one or more guardians. But this possibility is never considered. It is assumed that Laws is at best mistaken, at worst untruthful, though he refuses to accept any such judgement. 'I can positively say that I had not the grocery', he asserts, 'because I was then under those circumstances when I should have been glad of any little assistance whatever.' With equal conviction, Walsham insists, 'it is certain if you did not have it, somebody had it for you'.[366] The implication is that when common creatures like Laws dispute the word of eminent guardians and respectable grocers, the former must on principle be wrong. Clearly, the possibility that the poor may have been exploited in the way suggested, that they were virtually powerless to resist, and that they became alienated as a result, is just one of a number of meanings and connotations that could be imputed to the record of Laws's examination. The point, however, is that any such possibility is ruled out when stories like Laws's are excluded.

Less assertive than Grimditch and Laws but evidently no less alienated is the recently widowed Thomas Delves, who has also declined indoor relief. By presenting himself at the docks every day, Delves obtains work to the value of 10s. a week, but has had to leave his confined wife largely unattended. Because of illness, Mrs Delves had been awarded a small allowance but it was stopped when a parish doctor found that she had begun to rally and to consume less than she was given. Delves does not dispute her temporary remission but regrets that her relief was stopped precisely when 'she was a little better and wanted nourishment'. The allowance, he continues, was eventually restored, but she died soon afterwards of 'pulmonary consumption'.[367] During her illness, she purportedly complained to Douglas and other 'visitors' of being 'starved' and confided to a Mr Heale that Delves 'would not lose time to go' again to the parish. Perhaps, as Heale suggests, the woman intended to criticize her husband and might have survived had it not been for his 'indifference'. Perhaps she meant merely to acknowledge his effort to provide for her. Either way, it could be said that he found himself in an invidious position. When he applied to have his wife's allowance renewed he was offered the house but refused because he did not wish to be separated from her.[368] Possibly because of this precedent, he was convinced of the futility of any further application. Hence, he explains, '[t]he state of my wife's health was the reason why I did not come, because I knew she would not be alive long, and I wanted her with me'.[369] But his explanation is irrelevant. The Poor Law authorities are judged to have acted responsibly and the commissioners have no further use for him. Concluding with a discussion of whether, when his late wife's relief was suspended, a proper certificate had been issued for her removal, they effectively reduce his tragedy to a statistic.[370]

Unlike Grimditch and Delves, James Cutten seems prepared to recognize that the workhouse might be an acceptable alternative. The father of seven young children, Cutten had been relieved out of doors for incapacity. When told that to obtain further aid he must enter the house, he replied, 'before I would be parted from my children and my wife, I would put an end to our existence at once'.[371] Explaining that he said 'so on the impulse of the moment', being still unable to walk, he provokes the Reverend Parry to defend the ultimatum. The latter claims to have had 'sufficient information' to be sure that, 'at the close of a fortnight', the man 'would be well enough' to do without further assistance.[372] Cutten then tells of how he subsequently pawned his belongings to keep his family together. But in a lecture from the chair, Walsham condemns such foolishness. 'Although it is not a desirable thing for any person to come into the workhouse', he intones, it is

> a good house, good food, clothing, and education for your children . . .
> as to what you say about separation, begging your pardon, it is pure
> humbug, because we are all separated from our children; in every
> grade of life they are obliged to be knocked about and separated from
> us . . . The rich as well as the poor, the high as well as the low, have
> their home difficulties, their sorrows and discomforts; we cannot
> expect to have everything just as we like . . . It is the law of the land
> which says that able-bodied persons are only to be relieved in the
> workhouse . . . in your sphere of life, as well as in my sphere of life,
> there are many persons who shirk work if they can . . . if we were once
> to say that out-door relief was to be given to everybody, it would be
> very difficult to draw the distinction . . . [between] an honest, hard-
> working man [and] . . . a skulking idle fellow.[373]

Cutten appears to be reassured, observing that 'these things have [never before] been explained to me in this light'. Perhaps he is moved by Walsham's wisdom and the revelation that the rich and powerful are no less oppressed than himself. Yet his change of heart is sudden for one who has refused so steadfastly to be locked away in order to obtain assistance. In a concluding statement he suggests another possibility. 'It would give me more pleasure', he observes, 'to pay Dr. Morris than to have an order from the parish.' Perhaps his 'acquiescence' is therefore a ruse, calculated to relieve him of any further oppressive imposition.[374]

Regardless of this speculation and depending on one's historiographical inclinations, it might be thought that the unwillingness of these men to accept indoor relief exemplifies the neglect to which the commissioners attribute the undue suffering of their expectant wives. Such a judgement would seem inconsistent, however, with the responses of the women them-selves, who express as much determination as the men to avoid the house and are trenchant in their defence of absent husbands. One such woman is Ellen Mitchell and her testimony, like James Cutten's, might be inscribed with sev-eral meanings. When it is suggested by MacDowall, the district Relieving Officer, that she has been less than truthful, she responds indignantly that nei-ther she nor her husband would ever lie: 'we are poor', she continues, 'but . . . we are not . . . wicked . . . we are neither drunkards nor swearers, I assure you; we are two young people; we have been married for six years'.[375] Thus adduced, her statement could be used straightforwardly to illustrate her com-mitment to respectability. Yet the broader context of her interview can also sustain a different interpretation. The cited passage is part of her response to an allegation that her husband claims falsely to have applied for relief and to have been refused. She does not recall the exact date of his application but insists he made it and that neither he nor she would lie: 'I never do such things myself, nor my husband; we are poor, but . . . we are not . . . wicked'.[376] MacDowall produces evidence that the man was at work when he supposedly applied, and, as the interrogation proceeds, stops Mitchell periodically to advise her that her evidence is inconsistent with that of her husband. Each time she pleads confusion and changes her statement.[377] It may well be imagined, as Douglas insists, that she was 'half distracted with poverty'.[378] Alternatively, it may be thought that she deliberately lied, either to strengthen the case of Douglas, her benefactor, with or without his knowledge, or because she was implicated in a fraudulent plot calculated by her husband to secure relief while employed. Yet surely, if indeed the Mitchells perpetrated either of these deceits, risking the consequences of perjury for so little gain, they were driven by need. Ellen Mitchell conveys the sense of alienation and persecution which might attend such pressing need. Her credibility undermined, she asserts excitedly that she is beset by 'slanderers', 'friends' who have proven 'enemies' and have misrepresented her husband and herself to the authorities. They are bad and deceitful, not the Mitchells: 'we are poor, but I mean to say we are not so wicked as the generality of poor people are'.[379]

Doubtless the suggested constructions do not exhaust the range of meanings with which Mitchell's testimony could be imbued. But her immediate cir-cumstances, insofar as they can be ascertained from her own testimony and the broader context of the inquiry, appear to tie her to a lonely and contemptible status. Moreover, in her expressed alienation from those above and those around her – friends who have betrayed her and authorities who judge her deceitful – she appears to repudiate any collective affinity, either with a class or 'the people'. Most of the women interviewed are less voluble than Mitchell and imply their consensus on certain 'common' attitudes: loyalty to absent husbands; gratitude to Douglas without whose help, all agree, they might have perished; and determined resistance to the workhouse,[380] the most obvious and consistent sign that they were not utterly bereft of 'agency' or 'power'. Like Mitchell, however, they can be seen to evince a deep sense of social exclusion. Evidently most did not experience the terrible isolation to which she appears to have been reduced, for they acknowledge instances of practical help from sympathetic neighbours, notably nursing aid during their confinements. But despite their common attitudes and spontaneous acts of individual kindness, they do not participate in any visible 'network'. Indeed, they lack any obvious means around which they might organize collectively, thus to seek their own advantage. Instead, to use a Foucauldian expression, they seem at once total- ized and individualized, reduced by prevailing circumstances to a common condition yet 'tied to . . . [their] own identit[ies] in a constraining way'.[381] Highly suggestive of such an interpretation is the testimony of Sarah Ann Appleby.

Nine days after confinement with her fourth child, Appleby was forced to move with her family to new lodgings when the house at which they resided was sold. Soon afterwards, her husband suffered a crushed toe at work and she was assisted to the value of 8s. a week for four weeks. On the fifth week her husband reapplied but MacDowall refused him, observing that 'if every man had what he wanted, the house would be full, and the Board would be overrun with applications'.[382] Presumably he could have taken indoor relief, though MacDowall's comment indicates that the house was offered precisely because it was widely known that few would accept it. In any case, Appleby did not apply again, but he did, according to his wife, forward to MacDowall an order from the parish doctor for nursing aid. MacDowall denies any knowledge of such an order; Mrs Appleby swears that he was reminded of it several times. But because MacDowall has no record of the matter Walsham, the committee chairman, does not pursue it. He simply ascertains that Appleby was assisted by Douglas and a neighbour while confined. She, in turn, acknowledges the kindness shown to her but insists that she depended largely on her disabled husband who could move around only '[w]ith a stick, going by the chair and the table'.[383]

Despite his incapacity, Mr Appleby went once for her relief, but the next time she had no one to send. Hence, she explains, 'I left the baby and went down myself'. The day 'was very wet and very muddy' and 'I had no bottoms to my shoes'; 'I had to sit down on my stairs when I got back, or I should have fallen down'.[384] Prefiguring the committee's judgement, one of its members, Captain Howard, observes that she had not, on this occasion, sought help from the parish and that 'however affecting the picture may be, it has nothing to do with the question of this Board refusing relief'. Her 'fainting state', he continues, 'was owing to their own want of asking'.[385] Since Appleby's testimony is substantially about the consistency with which she has been denied relief, she might well discern a lack of correspondence between official rhetoric and official practice. And she might subsequently pause to reflect on the cynicism of her examiners, for despite her inability to 'get about the place at all' when her relief was terminated, MacDowall insists that she had already returned to good health.[386] Given these experiences, she is unlikely to return to the Board. Her husband, though not yet able to walk properly, has since gone back to his job and, while there is little work to be had, both he and she seem to have learned that they must look out for themselves.[387]

Describing similar attitudes and experiences, the other women interviewed reach similar conclusions. Some note that they have taken advice from sympathetic neighbours, suggesting the possibility of a collective response to a common condition. Yet beyond their evident need, what they appear most patently to share is the inability to translate mutual sympathy into practical help. Most have resisted offers of the house and might thus be seen to demonstrate a commitment to 'independence'. But it is scarcely the respectable independence of historiographical convention, for when their men are unemployed they seek out-relief, pledge their clothes or turn to Douglas for charity. They accept that they must do so if they are to maintain their families intact, and reject as foolish the notion that their husbands are 'neglectful' because they are away in search of work. Even Sarah Morgan, who agrees that she has been 'deserted', refuses the connotations of abandonment which her examiners impute to the term. She suggests instead that, had her absent husband been employed and able to send money, she would not have spent her confinement in the house, where her children contracted a skin disease of which three subsequently died. She discharged herself, she continues, to care for her two eldest, who had also taken ill, and was awarded relief of 8s. a week. After the death of her infants, however, her allowance was reduced to 5s. and she fed the rest by pawning her clothes. When pressed, Morgan expresses her gratitude to the Board, but her decision to relinquish her 'shelter' rather than to bring in her eldest two indicates that she found the uncertainty of life abroad to be a preferable alternative.[388]

Mary Gower, the only other woman to entertain the notion that she has been deserted, also appears to find the possibility difficult to accept and speculates that her husband, who has now been gone for four years, may be dead. Refused out-relief, she has since struggled to keep herself and three children on 2–3s. a week from sewing and laundering. They share one bed, have only the clothes they wear and her daughter is without under-garments, but she will not go indoors because she does 'not like to be separated from . . . [her] children'. When it is put to her that she might take what is offered and end her destitution, she simply repeats that she does 'not like the idea of coming into the house'.[389] Destitution, she implies, is less forbidding, a view reflected in the remaining testimonies. Sarah Myers, for example, states that she had out-relief to the value of 1s. and a medical order for her sick daughter. But she could not afford to have the doctor visit, 'the child was too sick to take', and she eventually obtained help from Douglas. She did not reapply to the parish for she was convinced that she would be offered the house and was not inclined to accept. Her husband, she continues, cannot find regular employment and has earned no more than £3 in the past six months. He has not attended the interview because he may lose work by doing so. Though she stresses that she has made no further claim on the parish, a committee member interjects to allege that 'the husbands are actually at work earning money when they are getting relief'. 'I thought I could do as well as my husband,' she replies, reminding him that Douglas is their benefactor and that neither she nor her spouse has returned to the Board.[390]

A further sixteen women are interviewed, some with more delicacy, some with less, but all regard as flawed the logic whereby their examiners attempt to hold them responsible for their wretchedness. Nor will they permit their men to be blamed, for the latter, they maintain, persistently seek work, both locally and abroad.[391] Some of these men, the fortunate few, are currently employed, like Caroline Sweetingham's partner, at an income of around 10s. a week.[392] Others have earned more but only for brief periods.[393] Most have managed no more than 2–3s. a week, or nothing at all. Jane Veasey's husband has joined 'droves' of others begging bread 'from house to house';[394] Henry May 'has walked 20 or 30 miles a day over London', seeking work and begging food along the way;[395] and George Thomas has also gone on the tramp with nothing to eat, determined to 'walk till he did get something'.[396] In Thomas's absence, his wife Mary applied for relief but to obtain it she had either to send him before the Board or to charge him with desertion, upon which he 'would be liable to three months' imprisonment'.[397] The purpose of his absence is evidently irrelevant. In MacDowall's words, 'it is tantamount to desertion, people going away and leaving their families starving'.[398] MacDowall effectively reduces the men and women in question to objects of contempt, the former by putting the worst possible interpretation on their departure, the latter by summarily dismissing their mitigating explanations. The husbands might seek work and even 'independence', thus to support their families and perhaps to endow them with a measure of 'respectability', but only at the risk of being charged with desertion. The wives must lay such a charge, however ludicrous, if they are to obtain relief. This construction, though doubtless one of many to which the cited evidence could be assimilated, is nevertheless compatible with contemporary literature about the extent to which the Poor Law was designed as a deterrent.[399] No less so is the contradictory logic suggested by MacDowall's judgement. Moreover, the language of the witnesses and the profound sense of frustration and alienation which it conveys are reflected in yet further testimonies.

Most women questioned, as already noted, have refused the house although some note with regret that they have been obliged to go in for their confinements.[400] Others are advised by their examiners that further out-relief might have been obtained had they only taken the trouble to reapply. But this suggestion, when set against statements about earlier treatment of respondents and their husbands by Poor Law authorities, seems simply to be one more expression of official cynicism. To the latter, however, the women are equal, for they point out that assistance was: extended in a threatening spirit which served to deter acceptance, as in the case of Mary Thomas; contingent on impossible conditions; or accompanied by verbal abuse, any defence against which was regarded as insolence. Given the likelihood that even after enduring such treatment they might receive no more than an order for the house, their reluctance to return is scarcely surprising. Agatha Martin, for example, testifies that she was bed-ridden for five months, apparently with a lung complaint, for she 'was raising a pint or a pint and a half a day of very bad stuff'.[401] The parish doctor recommended relief and MacDowall allowed it but insisted that, for anything further, the husband must apply to the Board. Martin explained that her partner was an epileptic, subject to fits and fainting spells, and not up to doing so, but MacDowall was unmoved. He judged that the man was fit enough to work and therefore able to comply with the instruction. The committee points out that the former does not necessarily imply the latter but nevertheless finds MacDowall to have acted responsibly.[402] That he may have prevented Martin from obtaining help to which she was apparently entitled is treated as an irrelevancy.

Of far greater importance is the failure of certain women and their partners to be suitably deferential. Indeed, the purported insolence of Mary Hillyard and her husband to parish authorities exercises her examiners far more than the pledging of her belongings to pay the parish doctor. It transpires that her husband's 'rudeness' consisted in observing to MacDowall, 'I am not going before the Board', and her own in electing to appear for him when told by another officer that 'he would be imprisoned for two years' if he did not attend.[403] These 'infelicities' are of sufficient moment altogether to displace the question of whether Hillyard was adequately relieved, yet the affected sensitivity of the Board's agents in this instance is belied by their own indelicate language in others. Hence, when Ann Boyle's spouse applied for relief after being injured at work, MacDowall informed him 'that he was worse than a common beggar'. The language was justified, MacDowall implies, because the man had spent time in prison 'for fighting and drinking'. Mrs Boyle denies the charge. She holds that her husband did no more than intervene when another 'man went to strike his wife' and was wrongly convicted. She concludes that such is the fate of '[m]any an innocent person'. But her interlocutor scoffs at this notion and the chair returns discussion to the question of relief, subsequently to terminate the interview by establishing that Boyle was offered the house and therefore had no cause for complaint.[404] Both MacDowall's abuse and Boyle's defence are overlooked. That she and her husband have been insulted is of no consequence.

The extent to which the needy were deterred by such experiences must remain a matter of conjecture; that they were so deterred is a less remote possibility, for virtually all witnesses emphasize widespread determination to endure everything short of perishing to avoid going indoors. Hence, women like Elizabeth Hyde and Elizabeth Patten, who picked oakum with their husbands to obtain a few shillings' relief, subsequently resorted to Douglas and the pawnshop to feed their children as their men set out again in search of work.[405] Hyde would not ask for further relief, for people said that she would only be given 'an order to come into the house'.[406] Patten concedes: 'I could not have seen myself and my children starved. I would have come here first.'[407] Attempting to obviate the need, however, she 'pawned everything' and managed thereafter on Douglas's charity.[408] When there was no more oakum to pick, Emily Mitchell sought relief but was refused. 'I did not apply for anything more', she observes, 'because if I was refused one thing, I should not apply for another.'[409] Rather than going indoors, she relied on Douglas for food, as did Elizabeth Cabby and a woman named Scott.[410] Sarah Gallifant and Sarah Cooper present their unredeemed pawntickets to suggest that the uncertainty of life out of doors is preferable to the shelter of the house.[411] It seems clear that people like the women depicted in this story could not survive independently of society at large. To sustain themselves they had to resort to social institutions: work when it was available, charity and the pawnshop when it was not. Yet in every other sense they appear to have been alienated. Respectable types, like the gentlemen who interrogate them, seem to have regarded them as another species which might be sheltered and fed 'humanely' in the workhouse, rather like domestic livestock for which there is no immediate practical use. They, in turn, express sensitivity both to their dependency and the contempt in which they are held, but their statements suggest that they preferred to negotiate with society from a position of qualified and uncertain liberty than to accept the house where families were unceremoniously divided and humanity denied.

Doubtless, if the above testimonies were adduced to a different set of interpretative practices, it could be argued that the choices of the people in question were shaped by a commitment to respectability.[412] Emily Mitchell's refusal to ask for assistance having once been rejected, for example, might be held to signify that she valued her dignity more highly than her material need. Yet her need was at least partially supplied by Douglas, reliance on whom seems to have denied her the 'independence' on which respectability was supposedly predicated. Should Douglas's charity have become exhausted, she may have been forced to reorder her priorities, to admit like Elizabeth Patten that she could not allow herself and her children to starve. She might then have returned to the Board. Alternatively she might have contemplated suicide and have taken the irrevocable step, as some evidently did, or have thought better of it, like James Cutten.[413] Many obviously continued to go indoors, for the minutes of a further inquiry indicate that workhouse populations remained substantial in the 1890s.[414] Possibly inmates came to associate the institution with a vision of 'social inclusiveness' which demanded provision for all members of the community. Possibly, as contemporary literature suggests, they continued to regard it as the 'bastille' where, reduced to paupers, they would be forced to endure the disdain not only of the better classes but, in some instances, of people little different from themselves.[415] Indeed, certain workingmen who appear before an 1894 Royal Commission on the Aged Poor and favour the introduction of an insurance or pension scheme for their own kind, recommend that the house be retained for tramps, malingerers and wastrels who are 'no better than dirt'.[416] Such vehement language seems clearly to signify contempt but it might also reflect a degree of fear, since unforeseen disadvantage could at any time have precipitated the speakers into destitution and have rendered them liable to a similar judgement. Perhaps, however, it is more appropriate to speculate, on the basis of the cited statements and others consulted in this narrative, that Victorian society was not as integrated and harmonious as labour historians would have it.[417]

Emphasis on particular commentaries which can be made to suggest that impoverished workers were despised for their condition and socially alienated as a consequence does not 'disprove' that a labour aristocracy existed; or that workers who acquired a 'respectable independence' came to support the *status quo*; or that some individuals regarded society as inclusive and harmonious. But since there are no independent or 'objective' criteria by which 'historical truth' might be measured, the very idea of 'proof' is quite meaningless. It seems clear from the above discussion, however, that for every document cited to confirm the reality of mid-Victorian social harmony, another can be found to suggest discord and alienation, that for every indication of popular conformity to a particular kind of social identity, another can be found to the effect that identity was fluid, complex and ambiguous. It might therefore be said that the conviction of any given story lies in its oversight of problematical or countervailing 'evidence', and that current conventions about harmony and consensus can be sustained only through the exclusion of information produced persistently, decade after decade, which speaks of powerlessness, alienation and social exclusion.

Like any particular piece of evidence, all of the above commentaries can be assumed to speak most directly to the particular historical moments in which they were advanced. From the briefest interview to the 150-odd pages of Storie's autobiography, all reflect the ways in which their speakers chose, at given times, to describe their experiences. They also reflect historically specific narrative conventions and signifying practices. The subjects whose discourses have been consulted might at different times have perceived and therefore have represented their condition and themselves differently. Depending on the circumstances of the moment, each presumably made her/his choices, acted, and identified in terms of, one or some of the complex range of subject positions available to them. But the degree of correspondence between their commentaries and the 'experiences' to which those commentaries speak cannot be measured objectively, nor can the 'intended' meaning of the language employed. Already, then, we are substantially removed from the context of lived experience. Moreover, even though the evidence constituted by these documents might be 'considered against' the context of all available evidence, the apparent meaning given by the context to particular units of information effectively dissolves when those statements are abstracted, removed to different contexts and subjected to different practices.[418] 'Analysis' of particular statements might enable speculation on the range of social identities available to their authors, and on the extent to which a particular statement suggests a particular state of consciousness or a particular way of identifying at a given moment. But to define the speakers by subject positions which they *might* momentarily have occupied and to extend this definition to collectivities assumed arbitrarily to have shared their experience(s), thus to explain a further assumption – *popular acquiescence in the* status quo – is surely to move beyond hermeneutics to creative writing.

Even were this reading of the historiography held to be wrong and it were insisted that the historians in question do no more than speculate on those traces of the past preserved as documents – an unlikely defence considering the language and tenor of the various theses – the coherence of their 'speculation' depends on the exclusion of other traces. When the excluded traces are addressed and given emphasis by and within different interpretative contexts, they facilitate the production of different stories, such as that illustrated above, because the possibilities for meaning are transformed when particular statements are moved from one context to another. Hence, abstracted statements adduced to particular kinds of history appear to confirm both the prevailing currency of particular kinds of social identity and explanations to which those identities are central. But returned to the contexts from which they have been drawn and which are themselves part of a larger and largely irrecoverable context, the abstracted statements acquire a different complexion, for they are juxtaposed with other statements which often contradict them and can in turn be abstracted to generate yet further contradictions. And even if the immediate context is insufficient to the purpose of producing a novel or contradictory account, then one need simply to investigate other traces which can be made to suggest less ambiguously the meaning one wishes to convey.

Perhaps, then, the question 'Who are "the people" in mid-Victorian labour history?' cannot be resolved. But were one to ask 'Who are the subjects?', the answer, it seems, would be the subjects of the statements one chooses to consult. But because such statements are, like all discourse, highly ambiguous, and because there are no 'independent' criteria against which any particular reading of them can be measured, the accuracy of the histories to which they are adduced must remain not only relative, but relative to something other than the past to which ostensibly they speak. This is to say that such histories must acquire their meaning elsewhere and that, as narratives of the past, they should be accorded the status of fiction or myth. To demonstrate and defend this claim, I will now proceed to a discussion of the narrative form in which the histories at issue are elaborated and the political content of that form, thus to suggest that their meaning is given largely by the contexts in which they emerge and that, whether accidentally or by design, they serve very particular, recognizable and immediate interests.

4

NARRATIVE HISTORY AND THE
POLITICS OF EXCLUSION

The above discussion, in its persistent claim that historical practice is present-centred and political, has been primarily concerned to suggest the contingency of historical truth. And in recognition of its own contingency my narrative has been made repeatedly 'to reflect on itself'. Effectively, however, its self-reflection is a rhetorical device calculated to enhance the conviction of an argument which is no more objectively true or false than those it criticizes. I have employed this artifice to illustrate that, even as the 'speaker' of my narrative denies the possibility of objective truth, the narrative form functions to produce 'truth effects'. By acknowledging the political predicates of my own position in an introductory discussion, then deferring substantially to a third-person narrator for whom no such admission is made, I have created, in a manner described by Roland Barthes in 1970, the illusion of objectivity.[1] Because the third-person narrative voice is self-concealing, its referent, the putative object of its discourse, appears to 'speak itself', independently of any authorial intent. Yet I am the architect of this commentary, the author of its intended meaning and I am therefore constrained to reiterate with all possible emphasis both its political conditioning and the provisional status of any truth effects it may generate.[2]

It might, of course, be argued that to talk about my intended meaning when I have argued that the meaning of historical texts is a function of the inter-pretative context is to contradict myself. But I would reject any such argument, for my epistemological assumptions do not preclude the possibility of meaningful communication at given times within given discursive regimes. They simply indicate that the understanding which can obtain in such communities is quite unlike that allegedly gained through conventional historical practice. The former is a function of shared dialogue which permits all interested agents to ask and respond to questions whereby ambiguity might be reduced and intended meaning clarified. Clarity is, of course, not guaranteed, and ambiguity is often artfully exploited, notably in the 'doublespeak' of political discourse. Moreover, to the extent that meaning is generated and mutually understood, it is contingent on identifications within particular regimes which in turn define themselves by what they exclude. Different regimes represent different meaning systems between which, even when they co-exist, dialogue is often difficult, perhaps impossible. Yet the dialogues which historians purport to establish are with communities often chronologically and culturally distant from their own. Hence, even were one to disregard the likely incommensurability of meaning from one system to another, their claims are dubious, for when they ask questions designed to generate meaning and understanding, they must imagine the answers.[3] Their putative correspondents, the authors of the documents they consult, have become mute, and to the request 'please explain' there can be no reply.

Hence I regard dialogue with the past to be little more than a rhetorical conceit, but suggest that, within given discursive systems, intended meaning can be grasped and truth effects generated, if only temporarily and contingently. Assuming this contingency, I submit to my own critique, reducing my thesis to a proposition, the conviction of which will depend on whether readers are disposed to share my assumptions and sympathize with my agenda. My proposition thus far has been that the meaning of narrative history is constructed rather than found and that different constructions reflect different political commitments. In addition, however, I have suggested that each construction, regardless of authorial intention or political orientation, functions to validate established political authority, either by representing nineteenth-century capitalism as just and equitable or by implying that the capitalist social order is inevitable. In this chapter I will explore these ideas further. I will begin with a survey of recent debates about historical discourse, its fictive quality and political contingency, which have been engendered by the scholarship of Hayden White. I take White as my point of departure partly because his work explores the politics of historical interpretation in great depth, and partly because it has provoked responses which precisely reflect the kind of politics which he describes.

HAYDEN WHITE AND THE POLITICS
OF INTERPRETATION

According to White, the narrative form is not politically inert or neutral but functions to determine what 'facts' are admissible and the meanings with which they are inscribed. Because the meaning of historical discourse inheres not in the facts but in the historian's narrative structure, he suggests, history is a form of fiction. Since his first major work was published in 1973, White has modified his views substantially, in ways which will be discussed below. But he has never resiled from the central premise of his original argument, the notion that historians attempt to explain the past by representing it. Elaborating this premise, he writes that

> [h]istorical accounts purport to be verbal models, or icons, of specific segments of the historical process. But such models are needed because

the documentary record does not figure forth an unambiguous image of the structure of events attested in them. In order to figure 'what *really* happened' in the past, therefore, the historian must first *pre*figure as a possible object of knowledge the whole set of events reported in the documents. This prefigurative act is *poetic* inasmuch as it is precognitive and precritical in the economy of the historian's own consciousness. It is also poetic insofar as it is constitutive of the structure that will subsequently be imaged in the verbal model offered by the historian as a representation and explanation of 'what *really* happened' in the past. But it is constitutive not only of a domain which the historian can treat as a possible object of (mental) perception. It is also constitutive of the *concepts* he will use *to identify the objects* that inhabit the domain and *to characterize the kinds of relationships* they can sustain with one another. In the poetic act which precedes the formal analysis of the field, the historian both creates his object of analysis and predetermines the modality of the conceptual strategies he will use to explain it.[4]

The historian's practice, White proceeds, involves three kinds of strategy: 'formal argument, explanation by emplotment and explanation by ideological implication'. Each of these strategies contains 'four possible modes of articulation' which relate in turn to four principal tropes or modes of consciousness: metaphor, metonymy, synechdoche and irony. Because these tropes function respectively to represent, to reduce, to integrate and to negate, each 'provides the basis for a distinctive linguistic protocol by which to prefigure the historical field and on the basis of which specific strategies of historical interpretation can be employed for "explaining" it'.[5] Although each produces a different 'explanatory affect [sic]', all purport to represent reality (or truthfully to reflect the historical record) and all appear, from a metahistorical perspective, to be equally plausible.[6] On the basis of this exposition, White urges historians to 'rethink their representational choices in light of their political and aesthetic commitments'.[7] They might begin, he suggests, by considering alternatives to 'irony' which in his view has been the dominant trope in twentieth-century historiography.

He then explores the limits of 'irony' as a narrative mode. 'Dialectical', he writes, in that it apprehends 'the capacity of language to obscure more than it clarifies in any act of verbal figuration', 'irony' forces figurative language to question 'its own potentialities for distorting perception' so that ironic characterizations seem self-critical, sophisticated and realistic. '[A] model of the linguistic protocol in which skepticism in thought and relativism in ethics are conventionally expressed', it appears, when '[e]xistentially projected into a full-blown world view . . . to be transideological'. It 'can be used *tactically*', he proceeds,

for defense of either Liberal or Conservative ideological positions, depending on whether the Ironist is speaking against established social forms or against 'utopian' reformers seeking to change the status quo. And it can be used offensively by the Anarchist and the Radical, to pillory the ideals of their Liberal and Conservative opponents. But, as the basis of a world view, Irony tends to dissolve all belief in the possibility of positive political actions. In its apprehension of the essential folly or absurdity of the human condition, it tends to engender belief in the 'madness' of civilization itself and to inspire a Mandarin-like disdain for those seeking to grasp the nature of social reality in either science or art.[8]

In one sense, the histories to which I have addressed myself seem to dispute this characterization of modern historiography. They reflect neither the disdain to which White refers nor the world view he describes. Their authors are centrally concerned with exploring the nature of social reality and could thus be said to engage in the very enterprise for which White's full-blown ironist must affect disdain. Indeed, they represent a society both orderly and inevitable, in which the *status quo* is accommodative (though implicitly inviolable), and in which workers effectively 'give in to win', acquiring 'independence' by accepting their subordination and dependency. According to White, however, such visions of order conceal the chaos in which historical data reside and 'deprive history of the kind of meaninglessness that alone can goad living human beings to make their lives different'.[9] But before pursuing these ideas further, I will consider critiques of White's scholarship, for it has been widely rejected by historians as formalist, relativist, devoid of any sensitivity to what they actually do, and overtly political.

Together these charges constitute a critical ensemble which suggests that the relativism whereby White reduces historical truth to a political function can be sustained only because he focuses on the narrative form of historical discourse to the exclusion of its content. As White himself puts it, the formalism whereby he holds 'that any historical object can sustain a number of equally plausible descriptions' is alleged effectively to 'deny the reality of the referent and [to] promote a debilitating relativism that permits any manipulation of the evidence as long as the account produced is structurally coherent'.[10] Hence Carlo Ginzburg suggests that White, because of his inattention to content and context, fails to appreciate that texts can be understood with 'reference to extra-textual realities' and that such realities can be controlled through careful textual criticism.[11] Casting his net more widely, Arthur Marwick includes White in an undifferentiated community of 'postmodernists'. The latter, Marwick observes, neglect to acquaint themselves with proper historical procedures and claim novelty for insights so ordinary that they might more properly be termed 'pre-modernist'.[12] In a similar vein Gertrude Himmelfarb insists that historians 'have always known what postmodernism professes to have just discovered – that any work of history is vulnerable on three counts: the fallibility and deficiency of the historical record . . . the fallibility and selectivity inherent in the writing of history; and the fallibility and subjectivity of the historian'. They have also been acutely aware, she adds, that their assumptions 'reflect the particular [culture,] race, gender and class to which they belong' and 'emanate from ideas and beliefs that are unique to themselves as individuals'.[13]

These 'relativist' insights may well be enjoyed by historians but they are not generally reflected in historical treatises which continue to be written as though their validity were transparent. Nor, to my knowledge, do postmodernists claim to have 'discovered' relativism, although they may suggest their novelty in other ways. Indeed, White notes repeatedly that his critique reflects one which emerged with the Enlightenment, when history sought to detach itself from literature, thus to acquire a status equal to that of the natural sciences. In any case, if his ideas speak significantly to historical practice – and my own thesis suggests that they do – it is difficult to understand why the vintage of those ideas should be an issue. The foregoing discussion seems clearly to illustrate that historical objects can sustain a variety of descriptions or meanings and that the latter are prefigured by the kinds of questions historians ask, questions politically (and ideologically) predicated, which order narrative history from within and induce particular kinds of representation. White himself explains that 'tropology is a theory of discourse, not of mind or consciousness. Although it assumes that figuration cannot be avoided in discourse, the theory, far from implying linguistic determinism, seeks to provide the knowledge necessary for a free choice among different strategies of figuration.'[14] It is in this connection that his work is relevant to historical practice, for although historians may refer to events, they deal in facts, or events under description. Their project is therefore discursive and as susceptible to 'formalist' analysis as any other discourse. White never denies the reality of events; he simply focuses his discussion on the range of possibilities for their description, on representation rather than referent. But historians are generally unmoved by such qualifications, insisting that they are calculated to obscure both the political purpose and the profound political implications of a postmodernism which they deplore.

Among the most recent critics to pursue this line are Arthur Marwick, as noted above, and Keith Windschuttle. Both regard White as an exemplar of postmodernism and postmodernism as nothing other than Marxism in disguise, an incubus spawned by the Left to destroy the humanities. History is especially vulnerable, writes Marwick, for the agents of this menace cultivate the belief that it is worthless ideology which must be replaced by one 'shaped to the needs of contemporary radical politics'. The very professionals on whom society depends to expose such propaganda, he warns, are thereby undermined.[15] Windschuttle is, if anything, even more explicit: 'Most young people today', he observes, are 'taught to scorn the traditional values of Western culture – equality, freedom, democracy, human rights – as hollow rhetoric used to mask the self-interest of the wealthy and powerful.'[16] He calls his book *The*

Killing of History and his subtitle proclaims that 'the discipline is being murdered by literary critics and social theorists'. Also implicated are semioticians,
cultural relativists, structuralists, poststructuralists, anti-humanists, genealo-
gists, discourse theorists, Hegelian and Marxist philosophers of history, new
historicists and hermeneuticists, who together comprise 'the old New Left
crowd from the 1960s'.[17] Portraying themselves as embattled outsiders, these
dissidents, according to Windschuttle, have infiltrated and hopelessly politicized the academy, diverting the humanities and social sciences from the
pursuit of objectivity and truth to the kind of relativism which White promotes.[18] Not all of White's critics are as strident as Marwick and
Windschuttle, yet even in more restrained commentaries his relativism has
been equated, as Kansteiner notes, with 'the ruthless pragmatics of fascist
politics'.[19]

In my view such charges are misdirected. The burden of White's scholarship
is neither to promote nor to spell out a political agenda, but to emphasize the
political contingency of all historical writing, and especially of the philosophy
of history which he himself practises. Unlike Marwick and Windschuttle, who
imply their own detachment by deploring the partisanship of postmodernists,
he does not pretend to be apolitical, but his politics, rather than reflecting fascism, are calculated to subvert the absolutes to which it appeals. As I have
indicated, the politics of interpretation and the political contingency of mid-
Victorian labour history constitute the primary concern of this chapter and
will be addressed with reference to White's scholarship. But because I am
morally and politically opposed to the Holocaust 'revisionism' which his relativism is alleged to invite, I will first evaluate the allegation and White's
response. To recapitulate, it is argued that White, in asserting the political
contingency of historical truth, rejects the possibility of factual verification
and renders any narrative emplotment of the past valid – for example, one
which denies that the Holocaust occurred – provided it is structurally coherent. In responding to this charge, White lacks his usual clarity, perhaps, as
Wulf Kansteiner suggests, because he is reluctant to destabilize a political
position opposed to fascism, a position which in principle he supports,
'although it might be based on illusory epistemological assumptions'.[20]
Hence, he pronounces the 'revisionist' denial of the Holocaust 'as morally
offensive as it is intellectually bewildering', and thereby seems to overlook his
own distinction between event and fact, or between the referent of historical
discourse and its linguistic description.[21] As a consequence, the 'fact', or the
'Holocaust', ceases to be 'an event under a description' and becomes an event
in itself. This formulation subverts the notion that all truth is conditional and
undercuts the democratic thrust of White's agenda, which explicitly is 'to provide the knowledge necessary for a free choice among different strategies of
figuration', and implicitly to illuminate the contingency of every interpretation so that each might be assessed on the basis of its political implications.[22]
But it also strains against the spirit and logic of everything else that he has

written. It occurs, in fact, in an essay which considers the possibility that history itself is meaningless, and therefore seems less a departure than an oversight.[23]

Consistently with White's characterization, it could be said that under the Nazi regime a multiplicity of atrocities was committed against European Jews, and each in its own right was an event capable of sustaining a range of descriptions. These events have been transformed descriptively and retrospectively into a fact called the Holocaust, the Genocide or the Shoah, and the fact, rather than the events to which it refers, has become the primary object of historical narrative. Hence, in the process of conferring meaning, description has transformed many events into a single fact which has subsequently displaced them in historical discourse. Advancing different descriptions, certain 'revisionists' have subsequently denied not only the fact but the events to which it refers, and insofar as they treat the Holocaust as a discursive construction, retrospectively imposed, their arguments are structurally coherent. But that coherence dissolves when they deny the reality of the referent, or of events exhaustively documented. The meaning of those events may depend on how the documents are interrogated, but their occurrence could be convincingly denied only if the documents ceased to exist.[24] White acknowledges that this kind of distinction might be difficult to make 'with respect to historical events less amply documented than the Holocaust',[25] but what historians seem most to object to is that the distinction itself fails to rule out structurally coherent histories sympathetic to Nazism which *do not* deny the reality of events.[26] When such objections are raised, their proponents invariably evade the problem which in White's view (and mine) renders all historical representation 'relativist': the absence of any necessary correspondence either between meaning imputed to historical artefacts and their putatively intrinsic meaning, or 'between factual statements and the means of emplotment which are employed to craft the narrative'.[27] It seems, therefore, that opposition to certain kinds of historical emplotment reflects something more or other than logic, and that it is not to relativism *per se* that White's opponents object, but to his illumination of their own relativist practices.[28]

Drawing similar conclusions, Kansteiner asks how 'unwanted emplotments of the past' might effectively be displaced 'without recourse to the concept of historical truth'.[29] In doing so he raises further questions which reflect the interpretative politics presently to be discussed: in the absence of any such concept, on what grounds other than those of morality, politics or taste could certain emplotments be judged undesirable or unwanted? Who would make such a judgement and on what authority? If one were to agree with Sande Cohen that White's purpose is to provide a new justification for history writing, then Kansteiner's question suggests that White has failed in the attempt, at least thus far.[30] Understood differently, however, White's project may be more useful. There is every indication that conflicting stories about the past will continue to be told, and every possibility that they will continue to reflect particular positions on a left–right political spectrum. By emphasizing another possibility, the meaninglessness of history itself, White identifies a position effectively outside the conventional historical paradigm from which it is possible to speculate on the contingency of historical narratives, the assumptions which inform them, the interests to which they correspond and the social consequences to which they conduce.[31] It is to this possibility that he addresses himself in a discussion of interpretative politics.

In this discussion White suggests that the ostensibly apolitical practices whereby historians impose order and meaning on the past function invariably to underwrite established political authority, and that their subordination to this function was a precondition of history's disciplinization in the nineteenth century.[32] While history remained a literary genre, he argues, the past remained a 'repository of tradition, moral exemplars, and admonitory lessons', all of which could be interpreted as widely 'as rhetorical practice, political partisanship and confessional variation admitted'.[33] Hence, with equal conviction, it could be made to figure forth stories of progress which valorized the prevailing social and political order, or 'a panorama of failure, duplicity, fraud, deceit, and stupidity' which justified utopian programmes of social and political reconstruction. Because such programmes abounded at the time and were informed by particular philosophies of history, it made eminently good sense, he finds, to constitute a discipline concerned solely with the facts of history whereby 'the objectivity, veridicality and realism' of each philosophy could be assessed.[34] Moreover, although the discipline conferred unmistakable ideological benefits on ascendant social classes and political constituencies, it could be justified theoretically and epistemologically with the claim that it opposed historical consciousness to utopian thinking and empirical rigour to metaphysical speculation.[35] But although the kind of historical knowledge subsequently produced became 'the standard of realism in political thought and action in general', he concludes, its theoretical and epistemological predicates are dubious.[36] At one level, they lend the appearance of political neutrality to a discipline which validates prevailing political authority by rejecting as 'metaphysical' the philosophies which authorize political alternatives. At another, they conceal the metaphysics of the 'realism' against which those philosophies are found wanting so that realism itself becomes merely a reflection of whatever currently prevails as educated common sense.

Paradoxically, history's disciplinization was justified on the basis that, as an empirical practice, it should be distinguished from literature. Hence, although it was not designated a science, its special status was ratified on the basis of its 'scientific' methodology.[37] Yet, as White indicates, it did not and never could attain 'to the theoretical and methodological regimentation that characterizes the physical sciences'.[38] Because the objects of historical study – humanity, society and culture – possess an element of autonomy, they cannot be 'explained' as instances of the operation of universal causal laws, in the way that physical scientists endeavour to explain natural phenomena. Historians therefore aspire to understand their objects through interpretation, and narrative history functions both as interpretative method and 'the mode of discourse in which a successful understanding of matters historical is represented'.[39] Attempts to transform history into a science have, in White's view, been undertaken almost invariably in the name of politics deemed progressive: liberalism in the case of positivism and socialism in that of Marxism. And invariably they have been resisted as political and utopian, though ironically, as noted above, resistance has been underpinned by 'values manifestly conservative or reactionary'. The politics of interpretation seem to turn, therefore, precisely on 'the question of the political uses to which knowledge thought to be specifically historical can and ought to be put'.[40] And it poses a problem which in his view lies 'not with philosophy of history, which is at least openly political, but with a conception of historical studies that purports to be above politics and at the same time rules out as unrealistic any political program or thought in the least tinged with utopianism'.[41] To illuminate this problem, White then examines more fully the proscriptions which disciplinization entailed.[42]

He begins this examination by citing Kant to the effect that what could be known from a study of history was reducible to three possibilities: 'that the human race was progressing continually'; that it 'was degenerating continually'; and that it 'remained at the same general level of development continually'.[43] While historical discourse remained subordinated to rhetoric, White observes, the historical field had to be viewed as chaotic, making 'no sense at all' or 'as many senses as wit and rhetorical talent could impose upon it', hence the likelihood that it would be conceived solely in terms of Kant's third alternative. Accordingly, if history was to become a distinctive kind of knowledge against which contending political programmes and their attendant philosophies could be evaluated, its rhetorical and fictive aspects had to be suppressed.[44] He regards the effort to do so as 'a rhetorical move in its own right'. Little more than a restatement of Aristotle's distinction between history and poetry, or between the study of 'real' and 'imagined' events, it served to affirm 'the fiction that the historian's stories are found in the evidence rather than invented'.[45]

Nevertheless, White proceeds, precisely because narrative histories take a rhetorical form – the declamative or deliberative mode of the middle style – they lend themselves to rhetorical analysis, which reveals them to entail stylistic exclusions and hence the exclusion of certain kinds of event: those deemed miraculous, magical or godly on the one hand, and those conceived to be the stuff of farce, satire and calumny on the other. These two orders of exclusion, he argues, constitute rules of evidence which serve to discipline the historical imagination, to limit 'what constitutes a specifically historical event', and to determine the ways in which the past can be described, since the categorization of events as real or imagined is always a function of 'what currently passes as educated common sense'.[46] Proceeding, White observes that the historical imagination takes a decidedly modern turn with the effort 'to enter sympathetically into the minds . . . of human agents long dead', and thus prefigures a conception of objectivity quite different from anything 'meant by that term in the physical sciences'.[47] The rules of evidence might possibly function as a rational constraint so that political and moral prejudice do not lead the historian to misread or misrepresent the documents, but 'sympathetic identification' defies rational measurement or verification. Moreover, when idiosyncratic views of 'what really happened' are set forth in narrative, the imagination functions precisely as it does in 'the activity of the poet or novelist', for an operation 'openly admitted to be literary supervenes'.[48] Because this operation is literary, its disciplinization 'entails an aesthetic regulation' whereby the beautiful displaces the sublime and the aesthetic sense, subordinated to 'judgements appropriate to the beautiful', is 'relegated to the rule of the cognitive and moral faculties'.[49] But if the literary character of this operation is acknowledged, its political character is not. It may seem possible to distinguish historical thinking from the kind which allows that the past can 'bear as many senses as wit and rhetorical talent' can devise, and, by investigating the mass of historical data available, to discern order and meaning in the past.[50] It might therefore be deemed appropriate to enhance any such investigation by discriminating between the rational and the irrational, the beautiful and the sublime, or real and imagined events. Yet neither the aesthetics which effects this displacement nor the logic which authorizes it should be seen as neutral, even though, according to White, they have generally been accepted as uncritically 'by Marxists as by their conservative and liberal counterparts'.[51] Indeed, he suggests, they are calculated to inhibit agency by 'restricting speculation on any ideal social order to some variant in which freedom [i]s apprehended less in an exercise of individual will than as a release of beautiful feelings'.[52]

To demonstrate that these effects have been apprehended historically, White refers to the writings of Friedrich von Schiller. For Schiller, the ascendant aesthetics reflected 'falsely construed forbearance' and 'effeminate taste' which served to 'cast a veil over the solemn face of necessity and, in order to curry favour with the senses, [to] *counterfeit* a harmony between good fortune and good behaviour of which not a trace is to be found in the actual world'. Schiller attributes this judgement to history, which he regards as a spectacle of change both terrifying and pathetic, 'which destroys everything and creates it anew, and destroys again'; and in which humanity 'wrestl[es] with fate, the irresistable [sic] illusiveness of happiness, confidence betrayed, unrighteousness triumphant and innocence laid low'.[53] In White's view, such conceptions had to be displaced if history was to serve as an object of knowledge and deprived of the terror it induced as a 'panorama of sin and suffering'. And displacement was achieved, he proceeds, by German idealism, which subsequently shaped both 'radical and conservative thought about the kind of utopian existence mankind could justifiably envisage as the ideal aim or goal of any putatively progressive historical process'.[54]

'Presid[ing] over the process in which historical studies are constituted as a . . . discipline', this aesthetic produces a number of consequences, according to White, for 'both the Left and the Right'.[55] It induces 'respect for the "individuality", "uniqueness", and "ineffability" of historical entities, sensitivity to the "richness" and "variety" of the historical field, and a faith in the "unity" that makes of finite sets of historical particulars comprehensible wholes'. It also informs a professional tendency to treat any "confusion" displayed by the historical record . . . [as] a surface phenomenon: a product of lacunae in the documentary sources, of mistakes in ordering the archives, or of previous inattention or scholarly errors'. And it predisposes historians to find something good or beautiful in everything human, to remain calm in current crises, to favour epistemological pluralism, to suspect reductionism, to eschew theory, to disdain jargon, and to affect contempt for 'any effort to discern the direction that the future development of [their] own society might take'.[56] Successfully countering every 'impulse to use history as the basis either of a science or a visionary politics' and thereby serving to proscribe histories of the sublime like Schiller's, these attitudes, White indicates, are politically domesticating. They create the impression that historical events are comprehensible or explicable and they do so by ruling out the possibility that they might be neither. Yet the 'proper historical understanding' which they supposedly reflect, he argues, is always revealed by analysis 'to be of an essentially aesthetic nature', a matter of taste and style. And it is inimical to a politics 'more concerned to endow social life with meaning than with beauty', because it denies what in White's view the theorists of the sublime correctly divined: that 'whatever dignity and freedom human beings could lay claim to could come only by way of what Freud called a "reaction-formation" to an apperception of history's meaninglessness'.[57]

To say that White's work is political, then, is to state the obvious, but to object to it on this basis looks suspiciously like special pleading, for under his scrutiny his critics, and the practices which they defend, seem equally political. They also seem unremittingly conservative, and even Marxism, according to White, is implicated, for as a philosophy of history it is anti-utopian and suggests like its bourgeois counterpart 'that history is not a sublime spectacle but a comprehensible process the various parts, stages, epochs and even individual events of which are transparent to a consciousness endowed with the means to make sense of it in one way or another'.[58] Moreover, the politics of interpretation which he describes appears indeed to proceed from an aesthetic which proscribes the 'sublime', the 'unmanageable', the 'chaotic', and generates the impression of order by privileging what prevailing common sense can render meaningful. My own analysis, in its emphasis on the exclusions from which orderly representation proceeds, suggests the operation of this aesthetic in the works I address. But the aspect of White's commentary which I find most compelling is one which parallels my emphasis on the absence of independent criteria whereby historians might determine whether the meanings imputed to historical artefacts and their putatively intrinsic meanings correspond. For even if one were to reject the aesthetic proposed by White and to attribute the historian's choice of illustrative material to other causes, one could not, insofar as I can tell, resolve the indeterminacy which, in Wulf Kansteiner's words, White has identified 'between different types of historical knowledge on the one hand and different narrative accounts written from incompatible theoretical and political positions on the other'.[59] It remains, now, to consider the ways in which the labour historians with whom I have engaged reflect in their interpretative practices the politics and the aesthetic which White describes.

THE CONTENT OF THE FORM
IN LABOUR HISTORY

In a sense, the focus of mid-Victorian labour history has been given by the historiography of Chartism. In accounts of Chartism, 1848 marks the end of organized mass protest and functions to effect narrative closure. The subsequent period is treated as little more than a postscript, a time during which attempts to revive the movement were unsuccessful and 'relative' political quietude prevailed. When the mid-Victorian decades became an object of historical interest in the 1950s and of vigorous debate in the 1970s, absence of conflict became the problematic, though one which was to remain 'underproblematized'. Like any object of explanation, it has shaped the narratives which describe it and these narratives subsequently function to confirm its historical reality. Description varies, and I have attempted to relate this variety to political orientation, but I have also proposed a deeper political effect whereby each representation, regardless of its apparent political predicates, suggests the inviolability of the capitalist system and the omnipotence of the interests which control it. This effect appears to be produced by a narrative mode which functions persistently to order the past according to present-centred logic, excluding as meaningless any 'evidence' which cannot service the dominant truths currently reflected in educated common sense. Existing power relations are thus projected into the past, futile attempts to subvert them are described and their permanence is confirmed.

As I indicated in Chapter 1, the first post-war labour historians to engage specifically with the mid-Victorian period were Marxists like Hobsbawm, Harrison and Foster, who endorsed an account of historical progress in which class consciousness and class struggle should culminate in the triumph of labour and the institution of proletarian dictatorship. Convinced that Chartism exemplified class struggle, these commentators assumed that its decline signified the diversion of working people to reformism, which they regarded as a manifestation of false consciousness.[60] The means by which this purported diversion was achieved then became the object of explanation. As relative absence of conflict was transformed prefiguratively into reformism, the qualifying term seemed to slip away and with it any suggestion that the postulated condition was not universal. The mid-Victorian period became an orderly spectacle in which even 'struggle' and 'conflict' were divested of any 'chaotic' possibility, an orchestrated contest in which 'revolution' was displaced by 'reformism'. The reason for this development was all that remained to be considered. Elaborated by committed Marxists during the 1950s and 1960s, when socialism seemed a viable alternative, this construction could be seen as an attempt to restore working people to revolutionary consciousness. But if such was the purpose of its architects, they would subsequently if tacitly concede defeat. They held their peace during the 1970s and for some years after the political Left had drawn its last breath. By the mid-1980s, however, they were deploring the tenacity of reformism and asking why labour 'had taken the path it had'.[61] Evidently they did not suspect that they may have facilitated the return of the Right by affirming, albeit inadvertently, the 'truth' of its historical superiority. Nor, it seems, did they allow that the 'absence' which they described as reformism, thus to construct their problematic, may have been susceptible of other descriptions with other, equally plausible, consequences.[62]

But other descriptions were imminent. As 1979 and the triumph of Thatcherism approached, former Marxist conventions looked increasingly fanciful, and one of the first to be abandoned was the concept of false consciousness. The latter, it was suggested, implied 'true' consciousness and articulated the past to an artificial and distorting teleology.[63] Hence revolution ceased to be the necessary end-point of class struggle. With this departure, the object of explanation was further transformed. The earlier equation of quietude with reformism was retained, but Marxists and liberals alike now described this condition as social stability and its predicates as negotiation and consensus. Stability was recognized in the first instance to have been 'relative' but the qualifier again quickly receded. When moments of discord were identified they were not investigated; they were simply said to have been 'contained' within existing social structures and of little overall significance to the prevailing condition. The possibility that discord was a manifestation of discontents to which reformism did not speak and which a reformist problematic might function to obscure was effectively discounted. Stability was then further finessed in some accounts to become social harmony and popular acquiescence in the prevailing social and political order.

Writing in 1976, for example, the liberal Trygve Tholfsen defined his object of enquiry as 'the relative quiescence of the age of equipoise'.[64] 'Although the mid-Victorian working man preserved his radicalism and independence', Tholfsen observed,

> he was nevertheless well integrated into a remarkably cohesive culture – a tightly knit structure of values, institutions, roles and ritual – built on a social base dominated by the middle classes. A firm

consensus on basic values had been established, especially on the over-riding importance of the moral and intellectual improvement of the individual.[65]

Stated as established fact, these remarks appeared, paradoxically, on the first two pages of an introductory chapter entitled 'Problems of Interpretation'. The subsequent narrative functioned to 'illustrate' the condition foreshadowed by these assertions and thus to 'explain' the negotiated consent of working people to middle-class predominance.

In the same year R.Q. Gray published a local study of Victorian Edinburgh which he introduced as an enquiry into 'the nature of class domi-nation in the nineteenth century'. He would proceed, he explained, by considering how 'the existence of the labour aristocracy helped to stabilize the class structure of capitalist society'. Electing to treat 'hegemony' and 'sta-bility' as historically given, he prefigured a past in which the prevailing condition was constituted as an orderly reflection of these concepts.[66] The question of why the purported condition obtained then shaped a narrative in which the negotiation of popular consent became a disciplined process of ideological incorporation: industrial conflict was 'contained within a society dominated by the bourgeoisie'; dissident values and practices were struc-turally transformed, and middle-class values, adapted to popular experience, became both the substance of working-class respectability and a means to independence. Towards the end of the century, Gray suggested, hegemony was eroded by socialist influences which served to revive class conscious-ness.[67] But a chronology which functioned to effect narrative closure precluded speculation on this development. Hence what seems to be an inconsistency, whereby hegemony is held to have been subverted yet power relations in which it was embodied remained and continue to remain intact, was not addressed.

Entering the debate in 1979, Geoffrey Crossick also began by assuming the 'relative stability' of mid-Victorian society. He introduced his commentary with a rejection of Tholfsen's argument but an endorsement of his conclusions, suggesting that 'stability' resulted from 'a process of continuing struggle, in which the features of a class society determined the outcome in only the most generalized way'.[68] His narrative then proceeded as a description of this sup-posed process and in most respects resembled Gray's. Their arguments, of course, were not identical: Crossick, for example, found that 'struggle' consti-tuted resistance to hegemony while Gray argued that it was hegemonically contained; and while Gray portrayed respectability as a solution to the 'prob-lems of economic survival', Crossick went further to suggest that it was also a way of coping with inequality.[69] But both elaborated narratives in which the stability foreshadowed by introductory assumptions was persistently stressed. By persistent assertion, stability had acquired the status of fact and was presently to be endowed with further connotations.

In the preface to his 1985 Marxist study of the mid-Victorian condition, Neville Kirk adopted Tholfsen's formulation, equating 'stability' with popular acquiescence in the *status quo*. As 'the broad features of the social system increasingly came to be seen as permanent', he asserted, 'workers sought their "emancipation" not in a "revolving of the whole system", but in gradual, limited, piecemeal reformism'.[70] His project, he observed, was a local study of Lancashire and Cheshire, but he would comment on the significance of developments such as the 'decline of class consciousness' and 'the overall stabilisation of British capitalism during the third quarter [of the nineteenth century]'.[71] Hence, before his analysis began, he outlined a conceptual economy in which apparent quietude became synonymous with 'acquiescence', 'social calm', 'social harmony', 'the decline of revolutionary class consciousness' and 'the stabilisation of British capitalism'. These terms functioned to predetermine, in a brief prefatory statement, not only a context and an object of analysis, but a narrative in which, by representation, the postulated condition would be 'explained' and confirmed.

Patrick Joyce adopted a similar procedure in 1991. Despite his claim to postmodern novelty, his introductory discussion betrayed not only a thoroughly modern understanding of language and discourse but a very conventional prefigurative strategy. Evidently unconcerned that his chosen period, 1840 to 1914, might be susceptible of a range of descriptions, he asserted unproblematically that 'the years from the decline of Chartism to the First World War do have a certain unity. They were bracketed by periods of crisis and conflict. They were, broadly, years of consolidation, the consolidation of industrial capitalism, of political democracy, of a new urban culture.'[72] There prevailed, he continued, a very powerful current of feeling, both utopian and religious. It was grounded in a shared vision of 'justice', 'fellowship' and 'human reconciliation', a vision in the likeness of which 'the people [and] the labouring poor . . . saw and made' themselves. These and similar statements were foundational. They constituted a 'landscape' within which the 'populism' envisaged by Joyce could be constructed, and were part of a knowledge which he insisted we 'need to extend'. They were not covered by the 'provisional' caveat which he attached to his authoritatively stated account of social identity.[73] With regard to the latter it is interesting to note, Joyce's designated focus on language notwithstanding, that the term 'populism', unlike the term 'class', is conspicuously absent from his illustrative material. The 'populist identity' foreshadowed in his introduction subsequently emerges as a product of his own narrative rather than of contemporary discourse, in traces of which references to 'the people' are characteristically ambiguous.

The decline of organized mass politics after 1848 is well documented, and the contemporary writings examined above seem, on face value, to indicate that certain mid-Victorian workingmen favoured a 'reformist' approach to the resolution of social problems. But the men consulted comprised a tiny minority and, although they may have been 'leaders' of working-class institutions, their outspoken emphasis on the alterity of their constituents suggests that they might not have represented the views of common workers. And even were one to accept that the Chartist movement was a manifestation of revolutionary class consciousness, it does not follow, as Marxists seem to assume, that its decline *necessarily* signified the broad conversion of working people to a 'reformist' mentality. 'Absence of conflict', as I have argued, can sustain a range of meanings. Hence, in Chapter 3, I illuminated a range of perceptions, sufficiently diverse in all but their pessimism, to mock any suggestion of order, progress or broad conformity to a particular mode of consciousness. The people whose statements I consulted say nothing about activism but a great deal about alienation and social fragmentation. Some convey a sense of reluctant resignation, others of desperate opportunism. Yet others hint that, beneath the façade of respectability, they may have engaged in practices deemed disreputable or illegal to sustain themselves. All describe a struggle for existence characterized by unremitting crisis and uncertainty, in which there was no 'time out' for reformism or any other social experiment.

The voices of such people are silenced by terms like 'reformism', 'stability' and 'harmony', which add considerable and significant content to what formerly was simply an absence. By using these terms, historians constitute a domain of mental perception, lend substance to the concepts (respectability and independence) by which its inhabiting objects will be identified, and confer meaning on the relationship (consensus and harmony) in which those objects will be said to exist. This arrangement precludes any serious consideration of discontent. Moreover, when it becomes the object of explanation in Marxist histories, it seems to subvert them politically, eliminating the possibility of historical progress towards a revolutionary utopia and thus repudiating a central Marxist tenet. Yet although the problematic is adopted by Marxists and liberals alike, it is never 'theorized' or defended; it is established prefiguratively, before analysis and debate begin. Some might, of course, argue that the represented condition is confirmed by the narratives which illustrate it, or by the collective scholarship of other historians. But to argue thus would simply be to concede that historians 'explain' the past by representing it, and the question of why they choose to describe 'relative absence' in a particular way would remain unanswered. The choice cannot be reduced to logic, for other equally plausible descriptions are available. And if its predicates are moral or political, then like morality and politics, it is ultimately a matter of taste. The choice therefore seems to reflect the aesthetic described by White, whereby events which do not lend themselves to orderly representation are excluded in an imaginative or poetic moment. Moreover, precisely as White argues, orderly representation is subject to change and, from one historiographical revision to the next, change is articulated to what currently passes for educated common sense. Hence, while socialist revolution seemed possible, the decline of Chartism could be attributed by those on the Left to false consciousness. But in the mid-1970s, when the political Left went into a period of crisis and decline, this possibility seemed remote, 'false consciousness' lost its explanatory appeal and 'revolution' faded from discussion.[74] Having dispensed with these conventions, Marxists found other ways of ordering the past.

Revisionists on the Left and Right have been equally discriminating at the theoretical level. They predicate their theses on paradigms or assumptions which imply the need for self-reflexivity but then exempt their own practices from scrutiny. Joyce, for example, assumes that the meaning of identity and experience is linguistically determined. Proceeding from this assumption, he treats the documents with which he engages as discourses, finds them rich with references to 'the people' and concludes that, in the nineteenth century, the prevailing social identity was populist. Yet he does not address the possibility that, if meaning is a function of discourse, then that of his own narrative might be given discursively in the 1990s rather than found in the historical record. Nor is this possibility explored in his recent publication, *Democratic Subjects*, a history of 'the self' and 'the social' in which he revisits certain evidence consulted in *Visions of the People*.[75] The evidence consists largely of writings by and about two supposedly representative individuals, the erstwhile workingman Edwin Waugh and the mill-owner John Bright. Adduced to a narrative which functions effectively to recapitulate Joyce's earlier thesis, they project persistent images of a 'populism' which transcended class and other social divisions.[76] Joyce nevertheless suggests that the volume is a departure informed by his increased sensitivity to postmodern insights and his recognition that language is not only determinative but constitutive.[77] As a consequence, he treats his sources as manifestations not of experience itself but of a 'protean social imaginary' to which discourse gave rise and which in turn prefigured categories like 'experience', 'society' and 'the people'. Whereas previously he thought of 'the people' as a foundational entity, a collective subject which pre-existed language and constructed meaning, he now understands that discourse constructs categories, meanings and subjects, and he interprets the former to understand the latter.[78]

This construction renders modern hermeneutics nicely into postmodern language, but it does not substantially alter Joyce's approach. His ongoing discussion of narrative might indicate a high level of theoretical sophistication, but his practice seems frequently to be at odds with the theory he espouses. He emphasizes, for example, that poverty and insecurity are manifestations not of an 'originary' experience but of 'culture'. To overlook the discursive character of such categories, he explains, is to obscure how experience was handled and constructed, or how people put it 'together in the first place'.[79] Yet the 'people' in his story remain anonymous and silent while their experience is 'constructed', 'handled' and 'circulated' in narratives such as those elaborated by Edwin Waugh.[80] With similar inconsistency, he disdains ontological foundationalism and 'essentialist' notions of an epistemological 'bottom line', then proceeds to speak persistently of foundations and essences.[81] Hence, as his account of identity and experience unfolds, he observes that Waugh's 'was an essential voice of the poor's condition'; that his narratives were 'an essential expression of the autodidact spirit'; that the latter was 'an essential spirit of the Victorian era'; and that narrative itself 'is *an ontological condition of social life*'.[82]

This theoretical inconsistency enables Joyce to produce characteristically modern truth effects, but it also signifies a lack of critical self-reflection, a lack further illustrated by his response to charges of linguistic determinism. In this instance he asserts that life is lived as a narrative and that the 'narratives' of Waugh and Bright are representative. To 'demonstrate' the first part of this claim he notes that life has a beginning, a middle and an end, and to justify the second part he suggests that, because his exemplars had high public profiles, they must have reflected and shaped popular perceptions.[83] Then, observing that formerly he had given too little emphasis to the prefigurative function of language, he purports to illustrate the reality of nineteenth-century life by interpreting his chosen narratives.[84] The mediating concept in his revised formula is 'imagination'. The procedure itself is supposed to subvert conventional distinctions between reality and representation by illuminating 'an imaginary that is not the image of something else, but without which there cannot be something else'.[85] Nothing, Joyce explains, can be experienced before it is first imagined, nor can it be 'understood outside discourse and the imaginary to which it gives rise'.[86] Whether this conceptual device helps to dissolve the binarism with which Joyce is concerned is debatable. But more significant, given his emphasis on the imaginative prefiguration of reality, is his persistent oversight of the possibility that the reality which he describes might be a product of *his own* imagination and hence of discursive imperatives in the 1990s.

This significance is underscored by a critique of Marxist historiography in which he notes the failure of recent Marxists to discern that, in the nineteenth century, 'class' and 'the people' were interchangeable collective identities. He links this problem to a preoccupation with class whereby the historians in question are unable to apprehend the 'storied' nature of their own narratives and those with which they engage.[87] Thus absorbed, he continues, they evince 'different chapters in their own story of class', in adding to which they do not report 'on what is out there in the real world' but instead elaborate 'a discursive means of handling an ever-evasive real'.[88] A useful comment on the epistemological contingency of Marxist 'knowledge', this critique nevertheless accentuates Joyce's inconsistency, for, when his discussion leads him to confront the contingency of his own thesis, he dismisses what he calls 'the epistemological question' as uninteresting and ultimately irrelevant. He acknowledges that this 'question' cannot be resolved because there is no independent measure by which the correspondence of representation to reality can be determined. But he then observes that there are other ways of 'discriminating accurate from inaccurate data, and tenable from untenable arguments', reverting to the evidence of 'experience' to point out that 'we do this all the time'.[89] The alternatives, it transpires, are 'widely differing protocols obtaining in different areas', the logic of which depends on 'consensus and social construction'.[90] Notwithstanding the difficulty of measuring 'consensus', this formulation is unexceptional as an account of how conventions are established within interpretative communities. But it cannot bridge the gap *between* discursive regimes. The epistemological problem which Joyce would like to dismiss as irrelevant therefore remains, for his interpretative strategy is grounded in one regime and the narratives to which he applies it in another.[91] In this regard, his practice seems indistinguishable from that of the writers he criticizes, and if their works are to be seen as histories of their own concerns, or discourses in which they are necessarily implicated, it is difficult to see why his should be regarded any differently.[92]

Similar oversights occur in the work of writers who employ Gramsci's theory of hegemony but ignore its significance for the historian as an intellectual. Gramsci distinguished hegemony from overt domination by representing it as a situation which can obtain only with popular consent, or when 'the general direction imposed on social life' by a ruling élite is broadly accepted.[93] Coercion of subaltern groups remains an option, but one to be used only should the prevailing view be disputed and popular consent withdrawn. Hegemony is implemented, he wrote, by a distinctive category of 'traditional' intellectuals who, on the basis of their historical continuity, affect independence from the currently dominant social group but are in fact its functionaries. In their various capacities as representatives of hegemonic institutions – religious, legal and educational – they construct, organize and persuade, mediating dominant truths and affirming their historical immutability. The triumph of capitalism, he suggested, was precisely commensurate with the bourgeoisie's ability to assimilate this stratum and to incorporate it ideologically.[94] He then postulated a category of 'organic' intellectuals which 'every new class creates alongside itself and elaborates in the course of its development'.[95] Linked dialectically to its constituents, this group plays a vital organizational role from which, in the case of the working class, liberation from the sway of dominant ideas proceeds.[96]

Gramsci also identified a third type, the outsider who joins a subaltern movement and merges with its organic intellectuals.[97] This type seems to account both for incorporated traditional intellectuals and for Gramsci himself, who had 'traditional' training but became a central participant – an educator, organizer and leader – in radical mass politics. Subsequently imprisoned for his subversive activities, he wrote his most-cited work not as an academic but as a convicted revolutionary.[98] Yet although his theory may have had the potential to transform popular radicalism into counter-hegemony in the early twentieth century, the historians with whom I have engaged use it to different effect. On the one hand, their debate about respectability is also a debate about hegemony, for the extent to which the former signified the latter is contested. On the other hand, all commentators seem to agree that the popular 'pursuit' of respectability reflected a prevailing conviction that the social order could not be changed, implying effectively that anything other than submission to middle-class predominance was meaningless.

This implication generates a significant ideological effect, for it tacitly affirms the immutability of power relations which are more or less identical to those which currently obtain: if acquiescence made sense then, it also makes sense now.[99] Moreover, the effect acquires an aura of objective validity because it appears to emerge 'spontaneously' from narratives which 'speak themselves'. Gramsci stressed the ideological potential of the intellectual, but the authors of these narratives understate or ignore this aspect of his theory and suppress their role as organizers and purveyors of knowledge, perhaps because they resemble his 'traditional' type so closely. They thereby suppress what seems clearly to be an ideological function, presenting as disinterested a vision which is profoundly political. Collectively contrived as an object of explanation, this vision has gradually crystallized as a historical given, a myth or meta-narrative of the mid-Victorian labour experience. Exempted from critique and debate, it has functioned politically to naturalize the hierarchy of capitalist society and thus to valorize dominant interests, regardless of the form in which those interests are represented. Hence, it reflected conservative nostrums during the 1970s and 1980s and is equally consistent with Labour Party rhetoric in the 1990s. This is not, of course, to say that Thatcherism, which was openly hostile to Marxism,[100] *proceeded from* the myth which I have described, a myth elaborated substantially by nominally Marxist historians. It is rather to suggest that the myth has evolved as a reflection of dominant ideas and has served persistently to validate them. But an adequate defence of this proposition requires some prior consideration of Thatcherite and recent Labour Party discourse.

FROM THATCHER TO BLAIR: DISCURSIVE CONVERGENCE IN BRITISH POLITICS

A persistent theme in Thatcherite discourse is the need to reinstate Victorian values which were exemplified, according to Thatcher, in the precepts of her childhood. 'We were taught', she observed,

> to work jolly hard. We were taught to prove yourself; we were taught self-reliance; we were taught to live within our income. You were taught that cleanliness is next to godliness. You were taught self-respect. You were taught always to give a hand to your neighbour.[101]

These values, she insisted, were both 'Victorian' and 'perennial'. The source of Britain's past greatness, they underpinned the Victorian 'burgeoning of free enterprise and philanthropy' and, depending on when she invoked them, would do so or were doing so again.[102] In 1977 she deplored their erosion by some thirty years of socialism which offered a choice 'between earning . . . [a] living and depending on the bounty of the State' but in her view encouraged the latter.[103] In 1979 she promised as Prime Minister that her government would correct this anomaly by 'rekindl[ing] the spirit which the Socialist years have all but extinguished'.[104] It would do so by reinstating Victorian values, by 'persuad[ing] our people that it's possible, through their own efforts, not only to halt our national decline, but to reverse it'.[105] We Britons 'have always had to go out and earn our living – the hard way', she intoned. 'In the past we did not hesitate . . . Our success wasn't based on Government hand-outs.' Nor was it based on 'envy or truculence or on endless battles between management and men, or between worker and fellow-worker. We didn't become the workshop of the world by being the nation with the most strikes.'[106] Prosperity, she explained, comes not from higher wages but from higher output.[107]

From the very outset, Thatcherism was promoted as a programme of national recovery. It would extirpate 'the Socialist disease'[108] which had all but decimated wealth-producing private enterprise to finance the growth of an inefficient, unproductive public sector.[109] And it would begin by attacking the 'debased rhetoric of fairness and equality' in which the disease reproduced itself.[110] Equality meant taxing industry and initiative to reward improvidence;[111] it meant wage increases which workers did not earn and services which they did not pay for but came to expect as 'a kind of manna from heaven';[112] it meant the irresponsible assertion of rights 'regardless of who ha[d] to pay';[113] and it meant that when the government had run 'out of other people's money' to spend, it supplied demand by printing and borrowing more.[114] The result was '[d]epressed profits, low investment, no incentive', spiralling inflation and escalating unemployment.[115] Unmoved by this crisis, 'a powerful vocal lobby', driven by envy and bourgeois guilt, continued to press 'for greater equality', but by 1975, according to Thatcher, most Britons had begun to revive 'a sober and constructive interest in the noble ideas of personal responsibility'.[116] Thatcherism would offer these people 'equity': equal opportunity and the freedom to choose. It would also protect their 'right to be unequal'.[117] This meant that those with special gifts should 'have their chance, because if the adventurers who strike out in new directions . . . are hobbled, there can be no advance'.[118]

Five years later, Thatcher completed her first year as Prime Minister, unemployment passed the 2 million mark and equity seemed a long way off. But she remained adamant that the Conservative Party would not be diverted from its mission. 'Decent people', she explained, 'want to do a proper job at work' and to give 'value for money'.[119] Her programme would enable them to do so by promoting free enterprise and cultivating a new respect for capitalism, which in her view was consistent not only with Victorian values but with Christian morality. In this equation capitalists, although few nowadays were willing to identify as such, exemplified Christ's injunction to act 'as stewards of the resources and talents' which God has given us.[120] They created jobs, prosperity, independence and the wealth whereby the Christian obligation of charity to the less fortunate could be met.[121] The Conservative government had extended the freedom necessary for these virtues to flourish by reversing the effects of socialism which, by investing all power and responsibility in the state, had curtailed liberty, discouraged community spirit and stifled self-reliance.[122] Indeed, she reminded the Small Business Bureau in 1984, she 'came to office with one deliberate intent: to change Britain from a dependent to a self-reliant society; from a give-it-to-me to a do-it-yourself nation; a get-up-and-go instead of a sit-back-and-wait-for-it Britain'.[123] And in 1988 she proclaimed her success. 'The habits of hard work, enterprise and inventiveness that made us great', she reported, 'are with us again.' By implementing policies conducive to such habits, her government had 'produced a standard of living undreamed of by our parents and the highest standard of social services this country has ever known'.[124] The enemies of prosperity might carp about materialism, greed and selfishness, but this was nonsense. The Conservative programme had brought out 'the best in human nature', making generous provision for the truly needy, offering the rest 'a wider choice . . . than ever before', and creating an environment in which industry, restraint and self-reliance were rewarded.[125]

Although this description of Thatcherite *discourse* is drawn entirely from Thatcher's own speeches, it reflects ideas embedded in Conservative policy which did not change substantially after she resigned and which seem since to have been adopted more widely.[126] Of course, there are alternative representations of Thatcherism and those advanced by the Left are less than gracious. To the notion of economic recovery, some critics have opposed accounts of economic misadventure which destroyed 'Britain's industrial productive capacity' and condemned some 4 million people to unemployment. Others have attacked the dismantling of the welfare state, the redistribution of wealth away from the most needy, the subversion of the labour movement and the cynical use 'of unemployment to compel workers to accept the "realism" of low wage settlements and the dole queue'.[127] Yet others have explored the language of Thatcherism to suggest that it functioned as a kind of Orwellian double-speak, denying the reality of the poverty and distress which Conservative initiatives were simultaneously creating.[128] By contrast, there are historians who have concerned themselves less with Thatcher*ism* than with the historical vision of its namesake. These writers have taken particular issue with Thatcher's account of Victorian values, explaining that it is hopelessly distorted by her omissions, but they have failed to note the extent to which her 'politics of exclusion' reflects their own, and have subsequently moved on to other things.[129]

Thatcher's response to critics was to castigate them as socialists who sought 'to destroy the free enterprise society and put a Marxist system in its place'.[130] They were thus found guilty by association with the 'Orwellian nightmare' which, under Labour Party auspices, had brought the nation to the brink of barbarism.[131] For over a generation, she observed, collectivist theory had predominated in intellectual and political life and its proponents, like the Labour Party, remained 'blind to the truth that all over the world, capitalism was achieving improvements in living standards and the quality of life, while Socialism was causing economic decay, bureaucracy . . . cruelty and repression'.[132] Assuming falsely that conscience could be collectivized, socialists urged the arrogation of all responsibility to the state and, claiming to eliminate 'class' in the name of a specious equality, produced 'the most stratified of all societies': one which consisted of *the powerful and the powerless*; the party bureaucratic élite and the manipulated masses'.[133] The consequence was economic decline and moral crisis, for not only did the socialist attack on free enterprise destroy opportunity and incentive, but it abrogated the individual responsibility on which morality was predicated. Hence thrift and industry were forced to subserve waste and idleness and when the latter gave rise to crime, 'Society' was held to account.[134]

To shed further light on the alien character of socialism, Thatcher compared it to a 'thoroughly British' conservatism. 'The Conservative Party', she observed, was integral to the British tradition, a 'part of the living flesh of British life over the generations'.[135] Steeped in Christianity, it embraced the spirit of capitalism (or 'free enterprise' as she preferred to call it),[136] for only in a free society could Britons make the moral choices on which their spiritual salvation depended. Moral judgement implied 'personal responsibility to self, family, firm, community and nation', and the market economy enabled people to exercise that responsibility. It also obliged them to serve the interests of others if they wished to serve their own, exemplifying 'the great truth that self-regard is the root of regard for one's fellows'.[137] Capitalism, she explained, 'produces a far higher standard of prosperity and happiness because it believes in incentive and opportunity, and because it is founded on human dignity and freedom'.[138] In 1988, with open contempt for her critics, she announced the success of the Conservative programme. 'Everybody' now knew, she declared, 'that our policies work and that Labour's don't'.[139] Free enterprise was thriving, 'the socialists' had been returned 'to square one'[140] and the Conservative Party to 'the common ground of British politics . . . where the great mass of the British people ha[d] pitched their tents'.[141]

Enhanced by its emphasis on the failure of socialist experiments abroad,[142] Thatcher's narrative identified discontent with the Labour government then transformed it discursively into a loss of popular confidence in British socialism. After 1979, left-wing commentators increasingly acknowledged the reality of this loss and attributed it to the gradual detachment of labour leaders from their constituents, suggesting that the latter, as a consequence, became susceptible to Thatcherite ideology.[143] But perhaps left-wing politicians and intellectuals were equally susceptible, for, after Thatcher's departure, their 'ideological' critique dissolved into a very pedestrian concern with issues like the government's decision to increase taxes, its indecision over European policy and the 'scandalous' behaviour of certain Tory MPs. Moreover, Thatcherite 'ideology' was subsequently to be reflected in the policies of a reconstituted Left. Hence, in the mid-1990s, the Labour Party distances itself from trade unionism, repudiates its commitment to collectivism and celebrates its movement into the middle ground of British politics. Abandoning any pretence at socialism, the Labour Party seems also to have abandoned its 'natural' and most vulnerable supporters. As a socialist party, its expressed purpose was to empower working people; instead, it empowered their leaders. The latter continue to enjoy the 'ruling lifestyles' which, as Thatcher was eager to point out, 'they rose to power by denouncing', while the former, consigned by the Conservative government to the tender mercies of 'the market', are offered little hope of redemption by a reconstituted Labour Party that directs its appeal to middle Britain.[144]

Like any historical phenomenon, British socialism lends itself to various representations. I propose, on the basis of the developments which I have described, that it has functioned as an agent of hegemony. Behind a façade of social reform, its leaders established their own independence by assuming control of 'collective' power and bartering it away until capital had no further use for compromise. This is not to say that they consciously and persistently betrayed their constituents to advance their own interests. It is rather to suggest that they may themselves have been betrayed by the logic of their own discourse and that the latter contributed inadvertently to the advent of Thatcherism. In the first place, socialism's expressed commitment to equality was inconsistent with its hierarchical structure. Inequality and hence the potential for popular disaffection were inherent in the distinction between the collective conformity to which it consigned its constituents and the relative autonomy which it reserved for their representatives. The representative role entailed making decisions and exercising power, exceptional responsibilities whereby socialist leaders resembled their capitalist counterparts more closely than their own followers, and in the discharge of which they may have been predisposed to regard (and reward) themselves as exceptional individuals. Second, the post-war compromise with capital (although some socialists may not have endorsed it) entailed a revision of socialist discourse in that it implied tacit recognition of the legitimacy of a phenomenon against which formerly socialism was held to define itself. This departure put socialism at an immediate disadvantage. Its advocates might well have adopted the view that co-operation would hasten the advent of a post-capitalist order, but to (big) capital the arrangement was simply a means of *containing* socialism until it could be eliminated. Finally, by opposing one hierarchical conception of society to another, to the exclusion of alternative possibilities, socialist discourse effectively conspired with liberal-conservatism to reduce political 'truth' to a choice between socialism and capitalism. Hence, when the former was defeated, the latter seemed inevitable. On the basis of this apparent inevitability, Thatcherism described a world view which has predominated ever since, affirmed by the Labour Party in its subsequent shift to the right and also by intellectual developments, notably in the historiography that is addressed above.

In juxtaposing Thatcherite discourse with the narratives elaborated by labour historians, I have indicated a series of correspondences in which the latter appear to authorize the former by depicting a past in which the Thatcherite vision is reflected and its promises realized. The most obvious of these correspondences relate to 'Victorian values' and the question of 'equity'. To recapitulate, in Thatcherite discourse Victorian values consist of self-respect, self-reliance, hard work, living within one's income and helping one's neighbours. To practise them is 'to prove' oneself, to exploit the opportunities to which Conservative policies have given rise, to prosper according to one's efforts and thus to contribute to the national good. The historical myth clearly suggests the wisdom of this formula, for not only do its protagonists, 'the people' and 'the working classes', exhibit the very qualities which Thatcher promotes – industry, thrift, restraint, self-respect, self-reliance and neigh-bourly co-operation, or 'mutual self-help' – but they also gain respectability and independence by doing so. Moreover, because they pursue and evidently attain their goals despite a prevailing climate of inequality – which they accept reluctantly or embrace, depending on the narrative in which they appear – they seem to demonstrate the 'truth' of Thatcher's claim that inequality and 'equity' are perfectly compatible. These corroborative effects can be traced to discursive strategies which predetermine and limit the meanings fig-ured forth by terms like inequality and poverty, and which reveal with particular clarity the politics of exclusion to which Thatcherite discourse and the historical myth conform.

According to Thatcherite discourse, British capitalism has eliminated real poverty and established an environment such that, as society prospers, 'it drag[s] the incubus of relative poverty with it up the income scale'. What 'poverty amounts to in the end', the narrative proceeds, 'is simply inequality' and Thatcherism, as Thatcher herself points out, celebrates inequality as a natural manifestation of human diversity.[145] In the historical myth, poverty has been simultaneously objectified and relativized. On the one hand, the implied predicate in discussions about the Poor Law, it has been characterized as a condition caused by unemployment or inadequate wages, marked by varying degrees of economic insufficiency and attended, especially in the pre-Victorian period, by a sharp increase in the cost of relief. On the other hand, it has been depicted as a phenomenon which mid-Victorian working people endured and in varying degrees transcended. But because stories which deny the possibility of 'transcendence' are excluded, poverty is reduced effec-tively to a condition which 'the working poor' left behind as they soldiered on, in the wake of their frugal, industrious and self-reliant 'representatives', towards respectability and independence.[146]

Patrick Joyce, in his latest intervention, claims to move beyond this kind of approach. Theorizing that reality is inseparable from representation, he proposes to illuminate the 'experience' of poverty by engaging with narratives in and by which it was constituted. '[W]hat matters', Joyce insists, is how contemporaries who identified or 'chose to be addressed' as 'poor' and 'insecure' understood such terms, and he discerns that understanding in a number of resoundingly Thatcherite narrative themes: 'the essential unity of all people'; 'stoical endurance'; 'putting up with the necessary limitations of poverty'; 'making something of yourself and not blaming or envying others'.[147] The narratives on which he focuses, however, are those of Edwin Waugh, who 'deserted the world of the workers for the "finer" life of literature', and John Hartley, 'editor of the big-selling Halifax *Illuminated Clock Almanack*' whose literary interest Waugh apparently inspired.[148] He is adamant that Waugh was a 'major force' in creating 'the meaning of poverty for himself and other[s]'[149] but the others are never consulted. Nor is the possibility that Waugh's readers may have construed his texts differently, that Joyce's interpretation is not definitive. In the end Joyce's thesis amounts to theoretical speculation, an idiosyncratic reading of certain dialect literature and the assertion that the latter 'gave' people their 'understandings of who they were'.[150] Like other versions of the historical myth, it excludes narratives such as those canvassed above in Chapter 3, which represent life as unremitting hardship, deprivation and alienation. Focusing instead on a handful of individuals who purportedly achieved a degree of respectability and independence, it employs categories like 'social identity' to transform them into representative figures, and thereby reduces poverty to insignificance.

The implications of this vision are the prescriptions of Thatcherism, which is ordered by a similar politics of exclusion. The myth depicts a capitalist society in which the poor remedied their condition through personal initiative. Thatcherism invites another generation of the poor to do likewise, repudiating social responsibility by repudiating *Society*. Just as Patrick Joyce suggests that 'society' is 'an historical construct' with which the subjects of his narrative 'were not usually in tune', Thatcherism declares that 'there is no such thing as Society' and the effect, in each case, is to valorize the self-reliant individual.[151] In Thatcherite narrative, the distinction between *Society* (a figment of the socialist imagination) and society (an ontological entity populated by self-reliant, independent individuals) is exploited to trivialize discordant voices when they cannot be silenced. Hence, as noted above, critiques which deplore the Conservative abrogation of social responsibility are dismissed as remnants of 'a specious argument left over from the Sixties' when it was fashionable to insist that '"society has a duty to me"', not "I have a duty to society"'; to ask 'why should I be less well off than he is' rather than 'have I earned the right to be better off than my neighbour?'; and to 'excuse violence on the grounds that it's not the criminal who is guilty – but the rest of us'.[152] The consistency of such assessments with 'public opinion' is then illustrated, as historical commentary is illustrated, with corroborative 'evidence'. In a 1977 speech, for example, Thatcher cites an unidentified correspondent to the Archbishop of Canterbury to the effect that

> [w]e wish to be self-reliant and do not want to be dependent on the State, nor do we want the State to take so great a proportion of our money in rates and taxes to decide for us what we shall have and not have . . . I may be wrong, but I think it weakens character when little by little our freedom of choice is taken from us.[153]

Expressing similar sentiments, 'the wife of a lower-paid worker' observes that, during years of struggle to buy a house,

> [w]e . . . have asked for nothing . . . What we have achieved we did ourselves. When we look round and see all the handouts people are getting from this Welfare State, we sometimes feel so sad that what should be a wonderful thing has really turned out to sap the goodness and initiative from so many of our people.[154]

And in 1979 there is the 'small businessman' who applauds Thatcherism's restoration of 'initiative' and its illumination of 'the basic common-sense fact that the country as a whole cannot continue to be paid more and more money for less and less work'.[155]

These comments might indeed be held to indicate that Thatcherism enjoyed popular support.[156] Their conviction, however, depends largely on the over-sight of other stories which speak not of order and optimism but of chaos and hopelessness. An extensive sample of these stories is consulted in a study which, politically opposed to Thatcherism, equates socialism with democracy and defends the logic of social responsibility. The sample includes complaints that Thatcherite initiatives, despite promises that they would not disadvantage the lowly paid, have reduced already meagre incomes by between £15 and £25 a week. In one such story, a supporting mother with three children describes her deprivation as a penalty for choosing to work rather than to stay 'at home and live . . . off social [security]'.[157] Other voices speak of disqualification from what Thatcher described as 'the highest standard of social services this country has ever known':[158] a pregnant woman because she surrendered a 'job which involved heavy lifting' and might, according to her doctor, cause her to miscarry; a man injured during short-term employment who subsequently left to find work which he could do while disabled; an asthmatic who resigned 'because the sawdust in the factory' where he worked exacerbated his condition; and a youth of seventeen who quit a job where he was compelled, in contravention of the Factory Act, 'to work over 12 hours a day including week-ends'.[159] In yet another example a Registered Disabled lady with no family, who survives on £20 a week maintenance from her ex-husband, describes her condition as anything but equitable. Because of Thatcherite economies, she observes,

> I have now lost all my special additions, i.e., diet, heating, laundry. I am also now having to pay £11.30 a month water rates. I have also lost my long-term high rate sickness benefit. There is no way that I can pay 20 per cent Poll Tax (what from?). I am already 57 years of age . . . I already live on porridge and roast potatoes four days a week to try to pay for some heat. My savings are £300. Dear Lord. Is suicide the only answer?[160]

This sense of futility becomes a direct indictment in the words of a man who has no need of scholarly language to characterize the politics of exclusion which I have been at pains to illuminate. Describing an alternative experience of Thatcherism, he explains that his father, incapacitated at sixty-two by an industrial injury, was awarded a modest pension and assured that it 'would be "safe"'. But it was '[n]ot safe', the man continues, 'from the cruel policies of the Conservative Party which is [sic] to let those who have, have more, and those who have tried but did not succeed be penalised for their failure'.[161] From this perspective, there is clearly no place for losers in the Thatcherite scheme of things.

Further examples include three women denied unemployment benefit, two because they could find no one to care for their infants during the evening and were therefore available for work only between 9.00 a.m. and 5.00 p.m.; and another because her part-time job made her unavailable for full-time work. Also disqualified were 'a man who had been unemployed for three years who refused to take a job which paid less than his supplementary benefit and which would not have covered his weekly expenditure; a man who had recently had a heart attack and was prepared to work only from 10.00 a.m. to 4.00 p.m.; three young mothers who, while being prepared to work from 8.30 a.m. to 5.00 p.m. were not prepared to travel more than ten miles to work; [and] a pregnant woman who said she would need time off to attend antenatal clinic'.[162] The authors of the volume to which this sample is adduced point out that, on applying for benefit, claimants are required

> to state the last three jobs they have had and then asked: 'What is the minimum weekly wage or salary you are willing to take?' If the answer is more than their recent earnings, and the rate being asked is more than the prevailing rate for the job sought in the area, or if the claimant's answer is deemed to be 'not sufficient', benefit officers are instructed to suspend payment, and benefit could then be disallowed. Thus, not only are claimants forced to take the lowest wages, but having once done so they cannot again seek work at a higher rate without putting their benefit in jeopardy.[163]

These procedures, the narrative concludes, are designed not to create a climate of equal opportunity but to 'squeeze claimants off the [unemployment] register, bring down the monthly employment statistics (while at the same time leaving the number of people unemployed unchanged) and underpin a low-wage economy'.[164]

The stories of uncertainty and despair adduced to this narrative seem clearly to demonstrate its central thesis: that 'for the successful to succeed [in Thatcher's Britain] it is inevitable that the weak must go to the wall'.[165] Without in any way seeking to diminish the experiences described by the various people consulted, I am nevertheless constrained to emphasize the political contingency of the volume itself. Unambiguously an attack on Thatcherism and a defence of socialism, it is also manifestly a promotion of the Labour Party as it was constituted in 1989 under the leadership of Neil Kinnock. A vindication of Kinnock's warnings to the populace 'not to fall sick' and 'not to grow old' in the present system of government, its foreword is contributed by Kinnock and it is co-written by one of his policy advisers. Designed, according to its authors, to tell the truth about Conservative policy, or to distinguish the rhetoric from the reality, it could be regarded as the definitive counter-discourse. As such, however, it is no more and no less plausible than Thatcherism, the discourse to which it is opposed. Each is consistent with the particular logic to which it appeals and each is illustrated with corroborative evidence. Together, however, they demonstrate the extent to which 'evidence' is constructed or invented, for each illuminates the politics of exclusion by which the meaning and conviction of the other is sustained. They also demonstrate that while truth effects proceed from particular exclusions, the exclusions themselves are dictated, like their historical counterparts, by a politics which overrides expressed political orientation.

The extent to which this politics of exclusion reflects 'dominant truth' is suggested by the evolution of the Labour Party's 'counter-discourse' in the 1990s. As an expression of this counter-discourse in 1989, the book under review, which is entitled *Punishing the Poor: Poverty under Thatcher*, proclaims Labour's commitment to eliminating poverty by reviving socialism. To justify this commitment, it valorizes narratives which Thatcherism assiduously ignores, narratives about how the young, the old, the infirm, the unemployed and people condemned to what amounts to sweated labour have been consigned to lives of chaos, oppression and uncertainty. Such stories continued to be told in 1995 but the Labour Party no longer consulted them. With electoral victory in sight, its most eminent spokesperson insisted that the place for Labour was in the middle ground of British politics. To secure this ground, Mr Blair and his colleagues courted capital and repudiated the principles for which, six short years before, the Labour Party supposedly existed. Their narrative was rewritten and the losers about whom their predecessors expressed such concern were effectively excluded, as they had been from Thatcherite discourse. The Labour Party apparently decided that the people who 'matter' were the respectable, the self-reliant and the independent of 'middle' Britain. Consistently with this reorientation, it embraced the dominant truth of economic rationalism. Aligning itself openly with capital, it pointed to the inevitability of capital*ism*. So too, by its narrative exclusions and organizing strategies, did the myth elaborated by labour historians.

LABOUR HISTORY AND THE POLITICS OF THATCHERISM

Just as Thatcherite discourse omits certain narratives to stress 'equity' as a defining feature of capitalism in the late twentieth century, the historical myth with which I have engaged omits stories of opportunity denied to suggest that Victorian capitalism was 'equitable', or at least sufficiently so to ensure social stability by rewarding industry and initiative with respectability and independence. Because of these exclusions, the images of equity figured forth confer on capitalism the implicit judgement that it is fair and just. Clearly the architects of the myth do not *explicitly* defend capitalism. But having suggested unexceptionably that equity is consistent with fairness and justice, they *do* describe a society in which independence was generally seen to be accessible to all and a populace which, because of this perception, acquiesced in a social order over which capital presided. The consequence, it is agreed, was social harmony.[166] In this formulation, 'representation' becomes 'explanation' and a purported popular perception becomes an indirect historical assessment. With similar subtlety, the myth conveys the impression that capitalism is inevitable, not explicitly as an object of debate but at the level of connotation, where meaning, although it is necessarily conditioned by the logic of the discursive regime in which the relevant narratives are produced and read, appears to emerge independently. In the first instance, this effect proceeds from a vision of nineteenth-century society in which capital predominates and hierarchically organized movements like liberal radicalism, 'labourism' and socialism are the only expressions of popular discontent. These movements then serve tacitly as alternatives against which the dynamism and resiliency of capitalism can be measured.

Tholfsen, for example, argues that 'merchants, manufacturers, and professional men . . . constituted a ruling class, exercising dominion over the wage earners below them' and securing popular acquiescence in 'their conception of consensus values and class relations'. Simply by acting as leaders and 'acclaiming the progress that was being made towards shared goals', he asserts, they justified 'their implicit claim to superiority', 'established a moral and cultural hegemony' and confirmed 'the legitimacy of underlying social and economic arangements'.[167] Hence, in a passage which does not so much as mention 'capitalism', Tholfsen nevertheless indicates that it was invincible by describing the 'hegemony' of its agents and of the social order over which it presided.

Nor, it seems, could socialism seriously disturb the stability to which these arrangements gave rise. Because 'revolutionary zeal' is an aberration 'which has to be imposed from the outside' and no such external influence emerged, he observes, reformism remained 'the norm'. Accordingly, socialism became at once synonymous with 'the various movements whose object was "to elevate the masses of Society"' by promoting 'mutual self-improvement', and so broadly defined that it could include 'just about any aspect of working-class activity'.[168]

Tholfsen's assessment, with its images of 'normal' and 'aberrant', is reflected in Joyce's revisionism, although for Joyce the normative agent is not ruling ideas but tradition, represented in an abundance of '[e]volutionary and biological metaphors'.[169] Joyce rejects the notion of bourgeois hegemony, but like Tholfsen he implies the invulnerability of capitalism by depicting it as sufficiently flexible to forestall the emergence of a genuinely subversive counter-discourse. In the nineteenth century, he suggests, capitalism persistently adapted to popular notions of tradition, independence and democracy, and its 'social and economic systems' remained 'for the most part unquestioned'.[170] Critique, such as it was, tended to be moral rather than economic, articulating a popular desire for '[c]heap food and stable employment' rather than 'welfare schemes', and a popular commitment to 'voluntary effort and independence' rather than class struggle.[171] 'There was little or no sense that the drive for profits systematically robbed the worker'; 'little or no notion of capitalist crisis or breakdown'; and 'no idea of capitalism's dissolution under its own contradictions'.[172] Similarly, according to Joyce, socialism was 'less about state intervention than self-help'. Informed by a tradition which it '[took] over intact' from Liberal radicalism, it embodied not a class critique of capitalism but a 'romantic, moral and aesthetic critique of industrialism'.[173] This tradition, on to which workingmen 'grafted their own visions of the past', fused with socialist thought and 'attach[ed] the sentiments of working people to the socialist cause', but it also engendered a conception of society 'in which the idea of "community" was uppermost' and sustained the 'belief that present society could evolve towards a reformed end'.[174] Hence, '[c]lass struggle was not the motive force of history, for what mattered 'was the moral energy of the whole people or the "commonwealth"'. The forms which society would eventually take were not specified, but although 'present' capitalism was expected to be overcome by 'collective ownership and social responsibility', they would not be 'those of class, for complementing socialist economic thought was a social analysis that ultimately denied class in the present or in the future'.[175]

In certain respects Marxist contributors disagree with both Joyce and Tholfsen but in their treatment of capitalism they point to similar conclusions. Crossick, for example, writes that the pursuit of respectability by Victorian workers was dictated by 'an economic and social system that seemed increasingly permanent'; Kirk adopts a similar formula to explain the Victorian

'decline of revolutionary class consciousness';[176] and R.Q. Gray treats capitalism as a historical given, a set of economic conditions within which class or
industrial struggle occurred and class interests were negotiated but which
was itself somehow untouchable.[177] Admittedly, these assessments are all
qualified, *contra* Joyce and Tholfsen, by emphases on a subsequent political
awakening in which labour re-evaluated capitalism, established its own independent political party and effectively resumed the class struggle. Crossick
observes that a range of national and local movements sprang up between
1880 and 1914 which signified 'an emerging labour consciousness' and drew
the various sections of the working class together 'into closer cooperation and
a sense of identity';[178] Gray notes the transmission of class identity 'to a wider
[working] class movement and culture' during the same period;[179] and Kirk
finds that, at the turn of the century, working-class divisions were increasingly
'being overshadowed by a renewed sense of class unity', with even the formerly
exclusive labour aristocracy moving 'into the ranks of the Labour Party, the
militant Shop Stewards Movement and the young Communist Party'.[180]
Hence, while Tholfsen and Joyce imply the immutability of capitalism by
denying the possibility of an effective counter-discourse – the former by
depicting bourgeois hegemony as total, the latter by suggesting a tradition-
inspired social cohesion so thorough that the question of subversion could not
arise – Marxists construe late nineteenth-century socialism as a genuine challenge to capitalism which exemplified both dissatisfaction with the *status quo*
and the partial or temporary character of ideological incorporation during the
Victorian period.

Yet precisely when these histories were being produced, the movements
which Marxism identified as convincing manifestations of popular resistance
to bourgeois hegemony and capitalist domination were weakening.
Communism had little more than a decade of life left, British socialism had
been compromised, the trade union base of labourism was under attack and the
Labour Party was sliding rightwardly into oblivion. Against the background
of these developments, the purported triumph of class consciousness and class
unity at the end of the nineteenth century looks singularly hollow. Moreover,
given that the populace, according to certain Marxist historians, had already
judged the prevailing social order to be both equitable and immutable, the
purported revival of class struggle at the turn of the century seems irrational,
futile and perhaps immoral. To correct this impression, Marxists might sus-
pend closure and introduce narratives like those consulted above in Chapter 3,
which contradict images of order, harmony and equity. By doing so, however,
they would compromise their Victorian portraits. Conversely, by adhering to
representational strategies which rule out such images, they conspire like
Tholfsen and Joyce in a discourse which suggests that Victorian capitalism was
invulnerable and that capitalism *per se* is immutable.

Given that capitalism has survived intact from the period under discussion
to the present, its immutability might, of course, appear to be self-evident.

But like the notion that it is equitable, this appearance is in my view an ideological effect which, in its Thatcherite formulation, has entered educated common sense and now shapes political and historical narrative. Its corollary is that any gesture of resistance or opposition to the prevailing order of things would be futile, and it thereby functions to reinforce dominant interests in the present. I do not suggest that these effects inhere in the histories themselves. Indeed, as I have argued above, I regard the meaning figured forth by any text to be simultaneously read into it. I do suggest, however, that the discursive regime in which the histories have been written and are currently read remains consistent with a Thatcherite world view, and that the truths proclaimed by that regime may seem inescapable. I have therefore attempted to identify another reading position from which the contingency of those truths can be discerned. I have done so not to predict the future of capitalism but to illuminate the rhetorical artifice by which the impression of its immutability is presently conveyed.

My purpose has been to suggest that those who find themselves disadvantaged by current social arrangements might consider the constructedness of the histories which seem to authorize their condition, the arbitrary and aesthetic character of the morality to which those histories enjoin them, and the possibility that acquiescence is not the only response. In taking historical texts as my object of enquiry, I have addressed discursive processes which conceal their political, ideological and epistemological contingency.[181] I have then argued that these processes, by excluding from discussion the assumptions which lend them consistency, produce truth effects and reproduce subjectivity, experience, agency and power in particular ways. Finally, I have attempted to demonstrate that the meaning of narrative history is given by these processes rather than found in the historical record, and that 'historically speaking', therefore, there are no true or false stories but only different stories which reflect and reproduce different interests. To the extent that my argument is convincing, it follows that history itself is meaningless and that narratives which reflect dominant interests have no special authority other than that of the power which they help to reproduce. It also follows that there is no compelling reason why British 'subjects' in the 1990s should not repudiate spurious truth claims and collaborate more actively in the constitution of their own myths and their own identities, thus to elaborate and pursue their own visions of order, dignity and freedom.

AFTERWORD

It should be clear from the foregoing commentary that I have not attempted to devise a better way of doing history. Instead I have invited speculation on the way a certain kind of history is done. Focusing on various constructions of the mid-Victorian labour experience, I have explored the artifice by which their evidence is constituted and their truth effects produced, thus to suggest that historical practice is present-centred, political, and productive of myths which function to naturalize and validate existing social arrangements, or prevailing power relations. Proceeding from the observation that there are no independent criteria against which competing truth claims can be evaluated, I have argued that all truth is contingent. I have then advanced my discussion as a proposition, the authenticity of which is contingent on the conviction that democracy and hierarchy are incompatible. To illustrate this proposition, I have explored the fluidity of meaning, the relativism of logic and the incommensurability of meaning systems. I have thus endeavoured to illuminate the ambiguity of historical information, the ramifications of selecting certain events and processes for description to the exclusion of others, and the ways in which meaning is generated. In particular, I have taken issue with theories of social identity and the representative figure of historical narrative, describing them as central components in a technology of power which serves to convey the impression that capitalism is just and equitable by excluding its casualties from history.

My work has been substantially influenced by the ideas of Michel Foucault, Joan Scott and Hayden White, all of whom have outlined possibilities whereby historical practice might be transformed. Foucault and Scott have urged that foundationalist concepts be made the focus of historical enquiry, and White has encouraged closer attention to the links between representational strategies and political commitments. In attempting to follow these suggestions I have clearly endorsed them, yet I am reluctant to do so explicitly or to make recommendations of my own, for a number of reasons. First, for over two decades, most mainstream historians have ignored such advice, equating it with a postmodernism which they either dismiss, like Arthur Marwick, as an unmitigated evil, or appropriate, in the manner of Patrick

Joyce, to give tired old practices a new look. Second, I think the egalitarianism to which Scott and White are committed would be better served were they to give less emphasis to alternative ways of speculating on the past and more to the artifice of historical production. By stressing the latter, they would in my view help to subvert a technology which has persistently functioned to frustrate the egalitarian politics they promote. Finally, I do not wish to enjoin special consideration of my own views. To do so, I suspect, would be to imply some notion of expertise and thus a hierarchy of knowledge, when my purpose is to undermine all such hierarchies.

It may seem that I have now put myself in an invidious position. On the one hand, if I discount the truth of my own observations, then what is the point of my discussion? On the other hand, if I say categorically that there is no possibility of objective truth, then am I not myself asserting an absolute? This dilemma reflects another. It is to people in general that I would like this book to speak, yet I am aware that because of its language, form and focus, only a minority of people are likely to read it. In this connection, my agency has been limited by my subject matter, the requirements of scholarly writing and my own understanding of those requirements. I am convinced, however, that the structural/discursive imperatives through which subjectivity and truth are constituted leave spaces in which agency can exert and increase itself. Because of this conviction, I am confident that the same ideas can be translated into more accessible forms. Moreover, although I am constrained to frame this book as a proposition, I am optimistic that some readers will be sympathetic to my prefigurative assumptions and will therefore find some use for my general argument. Should this prove to be the case, I hope my approach will be imitated to produce further genealogies, or histories of the present, which demystify historical practice in other areas. My optimism in both respects helps to explain a dual emphasis throughout this study on the constitution of people as subjects and the agency of subjects as people. It also helps to explain why my own project, according to one of my doctorate supervisors, 'is haunted by the ghost of a real alternative'. But rather than make explicit recommendations which might intrude on the agency of potential readers, I leave the ghost to hover and the reader to consider my narrative against others as a history of the present, a history of foundationalist concepts (though one which cannot escape creating new foundations), and a reflection of my own political commitments.

EVIDENCE OF WITNESSES

IN THE CASES OF

WILLIAM PEARCE AND JAMES BRISTOL,

WHO DIED AT BOLTON FROM WANT OF FOOD;

ALSO

ON THE GENERAL DISTRESS

IN THAT TOWN;

WITH REMARKS ON THAT SUBJECT

AND ON THE

ASSISTANT POOR-LAW COMMISSIONER'S REPORT

———————

BOLTON:
PRINTED BY J. GADSBY, FREE PRESS OFFICE, DEANSGATE.
MDCCCXLI.

INTRODUCTORY REMARKS

In presenting to the public the following pages, allow me, with as much brevity as possible, to offer the following observations; also, to republish Dr. Bowring's statement made in the House of Commons; that the public may see and be convinced that instead of the three cases being over-stated, they were very much under-stated. I shall also republish the evidence as given in Mr. Mott's report, in the case of William Pearce. The public will then see what an assistant poor-law commissioner calls "comfortable living" in Bolton.

It will also be seen that Mr. Mott was very careful not to examine any witnesses whose evidence was likely to show the real cause of these deaths; although he had been frequently requested to do so. He keeps to the old woman, although he knows she is little better than an idiot; and if one of his own witnesses did happen to slip a word likely to alarm his employers, he has taken care not to insert it in his report. For instance, I requested the clerk of the Board of Guardians to read to the relieving officer that part of the letter I sent to him which contained an account of the state we found the family in when we visited, them, and of which Dr. Bowring's statement, in the House of commons, was a verbatim copy. I then put the following questions to the relieving-officer in the presence of Mr. Mott: – First, "Was that the state we found the family in when we visited them?" His answer was, "Precisely so." Second, "Was it your opinion at the time that the man died from want?" Answer, "That is still my opinion." This occurrence does not appear in Mr. Brown's evidence, as given in Mr. Mott's report. The whole of his report is got up in the same way, and will serve for something to be pointed at at all times to show that government commissions are not intended to elicit truth, but to serve a party and special purpose.

With respect to Mr. Mott's remarks about the Anti-Corn Law League and politics, they are scarce worth notice. However, I may just observe that all these cases were visited by me some time previous to any meeting being held in Bolton under the sanction of the League. At the first meting that was held, I made a long speech in reference to the distress then existing in Bolton, a part of which was reported in several of the London and provincial newspapers. A few days previous to the election, when politics were running very high, I made a speech in the Temperance Hall, again alluding to the distress in Bolton; but on neither occasion did I allude to any of these cases. This proves that I did not visit the cases for the sake of serving the League, or for any political purpose: indeed, I never intended making any use of them, for I was convinced whilst I was a guardian, from what I saw at the board, and by visiting the poor, that deaths were occurring nearly every week in Bolton for want of the necessaries of life, – or, perhaps, more properly speaking, from sickness produced by want, and ending in death, which amounts to the same thing.

It will be seen by the evidence that the whole of the cases mentioned by Dr. Bowring are fully borne out by respectable witnesses, and that a verdict ought to have been recorded, both in the case of William Pearce and James Bristol: but they were very poor and must die, like dogs, unnoticed. Respecting the recording of the verdict in the case of William Pearce, I may just mention that one of the jury called upon me the day the inquest was held, knowing I had taken an active part in getting an inquest over the body, and stated they had returned a verdict "Died from want of food," and as a proof that that was the impression of the jury, Mr. Staton, reporter for the *Chronicle*, who was one of the jury, stated at the guardian meeting on Friday, the 10th Sept. last, in reply to a question from a guardian, "That he was on the jury, and they returned a verdict of 'Died from want of food.'" This proves that the jury were of that opinion, whether the coroner recorded the verdict or not. Of course I made no further inquiry into the matter: it was so notorious at the time that no one ever thought of disputing that the man had died from want.

Mr. Mot was apprised of and requested to attend the examination of these witnesses, but, to my surprise, instead of his attending, I received a letter from him, dated Friday, the 15th instant, in which he states, "that in accordance with the instructions I received, I made inquiries into the circumstances stated to have occurred, and, having reported the result to the Poor-Law Commissioners, I have received no directions to take any further proceedings." This proves that Mr. Mott's employers are well satisfied with what he has done, for a petition was sent by me to the House of Commons, stating that his report was a partial and unfair one, and praying for a full and fair inquiry. The petition was ordered to be printed, yet it appears he has received no instructions to make a further investigation.

W. NAISBY.

Bolton, October 18th, 1841.

Examination of witnesses, taken the 16th day of October, 1841, respecting the death of William Bristol, who died about two years ago.

CHARLES SKELTON says I recollect, about two years ago, Mr. Naisby calling upon me to visit the case of Bristol. On getting into the house, we inquired of the woman where her husband was, not knowing that he was dead. She stated that he was up stairs. Mr. Naisby replied, "I want to see him;" and she then said, "He is dead." Mr Naisby then went up stairs and looked at him. The woman had a very bad leg, and was quite unable to walk. There were two children lying in the corner of the house, on a bit of straw placed on the flags: one child was very much afflicted with St. Anthony's Fire, and all the other children were very ill and sickly. I asked Bristol's wife what food he had had lately, and she then stated that her husband had asked, the day before he died, for a bit of cheese and bread, but that she was unable to procure him any. An old woman, a neighbour, stated that Bristol had been "clammed to death."

CHARLES SKELTON.

ANN BRISTOL says my husband died about two years ago. I recollect, when he was laid out dead, Mr. Naisby then coming to visit us. My husband was laid out on the necessary door, up stairs, covered over with a sheet, which a neighbour had lent us. I was lame myself at the time, and could not walk. My child was blind at the time, having the St. Anthony's Fire: she was then nearly sixteen years of age. I had another daughter, very ill also, aged about thirteen years. I had four other children besides, the eldest of which was nearly eighteen years of age, the next nine years of age, the next seven years of age, and the other four years old: altogether I had six children. For three weeks previous to my husband's death we had nothing but three shillings per week coming in; and we had to live sometimes on potatoes, sometimes on porridge; but had only one meal a day, which we generally made about four o'clock in the afternoon. I think it was for a fortnight that we had to confine ourselves to one meal a day, sometimes having porridge and sometimes potatoes. When Mr. Naisby found us in this state, we got more food, otherwise I believe I should have lost more of my children, for we had got as far distressed as we well could be to be alive. About five months previous to my husband's death I had a child sucking, which died; and I feel sure that its death was occasioned by my not being able to give it suck, for want of sustenance. I had no bed, bedding, or anything whereon to lay, when Mr. Naisby visited us. I had only a stool whereon to sit, for myself. I had to shop where I could get provisions at: they all refused to give me credit. My husband wished for a bit of cheese and bread, the day before he died, but I was unable to procure him any.   HER

ANN ✗ BRISTOL.

MARK

BETTY BROWN says, I knew the last witness's husband previous to his death, also all the family for about two years. At the time of the death of Bristol, I laid him out, on the top of the necessary door. I assisted to undress him, he having died with his clothes on, in which he had laid for many weeks, having nothing besides to keep him warm; when I cut his trowsers legs and stocking legs open, there were large quantities of creeping filth, which had eaten quite into the flesh, and his legs were nothing but putrid flesh and scabs. He had nothing but straw to lie upon, which was spread on the floor. One of her children had the Saint Anthony's Fire, and the rest were all more or less very sickly and bad. They all slept together in one room, and the wife of Bristol had a great hole in her leg, and could not walk or assist her husband; but after she had received relief and had got bedding, she began to come round. I recollect Mr. Naisby coming down, when Bristol was laid out on the necessary door, and I then told him the man had died for want, and I know such to be the case.

HER

BETTY ✕ BROWN.

MARK

MARY ANN GRIMSHAW says, I recollect going in to see Bristol about two hours before he died; I found him laid on a bit of straw, without anything in the room, his wife laid beside him, with her back towards him, she had a hole in her leg and could not stand. He had his eyes open and was quite sensible; he was shaking as if he had got the ague. I said, James, how are you? and he replied, in a weakly and hollow voice, "I am very bad!" He died about two hours afterwards. From what I knew of the family for some weeks before, I am certain he died from starvation.

HER

MARY ANN ✕ GRIMSHAW.

MARK

JOSEPH REYNOLDS WOOD, of Great Bolton, gentleman, says, I was a Guardian at the time of Bristol's death, and recollect the case being brought before the Board of Guardians, and Mr. Naisby remarking to Mr. Benjamin Brown, the Relieving-officer, who was then present, "Why that poor fellow has died from want, Brown?" to which Brown made answer, "Yes, I believe he has."

JOSEPH R. WOOD.

KIRKMAN'S CASE

Examination of Witnesses, taken the 16th day of October, 1841, with respect to Kirkman's case, where seventeen people were residing in a house about four yards wide.

ANN KIRKMAN, wife of John Kirkman, labourer and bricklayer, Slater-fields, Bolton, says, about a year and a half ago I lived at the Willows, in Bolton. We were sold up there for rent: after we were sold up we removed to Robert Kirkman's, my husband's father's house, near Daubhill Bar. At this time there was my husband, and myself, and five children. There were two other brothers in the same house, one with a wife and three children, and the other with a wife and one child. Every one of us were out of work at the time. There were also the father and mother of my husband residing with us, making in the whole, seventeen residing in the house, which was about four yards square. We all slept in the room above, which was the same size. I recollect Mr. Naisby coming to the house and requesting either me or my husband to come down to the Guardian Meeting, on the Friday following. My husband went to the Guardian Meeting accordingly, and we had a bed and a few household requisites and some money given us, and we then removed to Fitton's Houses.

HER

ANN ✕ KIRKMAN.

MARK

After Ann Kirkman had made the above deposition she turned from the table as if to go away, but immediately turned round, and, bursting into tears, told Mr. Naisby that *there were thirteen of their family at home who had not broken their fasts that day, and were now starving.*

H. M. RICHARDSON.

PEARCE'S CASE

Examination of Witnesses, taken the 16th day of October, 1841, respecting the death of William Pearce, who died on the twenty-third day of Feb., 1840, in Howell-croft, Great Bolton.

THOMAS BRADSHAW deposes as follows — I was elected Relieving-officer to the Relief Fund Society, on the 22nd of February last year. On the Sunday following my appointment to such office, I was waited on by Mr. Coop, comb maker, of Great Bolton, who stated, that a man residing near his house was starving to death — that would be about eight o'clock in the evening. Mr. Coop requested that I would immediately go and see him. I did so. And when I got to the place alluded to by Mr. Coop, I found Mrs. Coop there and the man dead. I was informed he had been dead about a quarter of an hour. I felt the corpse, and it was still warm. I noticed the cellar to be in a very wretched state. Through the wall of the back part of the cellar, I perceived dirty filthy water oozing through the crevices of the bricks, which I afterwards found proceeded from a midden-stead adjoining the cellar. There was a nauseous smell and which I considered very unhealthy. All the furniture in the cellar, was a small three-legged table, an old chair with scarcely any bottom; and a three-legged stool, such as children use; there was a small bedstead, on which was placed some sacking, containing shavings, the shavings were quite visible through the sacking. There was no covering. The bed was quite wet with damp, and stunk with filth; so much so, that I gave orders for it to be burned; which, I believe, was done after deceased was buried. The corpse of Pearce lay out on a loom, without any covering, but Mrs. Coop lent them a pair of sheets. The value of the furniture altogether, I should consider, would not fetch 2s. if sold. I asked the woman and her daughters whether they had any food. They said, "They had not tasted that day. I went to my house, and brought them a quantity of broth, which they all devoured very voraciously. I was in the cellar whilst they partook of it, and one of the daughters, immediately after she had taken it, began to vomit very much; which I attributed to an excess of appetite and being kept without food so long previously. I may add, that previously to partaking of the broth, they began to quarrel amongst themselves, which had the greatest portion. I reported the case, and they were duly relieved. On the Tuesday following, the Committee sat, and they were ordered to be relieved. I now refer to the Book in which the "Distressed Cases" are entered, and I find that they were relieved with a grant of three shillings per week. I find the following entry, Pearce Ellen, widow, Howell-croft, to receive 3s. per week for an unlimited period; and the following entry in the remarks, "Husband supposed to have Died from Want." I inquired into the earnings of the whole family, and found they did not exceed three shillings per week. I have since, several times visited the old woman, Helen Pearce, and find that she is of very weak intellect; and any statements she might make, is not fit to be taken as evidence; and her daughters are the same. It appears that a dullness of intellect afflicts the whole family. I went to the Coroner's Inquest for the purpose of giving evidence, but not being called upon, I did not do so. Had my evidence been taken, I do not know how the jury could have done otherwise than returned a verdict that the deceased died from want.

THOMAS BRADSHAW.

JAMES WEBSTER says, I am Town Missionary at Bolton. My duty is to visit cases of sickness and distress. On Monday, the twenty-fourth of February last but one, from information I had received that a man had died from want in Howell-croft, I went there and made inquiry. The cellar of the deceased was pointed out to me, and on entering I saw the deceased dead, and laid out on his loom. I found the whole of the household requisites to consist of a small three legged table, a chair, almost without a bottom, a stool, and a bed with some sacking on. The whole of which were worthless, not worth carrying away – the bed was very filthy. I reported the case to the Benevolent Society, who gave the family 5s. I have seen the entry made in the Benevolent Society's book, and find Pearce's case is entered "Died from want of food," and this was my full impression immediately after I had examined into the case. On inquiring into their earnings I found they did not exceed three shillings per week. I have frequently visited and relieved the case since, and I consider them all, that is, the old woman (Mrs. Pearce) and her two daughters to be of such very weak intellect that it approximates very closely to insanity, and that they are totally incapable of giving evidence that could be depended upon. Whenever I have conversed with them I have always left them fully impressed that they were labouring strongly under a degree of insanity.

JAMES WEBSTER.

NANCY BESWICK, wife of Henry Beswick, weaver, Lever street, Great Bolton, says, I knew Pearce before he died for four years, and his family also. About three weeks previous to the death of Peace I stood against my own door step and saw Pearce coming towards my house. There are three steps up to my house. He looked very wan, and pale as death, and was so weakly, that to get on to my house floor he had to go down on his hands and knees and creep up. He had been in the habit of weaving for us some months before, and I had missed him for a month about, on the day I am now speaking of. When he got in, he said, "Nancy, do, bless you, make a sup of warm tea, for I am dying for want." I made him some tea and a little toast, and he devoured it very greedily. When he had done it he told me all that he had had for three or four weeks back, he had had nothing but a basin of gruel per day to subsist upon. In about a quarter of an hour after the old man had had the tea, he was seized with sickness, and I had to obtain the assistance of neighbours, for I thought he was dying. We reared him up in chairs with pillows, and in about three quarters of an hour he came round. I then asked him why he clammed himself to that degree, and he said as he did not belong to Bolton he could not get relief. He pulled up his trousers and showed me his legs, and they appeared nothing but skin and bone; and it was frightful to see him. He was taken home by my husband, and I and his wife went to the Overseers' Office to represent the case to them. We saw Bridge, the assistant to the Relieving Officer, and told him the case, and he was very saucy, and said we had better mind our own business. I gave in the name of Pearce to the officer myself, for although his wife was present *when the officer asked her husband's name she could not tell, and desired me to do so.* The officer said he would visit the case, but whether he ever did so or not I never ascertained and I never heard anything more until about three weeks afterwards, which was that he was dead. I heard this the same night that he died and went to the cellar. I there found them in a most shocking state, and the cellar smelled so much that I could not remain in it. He was laid out on the loom, with a sheet over him. I noticed in the back cellar there was a sewer, or midden channel, ran through, and the floor was covered with nauseous filth and water. All the goods in the house were a broken three-legged table, a stool, chair, and the bed, made of sacking, without covering. I went again on the Monday morning, and turned down the sheet to look at the corpse, and there were hundreds of creeping filth upon him. I pointed out the filth to his wife, and she appeared to be quite vacant. The daughters asked me to get them some light dresses and shawls, with purple spots in, as they were like to go the funeral of the old man – they did not call him their father – they laughed and appeared entirely out of their senses, and each of them had nothing wherewith to clothe them but canvass wrappering – without shoes, stockings, or wearing apparel of any description. There was not warp in the looms, but they stated that Messrs. Goodbrand had sent them some a week before, but they had sent for it back for fear the bailiffs should seize it. Before the inquest went over Pearce I was warned by a police man to go and give evidence before the jury at two o'clock. I went to the Britannia Inn where the jury was sitting, but was not called upon. I went precisely at two o'clock, but on going into the house the landlord told me that it was all over, and the old woman (Pearce's wife) was coming out at the door. Had I been called upon before the jury, as I expected I should have been, I am sure I should have proved that, to my knowledge, he had died from *want of food*. When the old woman was coming out of the public house, the man that showed her out said, "Well, mistress, go home, and take care that you don't die for want; look after something before you come to this, because you seem to have a dismal face." As I have stated before, I have known all the family for four years, and I always considered them not to be right in their minds. I have visited the family since the death of Pearce, and the old woman has often asked me *"if I knew what they were going to do with her, because several fellows had questioned her and inquired after her."* I told her I believed they did not intend to do anything with her, and she had no occasion to be frightened. She talked very irrationally, and said she believed they wanted to send her somewhere but that she would not go, but remain where she was. She appeared suspicious that some harm was meant towards her.

HER

NANCY ✕ BESWICK.

MARK

WILLIAM COOP, of Great Bolton, comb-maker, saith – At the time of the death of Pearce I was residing in the immediate neighbourhood, and had known the family well for some time previously. The first time that I had any acquaintance with Pearce he called to beg an old pair of shoes. I told him I gave my old clothes to my apprentice's father, whom I said was in great distress. He replied; "If they were as badly off as he was, God help them, for neither he nor any of his family had tasted food since yesterday." On questioning him I found him in a state of starvation. I went into the cellar and found him in the greatest distress. There was only one bed-stead for himself, wife, and two daughters. No bed covering: they were forced to sleep in their clothes. The seats they sat upon were bricks and stones, before I gave them two old stools to sit upon. This was about six months before he died – he died on Sunday. His wife came and stated she believed her husband had given over stirring. I went and found him dead. I went to the Relieving Officer for the Relief Fund Committee (Mr.

Bradshaw) and brought him down. He was laid out on a pair of looms, and my mistress found a sheet to lay over him. When it was returned, after Pearce had been buried, we were forced to burn it on account of there being hundreds of filth upon it. I have seen Pearce pick potatoes off the midden, which have been thrown away for being rotten; and afterwards having gone into the cellar, and found them boiled up, and they were eating them for dinner. There was no deceit in this, for I have gone frequently into the cellar, when they were not aware of my coming. It is my firm opinion that Pearce died from nothing but starvation. I consider all the family of the Pearce's to be to a great degree insane, and quite incompetent to give evidence. She has to my knowledge, although I know her to be in the most abject state of poverty, often stated she wants for nothing, and is fearful she will be sent to the Workhouse if she complains. She has told me many a time since her husband's death, that she shall fetch me if they offer to take her out of the cellar, and hopes I will protect her. Her aversion to going into the Workhouse, I am certain, would make her say and do anything to avoid going there.

WILLIAM COOP.

I, Henry M. Richardson, do make oath, that on the Sixteenth day of October 1841, the foregoing parties' examinations were taken before me fairly and fully as delivered by them, and that I wrote the same down as delivered by the several parties who have signed the same. As witness my hand, the day and year aforesaid.

H. M. RICHARDSON.

Sworn before us,   ROBT. HEYWOOD   ⎫
                     C. J. DARBISHIRE   ⎬   Justices of the Peace for
                     HENRY ASHWORTH   ⎭   the said Borough.

The examination of Richard Dunderdale, taken the 18th day of Oct., 1841.

Richard Dunderdale, of Great Bolton, tea-dealer, says – I was one of the overseers of the poor at the time of the death of Pearce. I recollect going with Mr. Naisby to the cellar at the time that Pearce lay dead on a pair of looms. From what I saw and heard from the old woman and her two daughters I felt convinced that the old man died from want. The old woman and her daughters appeared of very weak intellect.

RICHARD DUNDERDALE.

I, Henry Richardson, solemnly declare the above to be a true statement of Mr. Dunderdale's evidence.

HENRY RICHARDSON.

Taken before me, C. J. Darbishire.

FROM MR. MOTT'S REPORT.

"ELLEN PEARCE states that her husband's name was William Pearce; that he died last February twelve months; had been ailing eighteen weeks, but had worked occasionally during that time; that he was 65 years of age; that he had plenty of work if he could have done it; that he was a steady, sober man, and always brought his wages home; that they had two looms at home, on which she and her daughter worked; that her daughter Phœbe worked at Mr. Haslam's in Blackhorse-street, at that time; that she and her daughter earned about 9s. 6d. per week; that they never wanted food; "'they were comfortable then,'" and she had not applied for relief."

Ellen Pearce does not belong to Bolton, but her settlement cannot be ascertained; I found her inhabiting a cellar, in a dirty state. Her daughter Phœbe still works at weaving, and she receives 3s. per week of the Union for herself and daughter, a young woman of weak intellects; she did not make the least complaint of her husband having been neglected. I repeatedly asked her as to the state they were in when her husband died, and she answered, they did not want food; "that they were comfortable then."

In consequence of the statement made by William Coop, Ellen Pearce was again examined, and she confirmed the foregoing statement, and indignantly denied William Coop's story about the potatoes.

24 September, 1841   (Signed)   CHARLES MOTT

Extract from Dr. Bowring's Speech, in the House of Commons, on Wednesday, 25th August, 1841, on the Distress in Bolton.

Would the House bear with him while he detailed some cases of individual suffering, authenticated by the evidence of poor-law guardians and magistrates? "I visited, " says the informant, "a man and his wife, with four children; I found two of the children lying on a piece of straw, without any covering. I went up stairs and found the father dead on the boards, without bedding or bed. His wife told me that the day before he died he wished for a little bread and cheese, but in vain. The neighbours said he had died for want of food." Another wretched case. "A man, his wife, and two daughters (it is a guardian of the poor who speaks), lived in a cellar, the wife and daughters out of work; this man earned about four shillings per week by weaving; I was fetched by the neighbours, who told me the man had died of hunger; I found him lying dead on one of the looms; they had neither bed nor bedding. I caused a jury to be summoned: their verdict was, 'Died for want of food'" He felt a difficulty in selecting cases, from the many mournful examples he held in his hand. His correspondent had been called to visit a family which he was informed was in a state of starvation. He found the father had just sold all he had to pay his rent, and had removed, with his family, to his father's, whither he followed him, and found the man, his wife, and four children; another brother, his wife, and three children; a third brother, his wife, and one child, all the men out of work, all the women far advanced in pregnancy, in a house four and a half yards square; they all slept in a room above of the same size, and lay upon little but straw.

IS THE CONDITION OF THE POOR IMPROVED?

It may be said that these cases having occurred some time ago, that distress is not so great in Bolton at present. On that subject I beg to refer to a report which has been published and circulated in Bolton, within the last ten days, by the Committee of the Society for the Protection of the Poor, of which the Rev. J. Slade, vicar of this parish, is the president, and the Rev. J. S. Birley, vice-president, in which the following important information appears —

"Number of individuals constituting the families of applicants 2,656
Average income per week . . . . . 1s. 2¾d.
Average income per week of parties relieved . . . . . 10¼d."

W. N.

NOTES

INTRODUCTION

1   I should emphasize at the outset that, although the focus of the historiography to be addressed is often characterized as 'mid-Victorian', the term 'mid-Victorian' is used ambiguously, for discussion generally refers to a longer period, roughly 1830 to the 1890s. For an explanation of my own usage, see below, p.241 n.231.

2   Like 'the mid-Victorian period', the terms 'popular' and 'middle class' are ambiguous. I take 'popular' to signify the populace at large or at least a majority of its members. This generalization seems appropriate given that, even in discussions which focus predominantly on labour élites, notions of stability and harmony depend for their conviction on some variant of the view that élite workers led the rest into social consensus with the employing/ruling classes. Similarly, although the historians with whom I engage do not clearly identify 'the middle class', they seem to agree that the term 'middle-class hegemony' signifies the consolidation of a 'world view' consistent and compatible with the requirements of nineteenth-century industrial society. I therefore assume that, by the middle class, they mean the industrial employing class.

3   The temporal 'present' of my discussion is framed by the years 1975 and 1995, a period during which the histories that most concern me emerged. Following Michel Foucault, however, I engage with the present less as a period of time than as a distinctive discursive regime, or domain of rationality, which constitutes the enabling conditions on which truth effects are contingent. See Michel Foucault, 'Truth and Power', in *Power/Knowledge: Selected Interviews and Other Writings 1972–1977*, ed., Colin Gordon (New York, 1980), p.131; for a commentary on this construction, see Colin Gordon, 'Afterword', in *Ibid.*, p.241. See also Michel Foucault, 'The Subject and Power', in H.L. Dreyfus and P. Rabinow, *Michel Foucault: Beyond Structuralism and Hermeneutics* (London, 1982), pp.118–25.

4   Foucault, 'The Subject and Power', p.208.

5   *Ibid.*, pp.208–10.

6   Michel Foucault, 'The History of Sexuality', in *Power/Knowledge*, pp.183, 187–8; for a similar synthesis see Gordon, 'Afterword', in *Ibid.*, p.245.

7   Michel Foucault, *Language, Counter-memory, Practice, Selected Essays and Interviews by Michel Foucault*, ed., D.F. Bouchard (Ithaca, 1977), p.213; Foucault, 'The Subject and Power', p.221.

8   Michel Foucault, 'The Confessions of the Flesh', in *Power/Knowledge*, p.198; Foucault, 'The Subject and Power', pp.217, 220.

9   Foucault, 'The Subject and Power', pp.222–3.

10 *Ibid.*, pp.220–1; Foucault, *Language, Counter-memory, Practice*, p.213.

11 Foucault, 'Truth and Power', p.119.

12 *Ibid.*, p.133.

199

13 *Ibid.*, p.131.

14 *Ibid.*, pp.131–3.

15 Foucault refers to struggles against the power of men over women, parents over children, doctors over patients, teachers over students and employers over workers. Taking the medical profession as an example, he observes that it 'is not criticized primarily because it is a profit-making concern, but because it exercises an uncontrolled power over people's bodies, their health and their life and death' (Foucault, 'The Subject and Power', p.211).

16 *Ibid.*, p.211; Foucault, 'Truth and Power', p.133. For an overview of the kinds of question raised by Foucault's account of power, see Charles Taylor, 'Foucault on Freedom and Truth', in *Political Theory*, 12, 2, May 1984, pp.152–83; William E. Connolly, 'Taylor, Foucault, and Otherness', in *Political Theory*, 13, 3, August 1985, pp.365–76; Paul Patton, 'Taylor and Foucault on Power and Freedom', in *Political Studies*, 37, 1989, pp.260–76; Charles Taylor, 'Taylor and Foucault on Power and Freedom: A Reply', in *Political Studies*, 37, 1989, pp.277–81.

17 Foucault, 'The Subject and Power', pp.223–4.

18 *Ibid.*, p.184.

19 Salman Rushdie, *The Satanic Verses* (Dover, DE, 1988), p.168.

20 I use the term 'genealogy' as Foucault has defined it to denote a 'history of the present' which 'can account for the constitution of knowledges, discourses, domains of objects etc., without having to make reference to a subject which is either transcendental in relation to the field of events or runs in its empty sameness throughout the course of history'. This definition challenges the notion of history as a 'unitary body of theory which would filter, hierarchize, and order . . . in the name of some true knowledge and some arbitrary idea of what constitutes a science and its objects'. Foucault, *Power/Knowledge*, pp.83, 117.

21 My elision of the terms 'structure' and 'discourse' reflects the view that discourses invariably function structurally and that structures, in turn, are discursive phenomena, although structural imperatives may be implemented at a material level.

22 The subject is central to all of Foucault's work, but see, for example, Foucault, 'Truth and Power'; Foucault, 'The Subject and Power'. For a discussion of the representative figure, see Foucault, *Language, Counter-memory, Practice*, pp.205–17. Foucault's critique of modern ontology has since been taken up by a range of scholars, notably feminists, gay theorists and psychoanalytic theorists. The shift enacted by these scholars has in many ways prefigured my own approach and my work can be situated in the context of their debates. See, for example, Judith Butler, *Gender Trouble: Feminism and the Subversion of Identity* (New York, 1990); Teresa de Lauretis, *Technologies of Gender: Essays on Theory, Film and Fiction* (Bloomington, 1987); Teresa de Lauretis, 'Eccentric Subjects: Feminist Theory and Historical Consciousness', *Feminist Studies*, 16, 1, 1990; Joan W. Scott, *Gender and the Politics of History* (New York, 1988); Jeffrey Weeks, *Coming Out: Homosexual Politics in Britain from the Nineteenth Century to the Present* (London, 1977).

1 NARRATIVES OF THE PAST OR HISTORIES OF THE PRESENT?

1 By teleology I mean a rationale, based on the concept of final causes, which makes the present the end-point of historical explanation. Hence, any given teleology will prefigure a description of selected events in the past as the origin of a process which must terminate in a particular description of the present. See Michel Foucault, *The Archaeology of Knowledge*, transl., A.M. Sheridan Smith (London, 1969), pp.5, 8, 11–13, 16, 39, 70, 121, 125, 131, 201–3.

2 G.D.H. Cole, *A Short History of the British Working-class Movement, 1789–1947* (London, 1925; this edn, 1948), pp.104–5.

3   For an example of this contrast, see *Ibid.*, pp.96–119, and D. Thompson, *The Chartists: Popular Politics in the Industrial Revolution* (New York, 1984), pp.333–9. For further examples see below, pp.13–32.

4   More recent commentators seem nevertheless to agree that the movement's roots were firmly embedded in 'traditional' radicalism. See, for example, Thompson, *The Chartists*; Gareth Stedman Jones, 'The Language of Chartism', in J. Epstein and D. Thompson, eds, *The Chartist Experience: Studies in Working-class Radicalism and Culture, 1830–60* (London, 1982); Craig Calhoun, *The Question of Class Struggle: Social Foundations of Popular Radicalism during the Industrial Revolution* (Chicago, 1982); E.F. Biagini and A.J. Reid, eds, *Currents of Radicalism: Popular Radicalism, Organised Labour and Party Politics in Britain 1850–1914* (Cambridge, 1991).

5   E.P. Thompson, *The Making of the English Working Class* (Harmondsworth, 1968), pp.212–13.

6   *Ibid.*, pp.220–6.

7   See, for example, J.T. Ward, *Chartism* (London, 1973), pp.245–6; J. Foster, *Class Struggle and the Industrial Revolution: Early Industrial Capitalism in Three English Towns* (London, 1974), pp.6–7, 83–4; E. Royle and J. Walvin, *English Radicals and Reformers 1760–1848* (Brighton, 1982), pp.163–5; J. Saville, *1848: The British State and the Chartist Movement* (Cambridge, 1987), pp.15, 89; Calhoun, *The Question of Class*, pp.140–4. Even Gareth Stedman Jones, who argues that the 1830s did not give rise to a class-based critique, notes the class polarization of the period and seems thus to suggest that the middle and working classes came to define themselves against one another. G.S. Jones, *Languages of Class: Studies in English Working Class History 1832–1982* (Cambridge, 1983), pp.116–20, 170–1.

8   This is not to suggest a consensus among historians that 'class consciousness' was a 'real' link between the two periods, for there are various theories about when working-class consciousness emerged and how it responded to changing circumstances. I describe the concept as a 'historiographical' or 'interpretative' link because, whether engaged as a 'presence' or an 'absence', it is central to virtually all explanations of the transition from Chartism to mid-Victorian radicalism.

9   See, for example, Ward, *Chartism*, pp.54, 244–6.

10   As I will argue below, the problematic of mid-Victorian labour history, 'relative social stability', derives largely from the historiography of Chartism. Since that problematic was consolidated by 1985, I will discuss work on Chartism beyond that date only when it is relevant to my theoretical discussion.

11   By positivism I mean a mode of inquiry into the relationships between observable facts and phenomena which purports to preclude metaphysical speculation. It asserts that no statement can be meaningful in any objective sense unless it is verified by a reliable empirical test using the methods of logic and science. Positivist histories explore relationships between facts to explain the past, but they are shaped by important oversights. The first is that a fact is an event under description and that there is no independent way of ascertaining whether one description is more accurate than another. The second is that the methods of verification employed are themselves speculative, unstable and no less contingent on a particular world view than the statements referred to them. When this methodology is used to explain the past, it confers descriptions on its objects and then interprets the descriptions. In short, it explains itself to itself. The notion of correspondence between the description and some putative essence contained within the object described ultimately relies on faith. Hence, positivism does not exclude metaphysical speculation; it only excludes discussion of its enabling conditions, thus to obscure its own metaphysical contingency. These matters are discussed more fully in Chapter 4 below. See also Foucault, *Archaeology*, pp.202, 205.

12   R.G. Gammage, *History of the Chartist Movement: 1837–1854* (first published 1854; this edn, New York, 1969), pp.8–9.

13 *Ibid.*, pp.2–5, 8–9.

14 In Gammage's view, the movement's 'good' men, who were categorically opposed to all forms of violence – men such as Lovett, Vincent and O'Brien – were ultimately marginalized or driven out by self-serving individuals like O'Connor, Harney and Ernest Jones. The latter, he found, seduced the movement with clever, self-promotional rhetoric; divided it by canvassing irresponsibly the possibility of physical force; and ultimately undermined it with dishonest and deceitful practices. *Ibid.*, p.402. In its essential details, Gammage's account of the movement corroborated those of Cooper and Lovett. See Thomas Cooper, *The Life of Thomas Cooper, Written by Himself* (1st ed. London, 1872; this edition, with an introduction by John Sackville, Leicester, 1971); William Lovett, *Life and Struggles of William Lovett in his Pursuit of Bread, Knowledge and Freedom* (1st ed. London, 1876; this edition, London, 1920), vol. 1.

15 S. Webb and B. Webb, *The History of Trade Unionism* (first published, 1894; this edn, London, 1902), pp.157–61.

16 *Ibid.*, pp.160–1. The reference here is to Feargus O'Connor's 'land scheme'.

17 *Ibid.*, p.158. The Webbs were, of course, not categorically opposed to 'revolution'. Although they considered it inappropriate and futile in England, they supported and defended it in Russia. See S. Webb and B. Webb, *The Truth about Soviet Russia*, with a preface by Bernard Shaw (London, 1942).

18 *Ibid.*, p.164. This strength was exemplified for the Webbs in 'that system of authoritative mutual negotiation between the representatives of capital and labour which has become the distinctive feature of British Trade Unionism in the last half of the century' (*Ibid.*, p.172).

19 Like all 'Whig' historians, the Webbs failed to consider the possible ramifications of ignoring the fact that many who did not, like themselves, enjoy the blessings of 'progress', may not have been content to let history march 'independently' on. Paradoxically, they were not averse themselves to 'rewriting' history when it failed to march in the direction which they formerly predicted. Hence, between 1894 and 1920, as Theodore Rothstein illustrated, they changed their definition of trade unions and their account of trade union aims and strategies so substantially that they effectively reversed them. See T. Rothstein, *From Chartism to Labourism: Historical Sketches of the English Working Class Movement* (first published 1929; this edn, with an introduction by John Saville, London, 1983), pp.197–8.

20 The works included: J.L. Tildesley, *Die Entscheidung und die ökonomischen Grundsätze der Chartisten Bewegung* (Jena, 1898); H. Schlüter, *Die Chartisten-Bewegung: Ein Betrag zur Sozial-politischen Geschichte Englands* (New York, 1916); E. Dolléans, *Le Chartisme* (Paris, 1913). English language monographs to appear in America in the same period were F.F. Rosenblatt, *The Chartist Movement in its Social and Economic Aspects* (New York, 1916); H.U. Faulkner, *Chartism and the Churches: A Study in Democracy* (New York, 1916); P.W. Slosson, *The Decline of the Chartist Movement* (New York, 1916); Julius West, *A History of the Chartist Movement* (London, 1920).

21 As late as 1982, Gareth Stedman Jones referred to Hovell as the most influential historian of Chartism. See Jones, 'The Language of Chartism'.

22 Mark Hovell, *The Chartist Movement* (Manchester, 1925).

23 *Ibid.*, pp.300–12, esp. p.304.

24 *Ibid.*, p.1.

25 *Ibid.*, p.303.

26 Hovell nevertheless acknowledged that although 'the property qualification for members of Parliament' was abolished in 1858, vote by ballot 'established in 1872' and payment of Lower House members introduced in 1911, the remaining three points – universal male suffrage, equal electoral districts and annual elections – had not yet been implemented 'in their entirety'. *Ibid.*, pp.2, 300–1.

27 *Ibid.*, pp.300–12.

28 *Ibid.*, p.304.
29 *Ibid.*, p.307.
30 *Ibid.*, pp.304–7.
31 Hovell presumably meant that Parliament had undertaken to do so, and would pursue its commitment with the 1918 Representation of the People Act.
32 Hovell, *The Chartist Movement*, pp.301–2.
33 *Ibid.*, pp.259–62: Hovell saw the 1842 Plug Plot, for example, not as an initiative of the strikers themselves, but as 'a crafty device of the mill-owners of the Anti-Corn Law League to reduce wages and divert men's minds from the Charter'. Moreover, he attributed the plot's failure to lack of support from O'Connor, who 'dominated the movement to such an extent that a course of action of which he disapproved was condemned to futility'.
34 *Ibid.*, p.xxv.
35 I use the prefix 'proto' because the term 'Marxist' was not then in common usage.
36 G.D.H. Cole, *Chartist Portraits* (London, 1941), pp.29, 360. Cole did not elaborate on this judgement, nor did he address Rothstein's important observation that the suffrage was merely an instrument, the value of which depended on a clear understanding of how to use it. See Rothstein, *From Chartism to Labourism*, p.36, and below pp.18–20.
37 Cole, *History*, pp.96–7, 103, 111.
38 *Ibid.*, pp.94, 119.
39 Compare, for example, his assessments of Lovett – as a 'worthy', 'courageous', 'honest', 'industrious' and 'respectable' individual who 'would sooner have failed than have done any irrational or ignoble deed'; of Stephens, as a 'religious pariah'; and of O'Connor as a 'mob-orator' with 'a great deal of egoism' and 'a very small stock of ideas'. 'A thoroughly bad and rambling writer', he was also a leader unable to organize because he lacked the capacity for co-operation, he 'had no clear policy' and was, 'in truth, a disastrous leader'. Cole, *Portraits*, pp.62, 78, 336.
40 Cole, *History*, p.119.
41 *Ibid.*
42 *Ibid.*
43 *Ibid.*, p.120.
44 Asa Briggs, ed., *Chartist Studies* (first published 1959; this edn, London, 1965).
45 See, for example, Briggs, 'The Local Background of Chartism', *Ibid.*, pp.2, 6; Briggs, 'National Bearings', *Ibid.*, p.290; Donald Read, 'Chartism in Manchester', *Ibid.*, pp.31–3, 58–60, 63; J.F.C. Harrison, 'Chartism in Leeds', *Ibid.*, pp.172–3; R.B. Pugh, 'Chartism in Somerset and Wiltshire', *Ibid.*, pp.211, 218–19; Alex Wilson, 'Chartism in Glasgow', *Ibid.*, pp.279, 285; Joy MacAskill, 'The Chartist Land Plan', *Ibid.*, pp.340–1; Lucy Brown, 'The Chartists and the Anti-Corn Law League', *Ibid.*, pp.369–71; F.C. Mather, 'The Government and the Chartists', *Ibid.*, p.405.
46 Briggs, 'National Bearings', *Ibid.*, p.299.
47 *Ibid.*, p.301.
48 *Ibid.*, pp.291, 300.
49 Within a limited range of options, workers, in Rothstein's analysis, repeatedly made choices. They chose between leaders, sometimes acted independently of them and even rejected them when they were seen to have betrayed their constituents. Rothstein, *From Chartism*, pp.32, 75, 302.
50 F.C. Mather, *Chartism* (first published 1965; reprinted with revisions, London, 1975), pp.7–8.
51 *Ibid.*, pp.7–9; Donald Read, *The English Provinces, c1760–1960* (London, 1964), p.126; T.C. Barker and J.R. Harris, *A Merseyside Town in the Industrial Revolution, St. Helen's, 1750–1900* (London, 1959); W.H. Chaloner, *The Social and Economic Development of Crewe, 1780–1923* (Manchester, 1950); A.H. Birch, *Small-town Politics: A Study of Political Life in Glossop* (Oxford, 1959).

52   Mather, *Chartism*, p.10; E.P. Thompson, *The Making*, ch.8, *passim*.

53   Mather, *Chartism*, p.14.

54   *Ibid.*, p.11.

55   *Ibid.*, pp.13–14; A.R. Schoyen, *The Chartist Challenge: A Portrait of George Julian Harney* (London, 1958), p.20.

56   Briggs, *Chartist Studies*, ch.1 and p.348; Mather, *Chartism*, pp.17–20; Schoyen, *The Chartist Challenge*, p.183; I. Prothero, 'Chartism in London', *Past and Present*, 44, 1969, pp.76–105; B. Harrison and P. Hollis, 'Chartism, Liberalism and the Life of Robert Lowery', *English Historical Review*, 82, 1967, pp.503–35.

57   *Ibid.*, n.13; cited in Mather, *Chartism*, p.35.

58   A useful summary of these conclusions appears in *Ibid.*, pp.24–8.

59   *Ibid.*, pp.26–30.

60   Ward refers to Rothstein, *From Chartism*, and Reg Groves, *But We Shall Rise Again* (he does not include publication details). In his third reference, which is evidently to a lecture, he writes that '[i]n 1929 a young Oxonian, Hugh Gaitskell, taught the Workers' Educational Association that "Chartism, in its beginning the last and most violent protest of the new proletariat, reveals in its conclusion the triumph of a new bourgeoisie"' (Ward, *Chartism*, p.8).

61   *Ibid.*, p.8.

62   *Ibid.*, p.244.

63   *Ibid.*, p.245; West, *A History*, p.295.

64   Ward, *Chartism*, pp.245–6.

65   *Ibid.*, p.246.

66   *Ibid.*, pp.246–7.

67   *Ibid.*, p.247.

68   Royle and Walvin, *English Radicals*, p.192.

69   This disorder they saw as occasioned by the government's resignation in May and exacerbated by the 'Bedchamber Crisis'. Chartist delegates, they wrote, sought 'to rally the country in a series of mass meetings' and 'the forces of law and order were stretched to the limit', but most people refused either 'to contemplate serious violence' while the petition was under consideration, or to participate in a 'general strike' when it was rejected (*Ibid.*, pp.163–5).

70   *Ibid.*, p.180.

71   *Ibid.*, p.192.

72   'The line drawn' by the 1832 Reform Act 'for the exercise of the franchise was precisely made', Thompson stressed, 'to include all members of the middle and upper classes and to exclude all wage labourers'. As a consequence of the act, she continued, '[t]he interests of the manufacturers and shopkeepers which had seemed to many in 1832 to be allied to those of the working people now seemed to be being advanced in every area in which they conflicted with working-class interests'. This cleavage was further aggravated by the New Poor Law which, she tells us, 'divided the working-class radicals from the [bourgeois] Philosophical Radicals more sharply than any other issue'. Hence, in 1834, O'Brien could vilify former middle-class allies, remarking that '[i]n one respect the New Poor Law has done good. It has helped to open the people's eyes as to who are the real enemies of the working classes' (Thompson, *The Chartists*, pp.5, 28, 30; 35, citing O'Brien in the *Twopenny Dispatch*, 10 September 1836).

73   *Ibid.*, see preface, p.ii.

74   A similar observation was made with regard to Patrick Joyce's *Visions of the People* (see below). In a critique of this revisionist analysis, Philip Howell predicted accurately that Joyce's 'fiercest critics' would 'be those for whom class has been the master concept of their academic and personal careers'. See Philip Howell's review in *Journal of Historical Geography*, 17, 4, October 1991, p.469.

75 Thompson, *The Chartists*,, p.2. Notable among the latter was a volume of local studies which she edited with James Epstein in 1982. See Epstein and Thompson, *The Chartist Experience*.
76 Thompson, *The Chartists.*, p.12.
77 John Saville, review of Dorothy Thompson, *The Chartists*, in *Economic History Review*, 38, 1985, p.461.
78 Thompson, *The Chartists*, p.1.
79 *Ibid.*, pp.333–5.
80 *Ibid.*, pp.333–4.
81 *Ibid.*, p.335.
82 *Ibid.*
83 *Ibid.*
84 *Ibid.*, p.335.
85 *Ibid.*, pp.335–6.
86 *Ibid.*
87 *Ibid.*, p.336.
88 *Ibid.*
89 *Ibid.*, p.333.
90 *Ibid.*, pp.334, 337.
91 After 1850, Thompson observed, 'the working class' turned 'away from political solutions' and 'arrived at a non-political ideology'. They 'used the vote when they got it', she continued, 'to vote for the "non-political" Liberal Party' because 'the libertarian rhetoric of Gladstonian Liberalism' appealed to their new-found 'belief in the neutrality of political institutions' (*Ibid.*, pp.334–5).
92 *Ibid.*, p.337.
93 *Ibid.*, pp.2–3, 330.
94 O'Brien warned workers that the state was poised to become subordinated to capital, that the bill would oppose bourgeois interests to their own, and that their former allies, upon acquiring the franchise, would seek to withhold it from them. Most workers, however, remained confident both in the government's impartiality and in middle-class support for further reform. See Rothstein, *From Chartism*, pp.28–34.
95 *Ibid.*, pp.10–15, 26–34.
96 *Ibid.*, p.34.
97 *Ibid.*, p.7.
98 In Rothstein's view this awareness emerged fully only when the movement's centre of gravity shifted from Birmingham to the factory proletariat of Lancashire, Yorkshire and South Wales after the failure of the 1839 Convention. At Birmingham, he wrote, Chartism shed the last vestiges of middle-class influence and became a mature political party firmly based in the working classes. See *Ibid.*, pp.48–53.
99 *Ibid.*, p.7.
100 *Ibid.*, pp.51–3, 62–3, 75.
101 According to Rothstein, this 'backward-looking' thrust informed the two prevailing 'social views' within Chartism. One such view, elaborated by O'Connor, was of 'peasant proprietorship and class cooperation'. It was hostile to Socialism and Communism, the principles of which would, in O'Connor's opinion, 'destroy all incentives to industry', and it envisaged 'the three States of the Empire working harmoniously together, the people and the aristocracy reciprocally depending upon each other for comfort and advice, always recognising the right of property in its fullest sense to be the labour of the working classes'. By contrast, O'Brien sought the socialization of land and the means of production. 'In the direct gifts of nature', he insisted, 'there could be no private property', which was merely 'legalized plunder'. Neither of these formulations engaged the class 'structure' of society as a fundamental problem; both saw the power of 'capital' as merely 'knavery and plunder, which could be

stopped by legislation'; and both urged the subordination of industry to agriculture. See *Ibid.*, pp.51–2. In his citation of O'Connor, Rothstein's reference is to the *Northern Star*, 11 August 1836.

102 Rothstein, *From Chartism*, p.56.
103 *Ibid.*, pp.62–3.
104 *Ibid.*, p.63
105 *Ibid.*, p.64.
106 *Ibid.*, pp.61–4. The ulterior measures considered included 'a run on the banks, abstention from excise liquor, trade boycott of the opponents of the Charter, the arming of the people, and finally a one-month general strike'.
107 *Ibid.*, p.64.
108 *Ibid.*, p.75.
109 *Ibid.*, pp.66–7.
110 *Ibid.*, pp.68–9.
111 *Ibid.*, p.73–5.
112 *Ibid.*, p.75.
113 *Ibid.*, pp.76–8.
114 *Ibid.*, pp.81–3.
115 *Ibid.*, p.78.
116 *Ibid.*, p.90.
117 *Ibid.*, p.91.
118 *Ibid.*, p.355.
119 *Ibid.*, pp.354–5.
120 He meant specifically the 'political' labour movement and not the trades union movement. See *Ibid.*, pp.85–6.
121 *Ibid.*, pp.7, 92.
122 Gareth Stedman Jones, for example, set out in the 1970s to explore the 'language of Chartism'. But rather than producing a discursive or post-structuralist analysis, he simply engaged in a 'close reading' of a narrowly defined collection of Chartist newspapers, making virtually no allowance for the historical specificity of meaning. For critiques of his approach, see below, pp.36–8.
123 Just as Rothstein deplored the unscrupulous practices of supposedly independent and impartial scholars who excised whole periods of history, notably the Chartist era, to 'bolster up . . . frauds and villainous institutions', Hobsbawm castigated writers like W.H. Chaloner and W.O. Henderson, who, in their edition of Engels, supposedly 'whitewashed . . . the awful social and economic conditions of the working population in the first half of the nineteenth century'. See Rothstein, *From Chartism*, pp.93–4, and E.J. Hobsbawm, 'History and "The Dark Satanic Mills"', in *Labouring Men: Studies in the History of Labour* (London, 1964), pp.105–19, esp. p.106.
124 Hobsbawm, *Age of Revolution*, pp.249–54.
125 *Ibid.*, p.250.
126 *Ibid.*, p.255.
127 *Ibid.*, pp.255–6; E.J. Hobsbawm, 'Labour Traditions', in *Labouring Men*, pp.381–2.
128 E.J. Hobsbawm, 'Methodism and the Threat of Revolution in Britain', in *Ibid.*, p.24.
129 *Ibid.*; Hobsbawm, *Age of Revolution*, pp.256–7.
130 John Saville, 'The Christian Socialists of 1848', in *Democracy and the Labour Movement*, (London, 1954).
131 Saville, *1848*, pp.15, 89.
132 The force included a vast body of middle-class volunteers and some workers, although, in Saville's view, there is evidence that workers who participated did so reluctantly. See *Ibid.*, pp.102–26, esp. p.117.
133 *Ibid.*, p.125.
134 *Ibid.*, pp.170–4.

135 *Ibid.*, p.174.
136 *Ibid.*, p.202.
137 *Ibid.*, p.226.
138 The version of the dominant ideology thesis to which he refers describes 'the capacity of a dominant ideology to inhibit and confuse the development of the counter-ideology of a subordinate class' (Tom Bottomore, foreword to N. Abercrombie *et al.*, *The Dominant Ideology Thesis* (London, 1980), p.x). There is no doubt, according to Saville, that this theory is applicable to the 1850s (Saville, *1848*, p.226).
139 *Ibid.*, pp.220–7.
140 In mid-Victorian labour historiography, 'continuity' is indicated by the persistence of Chartist influence throughout the 1850s and of class tension and industrial conflict in the post-Chartist years. A.E. Musson finds that 'new model' trade unionism was not as innovative, pacifistic or 'capitalist-minded' as has been suggested and that the 'labour aristocracy', whose role is central to the most pessimistic accounts of 'change', had existed in one form or another long before the advent of the mid-Victorian period. See A.E. Musson, *British Trade Unions, 1800–1875* (London, 1972), *passim*; A.E. Musson, *Trade Union and Social History* (London, 1974), pp.9–11, 17–21, 70; A.E. Musson, 'Class Struggle and the Labour Aristocracy 1830–1860', *Social History*, 1, 3, 1976, *passim*. For a critique of Musson's view see Neville Kirk, *The Growth of Working-class Reformism in Mid-Victorian England* (London, 1985), pp.1–3, 9. For the 'novelty' of 'new model' trade unionism, see S. Webb and B. Webb, *History of Trade Unionism, passim*. For further emphasis on aspects of continuity, see I. Prothero, *Artisans and Politics in Early Nineteenth-century London: John Gast and His Times* (Folkestone, 1979); R.A. Leeson, *Travelling Brothers* (London, 1978).
141 V.I. Lenin, *Imperialism, the Highest Stage of Capitalism*, (Moscow, 1975), p.14. Rothstein advanced an account of the labour aristocracy which was similar to but less theorized than Lenin's. However, as John Saville has noted, he did so long before Lenin produced the analysis of reformism and labourism in which his theory of the labour aristocracy emerged. Although Rothstein's book was first published in 1929, the essays which it comprises were written between 1905 and 1929. They were informed, moreover, by journalistic work dating back to the 1890s in which he saw the labour aristocracy as central to British working-class politics. See Saville's introduction, pp.xxv–vi; Rothstein's preface, pp.1–5; the chapter entitled 'The Roots of Opportunism', pp.255–65; and Rothstein's long (not numbered) footnote, pp.261–3, in Rothstein, *From Chartism.*
142 Hobsbawm was subsequently to claim a similar subtlety for Lenin, suggesting that he situated the co-optation of labour leaders in a larger and more complex process of hegemony. See E.J. Hobsbawm, 'Lenin and the "Aristocracy of Labour"', *Marxism Today*, 14, 7, 1970, esp. p.208; V.I. Lenin, *What is to be Done?*, in *Selected Works*, vol. 1 (London, 1967), pp.120–33, 162–5.
143 Hobsbawm, 'The Labour Aristocracy in Nineteenth-century Britain', in *Labouring Men*, p.272.
144 *Ibid.*, pp.275, 290.
145 *Ibid.*, p.273.
146 *Ibid.*, pp.278–85.
147 *Ibid.*, pp.283–4, 288–91.
148 *Ibid.*, pp.285, 289, 290–1.
149 *Ibid.*, p.273.
150 *Ibid.*, p.275; the reference is to Thomas Wright, *Our New Masters* (1st ed. London, 1873; this edition, New York, 1984), pp.3, 6.
151 Hobsbawm, 'The Labour Aristocracy in Nineteenth-century Britain', in *Labouring*

Men, pp.273–4.

152 These included brassworkers, bookbinders, boot and shoe makers, compositors, painters, French polishers, iron-founders, fancy leather workers, shipwrights and typographers. See *Ibid.*, *p.289*.

153 *Ibid.*, p.287.

154 *Ibid.*, pp.290–1.

155 *Ibid.*, pp.290–3.

156 *Ibid.*, pp.294–7.

157 *Ibid.*, p.297.

158 *Ibid.*, p.298.

159 As variants of subcontracting he identified payment by result, piecework, 'buttying' and 'charter-mastering'. See *Ibid.*, pp.298–9.

160 *Ibid.*, pp.300–1.

161 Royden Harrison, *Before the Socialists: Studies in Labour and Politics 1861–1881* (London, 1965), p.5. The 'invention' thesis was advanced by Hugh Seton-Watson, *The Pattern of Communist Revolution* (London, 1953), p.341.

162 Harrison, *Before the Socialists*, p.5.

163 *Ibid.*, pp.3, 320.

164 *Ibid.*, pp.7–8, 36–8.

165 *Ibid.*, pp.5–8, 34.

166 *Ibid.*, pp.33–4. The quotation is from the *Fifth Report from the Royal Commission into Trade Unions*, vol. XXXIX, Minutes of Evidence, 1867 [3980–I], p.20, item 8753.

167 *Ibid.*, p.34, 37, 301. The quotation is from Thomas Brassey, 'Co-operative Production', *Contemporary Review*, July 1874, pp.215–16.

168 Harrison, *Before the Socialists*, p.6.

169 *Ibid.*, p.21. The reference is to Reform League, *To the Trade Unionists of the United Kingdom* (n.d. for the address, but first published 1865).

170 Harrison, *Before the Socialists*, p.32.

171 *Ibid.*, pp.6–7, 9.

172 *Ibid.*, pp.22–5.

173 *Ibid.*, pp.10, 25–7.

174 A. Marshall, 'The Future of the Working Classes: An Address Delivered on 25 November 1873', in A.C. Pigott, ed., *Memorials of Alfred Marshall* (London, 1925), p.105; cited in Harrison, *Before the Socialists*, pp.27–8.

175 'A Workingman', *Working Men and Women* (London, 1879), pp.111–12; cited in Harrison, *Before the Socialists*, p.28.

176 E. Eden, ed., *The Autobiography of a Workingman* (Edinburgh, 1862), p.49; cited in Harrison, *Before the Socialists*, p.29.

177 'A Working Man', *Reminiscences of a Stonemason* (1908), p.78; cited in Harrison, *Before the Socialists*, p.29.

178 Eden, ed., *The Autobiography of a Workingman*, p.54; cited in Harrison, *Before the Socialists*, p.29.

179 Harrison, *Before the Socialists*, p.29.

180 *Ibid.*, pp.30–7.

181 *Ibid.*, pp.38–9.

182 Foster, *Class Struggle*, pp.6–7.

183 *Ibid.*, p.7.

184 *Ibid.*

185 These determinants he listed as 'the closed shop, apprenticeship, higher ratios of skilled to unskilled, more men per job, [and] shorter hours' (*Ibid.*, p.48).

186 *Ibid.*, pp.48–9.

187 *Ibid.*, pp.48–52.

188 *Ibid.*, p.52.

189 *Ibid.*, p.72.
190 *Ibid.*, p.80. Those years were 1831, 1836, 1838, 1839, 1841, 1842, 1846, 1847 and 1848.
191 *Ibid.*, pp.81–3.
192 *Ibid.*, pp.83–4.
193 *Ibid.*, pp.118–19.
194 *Ibid.*, p.108.
195 *Ibid.*, p.109.
196 South Shields also experienced high unemployment and falling wages during the same period, Foster observed, as shipbuilding, its premier trade, began to be exported to Canada where labour costs were substantially cheaper. The town was not without a labour movement, but 'occupational solidarity' based on 'sectional shipping identity' prevailed, and impeded the further development of 'labour consciousness'. By contrast, employment in Northampton actually increased. A centre of cheap shoe-making to which London entrepreneurs had begun to remove their operations in the second decade of the century – because its workforce was unorganized, could subsist on less and was 'probably open to covert subsidy from the poor rates' – it absorbed a 'mass influx of rural immigrants in the 1850s' (*Ibid.*, pp.84–6, 106). However, the unmechanized shoe trade was a 'leader' among the sweated industries and although employment was high, conditions in Northampton were in many ways as wretched as those in Oldham (*Ibid.*, pp.86–7). Furthermore, the centre lacked a labour movement. '[A]ll that existed', wrote Foster, 'were small islands of organized workers amid a labour force whose main cultural ties were still with the countryside (72 per cent were immigrants in 1851) and whose immediate lives were often controlled by the small employers who gave them employment.' Hence, periodic attempts at unionization failed as, apparently, did 'every single strike' there between the 1830s and the 1850s. But this was to be expected, he concluded, because 'the whole pattern of Northampton's growth depended on the cheapness of its labour, its lack of militancy and the constant influx of workers from the surrounding countryside'. *Ibid.*, pp.102–3.
197 *Ibid.*, pp.123–4.
198 *Ibid.*, p.124.
199 *Ibid.*, pp.123–4.
200 *Ibid.*, p.147.
201 *Ibid.*, p.123–4.
202 *Ibid.*, p.149.
203 *Ibid.*
204 In Foster's view, 'economic recovery' was at best a partial explanation. In the cotton industry, he wrote, 'the pressure on wages was not relaxed till the early 1850s. The only development which *might* have had some effect was the lifting of the ban on machinery exports in 1842' as a result of which Oldham's engineering industry experienced 'very fast expansion, creating a relatively large sector of well-paid jobs as well as a labour force which was occupationally split into skilled and unskilled. But even here', he continued, 'the real dividends in terms of labour collaboration could only be drawn after the breaking of the old craft unions, and this did not take place until the engineering lockout of 1851. Up till then, the industry's rapid growth probably tended to intensify conflict' (*Ibid.*, pp.205–6).
205 *Ibid.*, pp.206–7.
206 *Ibid.*, pp.207–8.
207 *Ibid.*, pp.208–9.
208 *Ibid.*, pp.224–9.
209 *Ibid.*, pp.224–7.
210 *Ibid.*, p.227.

211 *Ibid.*, pp.229–33.

212 *Ibid.*, pp.234–5.

213 *Ibid.*, p.237.

214 *Ibid.*, p.229.

215 *Ibid.*, pp.237–8.

216 *Ibid.*, p.212.

217 See, for example, Geoffrey Crossick, *An Artisan Elite in Victorian Society* (London, 1978), p.14.

218 'Interview with E.J. Hobsbawm', in *Radical History Review*, 19, Winter 1978–9, pp.111–13, 116–17.

219 E.J. Hobsbawm, 'Trends in the British Labour Movement since 1850, in *Labouring Men*, p.330; E.J. Hobsbawm, *Revolutionaries* (London, 1973), p.251; H.J. Kaye, *The British Marxist Historians* (Cambridge, 1984), pp.132–5.

220 Reprinted in E.J. Hobsbawm, *Politics for a Rational Left* (London, 1989).

221 See Richard Price, 'The Future of British Labour History', in *International Review of Social History*, 36, 1991, p.251.

222 See, for example, Royden Harrison and Jonathan Zeitlin, *Divisions of Labour: Skilled Workers and Technological Change in Nineteenth Century Britain* (Brighton, 1985); John Foster, 'The Declassing of Language', in *New Left Review*, 150, March/April 1985, pp.29–46.

223 I have included Rothstein, Saville, Hobsbawm, Harrison and Foster in this category.

224 By this 'new breed of Marxists' I mean historians like Crossick, Gray and Kirk, who adhere to the materialist methodology of Marxism but affect a certain 'objectivity' towards capitalism which conveys the impression of intellectual and hence political detachment. See below, p.164, n62.

225 For my defence of these claims, see below, Chapter 4.

226 In a different context, Bryan Palmer has referred to this so-called broadening of historical analysis as the eclipse of materialism in the writing of history. He suggests that, by misappropriating E.P. Thompson's 'critical engagement with the inadequacies of the base-superstructure metaphor' and Raymond Williams's 'theoretical elaborations on "cultural materialism"', a particular species of post-structuralist analysis has 'denigrated the material' and 'reified the ideal'. See Bryan Palmer, 'The Eclipse of Materialism: Marxism and the Writing of Social History in the 1980s', in *The Socialist Register*, 1990, pp.114–15.

227 Some writers, like Trygve Tholfsen, accepted the theory in a 'limited' form. But he argued against total working-class capitulation to bourgeois values and insisted that 'cultural patterns cannot be 'derived' from a given social structure, however much they may reflect it'. Nor, he continued, 'can they be reduced to manifestations of something else presumed to be more fundamental', in this case the 'economic'. See T.R. Tholfsen, *Working Class Radicalism in Mid-Victorian England* (London, 1976), pp.157–8, 269, 278, 293. Others, like H. Pelling, rejected the theory altogether, arguing that the existence of the stratum has never convincingly been demonstrated, while A.E. Musson repudiated the notions both of 'revolutionary class consciousness' and of subsequent popular acquiescence in the *status quo*. See H. Pelling, 'The Concept of the Labour Aristocracy' in *Popular Politics and Society in Late Victorian England* (London, 1968); A.E. Musson, *British Trade Unions 1800–75* (London, 1972); A.E. Musson, *Trade Unions and Social History* (London, 1974); Musson, 'Class Struggle and the Labour Aristocracy 1830–1860'. Other contributors include H.F. Moorhouse, 'The Marxist Theory of the Labour Aristocracy', in *Social History*, 3, 1978, pp.61–82; Alastair Reid, 'Intelligent Artisans and Aristocrats of Labour: The Essays of Thomas Wright', in Jay Winter, ed., *The Working Class in Modern British History* (Cambridge, 1983). A useful survey of the debate appears in Gregor McLennan, *Marxism and the Methodology of History* (London,

1981), pp.206–66.

228 See for example, Takao Matsumura, *The Labour Aristocracy Revisited: The Victorian Flint Glass Makers 1850–80* (Manchester, 1983).

229 See, for example, Musson, 'Class Struggle and the Labour Aristocracy 1830–1860'; and G.S. Jones, 'Class Struggle and the Industrial Revolution', in *Languages of Class*, p.64.

230 Alastair Reid, 'Class and Organization', in *The Historical Journal*, 30, 1, 1987, p.224.

231 E.J. Hobsbawm, 'Debating the Labour Aristocracy' in *Worlds of Labour: Further Studies in the History of Labour* (London, 1984), p.217.

232 See, for example, Harrison's review of Geoffrey Crossick's, *An Artisan Elite in Victorian Society* (London, 1978), in *History*, 64, 1979, p.310; and Harrison and Zeitlin, *Divisions of Labour*, pp.1–18.

233 Norman McCord has insisted that we should not accept the labour aristocracy's existence simply because it was 'real' to contemporaries. Like 'class', he suggests, the labour aristocracy was one more popular superstition which 'enjoyed a kind of secondary reality as a source of inspiration'. Curiously, however, he also insists that, before the category of 'class' can legitimately be employed, it must be ascertained 'whether or not the workers of that period were generally conscious of belonging to the same social class as contemporary paupers'. If one assumes, as this second example indicates, that the subjective experience of contemporaries indeed constituted their 'reality', then it might be suspected that McCord is less concerned to represent the past as 'objectively' as possible than to invoke logic arbitrarily in defence of a particular version of it (Norman McCord, 'Adding a Touch of Class', in *History*, 70, 1985, pp.412–16).

234 See, for example, Kirk, *The Growth of Working-class Reformism in Mid-Victorian England*, p.1.

235 See, for example, G.S. Jones, *Outcast London: A Study in the Relationship between Classes in Victorian Society* (Oxford, 1971); G.S. Jones, 'Working-class culture and working-class politics in London, 1870–1900: notes on the remaking of a working class', in *Social History*, 7, 4, Summer 1974, republished in Jones, *Languages of Class*.

236 Jones, *Languages of Class*, pp.90–178, esp. pp.94–5.

237 *Ibid.*, pp.21–4, 179–82.

238 For comment on how '[t]he socio-political problems of the 1980s . . . [brought] renewed life to the long-standing debate about class in Britain', and on 'the defeats and retreats suffered by the labour movement under Thatcherism', see R.Q. Gray, 'The Deconstructing of the English working class', in *Social History*, 11, 3, 1986, p.363; and Neville Kirk, 'In Defence of Class: A Critique of Recent Revisionist Writing upon the Nineteenth-century English Working Class', in *International Review of Social History*, 32, 1987, p.3. See also David Mayfield and Susan Thorne, 'Social History and its Discontents: Gareth Stedman Jones and the Politics of Language', *Social History*, 17, 2, May 1992, pp.171–3.

239 Jones, *Languages of Class*, pp.237–8.

240 *Ibid.*, pp.90–9.

241 *Ibid.*, pp.99–100.

242 *Ibid.*, pp.100–1.

243 *Ibid.*, pp.93–5.

244 *Ibid.*, p.104.

245 *Ibid.*, pp.143–6.

246 *Ibid.*, pp.116–20, 170–1.

247 *Ibid.*, p.169.

248 *Ibid.*, pp.116–20, 170–1.

249 Jones, 'The Language of Chartism', pp.30–1.

250 *Ibid.*, pp.15, 51.

251 Jones, *Languages of Class*, p.178.
252 Calhoun, *The Question of Class Struggle*. See esp. pp.vii-xiv, 76, 118–34, 140.
253 Kirk, 'In Defence of Class', p.4.
254 *Ibid.*
255 Foster, 'The Declassing of Language', pp.29–45; see esp. p.43.
256 Bryan D. Palmer, *Descent into Discourse: The Reification of Language and the Writing of Social History* (Philadelphia, 1990), pp.128–33. Palmer himself describes his book as a 'polemic against historians' much-heralded utilization of what has come to be known as critical theory' (*Ibid.*, p.xiii).
257 *Ibid.*, pp.130–1.
258 *Ibid.*
259 *Ibid.*; p.133.
260 *Ibid.*
261 Joan Wallach Scott, 'On Language, Gender, and Working-Class History', in *Gender and the Politics of History* (New York, 1988), p.56. (This essay is a revised version of one originally published in *International Labor and Working Class History*, 31, 1987, pp.1–13.)
262 *Ibid.*, pp.57–9.
263 *Ibid.*, pp.57–8.
264 *Ibid.*, pp.58–9.
265 *Ibid.*, p.59.
266 *Ibid.*, p.60.
267 *Ibid.*, p.54.
268 Kirk, 'In Defence of Class', p.5.
269 R. Price, 'The Future of British Labour History', in *International Review of Social History*, 36, 1991, pp.252–3.
270 The explanatory significance of the labour aristocracy in earlier work was that, as an instrument of hegemony, it was also an agent of stability, mediating a middle-class world view to the rest of the working class and thereby procuring popular consent to middle-class rule. If the stratum did not function in this way, then the question of why (or whether) the majority of workers ceased to be troublesome remains unanswered and the stability postulated by historians remains unexplained. Beyond the implication that workers in general were immobilized because their leaders effectively deserted them, these problems are not addressed in the works under review. See, for example, Geoffrey Crossick, *An Artisan Elite in Victorian Society* (London, 1978), pp.13–19, 65; R.Q. Gray, *The Aristocracy of Labour in Nineteenth Century Britain* (London, 1981), p.38; R.Q. Gray, 'Bourgeois Hegemony in Victorian Britain', in J. Bloomfield, ed., *Class, Hegemony and Party* (London, 1977); R.Q. Gray, *The Labour Aristocracy in Victorian Edinburgh* (Oxford, 1976), p.7.
271 Crossick, *An Artisan Elite*, pp.16–19.
272 *Ibid.*, p.15.
273 *Ibid.*, p.18.
274 *Ibid.*
275 *Ibid.*, pp.45, 128.
276 *Ibid.*, pp.24–5, 58–9.
277 *Ibid.*, p.15.
278 *Ibid.*, pp.104–8, 130–8.
279 *Ibid.*, pp.136, 201–2. According to Crossick, the liberal commitment of politicized workers only began to falter in the 1870s when, during Gladstone's incumbency, they felt it had been betrayed. See *Ibid.*, pp.139, 212–27.
280 *Ibid.*, p.60.
281 *Ibid.*, pp.18–21.
282 *Ibid.*, pp.65–86.

283 *Ibid.*, pp.129, 136–7.

284 *Ibid.*, pp.136–7.

285 *Ibid.*, p.136.

286 *Ibid.*, pp.108, 111, 136.

287 *Ibid.*, pp.137–8.

288 *Ibid.*, p.136.

289 *Ibid.*, pp.111, 132, 134–6, 150–3.

290 *Ibid.*, p.153.

291 *Ibid.*, pp.60–87, 134, 161.

292 *Ibid.*, pp.129, 135, 249.

293 *Ibid.*, pp.138–9, 151.

294 *Ibid.*, p.136.

295 *Ibid.*, pp.108, 145.

296 *Ibid.*, pp.237–8.

297 *Ibid.*, pp.149–50.

298 *Ibid.*, pp.132, 135, 150.

299 *Ibid.*, pp.19–20. Notwithstanding the virtual absence from Crossick's account of the lower grades of workers, there is some suggestion that, where possible, they duplicated 'aristocratic' practices. Unskilled and semi-skilled dockworkers, for example, were shown to have elaborated a certain hierarchy whereby some kinds of work were held to be eminently superior to others. Hence, shipworkers enjoyed a higher status than shoreworkers, even though it may not have been adequate to denote respectability. And in the one friendly society examined which was apparently controlled by unskilled workers, the Irish were held to be inferior and therefore ineligible for membership. See *Ibid.*, pp.64–5, 186.

300 *Ibid.*, p.19.

301 *Ibid.*, pp.128, 130, 134. The synthesis of Crossick's discussion of 'meaning-systems' is borrowed from McLennan, *Marxism*, pp.222–3.

302 Crossick, *An Artisan Elite*, pp.19–20, 140, 150.

303 *Ibid.*, p.135.

304 *Ibid.*, pp.15, 19–20, 104.

305 I mean here that bourgeois hegemony implies a particular hierarchy; that to accept a privileged place in the hierarchy is to accept the hierarchy itself; and that to do so is to submit to the logic of bourgeois hegemony.

306 Crossick, *An Artisan Elite*, p.22.

307 *Ibid.*, p.20; McLennan, *Marxism*, pp.222–3.

308 *Ibid.*, p.222–3. According to Foucault, the phenomenological approach to which McLennan refers provides 'a means of communication between the space of the body and the time of culture, between the determinations of nature and the weight of history, but only on condition that the body, and, through it, nature, should first be posited in the experience of an irreducible spatiality, and that culture, the carrier of history, should be experienced first of all in the immediacy of its sedimented significations'. Foucault describes 'the analysis of actual experience' as 'a discourse of mixed nature: it is directed to a specific yet ambiguous stratum, concrete enough for it to be possible to apply to it a meticulous and descriptive language, yet sufficiently removed from the positivity of things for it to be possible, from that starting-point, to escape from that naïveté, to contest it and seek foundations for it. This analysis seeks to articulate the possible objectivity of a knowledge of nature upon the original experience of which the body provides an outline; and to articulate the possible history of a culture upon the semantic density which is both hidden and revealed in actual experience. It is doing no more, then, than fulfilling with greater care the hasty demands laid down when the attempt was made to make the empirical, in man, stand for the transcendental.' Such a project, he observes, can never be complete, for '[w]hat is

given in experience and what renders experience possible correspond to one another in an endless oscillation' (Michel Foucault, *The Order of Things: An Archaeology of the Human Sciences* (London, 1970), pp.321, 336).

309 Gray, *The Labour Aristocracy*, pp.1–4.

310 *Ibid.*, pp.3–4, 7. Gray argued that the labour aristocracy was embedded in specifically Victorian industrial structures whereby it transcended craft sectionalism thus to distinguish itself from labour élites of other periods. He also agreed that authority at work was one of the 'aristocracy's' fundamental defining features and 'the link between economic position and those forms of personal behaviour – such as saving – prescribed by influential social values'.

311 *Ibid.*, pp.1–3. Gray's specific reference here is to Lenin and Hobsbawm.

312 *Ibid.*, p.1.

313 *Ibid.*, pp.18–21.

314 *Ibid.*, pp.5–7, 19.

315 *Ibid.*, p.7.

316 *Ibid.*, pp.5–7.

317 *Ibid.*, p.137.

318 *Ibid.*, pp.142–5.

319 *Ibid.*, pp.18, 97, 121, 123, 126.

320 *Ibid.*, pp.159.

321 *Ibid.*, p.137.

322 *Ibid.*

323 *Ibid.*, pp.138–9.

324 *Ibid.*, p.138.

325 *Ibid.*, p.139.

326 *Ibid.*, p.184.

327 *Ibid.*, pp.141–3, 184.

328 *Ibid.*, pp.187–8. Gray cited Robert Michels as author of the 'classic statement' of the *embourgeoisement* thesis: see R. Michels, *Political Parties* (New York, 1959), p.276. Michels, he observed, attempts to explain 'the conservative influence of labour leaders' by suggesting that, as they become 'intermediaries' and professional experts, the 'pressures of *embourgeoisement* erode any commitment [they may have] to transforming society'. Then, noting the visibility of such processes 'in the history of the labour movement', Gray outlined their embeddedness in the wider processes of hegemony.

329 Gray, *The Labour Aristocracy*, pp.163, 167–9, 173–9.

330 *Ibid.*, p.179.

331 *Ibid.*, pp.185–6. The references are to *North Briton*, 25 March 1861; 5, 12 October 1864; and *Labour Chronicle*, October 1894.

332 Gray, *The Labour Aristocracy*, p.184.

333 *Ibid.*, p.3; Gray, 'The Labour Aristocracy', p.7. See also Gray, *The Aristocracy of Labour*, pp.13, 63–66.

334 T.W. Laqueur, *Religion and Respectability: Sunday Schools and Working Class Culture 1780–1850* (New Haven, 1976); Tholfsen, *Working Class Radicalism*. Tholfsen began his contribution in the early 1960s. See, for example, T.R. Tholfsen, 'The Transition to Democracy in Victorian England', in *International Review of Social History*, 6, 1961, pp.226–48.

335 It has, of course, been argued elsewhere that the earlier period *was* stable insofar as revolution was neither a reality nor a possibility. But in the works I address, it is the social unrest signified by Chartist agitation rather than total social collapse to which Victorian stability and 'harmony' are contrasted. For arguments about social stability in the late eighteenth century and the nineteenth, see, respectively, I.R. Christie, *Stress and Stability in Late Eighteenth Century Britain: Reflections on the British Avoidance of Revolution* (Oxford, 1984), and B. Harrison, *Peaceable Kingdom: Stability and Change in*

Modern Britain (Oxford, 1982).

336 Laqueur, *Religion and Respectability*, pp.xi–xv.
337 *Ibid.*, p.94. It has been argued that those sections of his book which relate to 'managerial personnel and finance' are 'short and inconclusive', and that the movement's independence of élite influence is doubtful. See C.G. Brown's critique in *Economic History Review*, 31, 1978, pp.302–3. It also seems doubtful that the upper-class philanthropists who originated the movement would have permitted devolution to teachers and administrators who did not conform rigidly to, and would therefore seek to perpetuate, carefully prescribed attitudes and values.
338 Laqueur, *Religion and Respectability*, pp.3–7, 214–15.
339 *Ibid.*, pp.2–4, 241–2.
340 *Ibid.*, p.9.
341 *Ibid.*, pp.8–9.
342 *Ibid.*, pp.8–11, 19–20.
343 *Ibid.*, p.217.
344 *Ibid.*
345 *Ibid.*, p.161.
346 *Ibid.*, p.139: 'Knowledge was either a great good in itself, expanding and invigorating the mind, or it was a means by which the poor man could improve his life and that of his family.'
347 *Ibid.*, pp.148, 156–7, 160–1.
348 *Ibid.*, p.19.
349 *Ibid.*, p.20.
350 *Ibid.*, pp.241–4.
351 *Ibid.*, p.243.
352 *Ibid.*, p.245.
353 *Ibid.*
354 Malcolm Dick, for example, argued in a sustained critique that Laqueur's conclusions were substantially at odds with his evidence. In a different reading of Laqueur's sources, Dick found that 'Sunday schools were evangelical and conservative institutions, promoted and staffed by individuals from [higher] social classes'; that they 'espous[ed] an ideology which attacked the . . . behaviour and radical inclinations of the poor'; that the schools 'do not seem to have promoted an identifiable working-class culture'; that they were far from indifferent to the politics of teachers and pupils; and that they were centrally concerned with cultivating deferential attitudes among working people (M. Dick, 'The Myth of the Working-class Sunday School', in *History of Education*, 9, 1, 1980, pp.27–41, esp. p.36).
355 See R.K. Webb's review in *American Historical Review*, 2, 82, 1977, pp.1250–1.
356 See C.G. Brown's review in *Economic History Review*, 31, 1978, pp.302–3. See also Nicholas Rogers's review in *History of Education Quarterly*, 19, 1979, pp.477–83. According to the *Children Employment Commission of 1842*, Rogers argued, most teachers were chosen, regardless of their class origins, 'on the grounds of moral and religious conduct [rather] than of any peculiar fitness for the office of teacher. Hence, he concluded, teachers 'were likely to have been vetted by their congregation and to have shared a basic affinity of interest with the school managers and other prominent members of their chapel or church'.
357 *Ibid.*, pp.482–3: questioning the economic independence of the schools, Rogers insisted that '[v]ery little is known about the finances of the Sunday schools and it is far from clear that middle-class contributions to the annual fund-raising sermons were inconsequential'. See also Webb's review, p.1251.
358 Rogers's review, pp.482–3.
359 Laqueur, *Religion and Respectability*, pp.241, 245.
360 *Ibid.*, p.219.

361 *Ibid.*, p.19.
362 *Ibid.*, p.20.
363 Tholfsen, *Working Class Radicalism*, preface and p.12.
364 *Ibid.*, pp.157–9.
365 *Ibid.*, p.13.
366 *Ibid.*, pp.23–5.
367 *Ibid.*, p.13.
368 *Ibid.*, pp.86, 121.
369 *Ibid.*, pp.61, 83,
370 *Ibid.*, pp.102, 120–1.
371 *Ibid.*, pp.217.
372 *Ibid.*, pp.243–9.
373 *Ibid.*, pp.246–9, 320, 325. Individuals might, of course, rise above the subaltern role and such men were idealized, according to Tholfsen, along with the virtues that purportedly elevated them. But although the independent workingman 'sought to mitigate . . . [the] effects' of class society, he did not attempt 'to change the class structure'. Hence, an individual might aspire to a higher status but the subordinate role of the working class was accepted, along with the social hierarchy. See *Ibid.*, pp.243–6.
374 See J.E. Cronin's critique in *Journal of Economic History*, 37, 1977, pp.848–9.
375 See Robert Storch's critique in *Labour History*, 20, 1979, pp.149–50.
376 Tholfsen, *Working Class Radicalism*, p.120.
377 Storch's critique, p.150; Joan W. Scott's review in *Journal of Modern History*, 51, 1979, p.566; Geoffrey Crossick, 'Reality of Power', in *New Society*, 39, 745, 13 January 1977, p.78.
378 Scott's review, pp.567–8.
379 *Ibid.*
380 Tholfsen, *Working Class Radicalism*, p.20.
381 Storch's critique, p.151.
382 Crossick, 'Reality of Power', p.78.
383 Tholfsen, *Working Class Radicalism*, pp.162–6.
384 *Ibid.*, p.164.
385 *Ibid.*, p.166.
386 *Ibid.*, p.167.
387 *Ibid.*, p.168.
388 Equality might, of course, have obtained within these exclusive institutions but the institutions themselves were not, in Tholfsen's narrative, the beginning and end of radicalism. If radicalism was characterized by the kind of exclusiveness which he describes, then, talk of an 'egalitarian' radical ethos is in my view little more than meaningless cant.
389 F.M.L. Thompson, *The Rise of Respectable Society: A Social History of Victorian Britain, 1830–1900* (London, 1988), p.360.
390 *Ibid.*, pp.98, 271, 360.
391 *Ibid.*, pp.355, 360.
392 *Ibid.*, pp.259–60.
393 *Ibid.*, p.352.
394 *Ibid.*, pp.200–4.
395 *Ibid.*, p.198.
396 *Ibid.*, p.199.
397 *Ibid.*, p.198.
398 *Ibid.*, pp.204–5.
399 *Ibid.*, pp.358–9.
400 *Ibid.*, p.359.

401 *Ibid.*

402 *Ibid.*, p.324.

403 The significance of gender and its oversight in the historiography under review is discussed in more detail below. See, for example, pp.64–5, 80–1, 125–6.

404 Michael Mason, 'Victorian Consumers', in *London Review of Books*, 11, 14, 16 February 1989, p.14.

405 Thompson, *The Rise*, p.361.

406 *Ibid.*, p.204.

407 *Ibid.*, p.359.

408 Patrick Joyce, *Work, Society and Politics: The Culture of the Factory in Later Victorian England* (Brighton, 1980), p.xiii.

409 Patrick Joyce, *Visions of the People: Industrial England and the Question of Class, 1840–1914* (Cambridge, 1991), pp.170, 337.

410 Joyce, *Work, Society and Politics*, pp.64, 73–4.

411 *Ibid.*, pp.11–12.

412 See T.R. Tholfsen's review in *Journal of Modern History*, 54, 1982, p.561.

413 Joyce, *Work, Society and Politics*, p.xiv.

414 *Ibid.*

415 *Ibid.*, pp.210–11.

416 *Ibid.*, p.81.

417 *Ibid.*, pp.62, 81.

418 *Ibid.*, p.xv.

419 *Ibid.*, pp.73–8.

420 *Ibid.*, pp.53, 62–3.

421 *Ibid.*, p.56.

422 *Ibid.*, pp.53–6.

423 *Ibid.*, pp.111, 116.

424 *Ibid.*, p.123.

425 *Ibid.*, pp.173–5.

426 *Ibid.*, pp.101, 209.

427 *Ibid.*, pp., 176–8.

428 *Ibid.*, pp.98–9.

429 *Ibid.*, pp.138–46. The generosity of one Keighley employer was so excessive, wrote Joyce, that it resulted in his bankruptcy (*Ibid.*, p.170). Workers were not deceived by superficial displays of largesse and would not be put off 'with a plate of beef and a glass of beer' when they believed a wage increase was in order. But, he noted, for kindly employers, whose concern for them was real, their affection was genuine and unreserved (*Ibid.*, p.149).

430 *Ibid.*, p.172.

431 *Ibid.*, pp.59, 98–100, 205, 210. According to Joyce, the majority turned out at election time 'by mills and wards' in the spirit of schoolboys playing 'cricket or football by "houses" or "forms"'. When political apostates were identified, they were shown less tolerance by their fellow operatives than by employers (*Ibid.*, p.220).

432 *Ibid.*, p.54.

433 *Ibid.*, p.55.

434 *Ibid.*, pp.229, 335–7.

435 Crossick, for example, observed that, although Joyce offered his analysis 'as the basis for reinterpretation of later Victorian relations', he was forced to acknowledge that not even the cities of Manchester, Liverpool and Leeds conformed to his paradigm. These cities, Crossick continued, contained the very 'forces for political and cultural independence so important in most urban areas'. See Geoffrey Crossick's review in *American Historical Review*, 86, 1981, p.841. See also Keith McClelland, 'Reviews and Enthusiasms', in *History Workshop Journal*, 11, 1981, pp.170–3.

436 *Ibid.*, pp.170–3.
437 Paul Thompson, 'Docile Workforce', in *New Society*, 54, 936, 23 October 1980, p.180.
438 *Ibid.*, p.173.
439 See T.R. Tholfsen's review essay in *Journal of Modern History*, 54, 1982, pp.562–3.
440 Patrick Joyce, 'Labour, Capital and Compromise: A Response to Richard Price', in *Social History*, 9, 1, 1984, p.74. This response emerged in the context of a debate between Joyce and Price in 1984 over the issues of structure, agency and historical change. The debate seems to have ended abruptly, however, and without resolution. See Price, 'The Labour Process and Labour History', pp.57–75; Joyce, 'Labour, Capital and Compromise', pp.67–76; Price, 'Conflict and Co-operation', pp.217–24; Joyce, 'Languages of Reciprocity and Conflict', pp.225–31.
441 Joyce, *Visions*, p.313.
442 See, for example, critiques of Patrick Joyce, ed., *The Historical Meanings of Work* (Cambridge, 1987), pp.1–30, by Michael Hanagan, in *Journal of Economic History*, 48, 1988, p.738; and Richard Price, in *International Review of Social History*, 34, 1989, p.332. The most consistent criticism of this volume was that Joyce and his contributors failed to attend adequately to popular agency and the dynamics of change. According to Price, the use of static linguistic and anthropological models by Joyce *et al.* served to displace rather than to expand 'labour history's traditional concern with class and power struggles' (*Ibid.*, p.332).
443 Joyce, *Visions*, pp.9, 11–12. In 1984 Joyce claimed to occupy a 'high ground' from which he looked 'down in puzzlement upon the wide reaches of accepted wisdom'. Clearly, in 1991, he was no less reluctant to situate himself at what he saw as the cutting edge of critical analysis. For his 1984 claim, see the debate between him and Price in Price, 'Conflict and Co-operation', p.224, and Joyce, 'Languages of Reciprocity', p.231.
444 One of the most persistent criticisms of Joyce has related to his misrepresentation of class analysis. See, for example, the reviews by H.J. Kaye in *American Journal of Sociology*, 98, 1, 1992, pp.221–3; Philip Howell in *Journal of Historical Geography*, 17, 4, October 1991, pp.468–70; Richard Price in *The Journal of Interdisciplinary History*, 23, 2, Autumn 1992, pp.338–40; Theodore Koditschek, *American Historical Review*, 97, 4, October 1992, pp.1217–18. Joyce observed that 'economic criteria' were uppermost in 'any definition of what the "working class" might mean', and, reducing class consciousness to a language of conflict and struggle which implied exploitation and resistance, argued that because that language was rarely spoken, class analysis was questionable. Joyce, *Visions*, pp.10–11, 16.
445 He 'pull[ed] back from the verge of denying class', not 'to retain the fig-leaf of Marxist decencies', but because 'class mattered'. 'It has its place,' he wrote, 'though it does from time to time need to be put in it'. The 'consciousness of *a class*', he intoned aphoristically, 'need not be the consciousness of *class*' (Joyce, *Visions*, pp.1, 5, 8, 15). Joyce rebuked other writers for failing to appreciate the extent to which language in general and dialect in particular generated 'meanings with which to manage daily life'. As a consequence, he wrote, they produced crude, bizarre historical fantasies about class traitors, labour aristocrats and 'other denizens of the nether world of false consciousness' (*Ibid.*, p.266).
446 *Ibid.*, p.16. Along with the historiography of 'class interests' he dismissed the categories of class analysis. The theory of hegemony, along with other 'Marxist notions of culture', were inadequate for his analysis of the symbolic structure of the social order (*Ibid.*, p.155). The 'labour aristocracy thesis', he found, failed to recognize that the labour aristocrat was no more than a 'rhetorical' and 'social' 'construct' (*Ibid.*, p.57). Yet the social construction of particular identity, albeit in a complex interaction of structure and agency, is scarcely news, and scarcely grounds for declaring that iden-

tity irrelevant. And given the profound importance which Joyce now accords to language, it seems highly inconsistent to trivialize an identity on the basis of its 'rhetorical construction'.

447 *Ibid.*, p.3. As examples of these 'new considerations', Joyce offered general references to M. Burawoy's *The Politics of Production* (Chicago, 1985) and *Manufacturing Consent* (Chicago, 1979), but his only *specific* reference was to himself: pp.6–8 of his introduction to *The Historical Meanings of Work*, in which he drew on Burawoy's work to suggest that co-operation and consent, rather than conflict, were the prevailing reality in the workplace.

448 Joyce, *Visions*, p.3.

449 *Ibid.*, p.3.

450 *Ibid.*, pp.5, 10, 113.

451 *Ibid.*, pp.100, 102.

452 *Ibid.*, p.17.

453 *Ibid.*, p.11.

454 *Ibid.*, pp.27–8.

455 *Ibid.*, pp.32, 51.

456 *Ibid.*, pp.13, 29.

457 *Ibid.*, p.30.

458 *Ibid.*, p.54.

459 *Ibid.*, p.40.

460 *Ibid.*, p.46.

461 *Ibid.*, pp.50–2.

462 *Ibid.*, p.87.

463 By 1991, Joyce had modified his earlier construction of 'deference'. He now saw it as 'less inward and more calculating' (*Ibid.*, p.313).

464 *Ibid.*, pp.93–4, 96.

465 *Ibid.*, pp.87, 90–1.

466 *Ibid.*, p.246.

467 *Ibid.*, p.94.

468 *Ibid.*

469 *Ibid.*, p.90.

470 *Ibid.*

471 *Ibid.*, pp.89–91.

472 *Ibid.*, pp.90–1, 112, 117.

473 *Ibid.*, pp.92, 109.

474 *Ibid.*, p.92.

475 *Ibid.*, p.145.

476 *Ibid.*, pp.147–8, 155.

477 *Ibid.*, p.228.

478 *Ibid.*, pp.155–8.

479 *Ibid.*, p.178. Italics added. In this passage, Joyce cites and endorses a view expressed by Mark Rutherford, author of the 1887 publication, *The Revolution in Tanner's Lane*.

480 *Ibid.*, p.170.

481 *Ibid.*, pp.171, 194, 199.

482 *Ibid.*, p.266.

483 *Ibid.*, pp.226–7.

484 Ballads inspired by the Tichborne agitation, wrote Joyce, were 'fuelled by the idea of "*vox populi, vox dei*", [and] . . . gave the people a sense of their own strength and agency'. The Tichborne case involved an unknown Australian, Charles Orton, who, in 1867, affronted the establishment by claiming to be the Tichborne heir. Joyce provides a brief account of the affair, emphasizing that the more Orton was resisted by the Tichborne family, the propertied and respectable, the more popular support he

attracted (*Ibid.*, pp.71, 253, 306).

485 *Ibid.*, p.323.

486 *Ibid.*, p.320.

487 *Ibid.*, pp.228, 260.

488 Perhaps the most generous in his praise is J.F.C. Harrison, who writes that '*Visions of the People* is a highly sophisticated and tightly argued presentation. At times it makes heavy reading and is somewhat repetitious. But this is a small price to pay for such a fine piece of scholarship' (J.F.C. Harrison, 'Top of the Pops', a review of Derek Fraser, *Cities, Class and Communication*, and Patrick Joyce, *Visions of the People*, in *History Today*, 41, July 1991, p.59). For more qualified praise, see Chris Waters, in *Social History*, 17, 3, October 1992, pp.513–16; Howell's review, pp.468–70; and J.G. Rule, in *The English Historical Review*, 107, 423, 1992, pp.414–15. Less favourably impressed are Harvey J. Kaye, in *American Journal of Sociology*, 98, 1, 1992, pp.221–3; Richard Price in *The Journal of Interdisciplinary History*, 23, 2, 1992, pp.338–40; and Koditschek's review, pp.1217–18.

489 See, for example, Price, in *The Journal of Interdisciplinary History*, 23, 2, 1992, p.339; and Koditschek's review, p.1218.

490 See the review by N.N. Feltes in *Victorian Studies*, 35, 4, Summer 1992, p.447.

491 As Richard Price observes, he takes *Reynold's Newspaper* 'to represent mid-nineteenth century working-class politics' and then uses it 'to confirm the liberal character of . . . [working-class] radicalism. But the same exercise using *The Beehive* might have produced a more conflict-ridden vision'. See Price's review in *The Journal of Interdisciplinary History*, 23, 2, Autumn 1992, p.340.

492 Koditschek's review, p.1218.

493 Feltes's review, p.447.

494 Joyce, *Visions*, pp.29, 334.

495 Koditschek's review, p.1218.

496 See the review by Waters, p.515. According to Richard Price, Joyce's workforce is the 'working class of the liberal imagination'. See the review by Price, p.339.

497 See Feltes's review, p.448. If, as suggested above, Dorothy Thompson's resistance to new theoretical approaches indicates her present-centredness, the adoption of such approaches by writers like Joyce and Stedman Jones can also be seen to reflect present-centredness. Politically, new forms serve to render the past compatible with currently dominant truths, while academically they facilitate the production of 'original contributions to knowledge' and thus enhance career opportunities.

498 This is not to say that various 'class' assumptions are not still current, but simply to suggest that 'class analysis' as critique of the social order has declined. For a useful account of the decline of class analysis, see E.M. Wood, *The Retreat from Class: A New 'True' Socialism* (London, 1986).

499 Biagini and Reid, *Currents of Radicalism*, p.9.

500 *Ibid.*, p.11.

501 See Wood, *The Retreat, passim.*

502 See W. Ferguson's review of Gray's *The Labour Aristocracy in Victorian Edinburgh*, in *History*, 63, 1978, p.141.

503 Virtually all nineteenth-century labour historiography, including the revisionist analyses, are fundamentally 'empiricist'. Although the latter employ sophisticated theories, they do so only as a way of shaping basically empiricist projects, finally subordinating their theories to empiricist methodology and thus assimilating them, as I will argue below, to a positivist epistemology which inevitably legitimizes the *status quo*. All seek to establish certain 'facts' about the past, but virtually all of the 'facts' available for consideration are those which were considered worthy of preservation by exceptional people who 'had a stake' in society. The powerless, if not all illiterate, were virtually all historically silent. Because their stories remain untold,

and only those of the more or less 'successful' are recorded, we get no real sense of those whom 'progress' passed by; hence the condition of the lower classes seems inexorably to have improved. Undoubtedly, 'empiricists' strive to make their enquiries as 'objective' as possible, but 'the past' surely speaks according to how it is interrogated, and the questions put to it always bear the imprint of the present – they are shaped by the subjective concerns of the historians who ask them. Because events in the 1980s cast doubt on earlier 'class' analyses of the nineteenth-century popular experience, Stedman Jones and Calhoun undertake to construct different teleologies, to elicit from the past different stories whereby current developments will be more intelligible. But despite their novel perspectives, they remain conventional in that they try to coax from the past some 'objective historical truth'. Steadfastly empiricist, Thompson suggests that, since the consciousness of nineteenth-century 'workers did not always conform to what theoreticians consider should have been correct for their stage of industrialisation, it may help to stand back a bit from theoretical preconceptions, and see what people actually were demanding, what they were defending, and why they took certain forms of action'. But, of course, empiricism, the 'science' of ordering 'facts' hierarchically and making educated inferences from them, is also theoretical. Transposed to the social sciences it consists in observing, selecting and arranging the 'facts' retrospectively 'to explain' problems or 'to answer' questions formulated in the present. And in the immediacy of Stedman Jones's, Calhoun's and Thompson's present, the besetting problem is to explain the decline of working-class consciousness which, purportedly revolutionary in the Chartist era, became 'reformist' in the mid-Victorian period and evidently conservative by the 1980s.

504 Remarkably, Stedman Jones said as much when in 1976, discussing the relationship between history and sociology, he observed that 'history, like any other "social science", is an entirely intellectual operation which takes place in the present and in the head' (Gareth Stedman Jones, 'From Historical Sociology to Theoretical History', in *British Journal of Sociology*, 27, 3, September 1976, p.296). Stedman Jones did not, however, pursue the implication embedded in his observation that history is also *about* the present and the subjective concerns of those who produce it, rather than about the past.

505 Cole, *Portraits*, pp.27, 360.

2 SOCIAL IDENTITY AND THE REPRESENTATION OF EXPERIENCE

1 The theory of interpellation is developed by Louis Althusser in his discussion of 'ideological state apparatuses'. He suggests that, through the medium of such apparatuses, 'all ideology hails or interpellates concrete individuals as concrete subjects'. But Althusser also suggests a tautology which rescues agency, at least partially. He observes that 'the category of the subject' is also 'constitutive of all ideology insofar as all ideology has the function (which defines it) of "constituting" concrete individuals as subjects'. See L. Althusser, *Lenin and Philosophy and Other Essays* (New York, 1971), pp.170–7; esp. pp.171–3.

2 One exception is the recent contribution by Margot Finn in which 'the nation' is suggested to have been a most compelling category. See Margot Finn, *After Chartism: Class and Nation in English Radical Politics 1848–1874* (Cambridge, 1993). Historians do not necessarily suggest that these categories were mutually exclusive. In each narrative, however, one predominates as the prevailing determinant of identity, and shapes the narrative accordingly.

3 Even liberal accounts which repudiate class as an important social determinant are forced to engage with class concepts and are elaborated largely in 'class language'.

4 To characterize class analysis in this way is not to diminish the importance which

Marx and his heirs have placed on the petit bourgeoisie.

5   In British labour history the term 'populism' has recently been employed by Patrick Joyce to dispute class constructions which emphasize division and conflict, even though populism itself usually signifies elements of conflict, social tension and revolution (or revolutionary potential): see G. Ionescu and E. Gellner, eds, *Populism: Its Meanings and National Characteristics* (London, 1969), and, in the English context, Michael Roe, *Kenealy and the Tichborne Cause: A Study in Mid-Victorian Populism* (Melbourne, 1972). Joyce cites both of these works and notes the departure of his own usage, but observes that a better alternative to populism is not available. The term must therefore be used, he writes, but 'purged as far as possible of associations automatically attaching to [it]'. He never satisfactorily explains, however, why those associations are inappropriate. (Patrick Joyce, *Visions of the People: Industrial England and the Question of Class*, 1840–1914 (Cambridge, 1991), pp.12–13.)

6   For critiques of this definition of populism see reviews of Joyce, *Visions*, by Richard Price in *Journal of Interdisciplinary History*, 23, 2, Autumn 1992, pp.337–8; and Theodore Koditschek in *American Historical Review*, 97, 4, October 1992, pp.1216–17.

7   See E.P. Thompson, *The Making of the English Working Class* (Harmondsworth, 1968); John Burnett, *Useful Toil: Autobiographies of Working People from the 1820s to the 1920s* (London, 1974); John Burnett, *Destiny Obscure: Autobiographies of Childhood, Education and Family from the 1820s to the 1920s* (London, 1982); David Vincent, *Bread, Knowledge and Freedom: A Study of Nineteenth-century Working-class Autobiography* (London, 1981); E.P. Thompson, *The Poverty of Theory and Other Essays* (London, 1978). See also B. Harrison, *Drink and the Victorians* (Pittsburgh, 1971).

8   See Chapter 1 above.

9   This 'corollary' is, of course, denied by proponents of élite theory which emerged in the late nineteenth century, notably in the writings of Vilfredo Pareto and Gaetano Mosca, had its heyday in the 1930s, and continues periodically to be revived. Opposed by its early champions to Marxian class analysis, élite theory is linked to the assumption that people are inherently unequal. It suggests that, in all societies, 'two classes of people appear – a class that rules and a class that is ruled. The first class, always the less numerous, performs all political functions, monopolizes power and enjoys the advantages that power brings, whereas the second, the more numerous class, is directed and controlled by the first, in a manner that is now more or less legal, now more or less arbitrary and violent'. Pareto attributed this distinction to the superior intellectual and moral endowments of individual members of the minority, proposing a direct correspondence between the degree to which one possessed these qualities and the extent of one's political and economic power. Mosca endorsed this view but added that superior individuals obeyed a single impulse to become organized, precisely because they were a minority, thus inevitably to exert their dominion 'over the unorganized majority'. In 1954 Lukács suggested that élite theory emerged to defend the *status quo* in countries 'where feudal elements were especially strong', Georg Lukács, *The Destruction of Reason*, trans. Peter Palmer (London, 1980) and various other writers, from Weber to Schumpeter and Karl Mannheim, attempted to reconcile élite theory to concepts of democracy. From a further term added by Mosca, 'the circulation of élites', they proceeded to the notion of equal opportunity, the implication always being, however, that opportunity would inevitably be seized by inherently superior individuals. In a detailed critique of élite theory, Tom Bottomore argues thus: even though societies may produce exceptional individuals, the notion that majorities are motivated only by external compulsion, that only minorities are capable of spontaneous individual effort, and the further notion that exceptional individuals who may advance societies form ruling élites, social élites or even necessarily acquire great social prestige, are unproven. Nor is there sufficient evidence, he continues, to support claims about the circulation of élites in past societies while, in

modern societies, the evidence tends to refute such claims. Finally, Bottomore points out the contradiction which inheres in the idea of equality of opportunity in an otherwise unequal society. 'Equality of opportunity, as the expression is habitually used', he writes, 'presupposes inequality, since "opportunity" means "the opportunity to rise to a higher level in a stratified society". At the same time, it presupposes equality, for it implies that the inequalities embedded in this stratified society have to be counteracted in every generation so that individuals can really develop their personal abilities; and every investigation of the conditions for equality of opportunity, for example in the sphere of education, has shown how strong and pervasive is the influence upon individual life-chances of the entrenched distinctions of social class. Equality of opportunity would become a reality only in a society without classes or élites, and the notion itself would then be otiose, for the equal life-chances of individuals in each new generation would be matters of fact, and the idea of opportunity would signify, not the struggle to rise into a higher social class, but the possibility for each individual to develop fully those qualities of intellect and sensibility which he or she has as a person, in an unconstrained association with others.' See Tom Bottomore, *Elites and Society* (first published 1964; this edn, London, 1993), pp.1–12, 102, 114–17. The purpose of this survey is neither to endorse nor to refute élite theory, but to emphasize that the historians under review do not invoke it (although there is a hint of sympathy with it in Patrick Joyce's work), and to suggest the implications of assuming that those historians accord agency only to the exceptional individuals whom they cite and discuss.

10 The Andover workhouse achieved notoriety when it was alleged that starving inmates who had been put to work converting bones into manure began to devour the rotten marrow and gristle. On the Poor Law, the workhouse and Andover, see N.C. Edsall, *The Anti-Poor Law Movement 1834–44* (Manchester, 1971), and J.R. Poynter, *Society and Pauperism: English Ideas on Poor Relief 1795–1834* (London, 1969)

11 I use the term 'subjective perception' to denote an individual subject's reflection on her/his 'experience', and the term 'subjective experience' to denote an individual subject's interpretation/negotiation, at any given moment, of structural/discursive imperatives. By contrast, I employ the term 'objective perception' to signify outwardly focused observations about other subjects or a putatively objective reality.

12 For a comprehensive survey of this literature see John Burnett, David Vincent and David Mayall, eds, *The Autobiography of the Working Class: An Annotated Critical Bibliography* (Brighton, 1984).

13 D. Thompson, *The Chartists: Popular Politics in the Industrial Revolution* (New York, 1984) p.ii., preface (italics added).

14 *Ibid.*, pp.94, 99–104, 375. The sources referred to are the autobiographies and/or correspondence of Harney, Frost, Fielden, Linton, O'Brien, O'Neil Daunt, Adam Rushton, Thomas Allsop and George White.

15 *Ibid.*, p.92.

16 This problem arises in all the histories with which I engage. It seems to reflect the reluctance of their authors to address the contingency of all knowledge and hence all hermeneutics. Those limits have been suggested by Michel Foucault, who writes that 'Historicism is a means of validating for itself the perpetual critical relation at play between History and the human sciences. But it establishes it solely at the level of the positivities: the positive knowledge of man is limited by the historical positivity of the knowing subject, so that the moment of finitude is dissolved in the play of a relativity from which it cannot escape, and which itself has value as an absolute. To be finite, then, would simply be to be trapped in the laws of a perspective which, while allowing a certain apprehension – of the type of perception or understanding – prevents it from ever being universal and definitive intellection.' It is in the very history of given lives, societies and languages, he continues, 'that knowledge finds the element enabling

it to communicate with other forms of life, other types of society, other significations: that is why historicism always implies a certain philosophy, or at least a certain methodology, of living comprehension (in the element of *Lebenswelt*), of interhuman communication (against a background of social structures), and of hermeneutics (as the re-apprehension through the manifest meaning of the discourse of another meaning at once secondary and primary, that is, more hidden but also more fundamental). By this means, the different positives formed by History and laid down in it are able to enter into contact with one another, surround one another in the form of knowledge, and free the content dormant within them; it is not, then, the limits themselves that appear, in their absolute rigour, but partial totalities, totalities that turn out to be limited by fact, totalities whose frontiers can be made to move, up to a certain point, but which will never extend into the space of a definitive analysis, and will never raise themselves to the status of absolute totality' (Michel Foucault, *The Order of Things: An Archaeology of the Human Sciences*, ed., R.D. Laing (London, 1970), pp.372–3). Foucault's epistemological approach is clearly at odds, then, with that of Hans-Georg Gadamer, who 'believe[s] that the universality of the hermeneutical viewpoint cannot be restricted even where it is a question of the multitude of historical concerns and interests subsumed under the science of history' (Hans-Georg Gadamer, *Truth and Method* (London, 1975), pp.xix–xx). For a guide to Foucault's discussion of hermeneutics see H.L. Dreyfus and P. Rabinow, *Michel Foucault: Beyond Structuralism and Hermeneutics* (London, 1982), p.228. For an extensive commentary on Gadamer's work, see J.C. Weinsheimer, *Gadamer's Hermeneutics: A Reading of Truth and Method* (New Haven, 1985). For a comparison of Foucault and Gadamer, see Q. Skinner, ed., *The Return of Grand Theory in the Human Sciences* (Cambridge, 1985), pp.21–39, 65–81.

17   Thompson, *The Chartists*, pp.123–5, 130–4.
18   *Ibid.*, pp.146–9.
19   *Ibid.*, p.136.
20   *Ibid.*, p.136 (italics added).
21   *Ibid.*, pp.136, 378.
22   It might, of course, be argued that educated inference is acceptable when it is consistent with a wider body of evidence, but since there are no independent evaluative criteria, either for the inference or the contextual information, such an argument would in my view be spurious.
23   It is possible, of course, that Ruthwell composed her own address and that it was published unaltered. But if this was the case, further problems arise. To what extent was the language in which she expressed it constitutive of the truths or conventions against which she spoke, and to what extent, therefore, might it have embedded her more firmly in the role which she sought to transcend? How firmly, for that matter, do our interpretative and deconstructive efforts tie us to the discourses within which those efforts are articulated? And, given the ambiguity of language and the fluidity of meaning, how can we ever know whether a late twentieth-century understanding of this 1845 newspaper report bears any relation to the meaning which Ruthwell sought to convey? These and similar questions will be explored further in Chapter 4.
24   Jutta Schwarzkopf, *Women in the Chartist Movement* (London, 1991).
25   *Ibid.*, pp.1–2.
26   *Ibid.*, esp. ch.4.
27   *Ibid.*, pp.101–22, 133–46, 301–2.
28   *Ibid.*, pp.280–2, 283–8.
29   *Ibid.*, pp.3, 35, 82.
30   *Ibid.*, pp.35–6.
31   E.F. Biagini and A.J. Reid, 'Introduction', in E.F. Biagini and A.J. Reid, eds, *Currents of Radicalism: Popular Radicalism, Organised Labour and Party Politics in Britain, 1850–1914* (Cambridge, 1991), p.5.

32 This is not to deny the extensive use by some contributors of 'primary' material. It is simply to reinforce the point that, if one is concerned with what people 'thought' and believes that their thoughts can be recovered, then one would presumably make every effort to consult critically the material which might, most directly, express their thoughts – material which they produced themselves.

33 E.F. Biagini, 'Popular Liberals, Gladstonian finance and the debate on taxation, 1860–1874', in Biagini and Reid, *Currents of Radicalism*, p.136.

34 A.J. Reid, 'Old unionism reconsidered: the radicalism of Robert Knight, 1870–1900', in Biagini and Reid, *Currents of Radicalism*, pp.214–43 *passim*.

35 John Shepherd, 'Labour and parliament: the Lib-Labs as the first working-class MPs, 1885–1906', in Biagini and Reid, *Currents of Radicalism*, p.187.

36 Biagini and Reid, 'Introduction', in *Currents of Radicalism*, pp.5–6.

37 Jonathan Spain, 'Trade unionists, Gladstonian Liberals and the labour law reforms of 1875', in Biagini and Reid, *Currents of Radicalism*, p.114.

38 Biagini and Reid, 'Introduction', in *Currents of Radicalism*, p.5.

39 *Ibid.*, p.5.

40 *Ibid.*, pp.5–6.

41 *Ibid.*, p.6.

42 *Ibid.*

43 *Ibid.*, p.5.

44 John Foster, *Class Struggle and the Industrial Revolution: Early Industrial Capitalism in Three English Towns* (London, 1974), pp.212–24.

45 T.W. Laqueur, *Religion and Respectability: Sunday Schools and Working Class Culture, 1780–1850* (New Haven, 1976), pp.170–239.

46 Neville Kirk, *The Growth of Working-class Reformism in Mid-Victorian England* (London, 1985), p.220.

47 F.M.L. Thompson, *The Rise of Respectable Society: A Social History of Victorian Britain, 1830–1900* (London, 1988), pp.355, 360.

48 T.R. Tholfsen, *Working Class Radicalism in Mid-Victorian England* (London, 1976), ch.8; R.Q. Gray, *The Labour Aristocracy in Victorian Edinburgh* (Oxford, 1976), ch.7; Geoffrey Crossick, *An Artisan Elite in Victorian Society: Kentish London 1840–1880* (London, 1978), chs 6 and 7.

49 Joyce, *Visions*, pp. 57–8, 156. Some of Joyce's emphases are reflected in a recent volume by Trevor Lummis, *The Labour Aristocracy 1851–1914* (Aldershot, 1994). The thrust of Lummis's argument is that 'the concept of the labour aristocracy is so seriously flawed that it should be modified or superseded'. He then challenges other 'labels – artisan, labourer, skilled, semi-skilled, unskilled, mechanic, handyman, craftsman', observing that 'these occupational categories display so many exceptions when used for the analysis of industrial, social and political experience within the working class that they should also be re-evaluated' (p.xii). To understand working-class experience and to explain 'the lack of revolutionary class action by the world's most developed working class', one must, in Lummis's view, consider other variables, relationships and experiences (pp.xi, 160–1). Adopting this procedure, he finds that it was women, in their capacity as domestic servants, rather than labour aristocrats, who functioned as the 'conduit for bourgeois values into the working class'. Women, he continues, were the authority figures who controlled families and initiated their children into class attitudes. With their 'system of support and regulation through family, friends and neighbours', women, he writes, also created stratification within the working class, 'establish[ing] their social level [within working-class neighbourhoods and communities] while their men were largely absent at the workplace' (p.162). Some historians may find Lummis's thesis provocative, but it is marked from the outset as a highly conventional and un-self-critical work. It begins with a statement of Lummis's prefigurative assumptions about his chosen period: 'there was

a social formation called the working class'; it 'had a shared sense of identity greater than the one they shared with the middle and upper classes'; '[c]lasses are not mere descriptions which categorise groups with different incomes and lifestyles but are active social formations which struggle for economic, political and social power in competition with other classes' (p.xi). Yet these assumptions are never problematized; he simply authorizes them with an appeal to convention. On the basis of this authority, he then substitutes one set of 'labels' for another, and the conviction of his analysis becomes contingent on the treatment of a whole range of categories as self-evident, ontological foundations.

50 See, for example, Michel Foucault, *Language, Counter-memory, Practice: Selected Essays and Interviews* (Ithaca, 1977); Michel de Certeau, *Heterologies: Discourse on the Other*, transl. by Brian Massumi (Minneapolis, 1986); Gayatri Chakravorty Spivak, *In Other Worlds: Essays in Cultural Politics* (New York, 1987).

51 Joan W. Scott, 'The Evidence of Experience', in *Critical Inquiry*, Summer 1991, pp.773–97.

52 *Ibid.*, pp.778–9.

53 *Ibid.*, p.782.

54 *Ibid.*

55 *Ibid.*, pp.786, 788.

56 *Ibid.*, p.790.

57 *Ibid.*, p790.

58 *Ibid.*, p.793.

59 *Ibid.*, pp.777, 793, 796.

60 *Ibid.*, p.796.

61 I should emphasize here that my main concern is with the constitution of experience *within* historical narrative. Although I identify concepts that are treated as foundations, I do not, as Scott recommends, attempt to grasp the experience of past actors. Instead, I suggest that any such attempt would be futile. For although Scott's critique of foundationalist history is thoroughly persuasive, her alternative is not consistent with that critique. At its most powerful, her argument seems to urge a relativist approach that is sensitive to the contingency of all categories, all orders of meaning and all discursive systems. Then, however, she steps back from the epistemological position to which her emphasis on contingency seems to point. She does so to propose a different kind of hermeneutics, or a different way of reading the evidence, which will supposedly give historians access to the experience that currently eludes them. What this move entails is a focus on discourse. By plotting the ways in which discursive terms are set and contested, she writes, historians can illuminate the possibilities and limits that language creates and thus the evidence by which experience can be understood. There are, I think, two serious problems with this alternative. The first is that it strains against Scott's very convincing argument that experience is not confined to a fixed order of meaning, that 'there are conflicts among discursive systems, contradictions within any one of them, multiple meanings for the concepts they deploy', and no guarantee that they will be understood by everyone in the same way. In suggesting that past experience can be grasped through discourse analysis, she seems to dismiss all these variables and to raise discourse itself to foundational status. Discourse may well shape experience, but if discourses generate meanings that can be understood by different subjects in different ways, then the character of experience may differ from one subject to the next. Moreover, even were we to entertain the possibility of a collective experience determined by discourse, how can we know that one discourse and not others was the most compelling determinant of experience at any given moment? The second problem is one I have already discussed at length and which hermeneutical analyses simply cannot escape. Although we might assume that historical evidence – including discourses inferred from historical documents – contains intrinsic and recoverable

meaning, there is no independent authority to verify that the meanings we impute to evidence are consistent with those it supposedly contains.

Other epistemologically sensitive studies are susceptible to the same critique. A notable example is the work of Mary Poovey. In a collection of essays on British cultural formation published in 1995, Poovey argues that twentieth-century mass culture was prefigured by certain domains of knowledge, each of which developed, complete with its own rationale, during the nineteenth century. Describing her approach as epistemological, she concedes the contingency of knowledge and the relativity of logic. And consistently with these concessions, she begins each essay by outlining certain foundational assumptions. She then consults various nineteenth-century documents to illustrate the currency of the discourses, or domains of knowledge, that concern her. Yet the evidence she adduces can be made to figure forth meanings very different from those she discerns simply by adducing them to different narratives. Moreover, since there is no independent authority to pronounce one construction more accurate than another, each, in effect, becomes a function of the narrative in which the evidence is construed. The conviction of Poovey's work rests, therefore, on an assumption that she does not acknowledge and cannot justify: the assumption that evidence contains intrinsic meaning which can be illuminated through analysis and interpretation. See Mary Poovey, *Making a Social Body: British Cultural Formation, 1830–1864* (Chicago, 1995), especially ch.1 and pp.25, 55, 74, 98–9, 115–16, 133–4, 156–7. For an alternative statement of the problems I have identified here see Robert F. Berkhofer Jr., *Beyond the Great Story: History as Text and Discourse* (Cambridge, MA, 1995), p.14. Other recent works that face these problems include J.R. Walkowitz, *City of Dreadful Delight: Narratives of Sexual Danger in Late-Victorian London* (Chicago, 1993); Antony Taylor, 'New Views of an Old Moral World: An Appraisal of Robert Owen', in *Labour History*, 36, Winter 1995, pp.88–94; Antony Taylor, 'Palmerston and Radicalism, 1847–1865', in *Journal of British Studies*, 33, April 1994, pp.157–179; Miles Taylor, 'Rethinking the Chartists: Searching for Synthesis in the Historiography of Chartism', in *The Historical Journal*, 39, June 1996, pp.479–95; Martin Hewitt, 'Radicalism and the Victorian Working Class: The Case of Samuel Bamford', in *The Historical Journal*, 34, December 1991, pp.873–92; Martin Hewitt, *The Emergence of Stability in the Industrial City: 1832–1867* (Aldershot, 1996); Dorothy Thompson, *Outsiders: Class, Gender and Nation (London,* 1993); Neville Kirk, ed., *Social Class and Marxism: Defences and Challenges* (Aldershot, 1996).

62   Laqueur, *Religion and Respectability*, pp.239–40, 245.

63   The term 'objective' is used to emphasize all material which is not self-reflective but describes the working classes from a supposedly detached position. Laqueur's objective sources include periodicals, local histories, parliamentary reports, Sunday school manuals, textbooks, sermons and works of fiction. See his bibliography in Laqueur, *Ibid.*, pp.261–87. Where working-class autobiographers explicitly or implicitly affect detachment in their commentaries, they are also held, in the present analysis, to claim an objective perspective.

64   *Ibid.*, pp.19–20, 85–6; James Hillocks, *Life Story: A Prize Autobiography* (London, 1860), p.20; F.W. MacDonald, *Reminiscences of my Early Ministry* (London, 1913), pp.20–2.

65   Laqueur, *Religion and Respectability*, pp.96, 119, 150, 156; Samuel Bamford, *Passages in the Life of a Radical*, vol. 1 (Manchester, 1844), p.7; Thomas Whittaker, *Life's Battles in Temperance Armour* (London, 1884), p.26; Joseph Livesey, *The Life and Teaching of Joseph Livesey, Comprising his Autobiography*, with an Introductory essay by John Pearce (London, 1885), p.42; Adam Rushton, *My Life, as a Farmer's Boy, Factory Lad, Teacher and Preacher 1821–1909* (Manchester, 1909), p.43.

66   Laqueur, *Religion and Respectability*, p.111; [Thomas Wright], *Some Habits and Customs of the Working Class by a Journeyman Engineer* (London, 1867), pp.15–16.

67 Laqueur, *Religion and Respectability*, p.102; Laqueur takes his reference to Barker from J.F.C. Harrison, *Learning and Living: A Study in the History of the Adult Education Movement*, 1790–1960 (London, 1961), p.45. Further references are to George Edwards, *From Crow Scaring to Westminster. An Autobiography* (London, 1922), p.21, and Tom Mann, *Memoirs* (London, 1923), p.13.

68 Laqueur, *Religion and Respectability*, pp.103, 107; Benjamin Brierley, *Home Memories and Recollections of a Life* (Manchester, 1886), pp.12, 38.

69 Laqueur, *Religion and Respectability*, p.153; Marianne Farningham, *A Working Woman's Life* (London, 1907), p.153.

70 Laqueur, *Religion and Respectability*, pp.156–7, 170; Thomas Cooper, *The Life of Thomas Cooper Written by Himself* (first published 1872; this edn, with an introduction by John Saville, Leicester, 1971), p.36; William Lovett, *Life and Struggles of William Lovett in His Pursuit of Bread, Knowledge and Freedom* (first published 1876; this edn, London 1920), p.7; Joseph McCabe, *Life and Letters of George Jacob Holyoake* (London, 1908), p.33; Tom Mann, *Memoirs*, p.4; Ben Tillett, *Memories and Reflections* (London, 1931), pp.26–8; John Saville, ed., *Dictionary of Labour Biography*, vol. 1 (1972), and vol. 2 (1974); George Edwards, *From Crow Scaring*, p.171. Thomas Carter, *Memoirs of a Working Man* (London, 1845), p.22.

71 Laqueur, *Religion and Respectability*, pp.136, 170; Lovett, *Life and Struggles*, pp.7–8.

72 Laqueur, *Religion and Respectability*, p.170; Edwards, *From Crow Scaring*, p.21; Carter, *Memoirs*, pp.18–19 (Laqueur gives the page number as p.22); Brierley, *Home Memories*, p.25. In this reference to Brierley, Laqueur provides a salutary example of the extent to which the selection of 'evidence' can shape the meaning of the 'evidence' selected. According to Laqueur, '[w]hen Benjamin Brierley's mother was very ill, he commented later that his first thought had been of "other boys who had been left motherless [and so] gone to rags both in clothing and in morals"'. This construction seems to imply very straightforwardly that Brierley was preoccupied with sympathy for such boys rather than with the contemplation of his own potentially imminent loss. If a larger part of the passage in which the quotation occurs is considered, however, the meaning generated by Laqueur can scarcely be sustained, for Brierley writes: 'She [his mother] was everything to me; and not all the romance that ever heated the blood of youth could have supplanted her in my affections. *When it was made known to me that the malady had reached a critical stage, I was overwhelmed with visions of what our home would be without her. I had known other boys who had been left motherless go to rags both in clothing and morals, and feared that such would be my fate*' (Brierley, *Home Memories*, p.25, italics added). This comment on Laqueur's usage may seem trivial insofar as he seeks, in this instance, merely to emphasize Brierley's commitment to a morality purportedly shared by respectable workers and fostered by the Sunday school. Laqueur's construction, however, imputes to Brierley a sense of community spirit such that the latter seems to think less of himself than of his fellows and to reflect thus the 'class' identity which Laqueur assigns him. But the larger quotation serves to suggest quite the reverse – that Brierley's first thoughts were for himself, that he was moved by self-interest rather than by any community spirit which might indicate his class identity.

73 Laqueur, *Religion and Respectability*, p.161; Thomas Burt, *An Autobiography* (London, 1924), p.44.

74 Laqueur, *Religion and Respectability*, pp.156–7; John Wilson, *Memories of a Labour Leader* (first published, 1910; this edn, with an introduction by John Burnett, Firle, 1980), pp.204–8.

75 Laqueur, *Religion and Respectability*, p.217; William Cobbett, *Advice to Young Men* (1829; facsimile edn, London, 1906), p.10.

76 Laqueur, *Religion and Respectability*, p.218; Thomas Cooper, *Eight Letters to Young Men of the Working Classes* (London, 1850), letter 2.

77 Laqueur, *Religion and Respectability*, pp.127–8; Joseph Barker, 'Minister of the Gospel' in *Mercy Triumphant, or Teaching the Children of the Poor to Write on the Sabbath Day . . .* (3rd edn, London, 1843), p.27.

78 Laqueur, *Religion and Respectability*, pp.xi–xv.

79 *Ibid.*, p.239

80 *Ibid.*, p.242.

81 *Ibid.*, p.245.

82 *Ibid.*, pp.241–2.

83 *Ibid.*, pp.241, 245.

84 *Ibid.*, pp.241–5.

85 Tholfsen, *Working Class Radicalism*, p.54.

86 *Ibid.*, pp.68–9.

87 *Ibid.*, p.88.

88 *Ibid.*, p.99.

89 *Ibid.*, p.71.

90 According to Tholfsen, these observations reflect 'an important aspect of the outlook of working men newly conscious of their own identity and worth, over against a middle-class that was not only bent on ruling them but on derogating their qualities as men' (*Ibid.*).

91 *Ibid.*, pp.216–21, 230–1.

92 *Ibid.*, pp.249–50, 258–9.

93 *Ibid.*, pp.124–5, 140–9. Tholfsen's references are to William Aitken's biography in *Oddfellows' Magazine*, July 1857, and Aitken's report to Lovett from Ashton-under-Lyne in 1839 in Add. MSS 34245A, f.19.

94 His good fortune might, of course, have made him more sensitive to distress and perhaps to class injustice, but his very success put him in a different relation than formerly to economic, social and political structures, and it is difficult to see how his identity was not changed accordingly.

95 Tholfsen, *Working Class Radicalism*, pp.113–15, 264; references are to G.J. Holyoake's correspondence to his father, 11 March 1842, MS Holyoake House, Manchester; *The Movement*, 1 January and 17 February 1844; *Reasoner*, June 1846; the *Leader*, 21 June 1851; *Workman*, 5 July 1861.

96 Tholfsen, *Working Class Radicalism*, p.312; Stan Shipley, *Club Life and Socialism in Mid-Victorian London*, History Workshop pamphlet (Oxford, 1971), pp.1–20; and Charles Murray, *A Letter to Mr George Jacob Holyoake* (London, 1854, Holyoake Collection, Bishopsgate Institute).

97 Tholfsen, *Working Class Radicalism*, p.313; reference is to Murray, *A Letter*.

98 Tholfsen, *Working Class Radicalism*, p.264; reference is to *Working Man*, 13 January 1866.

99 I do not, I repeat, deny that Holyoake could have remained sympathetic to his former equals. After all, sympathy was implicit in the views and initiatives of a range of middle-class activists from philanthropic reformers to radicals like Engels. But even as Engels, for example, theorized with Marx about proletarian dictatorship, he remained an industrial capitalist who exploited labour rather than a worker who sold it. One might express sympathy for those one exploits but so long as one continues to exploit them, then in effect one identifies against rather than with them.

100 Tholfsen, *Working Class Radicalism*, p.264; reference is to *Working Man*, 13 January 1866.

101 Tholfsen, *Working Class Radicalism*, pp.113–17, 149, 264–5, 312.

102 G.J. Holyoake, *Sixty Years of an Agitator's Life* (first published London, 1892; this edn, New York, 1984), vol. I, pp.42–3, 60, 178, 265, 271, 272; vol. II, pp.30, 40, 52–3, 67, 152, 157–9, 194.

103 Tholfsen, *Working Class Radicalism*, p.113.

104 Crossick, *An Artisan Elite*, p.107.

105 Gray, *The Labour Aristocracy*, p.121.

106 *Ibid.*, pp.5–7; Crossick, *An Artisan Elite*, pp.15, 19–20, 104.

107 See Ellen Chase, *Tenant Friends in Old Deptford* (London, 1929), pp.9–21, esp. pp.9–10; and Jane Connolly, *Old Days and Ways* (London, 1912), pp.1–12, esp. pp.1–3.

108 Crossick, *An Artisan Elite*, p.85; Chase, *Tenant Friends*, pp.47–8.

109 Crossick, *An Artisan Elite*, p.109; Chase, *Tenant Friends*, p.76.

110 Crossick, *An Artisan Elite*, pp.71–2; Connolly, *Old Days*, pp.104–5.

111 Crossick, *An Artisan Elite*, p.146; Connolly, *Old Days*, pp.104–5.

112 Crossick, *An Artisan Elite*, p.153; Connolly, *Old Days*, p.241.

113 I suggest two objects of speculation here. The first is that Chase's commentary, in its self-assured and self-important tone, is remarkably similar to speeches which Thatcher had been delivering with monotonous regularity for several years by the time Crossick's book was published. The second is that, for a Marxist ostensibly concerned with illuminating the consciousness and experience of nineteenth-century working people, a woman whose condescending 'objectivity' is so reminiscent of Thatcher's may not be the most appropriate source.

114 Crossick, *An Artisan Elite*, p.105; *Working Men and Women by a Workingman* (London, 1879), pp.36–7.

115 Crossick, *An Artisan Elite*, p.61; *Working Men and Women*, p.62.

116 Crossick, *An Artisan Elite*, p.129; *Working Men and Women*, p.111.

117 Crossick, *An Artisan Elite*, p.176; *Working Men and Women*, p.36.

118 Crossick, *An Artisan Elite*, p.136; *Working Men and Women*, p.32.

119 *Working Men and Women*, pp.viii–ix: although it might be suggested that he 'protesteth too much', he expressly assures 'all whom it may concern, that I am a working man. I was born of working-class parents, amid working-class surroundings; was educated in a working-class school, passed straight from school into the workshop, have lived all my life among working men and women, and – most explicit and conclusive evidence of all perhaps – have never earned a wage that has quite reached two pounds per week.'

120 Crossick, *An Artisan Elite*, p.201; Thomas Frost, *Forty Years Recollections* (London, 1880), pp.10, 28, 96.

121 Crossick, *An Artisan Elite*, p.220; F.M. Leventhal, *Respectable Radical: George Howell and Victorian Working Class Politics* (Cambridge, MA, 1971), pp.71–2.

122 Crossick, *An Artisan Elite*, pp.39, 156, 164, 154; references are, respectively, to [Thomas Wright], 'Riverside Visitor', 'Bundle-wood work and workers', in *Good Words*, 1883, pp.542–5; [Wright] 'Riverside Visitor', 'A Rookery District', in *Good Words*, 1883, p.545; Thomas Wright [Journeyman Engineer], *The Great Unwashed* (first published 1868; this edn, London 1970), pp.151–2; *Ibid.*, pp.11–12.

123 Crossick, *An Artisan Elite*, p.145; Wright, *The Great Unwashed*, pp.125–50: this specific comment appears on pp.125–7.

124 Crossick, *An Artisan Elite*, p.33; Crossick cites C.E. Buckley, 'Memoirs of Old Deptford', in *Transactions of the Greenwich and Lewisham Antiquarian Society*, 5, 1961, p.88.

125 Crossick, *An Artisan Elite*, p.119; Harry Gosling, *Up and Down Stream* (London, 1927), p.145.

126 Crossick, *An Artisan Elite*, p.63; Gosling, *Up and Down*, pp.7–8.

127 Crossick, *An Artisan Elite*, pp.74–6; [James Turnbull] 'Workingman', *Reminiscences of a Stonemason* (London, 1908), pp.76, 100.

128 Crossick, *An Artisan Elite*, p.199.

129 Gray, *The Labour Aristocracy*, p.37; Alexander Somerville, *The Autobiography of a Working Man* (first published 1848; this edn, London, 1951), p.88.

130 Gray, *The Labour Aristocracy*, p.53; *Fourth Report from the Select Committee on the Sweating System*, 1889, Minutes of Evidence, [331] XIV, p.80, item 26517.

131 Gray, *The Labour Aristocracy*, p.129; Wright, *The Great Unwashed*, pp.282–3.

132 Gray, *The Labour Aristocracy*, pp.137–9; Wright, *The Great Unwashed*, pp.6–20, 160.

133 Gray, *The Labour Aristocracy*, p.143; Wright, *The Great Unwashed*, p.126.

134 Gray, *The Labour Aristocracy*, p.91; L. Fleming, *An Octogenarian Printer's Reminiscences* (Edinburgh, 1893), p.21.

135 Gray, *The Labour Aristocracy*, p.92; Somerville, *Autobiography*, p.59 and H. Miller, *My Schools and Schoolmasters* (Edinburgh, 1854), pp.320–3.

136 Gray, *The Labour Aristocracy*, p.100; J.S. Blackie, *Notes of a Life*, ed. A.S. Walker (Edinburgh, 1908), p.228.

137 Gray, *The Labour Aristocracy*, p.135; reference is to a biographical sketch of Paterson in the *Reformer*, 6 May 1872.

138 Kirk, *Social Class and Marxism*, pp.220–2; Gray, *The Labour Aristocracy*, pp.5–7; Crossick, *An Artisan Elite*, pp.15, 19–20, 104.

139 See, for example, J.E. Cronin, 'The Wisdom of Conventional Wisdom', in *Journal of Economic History*, 47, 1987, p.776. See also the reviews by Theodore Koditschek in *Journal of Modern History*, 59, 1987, p.837 and A.L. Morton in *Science and Society*, 50, 1986–7, p.244.

140 Kirk, *The Growth*, pp.169, 220–2. A tendency simply to be rather dismissive of gender issues is suggested by Kirk's treatment of an article by Alice Wilson which appeared in the *Co-operator* in 1868. 'The very fact of a woman depending upon a man for her daily bread gives him power over her,' Wilson wrote, 'and in all but the very best natures, the man is thereby rendered egotistical, conceited and unjust.' Yet on the basis of a single reference to Dorothy Thompson, Kirk concludes that 'Wilson's views were far from typical', for '[w]omen's acceptance of "an image of themselves which involved both home-centredness and inferiority" was . . . an increasingly general feature of mid-Victorian society'. As noted above, Thompson's argument can be judged inadequate, even by her own criteria, and Kirk neither explains *why* he finds it convincing nor produces any evidence that the women in question accepted that they were inferior. Wilson's observation is from the *Co-operator*, 17 October 1868, pp.660–1.

141 Kirk, *The Growth*, p.219. See further comments on Kirk's treatment of William Marcroft in the following paragraphs.

142 The importance of such a consideration is argued persuasively by Joan Scott, who writes that 'concepts of class are created through differentiation' and that, historically, 'gender has provided a way of articulating and naturalizing difference'. Nineteenth-century languages of class, she continues, 'are built with, in terms of, references to sexual difference. In these references, sexual difference is invoked as a "natural" phenomenon; as such it enjoys a privileged status, seemingly outside question or criticism. Those who do criticize it (and there were those who did) have a difficult time challenging its authority for they seem to be disputing nature instead of social construction. Gender becomes so implicated in concepts of class that there is no way to analyze one without the other.' See Joan Scott, 'On Language, Gender and Working-class History', in *Gender and the Politics of History* (New York, 1988), p.60. This essay is a revised version of one first published in *International Labor and Working Class History*, 31, 1987, pp.1–13.

143 Kirk, *The Growth*, p.219.

144 Kirk, *The Growth*, pp.170–1; B. Wilson, *The Struggles of an Old Chartist* (Halifax, 1887), pp.40, 212, 229.

145 Kirk, *The Growth*, pp.179–80, 216; T.P. Newbould, *Pages From a Life of Strife, Being Some Recollections of W.H. Chadwick, the Last of the Manchester Chartists* (London, 1911); and C. Rowley, *Fifty years of Ancoats* (London, 1899), pp.5–9.

146 Kirk, *The Growth*, pp.216, 230, 163; Rowley, *Fifty Years*, pp.5–9, 8, 49, 50, 54.

147 Kirk, *The Growth*, p.88; Cooper, *The Life of Thomas Cooper*, p.393.

148 Kirk, *The Growth*, p.132; Leventhal, *Respectable Radical*, pp.113–19.

149 Kirk, *The Growth*, pp.225–6; B. Grime, *Memory Sketches* (Oldham, 1887), p.119.

150 Kirk, *The Growth*, pp.218, 156, 217; [Wright], *Some Habits*, pp.119, 35–6, 189.

151 Kirk, *The Growth*, pp.136–8; R.E. Tyson, 'William Marcroft (1822–94) and the Limited Liability Movement in Oldham', *Transactions of the Lancashire and Cheshire Antiquarian Society*, 80, 1979 (1980), pp.62, 64, 75; William Marcroft, *The Marcroft Family: A History of Strange Events* (Rochdale, 1889); J.C. Taylor, *The Jubilee History of the Oldham Industrial Co-operative Society Limited 1850–1900* (Manchester, 1900), pp.18, 37, 102, 129, 138, 170; *Co-operative News*, 15 September 1894; *Oldham Co-operative Record*, no. 3, July 1984; J.M. Bellamy and J. Saville, eds, *Dictionary of Labour Biography*, vols 1 and 2 (London, 1972 and 1974).

152 Kirk, *The Growth*, pp.217, 219; William Marcroft, *The Inner Circle of Family Life* (Manchester, 1886), pp.8–9, 11, 13ff.

153 Kirk, *The Growth*, p.217; Marcroft, *Inner Circle*, pp.29–30, 8–9.

154 Kirk, *The Growth*, p.138.

155 *Ibid.*, pp.137–8; Kirk declares Foster's claim open to question but evidently finds the question irrelevant for he fails to pursue it. See also Foster, *Class Struggle*, pp.212–24.

156 In Marcroft's own words, '[t]he capitalists are the parental fathers of the trade', and although 'labour workers have a power that can conquer a world of difficulties[,} . . . a forest of strength and a mine of intellect; . . . they are wanting in the tools and implements which father capitalists have got in their experience and opportunities'. William Marcroft, *A Co-operative Village: How to Conduct it and Where to Form it* (Manchester, ND), p.10.

157 *Ibid.*, pp.6–16.

158 William Marcroft, *Ups and Downs: Life in a Machine-making Works* (Oldham, 1889), pp.8–14, 50–5.

159 *Ibid.*, pp.20–2.

160 *Ibid.*, pp.29–30, 55–7, 59, 64–5.

161 *Ibid.*, p.66.

162 *Ibid.*, pp.36–7.

163 *Ibid.*, pp.37–8.

164 *Ibid.*, pp.43–4.

165 *Ibid.*, p.45.

166 *Ibid.*, p.39.

167 Kirk, *The Growth*, pp.197, 210, 214; Brierley, *Home Memories*, pp.49–50; Ben Brierley's Journal, June 1837, p.211.

168 Kirk, *The Growth*, pp.215–16; Brierley, *Home Memories*, pp.35–6, 50.

169 Kirk, *The Growth*, pp.214, 220–2; Brierly, op. cit, pp.14, 23, 45–9, 77–81.

170 *Ibid.*, pp.228–31. Kirk seems impressed by the sacrifices which his exemplars made in the pursuit of knowledge, but he considers neither the content of the knowledge which they pursued nor the extent to which it may have facilitated their 'ideological incorporation'. Hence it does not occur to him that Marcroft's patriarchal mentality, his proprietary attitude to his wife and family, and his advice to marriageable young men to choose their wives as they might choose an animal for purchase, may have been informed by a particular kind of knowledge engendered by and calculated to validate a social hierarchy which depended for its maintenance on both gender and class inequality.

171 In Kirk's view, 'whilst we possess a reasonably clear and detailed picture of the culture of the upper levels of the working class, our knowledge and understanding of the possibly wider appeal of respectability to a mass working-class constituency is

extremely limited'. He nevertheless concludes that there is sufficient evidence that many operatives were becoming more reasonable and that 'many working-class respectables, especially the leaders of the institutions of respectability, transmitted individualist values to the rest of the working class'. Apart from his 'leadership sample', however, all of his 'evidence' is 'objective'. It consists not only of the self-perceptions of the mass of working people whose identity he presumes to define, perceptions which might conceivably give some inkling of whether their world-view(s) approximated to those of their 'leaders', but also of constructions of such people by 'outsiders': politicians, middle-class observers and agents of the (mostly liberal) press. *Ibid.*, pp.135, 174, 176, 222.

172 This criticism is in one sense unreasonable, for 'to engage with the mass of working people' is, of course, impossible. But herein lies the fundamental flaw of a hermeneutics which aspires to contact 'the' consciousness and thus to delineate 'the' identity of a class.

173 Joyce, *Visions*, p.330.

174 *Ibid.*, p.17.

175 *Ibid.*, p.126. The reference is to J.R. Clynes, *The Right Honourable J.R. Clynes, P.C., M.P., D.C.L., Memoirs 1869–1924* (London, 1937), p.33.

176 *Ibid.*, pp.123, 156–7. The references are to Benjamin Brierley, 'A Christmas Dinner', in *A Bundle o' Fents from a Lancashire Loom* (Manchester, 1883) [page numbers not given]; Robert Roberts, *The Classic Slum: Salford Life in the First Quarter of the Century* (Manchester, 1971), ch.1; Joyce cites S. Reynolds, *Seems So! A Working-class View of Politics* (1911), ch.13, pp.116, 118.

177 *Ibid.*, pp.284–8, 293–4. The reference is to Benjamin Brierley, 'A Day at Bolton Abbey', in *Sketches*, vol. 3 [page numbers not given].

178 *Ibid.*, p.160. The reference is to J. Wilson, *Memoirs of a Labour Leader* (1980), pp.76–7, 95.

179 *Ibid.*, p.162. The reference is to W. Lovett, *The Life and Struggles of William Lovett . . .* (1920), pp.9–11.

180 *Ibid.* The reference is to T. Burt, *An Autobiography* (1924), p.125.

181 *Ibid.*, p.264. The references are to B. Turner, *About Myself 1863–1930* (1930), pp.19, 24, ch.2, pp.32–3, 48; and [Thomas Wright], *Some Habits*, part 2, pp.174–5.

182 *Ibid.*, p.57. The reference is to A. Reid, 'Hero of a Thousand Footnotes: Thomas Wright and the "Labour Aristocracy"', in J. Winter, ed., *The Working Class in Modern British History* (Cambridge, 1983), [page numbers not given].

183 *Ibid.*, p.61. The references are to W. Chadwick, *Pages from a Life of Strife* (London, 1911); Benjamin Grime, *Memory Sketches* (Oldham, 1887).

184 *Ibid.*, pp.80–1.

185 *Ibid.*, p.108. The reference is to an instalment of Aitken's autobiography which appeared in the *Ashton Reporter*, 2 October 1869. In the abstracted passage, Aitken observed: 'He would be a poor legislator and wretched well wisher to his country and his fellow man who could wish to permanently inure either capital or labour. Capital is the fruit of labour and all hoarded capital that is made reproductive proves advantageous to all classes of society . . . those who use their money in finding reproductive employment, in improving agriculture, in building mills, sinking mines, and all the various industries of the most industrial age the world has ever seen, are benefactors to all that come within their sphere of influence. The capitalist may benefit himself individually more than anyone else, but useful employment is found for others, blessings are multiplied more or less on every hand, and by their union and harmony they "make the desert blossom as the rose".' According to the copy of the *Ashton Reporter* which I obtained (and to which pagination has been added by hand), the passage quoted by Joyce is on p.3.

186 *Ibid.*, p.108. Although Joyce includes some references to literature in which are

emphasized 'notions of mutual interest and reciprocal obligations', his claim that such attitudes prevailed in the community-at-large remains unsubstantiated.

187 *Ibid.*, pp.108–9.

188 *Ibid.*, pp.108, 417. This literature consisted of several addresses: 'To the Factory Operatives of Oldham', 4 March 1853; 'To the Hand-mule Spinners of Ashton and Neighbourhood'; 'To the Master Cotton Spinners of Preston'; 'To the Manufacturers . . . Spinners in Your Employ' (title obscure, 1857?, 1858?). Other titles listed are 'The Late John Fielden of Todmorden'; 'On the Need for Discipline in the Mills'; and 'To the Self-acting Minders of the Hurst District' (near Ashton).

189 *Ibid.*, p.109.

190 *Ibid.*, p.235. The reference is to Benjamin Grime, *Memory Sketches* (Oldham, 1887). Commenting on popular rhymes and ballads, Grime observed that 'These rhyming outpourings of native talent please our fancy, and we highly appreciate them, and trust our readers will do the same. They reflect more than any ordinary epistle can do the sympathetic and party proclivities of the period. Attempts were made to depreciate these rhyming rhodomontades, but it was of no use. They were too expressive of the struggles and emotions that animated the body of the people during these periodical conflicts, and they enabled the great untaught to give vent to sarcasm and turbulent passions which ardour and zeal aroused in them. These rhymes were an easy way for the masses to express their sympathies and their antipathies. Reduced to verse in the native language of the locality, and adapted to some popular tune, the populace sang aloud or hummed their hopes and aspirations in a style of language suited to their intelligence.' The page number, excluded by Joyce, is p.168.

191 *Ibid.*, pp.234–5.

192 *Ibid.*, pp.235–6.

193 *Ibid.*, pp.122, 302.

194 *Ibid.*, p.302.

195 *Ibid.*

196 *Ibid.*

197 *Ibid.*, p.264.

198 *Ibid.*, pp.302–4.

199 *Ibid.*, p.303.

200 *Ibid.*, p.302.

201 *Ibid.*, p.262.

202 *Ibid.*, pp.18–19.

203 See Aitken's autobiography, serialized as 'Remembrances and Struggles of a working man for bread and liberty', in the *Ashton News*, 1869. The quoted reference to his father occurs on the first page of the 22 September 1869 edition. The reference to Aitken's having commenced work at eleven occurs in Tholfsen, *Working Class Radicalism*, p.249.

3 WHO ARE 'THE PEOPLE' IN MID-VICTORIAN LABOUR HISTORY?

1 The relevance of this last question is that all the arguments considered rely for their conviction on the notion of a common consciousness and a prevailing identity. Even Crossick and Gray, who state clearly that they are primarily interested in 'labour élites', argue that these élites mediated a particular world view to their underlings, thus effectively to incorporate them ideologically, or to assimilate them to a 'consensus' version of class identity. Indeed, it is the very extrapolation from exemplars to the wider community that makes each explanation of social harmony meaningful.

2 Even Patrick Joyce, who attempts to divorce respectability from economic considerations, seems constrained to acknowledge its economic connections, even if only to define it against them. See Patrick Joyce, *Visions of the People: Industrial England and the*

Question of Class, 1840–1914 (Cambridge, 1991), pp.78–9, 152–7.

3 See, for example, Neville Kirk, *The Growth of Working-class Reformism in Mid-Victorian England* (London, 1985), p.210.

4 Hugh Miller, *My Schools and Schoolmasters* (Edinburgh, 1893), pp.21–30, 41, 96, 103, 129, 141, 153.

5 *Ibid.*, pp.247, 358–9, 364.

6 *Ibid.*, pp.188, 338.

7 *Ibid.*, pp.286–8, 290.

8 *Ibid.*, p.367.

9 *Ibid.*, p.302.

10 *Ibid.*, pp.189–90, 311, 317–19, 367.

11 See above, p.79.

12 See, for example, Kirk, *The Growth of Working-class*, p.219, and Joyce, *Visions*, pp.35, 235.

13 Joyce, *Visions*, p.235.

14 Benjamin Grime, *Memory Sketches* (Oldham, 1887), pp.64–5.

15 *Ibid.*, p.14.

16 *Ibid.*, p.70.

17 *Ibid.*, p.119.

18 Kirk, *The Growth of Working-class*, pp.225–6.

19 Joyce, *Visions*, p.235; the phrase 'dialect idiom' is Joyce's, not Grime's.

20 *Ibid.*; Grime, *Memory Sketches*, pp.159–60, 168.

21 It bears repeating that the stress here is on ambiguity. If the writings of some individuals are seen to suggest that their authors regarded class as a political category, those individuals are not held to be representative. This construction should not, therefore, be seen to endorse any notion that class identity, albeit defined in political terms, prevailed among nineteenth-century workers.

22 Thomas Carter, *Memoirs of a Working Man* (London, 1845), p.130.

23 *Ibid.*, p.71.

24 *Ibid.*, p.87.

25 *Ibid.*, p.88.

26 *Ibid.*, p.142.

27 *Ibid.*, pp.142, 154.

28 *Ibid.*, p.163.

29 *Ibid.*, p.166.

30 *Ibid.*, pp.187, 201.

31 *Ibid.*, p.201.

32 *Ibid.*, p.23.

33 *Ibid.*, pp.43, 129–30, 218–19.

34 *Ibid.*, p.130.

35 *Ibid.*, p.71.

36 *Ibid.*, pp.21, 22–4, 60, 71–4, 87–8, 114.

37 J.I. Hillocks, *Life Story: A Prize Autobiography* (London, 1860), pp.23–4, 43.

38 *Ibid.*, pp.22; J.I. Hillocks, *Hard Battles for Life and Usefulness*, parts I and II (3rd edn, London, 1889), p.56.

39 Hillocks, *Autobiography*, pp.32–3; Hillocks, *Battles*, part I, p.56.

40 Hillocks, *Autobiography*, pp.32–3.

41 *Ibid.*, pp.35, 45, 61, 62–3, 66–9, 82–3.

42 Hillocks, *Battles*, part I, pp.139–46.

43 *Ibid.*, p.146.

44 *Ibid.*, pp.144–5; part II, p.110.

45 *Ibid.*, part I, pp.55–6; Hillocks, *Autobiography*, p.56.

46 Hillocks, *Battles*, part I, p.56.

47 Thomas Whittaker, *Life's Battles in Temperance Armour* (Manchester, 1884), p.69.
48 *Ibid.*, pp.70–1.
49 *Ibid.*, pp.21–2, 64–6.
50 *Ibid.*, p.148.
51 *Ibid.*, p.66.
52 *Ibid.*
53 *Ibid.*, pp.205–9.
54 Adam Rushton, *My Life, as Farmer's Boy, Factory Lad, Teacher and Preacher* (Manchester, 1909), pp.21–3, 32, 48, 143, 216–17.
55 *Ibid.*, pp.23, 49, 51–2, 60–2.
56 *Ibid.*, pp.223, 226, 236–8.
57 *Ibid.*, pp.48–52, 92.
58 *Ibid.*, pp.32, 140.
59 *Ibid.*, p.22.
60 *Ibid.*, pp.216–17.
61 *Ibid.*, p.92.
62 *Ibid.*, p.62.
63 *Ibid.*, pp.65–6. Though easily roused to demonstration, Rushton asserts, such people continued to purchase excisable articles and, reluctant to admit that they had deposits, would not join a run on the banks. He seems concerned here not to express regret that Chartism failed but rather to suggest that the people it sought to lead were scarcely worth the effort. If indeed Chartist strategies failed to inspire popular commitment, then perhaps the problem was that its leaders objectified its followers and refused to consider that their support might be contingent on judgements about how adequately the movement and its architects consulted and served them.
64 *Ibid.*, pp.140–1.
65 Marianne Farningham, *A Working Woman's Life: An Autobiography* (London, 1907), p.254.
66 *Ibid.*
67 *Ibid.*, pp.154, 203.
68 *Ibid.*, pp.203, 254.
69 *Ibid.*, pp.203, 254, 278.
70 *Ibid.*, p.92.
71 *Ibid.*, p.278.
72 *Ibid.*, p.77.
73 *Ibid.*, pp.33, 35.
74 *Ibid.*, p.254.
75 *Ibid.*
76 *Ibid.*, pp.45, 66, 75, 81, 191.
77 *Ibid.*, pp.131–4, 154–5, 156, 164–5, 170, 172, 179, 185, 187–8.
78 *Ibid.*, pp.12, 16, 19, 21–226, 28–32, 34, 35–6, 43–6.
79 This construction suggests 'totalization' as well as 'individualization', an equation formulated by Michel Foucault in his account of the alienation through which individuals are transformed into subjects. See Michel Foucault, 'The Subject and Power', in H.L. Dreyfus and P. Rabinow, eds, *Michel Foucault: Beyond Structuralism and Hermeneutics* (London, 1982), pp.211–16.
80 Alexander Somerville, *The Autobiography of a Working Man* (first published 1848; this edn, London, 1967), p.267.
81 *Ibid.*, p.266.
82 *Ibid.*, p.156.
83 *Ibid.*, pp.155–7. See also pp.267–79.
84 *Ibid.*, pp.270–9, 280–1.
85 *Ibid.*, p.287.

86 *Ibid.*, pp.155–6, 273–4.

87 The singular construction is Bamford's. See Samuel Bamford, *The Autobiography of Samuel Bamford: Passages in the Life of a Radical*, vol. II (first published 1839–40; this edn, with an introduction by W.H. Chaloner, London, 1967), part 2, p.248.

88 *Ibid.*, part 1, pp.6–7.

89 *Ibid.*, part 1, pp.7–8.

90 *Ibid.*, part 1, pp.266–7.

91 *Ibid.*, part 1, p.277.

92 *Ibid.*, part 1, p.281.

93 *Ibid.*, part 1, pp.277–8.

94 See, for example, the two pamphlets: Joseph Barker, *Aristocracy and Democracy, the Speech of Mr Barker at the Bolton Tea Party on Thursday Evening, September 28, 1848* (Wortley, Leeds, 1848); Joseph Barker, *The Triumph of Right over Might, or, A Full account of the Attempt made by the Manchester Magistrates and the Whig Government to Rob J. Barker of his Liberty, and Suppress his Publications and of the Signal Failure of that Attempt* (Wortley, Leeds, 1848).

95 Barker, *Aristocracy*, p.2.

96 *Ibid.*, p.6. The reader might find the gender bias in Barker's account of 'democracy' instructive, or my own emphasis on it anachronistic, depending, perhaps, on the importance which s/he attaches to gender issues and the extent to which s/he accepts that any meaning accorded to such documents is inscribed from the present and reflects present-centred political concerns.

97 Barker, *Triumph*, p.4.

98 Joseph Barker, *A Full Account of the Arrest, Imprisonment and Liberation on Bail, of Joseph Barker; together with an Account of His Triumphant Election For the Borough of Bolton* (Bolton, 1848), pp.1–8.

99 *Ibid.*, p.2.

100 See, for example, *Ibid.*, pp.2, 3, 4, 7; and Barker, *Triumph*, pp.3, 4.

101 Joseph Barker, *The History and Confessions of a Man, As put Forth by Himself – Showing how he became a Methodist and a Methodist preacher, and how, as he grew older, he gave up part of the old Methodist belief, and was expelled, and giving a true view of Methodism on both sides, the fair as well as the foul, the bright as well as the dark, together with a long and wonderful account of many other matters worthy to be read and thought upon* (London, 1846).

102 *Ibid.*, p.61.

103 *Ibid.*, pp.61, 67, 68–73.

104 *Ibid.*, pp.75–6.

105 *Ibid.*

106 *Ibid.*

107 See above and Chapter 2. See also Joyce, *Visions*, pp. 162, 178–9.

108 William Lovett, *Life and Struggles of William Lovett in his Pursuit of Bread, Knowledge and Freedom* (first published 1876; this edn, with an introduction by R.H. Tawney, London, 1920), vol. 2, pp.390, 449–50.

109 *Ibid.*, vol. 2, pp.449–50.

110 In 1836, Lovett writes, he drew up a petition to Parliament in which he expressed the conviction that '*the land itself cannot be given exclusively to any*'; 'that all the lands of this kingdom are in fact held *conditionally* of the king, as the executive of the people'; and that it is incumbent on those who occupy land to 'defray all the expenses of the army and the navy, of the household of the king, and other expenses attendant upon the carrying on of the Government and defending the country' (*Ibid.*, vol. 1, pp.92–3; italics in original).

111 *Ibid.*, vol. 1, p.74.

112 *Ibid.*, vol. 1, p.46.

113 *Ibid.*

114 *Ibid.*, vol. 1, p.45.

115 *Ibid.*, vol. 1, p.94.

116 *Ibid.*, vol. 1, pp.93–4.

117 *Ibid.*, vol. 1, p.94.

118 *Ibid.*, vol. 1, p.xxxi.

119 *Ibid.* See R.H. Tawney's introduction, p.vii.

120 Among those singled out for particular praise are William and Mary Howitt, who in 1856 engaged him as editor of their *People's Journal*, J.H. Parry, J.F. Mollett, and the Oldham MP William Fox who in 1848, to celebrate his 'public services' and 'private worth' arranged a testimonial and contributions to a presentation which included a silver tea service and a purse of 140 sovereigns (*Ibid.*, pp.328–9, 341–2, 368). The very occurrence of this testimonial seems to reflect a certain irony on the notion that Lovett and people like him embodied or exemplified a mass social identity, for the very honour accorded him, not to mention the gifts of silver and money, served to underline his exceptionality rather than his typicality.

121 Thomas Cooper, *The Life of Thomas Cooper Written by Himself* (first published 1872; this edn, with an introduction by John Saville, Leicester, 1971), pp. 34–5, 72, 89–91, 112–15, 128–32, 134–44, 154–64, 280–1, 286, 391.

122 Thomas Cooper, *Eight Letters to the Young Men of the Working Classes* (London, 1850), p.4.

123 Cooper, *Life*, pp.36, 145.

124 *Ibid.*, pp.138–42.

125 *Ibid.*, pp.182–4.

126 *Ibid.*, pp.212–18, 229–35; see also pp.16–17 of Saville's introduction.

127 See Chapter 2 for Laqueur and Kirk on Cooper's class identity.

128 See Cooper, *Letters*, p.11, for example, where Cooper urges his readers to emulate 'great men' but points out that some minds are suited to pedestrian labours, others to higher occupations, and that working people should be educated accordingly, accept their limitations and give their best in the work to which they are called. For an instance of Cooper's appeal to history, see *Letters*, p.31, where he points to historical and biographical works for '[e]xamples of perseverence, self-sacrifice, honour, uprightness, heroism, patriotism, philanthropy, and all true noble-ness'. For a shopping list of his 'great men' see *Letters*, pp.12, 14–15, 16–18, 20, and for his appeal to such figures to awaken the patriotism of young workers see Cooper, *Life*, pp.169–70.

129 Joyce, *Visions*, pp.178–9.

130 Cooper, *Life*, p.163.

131 *Ibid.*, p.179.

132 *Ibid.*, p.271.

133 *Ibid.*, p.277; the proposed plan was to accumulate funds co-operatively, by contribution, for the purchase of land which would gradually be redistributed in small workable allotments, thus to redeem factory operatives and to enable them to be self-sufficient.

134 *Ibid.*, pp.272–7, 303.

135 *Ibid.*, p.311.

136 *Ibid.*, pp.76–99.

137 *Ibid.*, p.99.

138 *Ibid.*, pp.100–1, 103–7.

139 *Ibid.*, pp.107–10.

140 *Ibid.*, pp.112, 122, 128–32.

141 Wright characterizes the majority of 'labour leaders' as lazy, inefficient, self-serving trouble-makers. [Thomas Wright], *Some Habits and Customs of the Working Classes* (London, 1867), part II, pp.36–8; [Thomas Wright], *The Great Unwashed by the*

Journeyman Engineer (first published 1868; this edn, London, 1970), pp.13, 52–3; [Thomas Wright], *Our New Masters* (first published 1873; this edn, New York, 1984), pp.70–6.

142 See Wright, *Unwashed*, pp.111–14; Wright, *Masters*, pp.v-vi; J. Hinton, *The First Shop Stewards' Movement* (London, 1973), pp.95–6; A. Reid, 'Intelligent artisans and aristocrats of labour: the essays of Thomas Wright', in Jay Winter, ed., *The Working Class in Modern British History: Essays in Honour of Henry Pelling* (Cambridge, 1983), pp.171–86.

143 Wright, *Unwashed*, pp.21–5.

144 *Ibid.*, pp.14–15.

145 *Ibid.*, pp.15–17.

146 *Ibid.*, p. 254; Wright, *Habits*, pp.118–24, 194, 240, 254.

147 *Ibid.*, pp.30–1.

148 *Ibid.*, p.32.

149 *Ibid.*, pp.34–5.

150 *Ibid.*, pp.37–8.

151 *Ibid.*, pp.39–41.

152 Joyce, *Visions* pp.263–4; Wright, *Habits*, pp.174–5.

153 *Ibid.*, pp.171, 174–5. Of eleven items on the predominantly 'classical' programme to which Wright refers, only three are 'readings' and none are in dialect. One is taken from Shakespeare's *The Merchant of Venice* and the other two are entitled 'Mr Pickwick and the Lady with Yellow Curl Papers' and 'The Rioters at the Maypole'. Wright commented on the 'popularity' of the second piece but attributed its warm reception to the superior reading skills of the Mr Smith who presented it rather than to its content. In this instance, therefore, Joyce seems clearly to have 'over-interpreted' his material.

154 *Ibid.*, pp.175–6.

155 Kirk, *The Growth*, p.156; Wright, *Habits*, pp.35–6.

156 Wright, *Masters*, p.25.

157 *Ibid.*, p.vii.

158 Wright, *Unwashed*, p.5.

159 Geoffrey Crossick, *An Artisan Elite in Victorian Society: Kentish London 1840–1880* (London, 1978), p.244.

160 *Ibid.*, pp.245–54.

161 *Ibid.*, pp.74, 76.

162 [James Turnbull], *Reminiscences of a Stonemason by a Working Man* (London, 1908), pp.75–6.

163 *Ibid.*, p.100.

164 *Ibid.*, pp.77, 115, 180, 188, 207–10, 238–40.

165 *Ibid.*, p.225.

166 *Ibid.*, pp.1–2.

167 *Ibid.*, pp.54, 69.

168 *Ibid.*, pp.182, 189, 207–8, 216–17.

169 *Ibid.*, p.193.

170 *Ibid.*, p.183.

171 *Ibid.*, pp.188–9, 192, 207–8.

172 *Ibid.*, pp.240, 247.

173 *Ibid.*, p.243.

174 Crossick, *An Artisan Elite*, p.76.

175 Turnbull, *Reminiscences*, p.240.

176 *Ibid.*, pp.115–65.

177 *Ibid.*, p.181.

178 *Ibid.*, p.231.

179 See below.
180 Thomas Burt, *An Autobiography, with Supplementary Chapters by Aaron Watson and a Foreword by Wilfred Burt* (London, 1924), p.156.
181 *Ibid.*, pp.163–4.
182 *Ibid.*, p.199.
183 *Ibid.*, pp.146–8.
184 *Ibid.*, pp.113, 121, 156, 166.
185 *Ibid.*, pp.155–6, 191–6.
186 *Ibid.*, pp.155, 177, 191–5, 205.
187 *Ibid.*, pp.177, 186, 196, 302–5.
188 *Ibid.*, pp.201–5.
189 *Ibid.*, p.204.
190 John Wilson, *Memories of a Labour Leader* (first published 1910; this edn, with an introduction by John Burnett, Firle, 1980), pp.62, 70, 72, 75, 118, 207, 214, 215, 218, 225–6, 227–32.
191 *Ibid.*, pp.207, 210, 214, 215, 225–7, 260–2.
192 *Ibid.*, pp.222–4, 231–2, 271–2.
193 *Ibid.*, p.316.
194 *Ibid.*, pp.244–8.
195 *Ibid.*, p.240.
196 *Ibid.*, p.319.
197 *Ibid.*, pp.318–19.
198 *Ibid.*, pp.194–6.
199 *Ibid.*, pp.227–9.
200 *Ibid.*, p.305.
201 Sir George Edwards, *From Crow Scaring to Westminster. An Autobiography* (London, 1922), pp.41–3, 61, 119, 121–22, 221–2.
202 Ben Turner, *About Myself 1863–1930* (London, 1930), pp.84, 163.
203 Ben Tillett, *Memories and Reflections* (London, 1931), pp.92, 116, 191.
204 Edwards, *From Crow Scaring*, pp.49, 100–5, 234–5, 231, 237; Tillett, *Memories*, pp.92, 108–9; Turner, *About Myself*, pp.81, 120, 122, 124, 136, 139–40, 163, 166, 179, 219–21, 239–40, 247–9, 270–4, 317–34; Harry Gosling, *Up and Down Stream* (London, 1927), pp.104, 110–12, 134, 153, 223, 230–1.
205 Tillett, *Memories*, pp.89, 11, 116. The resistance of skilled workers to unskilled organization has nevertheless been disputed. See, for example, Alun Howkins, *Poor Labouring Men: Rural Radicalism in Norfolk 1872–1923* (London, 1985).
206 Edwards, *From Crow Scaring*, pp.91–3.
207 *Ibid.*, pp.52–3, 82, 91–3.
208 *Ibid.*, p.105.
209 *Ibid.*, pp.99–105, 113.
210 Gosling, *Up and Down Stream*, pp.56–7, 104, 234.
211 *Ibid.*, p.104.
212 *Ibid.*, pp.111, 167, 189.
213 *Ibid.*, pp.189–92.
214 *Ibid.*, pp.117, 167, 191.
215 *Ibid.*, pp.196–7.
216 Turner, *About Myself*, p.50. It seems clear that, in the system which prevailed, unemployment would continue regardless of whether employed men gave up their overtime, but this point is overlooked by Turner and the historians who cite him. Nor does Turner define words like 'justice', 'fairness', 'honesty', 'truth' and 'poverty', though he uses them frequently.
217 *Ibid.*, pp.82–3, 90–1, 101, 118–19.
218 *Ibid.*, pp.133–5, 235–6.

219 *Ibid.*, pp.236, 339.

220 *Ibid.*, pp.233–4.

221 *Ibid.*, pp.105, 108–10, 120–2, 124.

222 *Ibid.*, pp.105, 108–10, 121.

223 For useful comments in this regard see Donald Read's introduction to Jacques Rancière, *The Nights of Labour: The Workers' Dream in Nineteenth-century France*, Transl. John Drury (first published 1981; this edn, Philadelphia, 1989), pp.xv–xxxvii.

224 Edwards, *From Crow Scaring*, pp.55–6, 105–11, 99–101; Tillett, *Memories*, pp.110–11; Gosling, *Up and Down Stream*, pp.143, 180, 168; Turner, *About Myself*, pp.94–101, 163, 186–91.

225 Turner, *About Myself*, p.131. See also Gosling, *Up and Down Stream*, p.189.

226 Edwards, *From Crow Scaring*, pp.82, 90–3; Tillett, *Memories*, p.210; Gosling, *Up and Down Stream*, pp.94, 138, 167, 199; Turner, *About Myself*, pp.152–4, 192, 196, 211, 233–4, 340.

227 Edwards, *From Crow Scaring*, pp.113, 121–2, 226–9, 234, 236; Tillett, *Memories*, pp.89, 111, 117, 210; Gosling, *Up and Down Stream*, pp.57–8, 117, 131, 148, 152, 164, 169, 191, 193, 209; Turner, *About Myself*, pp.105, 118–19, 239–40, 250, 339.

228 Edwards, *From Crow Scaring*, p.231; Tillett, *Memories*, pp.207–11; Gosling, *Up and Down Stream*, pp.221–3; Turner, *About Myself*, pp.264–5, 270–4.

229 *Ibid.*, p.16.

230 These questions in turn reflect ideological predicates and shape narratological practices, or narrative strategies which I will discuss in Chapter 4.

231 In the commentaries under discussion, there is no single set of dates by which the 'mid-Victorian' period is defined. Hence some evidence is drawn from the 1830s, some from the early decades of the twentieth century, some from the years in between. In taking issue with these works I have followed a similar procedure, focusing on the years 1840–95 to emphasize stories of distress which challenge notions of harmony and consensus, which were told persistently throughout the century, and which the works in question have persistently overlooked.

232 This practice is 'naturalized' by the narrative form of the discourses in which it is embedded so that the possibility of alternative constructions disappears, at least until other questions speak to other discourses conducive to the production of different meanings. See Chapter 4 below and Hayden White, *The Content of the Form: Narrative Discourse and Historical Representation* (Baltimore, 1987), pp.58–82.

233 I employ the term 'myth' to denote cultural meta-narratives and also to distinguish specific historical commentaries which, despite the fictive quality of the narratives by which they are constituted, are implied to contain or to reflect objective truth. In either form of usage I strive for clarity. Where it seems appropriate, I use the term 'fiction' but I prefer 'myth' because the stories under discussion function as ways of ordering perception, engaging with identity and making sense of the world, thereby producing important effects which, in my view, are not conveyed by the word 'fiction'.

234 *The Oxford English Dictionary*, second edn, prepared by J.A. Simpson and E.S.C. Weiner (Oxford, 1989), vol. III, p.760; vol. VI, p.1125; vol. XIV, pp.429–30. The historians under review usually qualify their statements by acknowledging that the condition they describe was 'relative', but as I will argue in Chapter 4, the qualifier invariably slips away.

235 It could be said that to define history as myth is indeed to diminish its status, and when historical truth is challenged the utility of history as a technology of power is certainly undermined. But although I advance such a challenge, I do not mean to devalue myth, to which, as a mechanism whereby subjects engage with their identities and construct their realities, I attribute profound importance.

236 White, *The Content*, p.58.

237 See Appendix.

238 In the title of Naisby's pamphlet, Bristol's Christian name is given as James but he is subsequently referred to as William. I have assumed that the title is correct and have therefore used 'James'.

239 W. Naisby, *Evidence of Witnesses In The Cases Of William Pearce And James Bristol, Who Died At Bolton From Want Of Food; Also On The General Distress In That Town; With Remarks On That Subject, And On The Assistant Poor-Law Commissioner's Report* (Bolton, 1841), pp.2–3, 8, (pp.189–91, 197–8 in Appendix, this volume).

240 *Ibid.*, pp.2–3, (pp.189–91 in Appendix, this volume). In a subsequent House of Commons debate, it was evidently accepted that Bristol and Pearce died of starvation and that distress in Bolton was very real. But these matters were of little relevance to the debate in their own right, for discussion focused on the extent to which distress had been exaggerated as a form of anti-Corn Law propaganda. According to the minutes, 'the question was not as to the extent of the distress, but as to the accuracy of certain statements of it'. See *Hansard's Parliamentary Debates*, Third Series, vol. LIX, 19 August to 7 October 1841, columns 219–24, 1017–30.

241 Naisby, *Evidence*, p.3, (p.191 in Appendix, this volume).

242 As in earlier chapters, I use the term *status quo* to signify the supposedly prevailing social and political order. When I refer to acceptance of or acquiescence in the *status quo*, I refer to a putative condition which the labour historians under review purport to explain.

243 Naisby, *Evidence*, p.4, (p.192 in Appendix, this volume).

244 *Ibid.*

245 *Ibid.*

246 I should stress here both the speculative character and the purpose of this analysis. I do not purport to offer insight into how women like Bristol and Kirkman saw the world and their place in it. Nor do I claim that they thought in terms of a social system, oppressive or otherwise (although they might have done). *They* describe their wretchedness; *I* suggest their indifference to a system which oppresses them. This apparent indifference might well be interpreted as acquiescence but it could not, in my view, be equated with the conscious consent to a negotiated arrangement which labour historians identify as the basis of social harmony. In making this judgement, I court two kinds of criticism: the first is that Naisby's pamphlet has nothing to do with the mid-Victorian period and the second is that the histories to which I address myself are concerned not with ordinary workers but with politically conscious labour élites. As I have already noted, however, I use the document to measure similar stories which in subsequent decades speak to the same condition and serve to counter conventions about harmony and consensus. Moreover, were the historians in question to reject my critique on the grounds that they are concerned only with labour élites, their own positions would be undermined, for the 'stability' or 'harmony' of a society can scarcely be explained by the attitudes and actions of a minority unless that minority is shown to be representative. Moreover, the theories of social identity from which the various narratives proceed are designed precisely to suggest such a connection.

247 Naisby, *Evidence*, p.2, (p.189 in Appendix, this volume).

248 *Ibid.*, p.5, (p.193 in Appendix, this volume).

249 *Ibid.*, pp.5–6, (pp.193–4 in Appendix, this volume).

250 *Ibid.*, p.6, (p.194 in Appendix, this volume).

251 *Ibid.*, p.7, (p.195 in Appendix, this volume).

252 *Ibid.*

253 *Ibid.*, pp.7–8, (pp.195–6 in Appendix, this volume).

254 *Ibid.*, p.2, (p.189 in Appendix, this volume).

255 *Ibid.*, p.8, (p.196 in Appendix, this volume).

256 *Ibid.*, pp.5–6, (pp.193–4 in Appendix, this volume). The dismissal of Pearce as incompetent can well be seen to illustrate a rhetorical strategy said to have been

predetermined in nineteenth-century medical and juridical discourse, which functioned to equate women, poverty and insanity, thus to marginalize women deemed to be in any way troublesome. For discussions of this view, see, for example, Michel Foucault, *Madness and Civilization: A History of Insanity in the Age of Reason* (New York, 1973); M. Duberman, M. Vicinus and G. Chauncey Jr, eds, *Hidden from History: Reclaiming the Gay and Lesbian Past* (London, 1989); F. Mort, *Dangerous Sexualities: Medico-Moral Politics in England since 1830* (London, 1987).

257 Elizabeth Storie, *The Autobiography of Elizabeth Storie, a Native of Glasgow* (Glasgow, 1859), p.2.

258 *Ibid.*, pp.1–3.

259 *Ibid.*, pp.6–10.

260 *Ibid.*, pp.10–12.

261 *Ibid.*, pp.15–16.

262 *Ibid.*, pp.23–5, 28.

263 *Ibid.*, p.29.

264 *Ibid.*, p.30.

265 *Ibid.*, p.55.

266 *Ibid.*, pp. 63, 75–6.

267 *Ibid.*, pp. 28, 64–70.

268 *Ibid.*, pp.145–7.

269 *Ibid.*, pp.149–50, 154.

270 *Ibid.*, pp.21, 76. Storie actually describes a form of legal aid for the poor, though one to which, by her account, access could be difficult (*Ibid.*, pp.76–9). An Act of Sederunt was an ordinance drawn up by the Court of Session to regulate its proceedings. See *The Concise Scots Dictionary* (Aberdeen, 1985), p.597.

271 *Ibid.*, pp.76–84.

272 *Ibid.*, pp.85–6.

273 *Ibid.*, pp.87–8.

274 *Ibid.*, pp.92–7.

275 *Ibid.*, pp.102–5.

276 *Ibid.*, pp.110–11.

277 *Ibid.*, p.112.

278 *Ibid.*, p.151.

279 *Ibid.*, pp.150–1 (Storie's italics).

280 *Ibid.*, p.153.

281 *Ibid.*, p.88.

282 *Ibid.*, p.148.

283 *Ibid.*, p.1.

284 *Ibid.*, p.2.

285 *Ibid.*, p.147.

286 *Ibid.*, pp.16, 24–5, 56, 146.

287 See above, pp.125–6.

288 For a survey of histories in which respectability is held to have been central to the identity of working people, see Chapter 2 above.

289 Although Storie notes that she obtained legal assistance by being entered on the Poor Roll, she gives no indication that she ever sought help to maintain herself.

290 *Report From The Select Committee On The Stoppage of Wages In The Hosiery Manufacture*, Minutes of Evidence, 1854–5 [421] XIV, pp.116–17, 119.

291 *Ibid.*, p.121.

292 *Ibid.*, p.108.

293 *Ibid.*, p.119.

294 *Ibid.*, p.117.

295 *Ibid.*, p.313. The net system is characterized by William Richmond, one of the

workingmen who testified at the inquiry, as a system in which a worker's wages are paid in full, without any stoppages or deductions (*Ibid.*, p.312). Frame rental and other stoppages were eventually abolished in 1874 by an act of Parliament, according to F.A. Wells, 'with little opposition'. By that time, Wells wrote, 'it was seen that factory production was bound to absorb an increasing proportion of the trade, and that with this development frame renting would tend automatically to disappear'. See F.A. Wells, *The British Hosiery and Knitwear Industry: Its History and Organization* (first published 1935; this edn, Newton Abbot, 1972), pp.122–3, 131–2.

296 *Select Committee on the Stoppage of Wages*, pp.109–10, 117, 240–1.
297 *Ibid.*, p.242.
298 *Ibid.*, p.241.
299 *Ibid.*, p.237.
300 *Ibid.*, p.241.
301 *Ibid.*, pp.118–21, 235.
302 *Ibid.*, pp.100–3, 120–3, 235–8, 242, 314–17, 320–22, 325, 331–5.
303 *Ibid.*, pp.117, 123.
304 *Ibid.*, pp.117–20.
305 *Ibid.*, pp.118–19.
306 *Ibid.*, p.118.
307 *Ibid.*, pp.100–4, Joseph Elliot; pp.229–40, John Sketchley; pp.241–2, John Ginns; pp.310–11, Mary Stevens; pp.312–27, William Richmond; pp.328–37, Thomas Newstead.
308 *Ibid.*, p.103.
309 *Ibid.*
310 *Ibid.*, pp.101–3.
311 Sir Joshua Walmsley was MP for Leicester from July 1847 to August 1848, for Bolton from January 1849 to July 1852, and again for Leicester from 1852 to 1857 (M. Stenton, ed., *Who's Who of British Members of Parliament, vol. I, 1832–1885* (Sussex, 1976), p.396).
312 *Select Committee on the Stoppage of Wages, 1854–55*, p.235.
313 *Ibid.*, pp.116–20. For a comparison with contemporary accounts of 1844 and earlier years, see K.E. Carpenter, ed., *The Framework Knitters and Handloom Weavers; Their Attempts to Keep up Wages: Eight Pamphlets 1820–1845* (New York, 1972).
314 *Select Committee on the Stoppage of Wages, 1854–55*, pp.100–2.
315 *Ibid.*, pp.102–3, 106.
316 *Ibid.*, pp.100–6.
317 Sketchley, Ginns, Newstead and Richmond, along with Abbott and Elliott, offer their accounts of the conditions experienced by workers in a particular industry. They do not claim, nor is it claimed on their behalf, that they are broadly representative. But framework-knitters constituted a substantial minority, for the industry in which they worked was an extensive one, and the cited statements coincide with those of virtually all operatives summoned to the inquiry. See, for example, the testimonies in *Ibid.*, of G. Buckby, p.83; T. Winters, p.285; M. Stevens, p.310; W. Emmerson, p.450; T. Greaves, p.468; E. Nicholson, p.505.
318 *Ibid.*, pp.229–37, 241–2, 333–6, 313–20.
319 *Ibid.*, pp.229–30, 234–5, 237.
320 *Ibid.*, pp.233, 237, 241.
321 William Lovett, *Life and Struggles of William Lovett in His Pursuit of Bread, Knowledge and Freedom*, vol. I (first published 1876; this edn London, 1920), p.45.
322 *Select Committee on the Stoppage of Wages*, pp.241–2.
323 *Ibid.*, pp.333–6.
324 *Ibid.*, pp.313–14.
325 *Ibid.*, pp.100–1, 233–4, 238–9, 320–3, 336–7.

326 *Ibid.*, pp.236–9, 319–21, 336–7.

327 *Ibid.*, pp.iii–iv.

328 See above and Chapter 2.

329 *Select Committee on the Stoppage of Wages*, p.123.

330 *Ibid.*, p.104.

331 *Ibid.*, pp.310–11.

332 *Ibid.*, p.337.

333 *Ibid.*, p.336.

334 *Ibid.*, p.336.

335 *Ibid.*, p.319.

336 *Ibid.*, p.105.

337 *Ibid.*, p.236.

338 *Ibid.*

339 *Ibid.*

340 *Ibid.*

341 *Ibid.*

342 *Ibid.*, pp.105, 238–9.

343 *Sixth Report From The Select Committee On Poor Relief (England)*, 1861 [474 – III] IX, Minutes of Evidence, p.873.

344 *Ibid.*, pp.859–60.

345 *Ibid.*, p.880.

346 *Ibid.*, pp.859–61.

347 *Ibid.*, pp.862–63, 868.

348 *Ibid.*, p.867.

349 *Ibid.*, pp.859–61, 867, 878–80, 885, 890, 893–4, 896, 899, 903.

350 The connection of the interlocutors in question to the inquiry is not revealed, although their statements suggest that they may have been Poor Law guardians.

351 *Select Committee On Poor Relief*, 1861, pp.875, 877, 879, 880.

352 *Ibid.*, p.880.

353 The chairman of the Select Committee was P.C. Villiers, son of the Earl of Clarendon, MP for Wolverhampton 1835–98 and President of the Poor Law Board 1859–66 (Stenton, *Who's Who*, pp.391–2). Sir John Walsham, a Poor Law Inspector, chaired proceedings held in the boardroom of the West Ham Union on 27 June 1861, the minutes of which form part of the 1861 report (*Select Committee On Poor Relief*, 1861, pp.869–71).

354 *Ibid.*, 1861, pp.922–3.

355 *Ibid.*, p.859.

356 *Ibid.*, p.943.

357 *Ibid.*, pp.910–12.

358 *Ibid.*, p.906.

359 *Ibid.*, p.879.

360 *Ibid.*, p.875.

361 *Ibid.*, pp.874, 881.

362 *Ibid.*, p.881.

363 *Ibid.*, pp.921, 927.

364 *Ibid.*, pp.921–4.

365 *Ibid.*, pp.923–4.

366 *Ibid.*, p.924.

367 *Ibid.*, pp.931–4.

368 *Ibid.*, pp.931–2.

369 *Ibid.*, p.933.

370 *Ibid.*, pp.933–4.

371 *Ibid.*, p.928.

372 *Ibid.*

373 *Ibid.*

374 *Ibid.*, pp.928–9.

375 *Ibid.*, p.912.

376 *Ibid.*

377 *Ibid.*, pp.912–14.

378 *Ibid.*, p.914.

379 *Ibid.*, pp.912–14. Mitchell's excited manner is not a product of my own literary artifice. It is commented on several times during the interview by Sir John Walsham, the committee chairman, the Rev. T. Parry, one of the examiners and the Rev. Herman Douglas.

380 *Ibid.*, p.913. Asked to confirm her insistence on a prior occasion that she 'never would apply to the parish', Mitchell observes, 'I said I never would go in'. See below for others equally determined.

381 Michel Foucault, 'The Subject and Power', in H.L. Dreyfus and P. Rabinow, eds, *Michel Foucault: Beyond Structuralism and Hermeneutics* (Chicago, 1982), pp.211–12.

382 *Select Committee On Poor Relief*, 1861, pp.881–4.

383 *Ibid.*, pp.883–5, 887–8.

384 *Ibid.*, pp.882–3.

385 *Ibid.*, p.885.

386 *Ibid.*, p.889.

387 *Ibid.*, pp.882, 884, 889.

388 *Ibid.*, pp.941–3.

389 *Ibid.*, pp.908–9.

390 *Ibid.*, pp.889–92.

391 *Ibid.*: Elizabeth Hyde, pp.892–5; Agatha Martin, pp.896–9; Ann Boyle, pp.900–2; Mary Wainwright, p.903; Elizabeth Patten, p.903; Mrs Scott, p.905; Sarah Galliphant, pp.907–8; Jane Veasey, p.910; Sarah Cooper, pp.915–17; Mary Ann Thomas, pp.918–20; Elizabeth Ann Cabby, pp.920–1; Mary Hillyard, pp.924–5; Emily Mitchell, pp. 929–31; Sarah Ann Haslam, pp.934–6; Caroline Sweetingham, pp. 936–9; Eliza May, pp.939–41.

392 *Ibid.*, p.937.

393 *Ibid.*, p.920.

394 *Ibid.*, p.909.

395 *Ibid.*, p.940.

396 *Ibid.*, p.920.

397 *Ibid.*, p.919.

398 *Ibid.*

399 See, for example, K.D.M. Snell, *Annals of the Labouring Poor: Social Change and Agrarian England 1660–1900* (Cambridge, 1985), esp. chs 1, 6 and 7.

400 Confinement indoors seems only to heighten their hatred of the place. To one such as Sarah Morgan (see above), who implicitly attributes the death of her children to their internment, the institution is less than salubrious. Knowledge of any such tragedy would surely have reinforced the determination of others to remain at large, although it is the denial of their humanity, the separation of parents from children as inmates are sorted like cattle, which seems most to deter the majority (*Select Committee On Poor Relief*, 1861, pp.941–3).

401 *Ibid.*, p.897.

402 *Ibid.*, pp.897–900.

403 *Ibid.*, pp.924–6.

404 *Ibid.*, pp.900–3.

405 *Ibid.*, pp.892–5, 903–5; see also Sarah Gallifant, pp.907–8, Sarah Cooper, pp.915–17, and Emily Mitchell, pp.929–31.

406 *Ibid.*, p.892.

407 *Ibid.*, p.905.

408 *Ibid.*, p.988.

409 *Ibid.*, p.930.

410 *Ibid.*, pp.929–31, 920–1, 905–6.

411 *Ibid.*, pp.907 and 917.

412 Yet another possibility, but only a possibility, is that for people such as Mitchell, respectability was little more than an air affected to ingratiate themselves with the likes of Douglas. As Peter Mandler writes in an essay on nineteenth-century poverty and charity, '[T]he task of the recipients was to fit themselves into the positions required by the donors at the moment of the transaction and then to apply the gift (so far as they were able) to their own needs' (see P. Mandler, 'Poverty and Charity in the Nineteenth-century Metropolis: An Introduction', in Peter Mandler, ed., *The Uses of Charity: The Poor on Relief in the Nineteenth-century Metropolis* (Philadelphia, 1990), pp.1–2).

413 *Royal Commission on the Aged Poor*, vol. III, Minutes of Evidence, 1895 [c.7684 – II] XV, p.825.

414 *Ibid.*, pp.818, 825–6, 901, 910.

415 *Ibid.*, see, for example, Edwin Noakes, gardener, pp.821–2, and William Webb, also a gardener, p.826.

416 *Ibid.*, p.826.

417 Again I stress that although the historians under discussion qualify their descriptions of consensus and harmony with the term 'relative', the qualifier slips away and stories of discord such as those to which I have referred are excluded.

418 This claim is illustrated above in my account of how statements by Thomas Wright acquire substantially different meanings in the context of Patrick Joyce's analysis. See above, p.110.

4 NARRATIVE HISTORY AND THE POLITICS OF EXCLUSION

1 Roland Barthes, 'Historical Discourse', in Michael Love, ed., *Structuralism: A Reader* (London, 1970), pp.145–55.

2 This admission simply reflects what has become 'a commonplace in the philosophy of the social and . . . hard sciences': the awareness that every utterance 'is traceable to a subject of enunciation' who, in turn, 'always has institutional affiliations, values . . . and . . . personal beliefs' (Philippe Carrard, *Poetics of the New History: French Historical Discourse from Braudel to Chartier* (Baltimore, 1992), p.97).

3 As I have indicated above, I regard historical explanation to be imaginative because, regardless of whether it is called analysis, interpretation or educated inference, there are no objective or independent criteria against which its truth can be measured.

4 Hayden White, *Metahistory: The Historical Imagination in Nineteenth-century Europe* (Baltimore, 1973), pp.2, 30–1.

5 *Ibid.*, pp.x–xi, 34.

6 *Ibid.*, pp.x–ix; Wulf Kansteiner, 'Hayden White's Critique of the Writing of History', in *History and Theory*, 32, 1993, pp. 277–8.

7 White, *Metahistory*, p.427; Kansteiner, 'Hayden White', p.278.

8 White, *Metahistory*, pp.37–8.

9 Hayden White, *The Content of the Form: Narrative Discourse and Historical Representation* (Baltimore, 1987), pp.65, 72.

10 *Ibid.*, p.76.

11 Carlo Ginzburg, 'Checking the Evidence: The Judge and the Historian', in *Critical Inquiry*, 18, 1991, p.84; Kansteiner, 'Hayden White', p.274.

12 Arthur Marwick, 'Two Approaches to Historical Study: The Metaphysical (Including Postmodernism) and the Historical', in *Journal of Contemporary History*, 30, 1995,

pp.5–6, 11–13, 19–21, 30. See also Hayden White, 'A Response to Arthur Marwick', in *Journal of Contemporary History*, 30, 1995, pp.233–46.

13 Himmelfarb neglects to distinguish between those postmodernists who seek to dispense with 'subject', 'object' and hence ontology, and others, like White, who consistently acknowledge an 'objective reality', albeit one to which, like 'objectively' existing historical artefacts, meaning is attributed. Gertrude Himmelfarb, 'Telling It as You Like It: Post-modernist History and the Flight from Fact', in *Times Literary Supplement*, 16 October 1992, pp.12–15.

14 Hayden White, '"Figuring the Nature of the Times Deceased": Literary Theory and Historical Writing', in Ralph Cohen, ed., *The Future of Literary Theory* (New York, 1989), p.34.

15 Marwick, 'Two Approaches', pp.5, 29–30.

16 Keith Windschuttle, *The Killing of History: How a Discipline is Being Murdered by Literary Critics and Social Theorists* (Sydney, 1994), p.10.

17 *Ibid.*, pp.2–3, 16–17.

18 *Ibid.*, pp.5, 8–10.

19 Kansteiner, 'Hayden White', p.274; Ginzburg, 'Checking the Evidence', pp.79–92; Carlo Ginzburg, 'Just One Witness', in S. Friedlander, ed., *Probing the Limits of Representation: Nazism and the 'Final Solution'* (Cambridge, MA, 1992), pp.82–96; Lionel Gossman, *Between History and Literature* (Cambridge, MA, 1990), p.303. Another possibility is that White points to the ruthless pragmatics of so-called liberal democratic politics. For massively documented speculation on the latter, see Noam Chomsky, *Turning the Tide: US Intervention in Central America and the Struggle for Peace* (Boston, 1985); Noam Chomsky, *On Power and Ideology: The Managua Lectures* (Boston, 1987); Noam Chomsky, *Deterring Democracy* (London, 1991); Noam Chomsky, *Year 501: The Conquest Continues* (Boston, 1993); Noam Chomsky, *Rethinking Camelot: JFK, the Vietnam War, and US Political Culture* (London, 1993).

20 Kansteiner, 'Hayden White', p.291.

21 White, *Content*, p.76.

22 White, 'Figuring', p.34.

23 *Ibid.*, p.30.

24 In this formulation I speculate that exhaustive documentation of the occurrence of an event is usually treated in the same way as eyewitness testimonies. If, for example, a substantial number of people witnessed an event in which someone fell to her death from a tall building, and a dead body was recovered which confirmed their subsequent testimonies, it would be difficult to argue that the event did not occur. But if spectators were positioned differently and therefore described the event differently (for example, one might have been on the roof of the building and have testified that the deceased had been pushed), then there could be some dispute about what constitutes a proper description of the event. The same would in my view apply to historical events so well documented that they cannot be denied but are the subject of ambiguous and conflicting descriptions.

25 White, *Content*, p.77.

26 See, for example, Kansteiner, 'Hayden White', p.292; Gossman, *Between History*, pp.303–20; Ginzburg, 'Checking the Evidence', pp.79–92; Ginzburg, 'Just One Witness', pp.82–96; Arnaldo Momigliano, 'The Rhetoric of History and the History of Rhetoric: On Hayden White's Tropes', in *Comparative Criticism*, 3, 1981, pp.259–68.

27 Kansteiner, 'Hayden White', p.293.

28 I should emphasize here that although I think White's event/fact distinction is useful, I nevertheless find it problematic. It serves to illustrate that an event can sustain a range of descriptions and thereby illuminates the contingency of meaning in historical narrative. Taken to its (semio)logical conclusion, however, the distinction dissolves

(thereby, in my view, enhancing rather than detracting from White's general argument). Semiologically speaking, a 'fact' may indeed be seen as an event under a description, but the term 'event' is also a description, albeit a simple one. 'Event' (the 'signifier') and 'fact' (the 'signified') are components of a semiological 'sign' which refers to something outside of itself (a referent). This referent is named by the signifier (as an 'event', a 'phenomenon', a 'process', etc.) and the name applied is then transformed through a more complex description into a 'fact' (the 'signified'). Because different names can be devised, the referent remains contested and elusive, while the signifier ('event'), like the signified ('fact'), remains a description. See Roland Barthes, *Writing Degree Zero and Elements of Semiology*, transl. Annette Lavers and Colin Smith (first published 1953; this edn, London, 1967), pp.101–19. See also Roland Barthes, *Mythologies*, transl., Annette Lavers (first published 1957; this edn, London, 1972), pp.109–58.

29 *Ibid.*, p.274.

30 *Ibid.*, p.278; Sande Cohen, *Historical Culture: On the Recoding of an Academic Discipline* (Berkeley, 1987), pp.81–7.

31 It can, of course, be said that terms like 'interest' and 'society' are remnants of a superannuated modernist discourse which has no relevance in today's postmodern world. But as I will presently argue, all critiques of modernity are themselves discourses which articulate both 'interest' and a social hierarchy.

32 White, *Content*, pp.58–62.

33 *Ibid.*, pp.64–5.

34 *Ibid.*, pp.60–1, 65

35 *Ibid.*, p.61.

36 *Ibid.*

37 It could, of course, be argued in response that, by 'scientific', historians simply mean 'organized rational knowledge'. But to do so would be to beg the question, 'Whose rationality?'

38 White, *Content*, p.59.

39 *Ibid.*, p.60.

40 *Ibid.*

41 *Ibid.*, p.63.

42 *Ibid.*, p.64.

43 The third alternative would seem to include cyclical theories of history.

44 White, *Content*, p.65.

45 *Ibid.*

46 *Ibid.*

47 *Ibid.*, p.67.

48 *Ibid.*, p.68.

49 *Ibid.*, pp.66–9.

50 *Ibid.*, p.65.

51 *Ibid.*, p.69.

52 *Ibid.*

53 Friedrich von Schiller, *Two Essays by Friedrich von Schiller: 'Naive and Sentimental Poetry' and 'On the Sublime'*, transl. Julius A. Elias (New York, 1966), pp.209–10, cited in White, *Content*, p.69.

54 *Ibid.*, p.70.

55 *Ibid.*

56 *Ibid.*, p.71.

57 *Ibid.*, pp.71–2.

58 *Ibid.*, p.73. I do not suggest that Marxist historiography is 'intended' to be politically conservative but I do suggest, consistently with White's characterization, that its effects are conservative because it adheres to conservative methodologies whereby the past and its unfolding are treated as comprehensible parts of a comprehensible historical

whole.

59 Kansteiner, 'Hayden White', p.274; White relates these different types of historical knowledge to the 'irreducible ideological component in every historical account of reality'. Proceeding, he observes that any 'claim to have distinguished a past from a present world of social thought and praxis, *implies* a conception of the form that knowledge of the present world must take, insofar as it is *continuous* with that past world. Commitment to a particular *form* of knowledge predetermines the *kinds* of generalizations one can make about the present world, the kinds of knowledge one can have of it, and hence the kinds of projects one can legitimately conceive for changing that present or for maintaining it in its present form indefinitely' (White, *Metahistory*, p.21).

60 See discussion of the contributions by Hobsbawm, Harrison and Foster in chapters 1 and 2 above.

61 E.J. Hobsbawm, 'Labour's Forward March Halted?', in E.J. Hobsbawm, *Politics for a Rational Left* (London, 1989); Royden Harrison and Jonathan Zeitlin, *Divisions of Labour: Skilled Workers and Technological Change in Nineteenth Century Britain* (Brighton, 1985); John Foster, 'The Declassing of Language', in *New Left Review*, 150, March/April 1985, pp.29–46.

62 One such possibility would have been to focus on sources like those I have used to represent the period as one in which prevailing authority insured an orderly existence for some contemporaries by committing others to lives of wretchedness and despair. Such an emphasis was maintained by older Marxists like Hobsbawm, and the outcome was an account of how capitalist power relations might be challenged and subverted. But subsequent Marxists, affecting political neutrality, have ignored such sources to depict nineteenth-century capitalism as an immutable but benign system under which respectable independence was generally accessible. The outcome of this departure is the implication that capitalism cannot be subverted and might just as well, therefore, be accepted.

63 For a general discussion of this view, see A. Cutler, B. Hindess, P. Hirst and A. Hussain, *Marx's Capital and Capitalism Today* (Boston, 1977). This approach to the question of 'consciousness' is implicit in the work of Crossick, Gray and Joyce, all of whom insist on the cultural mediation of ideas and on social consensus, rather than on notions of ideological mystification and the manufacture of consent, which imply true and false consciousness. See G. Crossick, *An Artisan Elite in Victorian Society: Kentish London 1840–1880* (London, 1978), p.15; R.Q. Gray, *The Labour Aristocracy in Victorian Edinburgh* (Oxford, 1976), pp.1–4; Patrick Joyce, *Visions of the People: Industrial England and the Question of Class* (Cambridge, 1991), ch. 3 and *passim*.

64 T.R. Tholfsen, *Working Class Radicalism in Mid-Victorian England* (London, 1976), p.11.

65 *Ibid.*, p.12.

66 Gray, *Labour Aristocracy*, pp.1–4.

67 *Ibid.*, pp.1–6, 121.

68 Crossick, *An Artisan Elite*, pp.13–15.

69 Gray, *Labour Aristocracy*, p.121; Crossick, *An Artisan Elite*, p.107.

70 Neville Kirk, *The Growth of Working-class Reformism in Mid-Victorian England* (London, 1985), p.xii.

71 *Ibid.*, pp.ix–xii.

72 Joyce, *Visions*, p.19.

73 *Ibid.*, pp.22–3.

74 For different perspectives on the Labour Party's decline between 1974 and 1979, see the collected essays in Stuart Hall and Martin Jacques, eds, *The Politics of Thatcherism* (London, 1983).

75 Patrick Joyce, *Democratic Subjects: The Self and the Social in Nineteenth-century England* (Cambridge, 1994).

76 *Ibid.*, p.10

77 *Ibid.*, pp.6, 10–11.

78 *Ibid.*

79 *Ibid.*, p.12.

80 *Ibid.*, pp.12, 150.

81 *Ibid.*, pp.6–8.

82 *Ibid.*, pp.80–2, 153, 176. The assertion that narrative *'is an ontological condition of social life'* is italicized by M.R. Somers and G.D. Gibson in an adduced quotation which, in Joyce's view, 'helps validate the high claims for narrative made in . . . [his] introduction'. The essay from which the quotation is taken is M.R. Somers and G.D. Gibson, 'Reclaiming the Epistemological "Other": Narrative and the Social Constitution of Identity', in Craig Calhoun, ed., *Social Theory and the Politics of Identity* (Oxford, 1994).

83 Joyce, *Democratic Subjects.*, pp.12, 63, 148, 154, 185.

84 *Ibid.*, p.11.

85 *Ibid.*, pp.2–4.

86 *Ibid.*, p.4.

87 *Ibid.*, pp.159–61.

88 *Ibid.*, p.160.

89 *Ibid.*, p.9.

90 *Ibid.*

91 It should be clear from the attention I have given to Joyce's work that I do not dismiss it lightly. And to give credit where it is due, it is Joyce more than anyone else apart from Gareth Stedman Jones who has cultivated an interest in the linguistic turn among British labour historians. In doing so, however, he seems to have passed on his disdain for epistemology to a new generation of scholars, notably his protégé, James Vernon. Vernon describes his 1993 publication, *Politics and the People*, as a history of 'subjectivities and identities' that illuminates 'the ways in which politics defined and imagined people'. Like Joyce, he attempts to identify a political 'master narrative' through which popular identity was constituted, and in this connection provides a sophisticated reading of a wide range of texts. Yet notwithstanding two chapters that supposedly deal with the popular reception of certain postulated identities, both the currency of those identities and how they may have been taken on remain matters of conjecture. As with Joyce's work, it is here that epistemological questions demand to be asked. How do we know that 'the people' adopted the subject positions that supposedly beckoned them? How do we know that they interpreted political narratives and various other texts as Vernon does? What unstated assumptions prefigure Vernon's narrative? How does he know what he knows? By refusing to engage with such questions, writers like Vernon and Joyce can recognize the constitutive character of discourse, take narrative as their object of analysis and claim to illuminate exciting new possibilities. In the process, however, they generate highly conventional truth effects and oppose themselves to the postmodernism they want to embrace, for postmodernism repudiates the very truth effects they produce. See James Vernon, *Politics and the People: A Study in English Political Culture c.1815–1867* (Cambridge, 1993), esp. the introduction and chs 6–8.

92 During the past decade, many labour and social historians have begun the shift to cultural history and some, like Joyce and Vernon, have signalled the shift by adopting the language of poststructuralism or postmodernism. Among the most notable of these works are Sonya O. Rose, *Limited Livelihoods: Gender and Class in Nineteenth-century England* (Berkeley and Los Angeles, 1992); Lenard Berlanstein, ed., *Rethinking Labour History: Essays on Discourse and Class Analysis* (Urbana, 1993); Kathleen Canning, 'Feminist History after the Linguistic Turn: Historicizing Discourse and Experience', in *Signs*, 19, 2, 1994, pp.368–404; Mary Poovey, *Making a Social Body:*

British Cultural Formation, 1830–1864 (Chicago, 1995); Jacques Rancière, *The Nights of Labour: The Workers' Dream in Nineteenth-century France*, transl. John Drury (first published 1981; this edn, Philadelphia, 1989). Neither these nor any other recent works that I am aware of, however, address the hermeneutical problem of how their studies can be independently verified, or the epistemological possibility that the past is unknowable. In an eloquent critique of Joyce, Vernon and Stedman Jones, Neville Kirk touches on these problems but does not consider their implications for the realist history he defends. See Neville Kirk, 'Class and the "Linguistic Turn" in Chartist and Post-Chartist Historiography', in Neville Kirk, ed., *Social Class and Marxism: Defences and Challenges* (Aldershot, 1996), pp.87–134. Even so-called new historicists come up against these problems. They engage in textual interpretation and turn to history, as Hayden White points out, 'for the kind of knowledge that a specifically historical approach to' the study of literature might yield. Yet, as White explains, 'there is no such thing as a specifically historical approach to the study of history, but a variety of such approaches, at least as many as there are positions on the current ideological spectrum'. Hence, 'to embrace a historical approach to the study of anything entails or implies a distinctive philosophy of history' which in turn 'is a function as much of the way one construes one's own special object of scholarly interest as it is of one's knowledge of "history" itself' (Hayden White, 'New Historicism: A Comment', in Aram H. Veeser, ed., *The New Historicism* (London, 1989), p.302).

93 Antonio Gramsci, *Selections from the Prison Notebooks of Antonio Gramsci* (London, 1978), p.12.

94 *Ibid.*, pp.5–20.

95 *Ibid.*, p.6.

96 *Ibid.*, pp.6–18.

97 *Ibid.*, p.16.

98 For a brief chronology of Gramsci's life see Josef V. Femia, *Gramsci's Political Thought: Hegemony, Consciousness, and the Revolutionary Process* (Oxford, 1981), p.xiii.

99 This claim is pursued in more detail below on pp.175–84.

100 Margaret Thatcher, 'The Iain Macleod Memorial Lecture', Caxton Hall, 4 July 1977. Reprinted in A.B. Cooke, compiler/ed., *Margaret Thatcher – The Revival of Britain: Speeches on Home and European Affairs 1975–1988* (London, 1989), p.52.

101 Cited in the *Standard*, 15 April 1983.

102 Thatcher, 'The Iain Macleod Memorial Lecture', in Cooke, *Margaret Thatcher*, p.57.

103 *Ibid.*, p.55.

104 Thatcher, 'The Conservative Party Conference', Blackpool, 12 October 1979, in Cooke, *Margaret Thatcher*, p.99.

105 *Ibid.*

106 *Ibid.*, p.98.

107 *Ibid.*, p.101.

108 Thatcher, 'The Conservative Party Conference', Blackpool, 10 October 1975, in Cooke, *Margaret Thatcher*, p.20.

109 Thatcher, 'The Institute of Socio-Economic Research', New York, 15 September 1975, in Cooke, *Margaret Thatcher*, p.12.

110 *Ibid.*, p.13.

111 *Ibid.*, p.10

112 *Ibid.*, p.8; Thatcher, 'The Conservative Party Conference', Blackpool, 12 October, 1979, in *Ibid.*, p.101.

113 Thatcher, 'The Institute of Socio-Economic Research', in Cooke, *Margaret Thatcher*, p.13.

114 Thatcher uses terms like 'running out of other people's money', 'bleeding the wealth-producers dry', and 'the Socialist disease' in preference to the less provocative 'exhausting tax-revenue'. Thatcher, 'Institute of Socio-Economic Research', in Cooke,

Margaret Thatcher, p.11; Thatcher, 'Conservative Party Conference', Blackpool, October 1975, in Cooke, *Margaret Thatcher*, p.20; Thatcher, 'Conservative Party Conference', Blackpool, October 1979, in Cooke, *Margaret Thatcher*, p.101.

115 Thatcher, 'Institute of Socio-Economic Research', in Cooke, *Margaret Thatcher*, pp.8–10; Thatcher, 'Conservative Party Conference', Blackpool, October 1975, in Cooke, *Margaret Thatcher*, pp.19–20, 25.

116 Thatcher, 'Institute of Socio-Economic Research', in Cooke, *Margaret Thatcher*, pp.3, 6.

117 Thatcher, 'Conservative Party Conference', Blackpool, October 1975, in Cooke, *Margaret Thatcher*, pp.25–6.

118 *Ibid.*, p.26.

119 Thatcher, 'Conservative Party Conference', Brighton, 10 October 1980, in Cooke, *Margaret Thatcher*, p.116.

120 Thatcher, speech at 'St Lawrence Jewry', City of London, 4 March 1981, in Cooke, *Margaret Thatcher*, pp.126–8.

121 *Ibid.*, p.101; Thatcher, 'The Conservative Party Conference', Brighton, 10 October 1980, in Cooke, *Margaret Thatcher*, p.116; Thatcher, 'The Bow Group: The Royal Commonwealth Society', London, 6 May 1978, in Cooke, *Margaret Thatcher*, pp.72–3; Thatcher, 'The Conservative Party Conference', Blackpool, 10 October 1975, in Cooke, *Margaret Thatcher*, p.21; Thatcher, 'The Institute of Directors', Royal Albert Hall, 11 November 1976, in Cooke, *Margaret Thatcher*, p.41.

122 Thatcher, 'The Bow Group: The Royal Commonwealth Society, London', 6 May 1978, in Cooke, *Margaret Thatcher*, p.81; Thatcher, 'The Conservative Party Conference', Blackpool, 12 October 1979, in Cooke, *Margaret Thatcher*, p.99; Thatcher, 'The Conservative Party Conference', Brighton, 14 October 1988, in Cooke, *Margaret Thatcher*, pp.267–70.

123 Margaret Thatcher, address to the Small Business Bureau, 8 February 1984, cited in Kay Andrews and John Jacobs, *Punishing the Poor: Poverty under Thatcher* (London, 1990), p.3.

124 Thatcher, 'The Conservative Party Conference', Brighton, 14 October 1988, in Cooke, *Margaret Thatcher*, pp.268–71.

125 *Ibid.*, pp.268–9.

126 See below.

127 See, for example, Hall and Jacques, *Politics*, pp.11–12 and *passim*.

128 Andrews and Jacobs, *Punishing*, *passim*.

129 See, for example, Patrick Middleton, 'For "Victorian", read "Georgian": Mrs Thatcher Corrected', in *Encounter*, 67, July/August 1986, pp.5–9; Jeffrey Richards, 'A Reply to Patrick Middleton: Victorian Values Revisited', (and Middleton's response), in *Encounter*, 68, March 1987, pp.73–8; Raphael Samuel, 'Soft Focus Nostalgia', in *New Statesman*, 27 May 1983, pp.ii–iv; Raphael Samuel, 'Cry God for Maggie, England and St George', in *New Statesman*, 27 May 1983, pp. iv–vi; Mary Chamberlain and Ruth Richardson, 'Pawnographic Values', in *New Statesman*, 27 May 1983, p.vii; Michael Ignatieff, 'Law and Order in a City of Strangers', in *New Statesman*, 27 May 1983, pp.viii–x; Gareth Stedman Jones, 'Poor Laws and Market Forces', in *New Statesman*, 27 May 1983, pp.x–xiii; Leonore Davidoff and Catherine Hall, 'Home Sweet Home', in *New Statesman*, 27 May 1983, pp.xiv–xvi. See also R.Q. Gray, 'The Deconstructing of the English Working Class', in *Social History*, 11, 3, October 1986, p.363; Neville Kirk, 'In Defence of Class: A Critique of Recent Revisionist Writing upon the Nineteenth-century Working Class', in *International Review of Social History*, 32, 1987, pp.2–47.

130 Thatcher, 'The Conservative Party Conference', Blackpool, 10 October 1975 in Cooke, *Margaret Thatcher*, p.20.

131 Thatcher, 'The Conservative Party Conference', Brighton, 10 October 1980, in Cooke, *Margaret Thatcher*, p.121; Thatcher, 'The Swinton Lecture' in Cooke, *Margaret Thatcher*, p.85.

132 *Ibid.*, pp.85–8.

133 Thatcher, 'The Iain Macleod Lecture', in Cooke, *Margaret Thatcher*, p.56.

134 *Ibid.*, p.54; Thatcher, 'The Conservative Party Conference', Brighton, 14 October 1988, in Cooke, *Margaret Thatcher*, p.274.

135 Thatcher, 'The Iain Macleod Lecture', in Cooke, *Margaret Thatcher*, p.52.

136 *Ibid.*, p.50.

137 *Ibid.*, pp.52–3.

138 Thatcher, 'The Conservative Party Conference', Blackpool, 10 October 1975, in Cooke, *Margaret Thatcher*, p.21.

139 Thatcher, 'The Conservative Party Conference', Brighton, 14 October 1988, in Cooke, *Margaret Thatcher*, p.268.

140 *Ibid.*, p.268.

141 *Ibid.*, pp.279–80.

142 Thatcher, 'The Iain Macleod Lecture', in Cooke, *Margaret Thatcher*, pp.57–9; Thatcher, 'The Bow Group', in Cooke, *Margaret Thatcher*, p.72; Thatcher, 'The Swinton Lecture', in Cooke, *Margaret Thatcher*, p.8.

143 See, for example, Hall and Jacques, *Politics*. According to Hall, Labour has always 'refused like the plague the mobilization of democratic power at the popular level', using the state machine 'to reform conditions for working people' only when 'this did not bite too deeply into the "logic" of capitalist accumulation'. After Labour was returned to power in 1974, however, its contradictions became increasingly obvious. There were 'glaring discrepancies between the redistributive language of the Social Contract', which it initiated 'to graft powerful social and economic objectives onto the "price" of limiting wage demands', and 'its actual disciplinary character'. These contradictions 'bit deeper and deeper into the Labour/trade union alliance' until there was a 'revolt against incomes policy and in favour of "collective bargaining"'. The contradictions also became an 'index', he concluded, 'of how "the state" under corporatist management came to be experienced as "the enemy of the people"', eventually 'undermin[ing] the credibility and *raison d'être* of Mr Callaghan's government itself' (Stuart Hall, 'The Great Moving Right Show', in *Ibid.*, pp.32–3). In Jacques's view, these developments, the central element of which was to secure 'working-class acquiescence to cuts in real wages and public expenditure together with rising unemployment[,] . . . paved the way for the more doctrinaire attack of Thatcherism' (Martin Jacques, 'Thatcherism – Breaking Out of the Impasse', in *Ibid.*, pp.49–50).

144 Thatcher, 'The Iain Macleod Lecture', in Cooke, *Margaret Thatcher*, p.57.

145 John Moore MP, Conservative Secretary of State for Social Security, 11 May 1989, cited in Andrews and Jacobs, *Punishing*, p.xvii; Thatcher, 'The Conservative Party Conference', Blackpool, 10 October 1975, in Cooke, *Margaret Thatcher*, pp.25–6.

146 See, for example, Gray, *Labour Aristocracy*, pp.49–51, 55; Crossick, *An Artisan Elite*, pp.108–13, 136; Tholfsen, *Working Class Radicalism*, pp.189–95; Kirk, *Growth*, pp.103–8.

147 *Ibid.*, pp.76–8.

148 *Ibid.*, pp.24, 64.

149 *Ibid.*, p.24.

150 *Ibid.*, p.26.

151 *Ibid.*, p.5; Margaret Thatcher, cited in Andrews and Jacobs, *Punishing*, p.xviii.

152 Thatcher, 'The Institute of Socio-Economic Research', in Cooke, *Margaret Thatcher*, p.13; Thatcher, 'The Conservative Party Conference' Brighton, 14 October 1988, in Cooke, *Margaret Thatcher*, p.274.

153 'Cited' by Thatcher, 'The Iain Macleod Memorial Lecture', in Cooke, *Margaret Thatcher*, p.55.

154 *Ibid.*

155 Thatcher, 'The Conservative Party Conference' Blackpool, 12 October 1979, in Cooke, *Margaret Thatcher*, p.104.
156 It might also be argued that support for Thatcherism could be measured by polling data, but the relevance of polls (or at least of those published) is, of course, widely and convincingly disputed on a number of grounds, notably their targeting and the pre-determination of their results by the questions they ask.
157 Cited in Andrews and Jacobs, *Punishing*, p.64.
158 Thatcher, 'The Conservative Party Conference', Brighton, 14 October 1988, in Cooke, *Margaret Thatcher*, pp.268–71.
159 Andrews and Jacobs, *Punishing*, p.153.
160 *Ibid.*, pp.114–15.
161 *Ibid.*, p.141.
162 *Ibid.*, pp.161–2.
163 *Ibid.*, p.160.
164 *Ibid.*
165 *Ibid.*, p.289.
166 See above, pp.61, 163–6.
167 Tholfsen, *Working Class Radicalism*, p.197.
168 *Ibid.*, pp.22, 256.
169 Joyce, *Visions*, p.78.
170 *Ibid.*, p.76.
171 *Ibid.*, pp.75, 78.
172 *Ibid.*, p.78.
173 *Ibid.*, pp.77–9.
174 *Ibid.*, pp.77, 78,
175 *Ibid.*, p.78.
176 Crossick, *An Artisan Elite*, p.107; Kirk, *Growth*, p.xii.
177 Gray, *Labour Aristocracy*, pp.144–5.
178 Crossick, *An Artisan Elite*, pp.244–5.
179 Gray, *Labour Aristocracy*, p.190.
180 Kirk, *Growth*, p.231.
181 In a similar critique, Robert Berkhofer Jr writes that '[t]he literary job of normal historical realism is to make the structure of interpretation appear to be (the same as) the structure of factuality. The effect of such a representation is to impress the reader that the structure of interpretation is the structure of factuality, thereby reconciling and transcending the various supposed dichotomies endemic to the discipline. Rather than showing the reader how the (re)presentation is structured to *look like* total factuality, the normal historian's job is to make it appear *as though* the structure of factuality itself had determined the organizational structure of her or his account. Such a fusion of representation and referentiality is meant to convey the illusion of realism' (Robert F. Berkhofer Jr, *Beyond the Great Story: History as Text and Discourse* (Cambridge, MA, 1995), p.60).

BIBLIOGRAPHY

PRIMARY SOURCES

Periodicals

Ashton Reporter
Ashton-under-Lyne News
Bronterre's National Reformer
Christian Socialist
Cobbett's Weekly Political Register
Co-operative News
Cooperator
Good Words
Leader
London Chartist Monthly Magazine
McDouall's Chartist and Republican Journal
Morning Star
Movement
Northern Liberator
Northern Star
Oddfellows' Magazine
Oldham Co-operative Record
Reasoner
Reynold's Weekly Newspaper
Standard
Star of Freedom
Working Man
Workman

Parliamentary papers

Report from the Select Committee on the Stoppage of Wages in the Hosiery Manufacture, Minutes of Evidence, 1854–5 [421] XIV.
Sixth Report from the Select Committee On Poor Relief (England), 1861, Minutes of Evidence, [474 – III] IX.
Fifth Report from the Royal Commission into Trade Unions, vol. XXXIX, Minutes of Evidence, 1867–8 [3980 – I].

Fourth Report from the Select Committee on the Sweating System, 1889, Minutes of Evidence [331] XIV.

Royal Commission on the Aged Poor, vol. III, Minutes of Evidence, 1895 [c.7684 – II] XV.

Hansard Parliamentary Debates, Third Series, 19 August to 7 October 1841, vol. LIX, cols 219–24, 1017–30.

Printed sources by or about nineteenth-century working people (some of which were not published until the twentieth century)

Adams, W.E., *Memoirs of a Social Atom* (London, 1903).

Aitken, William, Autobiography, serialized as 'Remembrances and Struggles of a working man for bread and liberty', in the *Ashton News*, 1869.

Aitken, William, Biography in *Oddfellows' Magazine*, July 1857.

Andrew, S., *Fifty Years in the Cotton Trade* (Oldham, 1887).

Anon., *Scenes from my Life, by a Working Man* (London, 1858).

Anon., *Working Men and Women by a Workingman* (London, 1879).

Arch, J., *Joseph Arch: The Story of His Life, Told by Himself and Edited with a Preface by the Countess of Warwick* (London, 1898).

Bamford, Samuel, *The Autobiography of Samuel Bamford: Passages in the Life of a Radical*, vols I and II (London, 1844).

Barker, Joseph, 'Minister of the Gospel' in *Mercy Triumphant, or Teaching the Children of the Poor to Write on the Sabbath Day . . .* (3rd edn, Bolton, 1843).

Barker, Joseph, *The History and Confessions of a Man, As put Forth by Himself – Showing how he became a Methodist and a Methodist preacher, and how, as he grew older, he gave up part of the old Methodist belief, and was expelled, and giving a true view of Methodism on both sides, the fair as well as the foul, the bright as well as the dark, together with a long and wonderful account of many other matters worthy to be read and thought upon* (London, 1846).

Barker, Joseph, *A Full Account of the Arrest, Imprisonment and Liberation on Bail, of Joseph Barker; together with an Account of His Triumphant Election For the Borough of Bolton* (Bolton, 1848).

Barker, Joseph, *Aristocracy and Democracy, the Speech of Mr. Barker at the Bolton Tea Party on Thursday Evening, September 28, 1848* (J. Barker: Wortley, Leeds, 1848).

Barker, Joseph, *The Triumph of Right over Might, or, A Full account of the Attempt made by the Manchester Magistrates and the Whig Government to Rob J. Barker of his Liberty, and Suppress his Publications and of the Signal Failure of that Attempt* (J. Barker: Wortley, Leeds, 1848).

Barnes, G.N., *From Workshop to War Cabinet, with an Introduction by the Right Honourable D. Lloyd George, M.P.* (London, 1924).

Blackie, J.S., *Notes of a Life*, ed. A.S. Walker (Edinburgh, 1908).

Bower, F., *Rolling Stonemason: An Autobiography by Fred Bower, With a Foreword by John Brophy* (London, 1911).

Brierley, Benjamin, *Home Memories and Recollections of a Life* (Manchester, 1886).

Buckmaster, J.C., ed., *A Village Politician: The Life Story of John Buckley* (London, 1897).

Burgess, Joseph, *John Burns: The Rise and Progress of a Right Honourable* (Glasgow, 1911).

Burt, Thomas, *An Autobiography, with Supplementary Chapters by Aaron Watson and a Foreword by Wilfred Burt* (London, 1924).

Bussy, J.F.M., *From E.C. to P.C: A Biographical Sketch of the Right Honourable J.H. Thomas, M.P.: General Secretary of the National Union of Railwaymen* (London, 1917).

Carter, Thomas, *Memoirs of a Working Man* (London, 1845).

Chadwick, W., *Pages from a Life of Strife* (London, 1911).

Chase, Ellen, *Tenant Friends in Old Deptford* (London, 1929).

[Chatterton, Daniel], 'Chat', *Biography of Dan. Chatterton. Atheist and Communist* (London, 1891).

Clynes, J.R., *The Right Honourable J.R. Clynes, P.C. M.P. D.C.L., Memoirs 1869–1924* (London, 1937).

Cobbett, William, *Advice to Young Men* (1829; facsimile edn, 1906).

Collison, W., *The Apostle of Free Labour: The Life Story of William Collison, Founder and General Secretary of the National Free Labour Association, Told by Himself* (London, 1913).

Connolly, Jane, *Old Days and Ways* (London, 1912).

Cooper, Thomas, *Eight Letters to the Young Men of the Working Classes* (first published in *The Plain Speaker* between December 1848 and August 1849; London, 1850).

Cooper, Thomas, *The Life of Thomas Cooper Written by Himself* (first published 1872; this edn, with an introduction by John Saville, Leicester, 1971).

Eden, E., ed., *The Autobiography of a Workingman* (Edinburgh, 1862).

Edwards, George, *From Crow Scaring to Westminster. An Autobiography* (London, 1922).

Engels, F., *The Condition of the Working Class in England* (first published 1845; this edn, with an introduction by David McLellan, Oxford, 1993).

Farningham, Marianne, *A Working Woman's Life: An Autobiography* (London, 1907).

Fleming, L., *An Octogenarian Printer's Reminiscences* (Edinburgh, 1893).

France, R.S., ed., *The Diary of John Ward of Clitheroe, Weaver, 1860–64* (first published Liverpool, 1953)

Frost, Thomas, *Forty Years' Recollections* (London, 1880).

Gallacher, William, *Revolt on the Clyde: An Autobiography* (London, 1927).

Gammage, R.G., *History of the Chartist Movement: 1837–1854* (first published 1854; this edn, New York, 1969).

Gosling, Harry, *Up and Down Stream* (London, 1927).

Grime, Benjamin, *Memory Sketches* (Oldham, 1887).

Harrison, F., *Autobiographic Memoirs by Frederic Harrison, D.C.L., Litt. D., LL.D., Honorary Fellow of Wadham College, Oxford*, vol. 1 (London, 1911).

Hillocks, James, *Life Story: A Prize Autobiography* (London, 1860).

Hillocks, J.I., *Hard Battles for Life and Usefulness*, parts I and II (third edn, London, 1889).

Hodge, J., *Workman's Cottage to Windsor Castle by the Right Honourable John Hodge, P.C., First Minister of Labour and Ex-Minister of Pensions, Ex-President of Iron and Steel Trades Confederation* (London, 1931).

Hodges, Frank, *My Adventures as a Labour Leader* (London, 1925).

Holyoake, G.J., *Sixty Years of an Agitator's Life* (first published London, 1892; this edn, New York, 1984).

Holyoake, G.J., *Bygones Worth Remembering* (London, 1905).

Hopkinson, James, *Victorian Cabinet Maker: The Memoirs of James Hopkinson 1819–1894*, ed., J. Baty Goodman (first published London, 1968).

Kirkwood, David, *My Life of Revolt* (London, 1935).

Leatherland, J.A., *Essays and Poems with a Brief Autobiographical Memoir* (London, 1862).

Leno, J.B., *The Aftermath: With Autobiography of John Bedford Leno* (London, 1892).

Livesey, Joseph, *The Life and Teaching of Joseph Livesey, Comprising his Autobiography*, with an introductory essay by John Pearce (London, 1885).

Lovett, William, *Life and Struggles of William Lovett in his Pursuit of Bread, Knowledge and Freedom*, vols I and II (first published 1876; this edn, with an introduction by R.H. Tawney, London, 1920).

Mann, Tom, *From Single Tax to Syndicalism* (London, 1913).

Mann, Tom, *Memoirs* (London, 1923).

Marcroft, William, *A Co-operative Village: How to Conduct it and Where to Form it* (Manchester, ND).

Marcroft, William, *The Inner Circle of Family Life* (Manchester, 1886).

Marcroft, William, *The Marcroft Family: A History of Strange Events* (Rochdale, 1889).

Marcroft, William, *Ups and Downs: Life in a Machine-making Works* (Oldham, 1889).

McCabe, Joseph, *Life and Letters of George Jacob Holyoake* (London, 1908).

Miall, A., *Life of Edmund Miall by his Son, Arthur Miall* (London, 1884).

Miller, Hugh, *My Schools and Schoolmasters* (Edinburgh, 1854).

Miller, Hugh, *My Schools and Schoolmasters* (Edinburgh, 1893).

Naisby, W., *Evidence of Witnesses in the Cases of William Pearce and James Bristol, Who Died at Bolton from Want of Food; Also on the General Distress in that Town; with Remarks on that Subject, and on the Assistant Poor-Law Commissioner's Report* (Bolton, 1841).

Newbould, T.P., ed., *Pages From a Life of Strife, Being Some Recollections of W.H. Chadwick, the Last of the Manchester Chartists* (London, 1911).

Owen, Robert, *The Life of Robert Owen, Written by Himself* (first published London, 1857; this edn, London, 1971).

Rennie, J., *The Converted Shepherd Boy: The Life of James Rennie* (London, 1878).

Rowley, C., *Fifty Years of Ancoats* (London, 1899).

Rowley, C., *Fifty Years of Work without Wages* (London, 1911).

Rushton, Adam, *My Life, as Farmer's Boy, Factory Lad, Teacher and Preacher* (Manchester, 1909).

Smillie, R., *My Life for Labour by Robert Smillie, M.P.* (London, 1924).

Smith, C.M., *The Working Man's Way in the World* (London, 1857).

Somerville, Alexander, *The Autobiography of a Working Man* (first published London, 1848; later edns, London, 1951 and 1967).

Storie, Elizabeth, *The Autobiography of Elizabeth Storie, a Native of Glasgow* (Glasgow, 1859).

Thomas, J.H., *By the Right Honourable J.H. Thomas, My Story* (London, 1937).

Thomson, C., *The Autobiography of an Artisan* (London, 1847).

Thorne, Will, *My Life's Battles* (London, 1925).

Tillett, Ben, *Memories and Reflections* (London, 1931).

[Turnbull, James], *Reminiscences of a Stonemason by a Working Man* (London, 1908).

Turner, Ben, *About Myself 1863–1930* (London, 1930).

Whittaker, Thomas, *Life's Battles in Temperance Armour* (Manchester, 1884).

Wilson, B., *The Struggles of an Old Chartist* (Halifax, 1887).

Wilson, John, *Memories of a Labour Leader* (first published 1910; this edn, with an introduction by John Burnett, Firle, 1980).

[Wright, Thomas], *Some Habits and Customs of the Working Classes by a Journeyman Engineer* (London, 1867).

Wright, Thomas, *The Great Unwashed by the Journeyman Engineer* (first published 1868; this edn, London, 1970).

[Wright, Thomas], *Our New Masters* (first published London, 1873; this edn, New York, 1984).

[Wright, Thomas], 'Riverside Visitor', 'A Rookery District', 'Bundle-wood work and workers', in *Good Words*, 1883.

Younger, J., *Autobiography of John Younger, Shoemaker, St. Boswells* (Edinburgh, 1881).

SECONDARY SOURCES

Books

Abercrombie, N., *et al.*, *The Dominant Ideology Thesis* (London, 1980).

Althusser, L., *For Marx* (New York, 1969).

Althusser, L., *Lenin and Philosophy and Other Essays* (New York, 1971).

Althusser, L., *Montesquieu, Rousseau, Marx: Politics and History*, transl. B. Brewster (London, 1972).

Andrews, K. and Jacobs, J., *Punishing the Poor: Poverty under Thatcher* (London, 1990).

Barker, T.C. and Harris, J.R., *A Merseyside Town in the Industrial Revolution, St. Helen's, 1750–1900* (London, 1959).

Barthes, R., *Writing Degree Zero and Elements of Semiology*, transl. A. Lavers and C. Smith (first published 1953; this edn, London, 1967).

Barthes, R., *Mythologies*, transl. A. Lavers (first published 1957; this edn, London, 1972).

Bellamy, J. and Saville, J., eds, *Dictionary of Labour Biography*, vols 1 and 2 (London, 1972 and 1974).

Benson, J., *The Working Class in England 1875–1914* (London, 1985).

Berkhofer Jr, R.F., *Beyond the Great Story: History as Text and Discourse* (Cambridge, MA, 1995)

Berlanstein, L., ed., *Rethinking Labor History: Essays on Discourse and Class Analysis* (Urbana, 1993).

Biagini, E.F., and Reid, A.J., eds, *Currents of Radicalism: Popular Radicalism, Organised Labour and Party Politics in Britain 1850–1914* (Cambridge, 1991).

Birch, A.H., *Small-town Politics: A Study of Political Life in Glossop* (Oxford, 1959).

Bloomfield, J., ed., *Class, Hegemony and Party* (London, 1977).

Bottomore, T., *Elites and Society* (first published 1964; this edn, London, 1993).

Bottomore, T., ed., *A Dictionary of Marxist Thought* (Oxford, 1983).

Briggs, A., ed., *Chartist Studies* (first published 1959; this edn, London, 1965).

Burawoy, M., *Manufacturing Consent* (Chicago, 1979).

Burawoy, M., *The Politics of Production* (Chicago, 1985).

Burke, P. and Porter, R., eds, *Language, Self and Society: A Social History of Language* (Cambridge, 1991).

Burnett, J., *Useful Toil: Autobiographies of Working People from the 1820s to the 1920s* (London, 1974).

Burnett, J., *Destiny Obscure: Autobiographies of Childhood, Education and Family from the 1820s to the 1920s* (London, 1982).

Burnett, J., Vincent, D. and Mayall, D., eds, *The Autobiography of the Working Class: An Annotated Critical Bibliography* (Brighton, 1984).

Butler, J., *Gender Trouble: Feminism and the Subversion of Identity* (New York, 1990).

Calhoun, C., *The Question of Class Struggle: Social Foundations of Popular Radicalism during the Industrial Revolution* (Chicago, 1982).

Carpenter, K.E., ed., *The Framework Knitters and Handloom Weavers; Their Attempts to Keep up Wages: Eight Pamphlets 1820–1845* (New York, 1972).

Carrard, P., *Poetics of the New History: French Historical Discourse from Braudel to Chartier* (Baltimore, 1992).

Certeau, M. de, *Heterologies: Discourse on the Other*, transl. by B. Massumi (Minneapolis, 1986).

Chaloner, W.H., *The Social and Economic Development of Crewe, 1780–1923* (Manchester, 1950).

Chandler, J., Davidson, A.I. and Harootunian, H., *Questions of Evidence: Proof, Practice, and Persuasion across the Disciplines* (Chicago, 1991).

Chomsky, N., *Turning the Tide: US Intervention in Central America and the Struggle for Peace* (Boston, 1985).

Chomsky, N., *On Power and Ideology: The Managua Lectures* (Boston, 1987).

Chomsky, N., *Deterring Democracy* (London, 1991).

Chomsky, N., *Rethinking Camelot: JFK, the Vietnam War, and US Political Culture* (London, 1993).

Chomsky, N., *Year 501: The Conquest Continues* (Boston, 1993).

Christie, I.R., *Stress and Stability in Late Eighteenth Century Britain: Reflections on the British Avoidance of Revolution* (Oxford, 1984).

Claeys, G., *Machinery, Money and the Millennium: From Moral Economy to Socialism 1815–1860* (Cambridge, 1987).

Cohen, R., ed., *The Future of Literary Theory* (New York, 1989).

Cohen, S., *Historical Culture: On the Recoding of an Academic Discipline* (Berkeley, 1987).

Cole, G.D.H., *Chartist Portraits* (London, 1941).

Cole, G.D.H., *A Short History of the British Working-class Movement, 1789–1947* (London, 1948).

Cooke, A.B., compiler/ed., *Margaret Thatcher – The Revival of Britain: Speeches on Home and European Affairs 1975–1988* (London, 1989).

Crossick, G., *An Artisan Elite in Victorian Society: Kentish London 1840–1880* (London, 1978).

Cutler, A., Hindess, B., Hirst, P. and Hussain, A., *Marx's Capitalism and Capitalism Today* (Boston, 1977).

Dinwiddy, J.R., *Chartism* (London, 1987).

Donajgrodski, A.P., ed., *Social Control in Nineteenth-century Britain* (Totawa, NJ, 1977).

Dreyfus, H.L. and Rabinow, P., *Michel Foucault: Beyond Structuralism and Hermeneutics* (London, 1982).

Duberman, M., Vicinus, M. and Chauncey Jr, G., eds, *Hidden from History: Reclaiming the Gay and Lesbian Past* (London, 1989).

Edsall, N.C., *The Anti-Poor Law Movement 1834–44* (Manchester, 1971).

Elders, F., *Reflexive Waters: The Basic Concerns of Mankind* (London, 1974).

Epstein, J. and Thompson, D., eds, *The Chartist Experience: Studies in Working-class Radicalism and Culture, 1830–60* (London, 1982).

Faulkner, H.U., *Chartism and the Churches: A Study in Democracy* (New York, 1916).

Femia, J.V., *Gramsci's Political Thought: Hegemony, Consciousness, and the Revolutionary Process* (Oxford, 1981).

Finn, M., *After Chartism: Class and Nation in English Radical Politics 1848–1874* (Cambridge, 1993).

Foster, J., *Class Struggle and the Industrial Revolution: Early Industrial Capitalism in Three English Towns* (London, 1974).

Foucault, M., *The Archaeology of Knowledge*, transl., A.M. Sheridan Smith (London, 1969).

Foucault, M., *The Order of Things: An Archaeology of the Human Sciences*, ed., R.D. Laing (London, 1970).

Foucault, M., *Power/Knowledge: Selected Interviews and Other Writings 1972–1977*, ed., Colin Gordon (New York, 1980).

Foucault, M., *Madness and Civilization: A History of Insanity in the Age of Reason* (New York, 1973).

Foucault, M., *The Birth of the Clinic: An Archaeology of Medical Perception*, transl., A.M. Sheridan Smith (New York, 1975).

Foucault, M., *Language, Counter-memory, Practice: Selected Essays and Interviews by Michel Foucault*, ed., Donald F. Bouchard (Ithaca, 1977).

Foucault, M., *Discipline and Punish: The Birth of the Prison*, transl., A.M. Sheridan (New York, 1979).

Foucault, M., *The History of Sexuality Volume I: An Introduction*, transl., R. Hurley (New York, 1980).

Foucault, M., *The Use of Pleasure: The History of Sexuality Volume II* (New York, 1990).

Friedlander, S., ed., *Probing the Limits of Representation: Nazism and the 'Final Solution'* (Cambridge, MA, 1992).

Gadamer, H.G., *Truth and Method* (London, 1975).

Gossman, L., *Between History and Literature* (Cambridge, MA, 1990).

Gramsci, A., *Selections from the Prison Notebooks of Antonio Gramsci* (London, 1978).

Gray, R.Q., *The Labour Aristocracy in Victorian Edinburgh* (Oxford, 1976).

Gray, R.Q., *The Aristocracy of Labour in Nineteenth Century Britain* (London, 1981).

Hall, S. and Jacques, M., eds, *The Politics of Thatcherism* (London, 1983).

Harrison, B., *Drink and the Victorians* (Pittsburgh, 1971).

Harrison, B., *Peaceable Kingdom: Stability and Change in Modern Britain* (Oxford, 1982).

Harrison, J.F.C., *Learning and Living: A Study in the History of the Adult Education Movement, 1790–1960* (London, 1961).

Harrison, R., *Before the Socialists: Studies in Labour and Politics 1861–1881* (London, 1965).

Harrison, R. and Zeitlin, J., *Divisions of Labour: Skilled Workers and Technological Change in Nineteenth Century Britain* (Brighton, 1985).

Hewitt, M., *The Emergence of Stability in the Industrial City: Manchester 1832–1867* (Aldershot, 1996).

Hinton, J., *The First Shop Stewards' Movement* (London, 1973).

Hobsbawm, E.J., *The Age of Revolution: 1789–1848* (New York, 1962).

Hobsbawm, E.J., *Labouring Men: Studies in the History of Labour* (London, 1964).

Hobsbawm, E.J., *Revolutionaries* (London, 1973).

Hobsbawm, E.J., *Worlds of Labour: Further Studies in the History of Labour* (London, 1984).

Hobsbawm, E.J., *Politics for a Rational Left* (London, 1989).

Hoggart, R., *The Uses of Literacy* (Harmondsworth, 1957).

Hollis, P., *Women in Public 1850–1900: Documents of the Victorian Women's Movement* (London, 1979).

Hovell, M., *The Chartist Movement* (Manchester, 1925).

Howkins, A., *Poor Labouring Men: Rural Radicalism in Norfolk 1872–1923* (London, 1985).

Ionescu, G. and Gellner, E., eds, *Populism: Its Meanings and National Characteristics* (London, 1969).

Jenkins, K., *Rethinking History* (London, 1991).

Jones, G.S., *Outcast London: A Study in the Relationship between Classes in Victorian Society* (Oxford, 1971).

Jones, G.S., *Languages of Class: Studies in English Working Class History 1832–1982* (Cambridge, 1983).

Joyce, P., *Work, Society and Politics: The Culture of the Factory in Later Victorian England* (Brighton, 1980).

Joyce, P., ed., *The Historical Meanings of Work* (Cambridge, 1987).

Joyce, P., *Visions of the People: Industrial England and the Question of Class, 1840–1914* (Cambridge, 1991).

Joyce, P., *Democratic Subjects: The Self and the Social in Nineteenth-century England* (Cambridge, 1994).

Kaye, H.J., *The British Marxist Historians* (Cambridge, 1984).

Kaye, H.J., *The Powers of the Past* (Minneapolis, 1991).

Kirk, N., *The Growth of Working-class Reformism in Mid-Victorian England* (London, 1985).

Kirk, N., ed., *Social Class and Marxism: Defences and Challenges* (Aldershot, 1996).

LaCapra, D., *Rethinking Intellectual History: Texts, Contexts, Language* (Ithaca, 1983).

Laqueur, T.W., *Religion and Respectability: Sunday Schools and Working Class Culture, 1780–1850* (New Haven, 1976).

Lauretis, T. de, *Technologies of Gender: Essays on Theory, Film and Fiction* (Bloomington, 1987)

Leeson, R.A., *Travelling Brothers* (London, 1978).

Lenin, V.I., *Selected Works*, vol. 1 (London, 1967).

Lenin, V.I., *Imperialism, the Highest Stage of Capitalism* (Moscow, 1975).

Leventhal, F.M., *Respectable Radical: George Howell and Victorian Working Class Politics* (Cambridge, MA, 1971).

Loane, M., *Neighbours and Friends* (London, 1910).

Love, M., ed., *Structuralism: A Reader* (London, 1970).

Lukács, G., *The Destruction of Reason*, transl., P. Palmer (London, 1980).

Lukes, S., *Individualism* (New York, 1973).

Lummis, T., *The Labour Aristocracy 1851–1914* (Aldershot, 1994).

MacDonald, F.W., *Reminiscences of my Early Ministry* (London, 1913), pp.20–2.

Macdonell, D., *Theories of Discourse: An Introduction* (London, 1986).

MacIntyre, A., *After Virtue: A Study in Moral Theory* (London, 1985).

MacIntyre, A., *Whose Justice? Which Rationality* (Indiana, 1988).

Mandler, Peter, ed., *The Uses of Charity: The Poor on Relief in the Nineteenth-century Metropolis* (Philadelphia, 1990).

Mather, F.C., *Chartism* (first published 1965; this edn, London, 1971).

Matsumura, T., *The Labour Aristocracy Revisited: The Victorian Flint Glass Makers 1850–80* (Manchester, 1983).

McLennan, G., *Marxism and the Methodology of History* (London, 1981).

McLeod, H., *Religion and the Working Class in Nineteenth-century Britain* (London, 1984).

Michels, R., *Political Parties* (New York, 1959).

Mitchell, J. and Oakley, A., eds, *The Rights and Wrongs of Women* (Harmondsworth, 1976).

Mort, F., *Dangerous Sexualities: Medico-moral Politics in England since 1830* (London, 1987).

Musson, A.E., *British Trade Unions 1800–1875* (London, 1972).

Musson, A.E., *Trade Unions and Social History* (London, 1974).

Palmer, B.D., *Descent into Discourse: The Reification of Language and the Writing of Social History* (Philadelphia, 1990).

Parkin, F., *Class, Inequality and Political Order* (New York, 1971).

Pelling, H., *Popular Politics and Society in Late Victorian England* (London, 1968).

Poovey, M., *Making a Social Body: British Cultural Formation, 1830–1864* (Chicago, 1995).

Poster, M., *Foucault, Marxism and History: Mode of Production versus Mode of Information* (Cambridge, 1984).

Poynter, J.R., *Society and Pauperism: English Ideas on Poor Relief, 1795–1834* (London, 1969).

Prothero, I., *Artisans and Politics in Early Nineteenth-century London: John Gast and His Times* (Folkestone, 1979).

Rancière, J., *The Nights of Labour: The Workers' Dream in Nineteenth-century France*, transl., John Drury (first published 1981; this edn, Philadelphia, 1989).

Read, D., *The English Provinces, c1760–1960* (London, 1964).

Reid, A.J., *Social Classes and Social Relations in Britain, 1850–1914* (London, 1992).

Roberts, R., *The Classic Slum: Salford Life in the First Quarter of the Century* (Manchester, 1971).

Roe, M., *Kenealy and the Tichborne Cause: A Study in Mid-Victorian Populism* (Melbourne, 1974).

Rorty, R., *Philosophy and the Mirror of Nature* (Princeton, 1980).

Rose, S.O., *Limited Livelihoods: Gender and Class in Nineteenth-century England* (Berkeley and Los Angeles, 1992).

Rosenau, P.M., *Post-modernism and the Social Sciences: Insights, Inroads and Intrusions* (Princeton, 1992).

Rosenblatt, F.F., *The Chartist Movement in its Social and Economic Aspects* (New York, 1916).

Rothstein, T., *From Chartism to Labourism: Historical Sketches of the English Working Class Movement*, with an introduction by John Saville (first published 1929; this edn, London, 1983).

Royle, E. and Walvin, J., *English Radicals and Reformers 1760–1848* (Brighton, 1982).

Rushdie, S., *The Satanic Verses* (Dover, DE, 1988).

Samuel, R., ed., *Village Life and Labour* (London, 1975).

Samuel, R. and Jones, G.S., *Culture, Ideology and Politics: Essays for Eric Hobsbawm* (London, 1982).

Savage, M. and Miles, A., *The Remaking of the British Working Class 1840–1940* (London, 1994).

Saville, J., ed., *Democracy and the Labour Movement* (London, 1954).

Saville, J., ed., *Dictionary of Labour Biography*, vol. 1 (London, 1972) and vol. 2 (London, 1974).

Saville, J., *1848: The British State and the Chartist Movement* (Cambridge, 1987).

Schiller, F. von, *Two Essays by Friedrich von Schiller: 'Naive and Sentimental Poetry' and 'On the Sublime'*, transl., Julius A. Elias (New York, 1966).

Schlüter, H., *Die Chartisten-Bewegung: Ein Betrag zur Sozial-politischen Geschichte Englands* (New York, 1916).

Schoyen, A.R., *The Chartist Challenge: A Portrait of George Julian Harney* (London, 1958).

Schwarzkopf, J., *Women in the Chartist Movement* (London, 1991).

Scott, J.W., *Gender and the Politics of History* (New York, 1988).

Seton-Watson, H., *The Pattern of Communist Revolution* (London, 1953).

Shipley, S., *Club Life and Socialism in Mid-Victorian London*, History Workshop pamphlet (Oxford, 1971).

Sigsworth, E.M., *In Search of Victorian Values: Aspects of Nineteenth-century Thought and Society* (Manchester, 1988).

Skinner, Q., ed., *The Return of Grand Theory in the Human Sciences* (Cambridge, 1985).

Slosson, P.W., *The Decline of the Chartist Movement* (New York, 1916).

Smith, F.B., *Radical Artisan: William James Linton 1812–1897* (Manchester, 1973).

Smith, P., *Discerning the Subject* (Minneapolis, 1988).

Snell, K.D.M., *Annals of the Labouring Poor: Social Change and Agrarian England 1660–1900* (Cambridge, 1985).

Spivak, G.C., *In Other Worlds: Essays in Cultural Politics* (New York, 1987).

Stenton, M., ed., *Who's Who of British Members of Parliament*, vol. I, 1832–1885 (Sussex, 1976).

Taylor, C., *Sources of the Self: The Making of the Modern Identity* (Cambridge, 1989).

Taylor, J.C., *The Jubilee History of the Oldham Industrial Co-operative Society Limited 1850–1900* (Manchester, 1900).

Tholfsen, T.R., *Working Class Radicalism in Mid-Victorian England* (London, 1976).

Thompson, D., *The Chartists: Popular Politics in the Industrial Revolution* (New York, 1984).

Thompson, D., *Outsiders: Class, Gender and Nation* (London, 1993).

Thompson, E.P., *The Making of the English Working Class* (Harmondsworth, 1968).

Thompson, E.P., *The Poverty of Theory and Other Essays* (London, 1978).

Thompson, F.M.L., *The Rise of Respectable Society: A Social History of Victorian Britain, 1830–1900* (London, 1988).

Veeser, H.A., ed., *The New Historicism* (London, 1989).

Vernon, James, *Politics and the People: A Study in English Political Culture c.1815–1867* (Cambridge, 1993).

Vincent, D., *Bread, Knowledge and Freedom: A Study of Nineteenth-century Working-class Autobiography* (London, 1981).

Walkowitz, J.R., *City of Dreadful Delight: Narratives of Sexual Danger in Late-Victorian London* (Chicago, 1993).

Ward, J.T., *Chartism* (London, 1973).

Webb, S. and Webb, B., *The History of Trade Unionism* (first published 1894; this edn, London, 1902)

Webb, S. and Webb, B., *The Truth about Soviet Russia*, with a preface by G.B. Shaw (London, 1942).

Weeks, J., *Coming Out: Homosexual Politics in Britain from the Nineteenth Century to the Present* (London, 1977).

Weinsheimer, J.C., *Gadamer's Hermeneutics: A Reading of Truth and Method* (New Haven, 1985).

Wells, F.A., *The British Hosiery and Knitwear Industry: Its History and Organization* (first published 1935; this edn, Newton Abbot, 1972).

West, J., *A History of the Chartist Movement* (London, 1920).

White, H., *Metahistory: The Historical Imagination in Nineteenth-century Europe* (Baltimore, 1973).

White, H., *Tropics of Discourse: Essays in Cultural Criticism* (Baltimore, 1978).

White, H., *The Content of the Form: Narrative Discourse and Historical Representation* (Baltimore, 1987).

Wiener, M.J., *English Culture and the Decline of the Industrial Spirit, 1850–1980* (Cambridge, 1981).

Williams, R., *Culture and Society 1780–1950* (Harmondsworth, 1963).

Windschuttle, K., *The Killing of History: How a Discipline is Being Murdered by Literary Critics and Social Theorists* (Sydney, 1994).

Winter, J., ed., *The Working Class in Modern British History: Essays in Honour of Henry Pelling* (Cambridge, 1983).

Wood, E.M., *The Retreat from Class: A New 'True' Socialism* (London, 1986).

Journal articles

Ackroyd, P., 'Who Owns the Victorians?', in *The Spectator*, 28 May 1983.

Ankersmit, F.R., 'Historiography and Postmodernism', in *History and Theory*, 28, 1989.

Bailey, P., '"Will the Real Bill Banks Please Stand Up?" Towards a Role Analysis of Mid-Victorian Working-class Respectability', in *Journal of Social History*, 12, 1978–9.

Bailey, P., review of P. Joyce, *Work, Society and Politics*, in *Journal of Social History*, 15, 1981–2.

Bailey, P., 'Ally Sloper's Half-holiday: Comic Art in the 1880s', in *History Workshop*, 16, 1983.

Behagg, C., 'Custom, Class and Change: The Trade Societies of Birmingham', in *Social History*, 4, 3, 1979.

Breuilly, J., 'Avoiding Post-Modernism', in *Teaching History*, 75, 1994.

Breuilly, J., 'The Labour Aristocracy in Britain and Germany: A Comparison', in *Bulletin of the Society for the Study of Labour History*, 48, 1984.

Brown, C.G., critique of T.W. Laqueur, *Religion and Respectability*, in *Economic History Review*, 31, 1978.

Bythell, D., review of Neville Kirk, *The Growth of Working-class Reformism in Mid-Victorian England*, in *American Historical Review*, 91, 1986.

Cannadine, D., 'British History: Past, Present – and Future?' in *Past and Present*, 116, 1987.

Canning, Kathleen, 'Feminist History after the Linguistic Turn: Historicizing Discourse and Experience', in *Signs*, 19, 2, 1994.

Chamberlain, Mary and Richardson, Ruth, 'Pawnographic Values', in *New Statesman*, 27 May 1983.

Chapman, S.D., review of P. Joyce, *Work, Society and Politics*, in *Economic History Review*, 34, 1981.

Claeys, G., 'The Triumph of Class-conscious Reformism in British Radicalism 1790–1860', in *Historical Journal*, 26, 4, 1983.

Clark, A., 'The Rhetoric of Chartist Domesticity: Gender, Language, and Class in the 1830s and 1840s', in *Journal of British Studies*, 31, 1, 1992.

Connolly, W.E., 'Taylor, Foucault, and Otherness', in *Political Theory*, 13, 3, August 1985.

Cronin, J.E., critique of T.R. Tholfsen, *Working Class Radicalism*, in *Journal of Economic History*, 37, 1977.

Cronin, J.E., 'The Wisdom of Conventional Wisdom', in *Journal of Economic History*, 47, 1987.

Crossick, G., 'The Labour Aristocracy and its Values: A Study of Mid-Victorian Kentish London', in *Victorian Studies*, March, 1976.

Crossick, G., 'Reality of Power', in *New Society*, 39, 745, 13 January 1977.

Crossick, G., review of Patrick Joyce, *Work, Society and Politics*, in *American Historical Review*, 86, 1981.

Crossick, G., 'Classes and the Masses in Victorian England', in *History Today*, 37, 1987.

Davidoff, L. and Hall, C., 'Home Sweet Home', in *New Statesman*, 27 May 1983.

Davis, J., 'A Poor Man's System of Justice: The London Police Courts in the Second Half of the Nineteenth Century', in *Historical Journal*, 27, 2, 1984.

Davis, R.W., review of F.M.L., Thompson, *The Rise of Respectable Society*, in *Victorian Studies*, 33, 1989–90.

Dick, Malcolm, 'The Myth of the Working-class Sunday School', in *History of Education*, 9, 1, 1980.

Draper, H., 'The Concept of the "Lumpenproletariat" in Marx and Engels', in *Economies et Sociétiés Cahiers de: l'ISEA*, 5, 15, 1972.

Feltes, N.N., review of Patrick Joyce, *Visions of the People*, in *Victorian Studies*, 35, 4, Summer 1992.

Ferguson, W., review of R.Q. Gray, *The Labour Aristocracy in Victorian Edinburgh*, in *History*, 63, 1978.

Foster, J., review of R.Q. Gray, *The Labour Aristocracy in Victorian Edinburgh*, in *British Journal of Sociology*, 29, 1978.

Foster, J., 'The Declassing of Language', in *New Left Review*, 150, 1985.

Gadian, D.S., 'Class Consciousness in Oldham and Other North-West Industrial Towns 1830–1850', in *Historical Journal*, 21, 1, 1978.

Gagnier, R., 'Social Atoms: Working-class Autobiography, Subjectivity, and Gender', in *Victorian Studies*, Spring 1987.

Geras, N., 'Althusser's Marxism: An Account and Assessment', in *New Left Review*, 71, 1972.

Geras, N., 'Language, Truth and Justice', in *New Left Review*, 209, 1995.

Ginzburg, C., 'Checking the Evidence: The Judge and the Historian', in *Critical Inquiry*, 18, 1991.

Gray, R.Q., 'The Political Incorporation of the Working Class', in *Sociology*, 9, 1975.

Gray, R.Q., 'The Labour Aristocracy: Comments on the Recent Debate', in *Bulletin of the Society for the Study of Labour History*, 40, Spring 1980.

Gray, R.Q., 'The Deconstructing of the English Working Class', in *Social History*, 11, 3, 1986.

Gray, R.Q., review of Neville Kirk, *The Growth of Working-class Reformism in Mid-Victorian England*, in *Economic History Review*, 39, 1986.

Hanagan, M., review of Patrick Joyce, *The Historical Meanings of Work*, in *Journal of Economic History*, 48, 1988.

Harrison, B., 'The Sunday Trading Riots of 1855', in *Historical Journal*, 7, 2, 1965.

Harrison, B. and Hollis, P., 'Chartism, Liberalism and the Life of Robert Lowery', in *English Historical Review*, 82, 1967.

Harrison, J.F.C., review of T.W. Laqueur, *Religion and Respectability: Sunday Schools and Working-class Culture 1780–1850*, in *Journal of Economic History*, 38, 1978.

Harrison, J.F.C., 'Top of the Pops', a review of Derek Fraser, *Cities, Class and Communication*, and Patrick Joyce, *Visions of the People*, in *History Today*, 41, July 1991.

Harrison, R., review of G. Crossick, *An Artisan Elite*, in *History*, 64, 1979.

Hewitt, M., 'Radicalism and the Victorian Working Class: The Case of Samuel Bamford', in *The Historical Journal*, 34, December 1991.

Himmelfarb, G., 'Telling It as You Like It: Post-modernist History and the Flight from Fact', in *Times Literary Supplement*, 16 October 1992.

Hobsbawm, E.J., 'Lenin and the "Aristocracy of Labour"', in *Marxism Today*, 14, 7, 1970.

Hobsbawm, E.J., 'Interview', in *Radical History Review*, 19, Winter 1978–9.

Howell, P., critique of Patrick Joyce, *Visions of the People*, in *Journal of Historical Geography*, 17, 4, October 1991.

Howes, G., 'The Work Ethic', a review of T.W. Laqueur, *Religion and Respectability: Sunday Schools and English Working-class Culture 1780–1850*, in *New Society*, 39, 747, 1977.

Ignatieff, M., 'Law and Order in a City of Strangers', in *New Statesman*, 27 May 1983.

Jenkins, K., 'Beyond the Old Dichotomies: Some Reflections on Hayden White', in *Teaching History*, 74, 1994.

Jones, G.S., 'Working-class culture and Working-class Politics in London, 1870–1900: Notes on the Remaking of a Working Class', in *Social History*, 7, 4, 1974.

Jones, G.S., 'From Historical Sociology to Theoretical History', in *British Journal of Sociology*, 27, 3, September 1976.

Jones, G.S., 'Society and Politics at the Beginning of the World Economy', in *Cambridge Journal of Economics*, 1, 1977.

Jones, G.S., 'Poor Laws and Market Forces', in *New Statesman*, 27 May 1983.

Jones, G.S., 'The Declassing of Language', in *New Left Review*, 149–51, 1985.

Jones, T., 'A Return to Victorian Values? Fings Ain't What They Used To Be', in *Listener*, 11 July 1985.

Joyce, P., 'Labour, Capital and Compromise: A Response to Richard Price', in *Social History*, 9, 1, January 1984.

Joyce, P., 'Languages of Reciprocity and Conflict: A Further Response to Richard Price', in *Social History*, 9, 2, May 1984.

Kansteiner, W., 'Hayden White's Critique of the Writing of History', in *History and Theory*, 32, 1993.

Kaye, H.J., critique of Patrick Joyce, *Visions of the People*, in *American Journal of Sociology*, 98, 1, 1992.

Kellner, H., '"Never Again" Is Now', in *History and Theory*, 33, 2, 1994.

Kent, C., 'Presence and Absence: History, Theory, and the Working Class', in *Victorian Studies*, 29, 1985–6.

Kirk, N., '"Traditional" Working-class Culture and "the Rise of Labour": Some Preliminary Questions and Observations', in *Social History*, 16, 2, 1991.

Kirk, N., 'In Defence of Class: A Critique of Recent Revisionist Writing upon the Nineteenth-century English Working Class', in *International Review of Social History*, 32, 1987.

Koditschek T., review of G. Crossick, *An Artisan Elite*, in *Journal of Modern History*, 59, 1987.

Koditschek, T., critique of Patrick Joyce, *Visions of the People*, in *American Historical Review*, 97, 4, October 1992.

Koditschek, T., 'A Tale of Two Thompsons', in *Radical History Review*, 56, 1993.

Lauretis, T. de, 'Eccentric Subjects: Feminist Theory and Historical Consciousness', in *Feminist Studies*, 16, 1, 1990.

Lazarus, N., 'Doubting the New World Order: Marxism, Realism, and the Claims of Postmodernist Social Theory', in *Differences: A Journal of Feminist Cultural Studies*, 3, 3, 1991.

Lazonick, W., 'Industrial Relations and Technical Change: the Case of the Self-acting Mule', in *Cambridge Journal of Economics*, 3, 1979.

Marshall, G., 'Distributional Struggle and Moral Order in a Market Society', in *Sociology*, 21, 1, 1987.

Marwick, A., 'Two Approaches to Historical Study: The Metaphysical (Including Postmodernism) and the Historical', in *Journal of Contemporary History*, 30, 1995.

Mason, M., 'Victorian Consumers', in *London Review of Books*, 11, 14, 16 February 1989.

Mayfield, D. and Thorne, S., 'Social History and its Discontents: Gareth Stedman Jones and the Politics of Language', in *Social History*, 17, 2, May 1992.

McClelland, K., 'Reviews and Enthusiasms', in *History Workshop Journal*, 11, 1981.

McCord, N., 'Adding a Touch of Class', in *History*, 70, 1985.

McKibbin, R., 'Why Was There no Marxism in Great Britain?', in *English Historical Review*, April 1984.

McNutt, R., 'History and Text: Chartism, the Middle Class, and Narrative Containment', in *Semiotica*, 59, 1986.

Megill, A., 'Foucault, Structuralism, and the Ends of History', in *Journal of Modern History*, 51, 1979.

Middleton, P., 'For "Victorian", read "Georgian": Mrs Thatcher Corrected', in *Encounter*, 67, July/August 1986.

Momigliano, A., 'The Rhetoric of History and the History of Rhetoric: On Hayden White's Tropes', in *Comparative Criticism*, 3, 1981.

Moorhouse, H.F., 'The Political Incorporation of the British Working Class: An Interpretation', in *Sociology*, 7, 3, 1973.

Moorhouse, H.F., 'The Marxist Theory of the Labour Aristocracy', in *Social History*, 3, 1978.

Morton, A.L., review of G. Crossick, *An Artisan Elite*, in *Science and Society*, 50, 1986–7.

Morton, A.L., review of Ivor Wilks, *South Wales and the Rising of 1839*, in *Science and Society*, 50, 1986–7.

Musson, A.E., 'Class Struggle and the Labour Aristocracy 1830–1860', *Social History*, 1, 3, 1976.

Palmer, B.D., 'Critical Theory, Historical Materialism, and the Ostensible End of Marxism: The Poverty of Theory Revisited', in *International Review of Social History*, 38, 1983.

Palmer, B.D., 'The Eclipse of Materialism: Marxism and the Writing of Social History in the 1980s', in *The Socialist Register*, 1990.

Patton, P., 'Taylor and Foucault on Power and Freedom', in *Political Studies*, 37, 1989.

Pickering, P.A., 'Class without Words: Symbolic Communication in the Chartist Movement', in *Past and Present*, 112, 1986.

Price, R., 'The Other Face of Respectability: Violence in the Manchester Brickmaking Trade 1859–1870', in *Past and Present*, 66, 1975.

Price, R., 'The Labour Process and Labour History', in *Social History*, 8, 1, January 1983.

Price, R., 'Conflict and Co-operation: A Reply to Patrick Joyce', in *Social History*, 9, 2, May 1984.

Price, R., review of Patrick Joyce, *The Historical Meanings of Work*, in *International Review of Social History*, 34, 1989.

Price, R., 'The Future of British Labour History', in *International Review of Social History*, 36, 1991.

Price, R., review of Patrick Joyce, *Visions of the People*, in *The Journal of Interdisciplinary History*, 23, 2, Autumn 1992.

Prothero, I., 'Chartism in London', in *Past and Present*, 44, 1969.

Prothero, I., review of T.R. Tholfsen, *Working-class Radicalism in Victorian England*, in *History*, 63, 1978.

Purvis, M., 'The Development of Co-operative Retailing in England and Wales, 1851–1901: A Geographical Study', in *Journal of Historical Geography*, 16, 3, 1990.

Reid, A., 'Politics and Economics in the Formation of the British Working Class: A Response to H.F. Moorhouse', in *Social History*, 3, 3, 1978.

Reid, A., 'Class and Organization', in *The Historical Journal*, 30, 1, 1987.

Richards, J., 'A Reply to Patrick Middleton: Victorian Values Revisited', (and Middleton's response), in *Encounter*, 68, March 1987.

Rogers, N., 'Class and Popular Education in Nineteenth-century Britain', a review of T.W. Laqueur, *Religion and Respectability: Sunday Schools and Working-class Culture 1780–1850*, in *History of Education Quarterly*, 19, 1979.

Rootes, C.A., 'The Dominant Ideology Thesis and its Critics', in *Sociology*, 15, 3, 1981.

Rose, S.O., 'Gender Antagonism and Class Conflict: Exclusionary Strategies of Male Trade Unionists in Nineteenth-century Britain', in *Social History*, 13, 1988.

Royle, E., 'Mechanics Institutes and the Working Classes, 1840–1860', in *Historical Journal*, 14, 2, 1971.

Rule, J.G., review of P. Joyce, *Visions of the People*, in *English Historical Review*, 107, 423, 1992.

Said, E.W., 'Opponents, Audiences, Constituencies, and Community', in *Critical Inquiry*, 9, 1982.

Samuel, R., 'Cry God for Maggie, England and St George', in *New Statesman*, 27 May 1983.

Samuel, R., 'Soft Focus Nostalgia', in *New Statesman*, 27 May 1983.

Samuel, R., 'Reading the Signs', in *History Workshop*, 32, 1991.

Samuel, R., 'Reading the Signs II: Fact-grubbers and Mind-readers', in *History Workshop*, 33, 1992.

Saville, J., review of D. Thompson, *The Chartists*, in *Economic History Review*, 38, 1985.

Scott, J.W., review of T.R. Tholfsen, *Working Class Radicalism*, in *Journal of Modern History*, 51, 1979.

Scott, J.W., 'On Language, Gender, and Working-class History', in *International Labor and Working-class History*, 31, 1987.

Scott, J.W. 'A Reply to Criticism', in *International Labor and Working-class History*, 32, 1987.

Scott, J.W., 'The Evidence of Experience', in *Critical Inquiry*, Summer 1991.

Shapiro, I., 'Realism in the Study of the History of Ideas', in *History of Political Thought*, 3, 3, 1982.

Smith, S., 'Who's Talking/Who's Talking Back? The Subject of Personal Narrative', in *Signs*, Winter 1993.

Stansky, P., review of F.M.L. Thompson, *The Rise of Respectable Society*, in *Journal of Interdisciplinary History*, 20, 1989–90.

Storch, R., 'The Plague of the Blue Locusts: Police Reform and Popular Resistance in Northern England, 1840–57', in *International Review of Social History*, 20, 1976.

Storch, R., review of T.R. Tholfsen, *Working Class Radicalism*, in *Labour History*, 20, 1979.

Taylor, A., 'Palmerston and Radicalism, 1847–1865', in *Journal of British Studies*, 33, April 1994.

Taylor, A., 'New Views of an Old Moral World: An Appraisal of Robert Owen', in *Labour History*, 36, Winter 1995.

Taylor, C., 'Foucault on Freedom and Truth', in *Political Theory*, 12, 2, May 1984.

Taylor, C., 'Taylor and Foucault on Power and Freedom: A Reply', in *Political Studies*, 37, 1989.

Taylor, M., 'Rethinking the Chartists: Searching for Synthesis in the Historiography of Chartism', in *The Historical Journal*, 39, June 1996.

Tholfsen, T.R., 'The Transition to Democracy in Victorian England', in *International Review of Social History*, 6, 1961.

Tholfsen, T.R., 'The Intellectual Origins of Mid-Victorian Stability', in *Political Science Quarterly*, 86, 1971.

Tholfsen, T.R., review of R.Q. Gray, *The Labour Aristocracy in Victorian Edinburgh*, in *American Historical Review*, 1, 82, 1977.

Tholfsen, T.R., review of G. Crossick, *An Artisan Elite in Victorian Society*, in *American Historical Review*, 2, 84, 1979.

Tholfsen, T.R., 'Moral Education in the Victorian Sunday School', in *History of Education Quarterly*, 20, 1980.

Tholfsen, T.R., review of Patrick Joyce, *Work, Society and Politics*, in *Journal of Modern History*, 54, 1982.

Thompson, F.M.L., 'Social Control in Victorian Britain', in *Economic History Review*, 34, 2, 1981.

Thompson, P., 'Labour Aristocracy', a review of G. Crossick, *An Artisan Elite in Victorian Society*, in *New Society*, 46, 845, 1978.

Thompson, P., 'Docile Workforce', in *New Society*, 54, 936, 23 October 1980.

Tyson, R.E., 'William Marcroft (1822–94) and the Limited Liability Movement in Oldham', in *Transactions of the Lancashire and Cheshire Antiquarian Society*, 80, 1979 (1980).

Waters, C., review of Patrick Joyce, *Visions of the People*, in *Social History*, 17, 3, October 1992.

Webb, R.K., review of T.W. Laqueur, *Religion and Respectability*, in *American Historical Review*, 2, 82, 1977.

White, H., 'Foucault Decoded: Notes from Underground', in *History and Theory*, 12, 1975.

White, H., 'The Discourse of History', in *Humanities in Society*, 2, 1979.

White, H., 'The Politics of Historical Interpretation: Discipline and De-sublimation', in *Critical Inquiry*, 9, 1982.

White, H., 'Introduction', in *Stanford Literature Review*, 6, 1989.

White, H., 'Writing in the Middle Voice', in *Stanford Literature Review*, 9, 1992.

White, H., 'A Response to Arthur Marwick', in *Journal of Contemporary History*, 30, 1995.

Wiener, J.H., review of F.M.L. Thompson, *The Rise of Respectable Society*, in *Journal of Social History*, 24, 1990–1.

Williams, G.A., 'The Concept of "Egemonia" in the Thought of Antonio Gramsci: Some Notes on Interpretation', in *Journal of the History of Ideas*, 21, 4, 1960.

Zammito, J.H., 'Are We Being Theoretical Yet? The New Historicism, the New Philosophy of History, and "Practising Historians"', in *Journal of Modern History*, 65, 1993.

INDEX

aesthetic: of history 161–3

aged: attitudes to 135, 136, 137

agency *see* popular agency

alienation *see* the poor: alienation of; social exclusion

artisans *see* labour aristocracy; working classes

autobiographers: attitudes to class 96–102, 104–8, 110–12, 113, 115, 116–17, 118; attitudes to reform 105–6; attitudes to working classes 96–7, 99, 100, 101, 102–4, 106–7, 109–10, 111, 113–17, 118; individualism in 105–6, 107, 112–13; representativeness of 70, 72–3, 75, 76–7, 78, 81–2, 83–4, 85, 86–7, 89, 90–1, 92, 94–9, 100, 107–8, 111, 113, 115–16, 118–19, 166–7, 168–9, 177

autobiographies: of labour leaders 113–19; *see also* popular agency

ballads: function 57, 87

benefits *see* New Poor Law; the poor; poverty; welfare benefits; workhouses

Biagini, E.: on populism 66–7

Blair, T. *see* Labour Party

Bolton: poverty in 121–5, 187–98

bourgeois hegemony *see* class hegemony

bourgeoisie *see* middle classes

Briggs: A., on Chartism 13, 14–15

Calhoun, C.: on failure of Chartism 36

capitalism: and class hegemony 181; development of 181, 182–4; discourses on 182–3; equity of 181; and wages 24–5

capitalists *see* middle classes

Chartism: 1848 revival 19–20, 22; achievements 11–12, 14, 15, 16–17, 20; causes of failure 10–11, 12–14, 15, 16, 18–19, 21, 22, 35–6; class analysis 22–3, 37; decline 19, 20; definitions of 16, 18; divisions within 12–14; effects of reform 35–6; and gender 64–5; interpretations of 8, 20–1, 35; Marxist interpretations 15–20, 21–34; and middle class radicals 14, 15; objectives 10, 11, 12–13, 48; political ideology 35–6, 37; as a precursor of Communism 20; and radicalism 14, 15, 36; strikes 19; and working class consciousness 8–9, 14, 15, 34, 70

Chartist Convention: dissolution 19

Chartist riots 19–20

Christian Socialism: development 20, 22

class: attitudes of autobiographers 96–102, 104–8, 110–12, 113, 115, 116–17, 118; definitions of 96; and discrimination 127–8; and liberalism 55; and radicalism 55; *see also* social identity; working class consciousness

class analysis: and Chartism 22–3, 37; and gender 80; and social identity 35, 60–2, 71, 74–80, 84–5, 111–12, 129, 135; structural 61–2, 70; and the Sunday school movement 96; and working class values 67–8, 72; *see also* trade status

class consciousness *see* working class consciousness

class hegemony: and capitalism 181; and the labour aristocracy 42–4, 165; as an object of explanation 165; and radicalism 21–2; and the Sunday school movement 45; and the working classes 45, 46, 49, 52, 70, 84–5

co-operative movement *see* mutualism

Cole, G.D.H.: on Chartism 12–13, 14–15

Communism: Chartist roots 20; failure of 32; *see also* headings beginning Marxist

community support: for families 135; for women 144, 145

consensus values: and radicalism 48–9; reality of 137; *see also* social stability

conservatism: in historiography 58, 59, 61; of the labour aristocracy 24, 25; value of 174; of the working classes 34–5, 36

Conservative Government: criticisms of 173, 178–80; policies 171–3; *see also* Thatcher, M.

contexts: and historical evidence 150

cotton industry *see* textile industry

counter-discourses *see* discourses

Crossick, G.: on the labour aristocracy 38–42; on social identity 111–12; on social stability 165; on working class values 67, 73–4, 77–9, 182

cultural change: and technological innovation 52–3

culture: working class 51–8, 67–8; *see also* values

democracy: attitudes to 67; progress of 12, 16–17; *see also* working classes, empowerment

dependence *see* independence

depressions *see* economic depressions

dialect: and populism 88, 95

dialogue: in historical interpretation 152–3

discourses: on capitalism 182–3; and experience 68–9, 89–90; and historiography 60; Labour Party 174–5, 180–1; and meaning 168; and social identity 54–7; Thatcherite 171–4, 176, 177–8; theories of 68–70

discrimination: against women 123–9; and class 127–8; *see also* gender

Durkheim, É.: on liberalism 49–50

economic conditions *see* material conditions

economic depressions: nineteenth century 29–30

economic social identity 132–3, 135

Edinburgh: labour aristocracy in 42–3, 165

empiricism: and historiography 65; *see also* historical evidence

employees *see* working classes

employers *see* labour aristocracy; middle classes

employment patterns: nineteenth century 25, 31–2, 39, 52–4

empowerment *see* Chartism; democracy; radicalism; working classes: empowerment

environment: and working class consciousness 72–3

equality: and law 58; *see also* inequality

equity: of capitalism 181; and inequality 176; *see also* inequity

events: compared to facts 157–8

evidence *see* historical evidence

experience: and discourses 89–90; and historical evidence 68–9; *see also* subjectivity

exploitation: of poor people 131–2, 133–6, 137, 141

factories: and families 52–4

facts: compared to events 157–8; *see also* historical evidence

false consciousness: concept of 163, 164, 167–8

families: and community support 135; and factories 52–4

fiction: in historical narratives 153–4, 161

Foster, J.: on Chartism 23, 70; on the linguistic approach to historiography 36; on nineteenth-century industry 28–32; on working class values 67, 70, 82

Foucault, M.: on power 2–4

franchise *see* democracy

free will *see* individualism

Gammage, R.G.: on Chartism 10

gender: and Chartism 64–5; and class analysis 80; *see also* women

Gramsci, A.: on hegemony 49, 170–1

Gray, R.Q.: on capitalism 183; on a labour aristocracy 42–4, 165; on working class values 67, 73–4, 77, 79–80

Harrison, B.: on Chartism 14

Harrison, R.: on Chartism 23; on a labour aristocracy 26–8, 33–4

hegemony: and socialism 175–6; theories of 49, 170–1; *see also* class hegemony

historical concepts: definitions of 47, 49, 50, 73

historical evidence: and contexts 150;
exclusion of 39, 41, 47, 51, 53–4,
63–4, 70, 85, 89, 121, 122, 124–5,
128, 130–1, 149, 150, 167, 168, 177,
178, 180–1, 188; and experience 68–9;
from 'ordinary' people 67, 121–4,
125–8, 130–2, 133–4, 135–7, 139–49,
167, 178–9, 189–96; and popular
agency 63–8; subjectivity of 68–71, 74,
77–80, 95–6, 132, 149–50, 177, 178;
value of 61, 149; *see also*
autobiographies; empiricism; facts;
women
historical interpretation: ambiguities in
44, 73, 79–80, 88, 94, 103–4, 121,
130, 132, 142–3; dialogue in 152–3;
and the interpretative context 32–3,
110–11, 129, 176–7, 184; irony in
154–5; limitations 122, 128;
politicization of 42, 47, 51, 58–9, 153,
156–7, 159, 162–3, 164, 171, 177,
181; and relativism 156–8; subjectivity
57–8, 65, 70; theories of 16, 153–63,
167–8, 169–70, 177
historical methodology 159–60
historical narratives: literary nature
153–4, 161; as myths 119–21, 129,
150–1, 176, 177, 181; and truth 61,
152–3
historical strategies 154
historiography: conservatism in 58, 59,
61; and discourses 60; and empiricism
65; and ideology 59; liberal 61;
linguistic approach 34–8, 54, 57, 87–8,
168–9; Marxist *see* Marxist
historiography; objectivity of 33;
objects of explanation in 163–7, 171;
and popular agency 60; post-
structuralist 51, 54, 57–8, 90; and
power 3–4; revisionist 34, 47–8, 61,
157–8, 168–70
history: aesthetic of 161–3; as a discipline
159–62; imagination in 169; rhetorical
analysis of 160; as a science 159–60;
and verification of facts 157
Hobsbawm, E.J.: on Chartism 21–2; on a
labour aristocracy 23–6, 33; on working
class empowerment 32–3
Hollis, P.: on Chartism 14
Holocaust: verification of 157–8
hosiery industry: regulation 130–2,
133–6
Hovell, M.: on Chartism 11–12

ideological control: and the labour
aristocracy 22, 23, 38, 43, 52, 67
ideology: and historiography 59
imagination: in history 169
independence: and respectability 138; and
the working classes 138, 140, 145, 146;
see also respectability
individualism: in autobiographers 105–6,
107, 112–13
individuality: and social identity 62–3,
72–3
indoor relief *see* workhouse
industrial conditions: nineteenth century
28–32
industrial development: and cultural
change 52–3
industrial disputes *see* strikes
industrial structure: nineteenth century *see*
employment patterns
inequality 176; *see also* equality; social
exclusion
inequity: structural 137; *see also* equity
intellectuals: and hegemony 170–1
interpretation: of history *see* historical
interpretation; of poverty 176–7
irony: in historical interpretation 154–5

Jones, G. Stedman *see* Stedman Jones, G.
Joyce, P.: on capitalism 182, 183; on
historical interpretation 169–70; on
poverty 177; representativeness of
evidence 85–91; on social identity 85,
90, 95, 110, 166; on social stability
166; on working class culture 51–8,
67–8; on working class values 67–8,
86–8

Kirk, N.: on linguistic approach to
historiography 36; on social stability
166; on working class consciousness
182–3; on working class values 67,
73–4, 80–5, 110–11
knitting frames: rental for 131–2

labour aristocracy: changes in role 26–7;
and class consciousness 23; and class
hegemony 42–4, 165; conservatism 24,
25; decline 25, 31; definition 23–4,
38–9; in Edinburgh 42–3, 165; and
ideological control 22, 23, 38, 43, 52,
67; liberalism 39, 43; in London 38–9;
and the middle classes 28, 32, 39,
40–1, 42, 43; and mutualism 40–1, 43;

labour aristocracy – *continued*
  thesis questioned 33–4, 38, 44, 52;
  values 39, 40–1, 43, 67; wages 24–5,
  27, 28; and the working classes 25,
  26–7, 28, 39
labour consciousness *see* working class
  consciousness
labour leaders: attitudes to strikes
  117–18; attitudes to working classes
  113–17, 118; autobiographies of
  113–19; and trade unions 114–15,
  116–17
Labour Party: discourses 174–5, 180–1
language: of radicalism 30
Laqueur, T.W.: on working class values
  44–7, 67, 70–3, 96–102
law: and equality 58
liberal historiography 61
liberalism: and class 55; of the labour
  aristocracy 39, 43; of the working
  classes 18, 44, 49–50
linguistic approach to historiography
  34–8, 54, 57, 87–8, 168–9
literacy education: effects 71–2, 73; *see also*
  Sunday school movement
literary nature: of historical narratives
  153–4, 161
literature: and populism 88; and social
  identity 56–7; *see also* ballads; dialect
London: labour aristocracy in 38–9; *see also*
  West Ham

Marxist historiography 9–10, 15, 32–3,
  58, 61, 164, 167–8, 183; criticisms 33,
  169–70; philosophy of 162; *see also*
  revisionist historiography
Marxist interpretations: of Chartism
  15–20, 21–34
material conditions: and working class
  values 72–3, 74, 75–7, 80, 82–3
Mather, F.C.: on Chartism 14
meaning: and discourses 168
mechanization *see* industrial development
middle class radicals: and Chartism 14,
  15
middle classes: appropriation of radical
  concerns 31–2; and the labour
  aristocracy 28, 32, 39, 40–1, 42, 43;
  and the working classes 48, 49, 53,
  75–7, 82–3
miners: trade unions 114–15
mutualism: and the labour aristocracy
  40–1, 43; and the working classes 17,

55–6; *see also* trade unions
myths: in historical narratives 119–21,
  129, 150–1, 176, 177, 181

narratives *see* discourses; historical
  narratives
New Poor Law: administration of 137–49,
  188–9; attitudes to 104–5; effects 18,
  35; and women 143–8; *see also*
  workhouses

objectivity: of historiography 33; *see also*
  subjectivity
objects of explanation: in historiography
  163–7, 171
older people *see* aged
Oldham: industrial conditions
  28–32
oral culture: and social identity 56–7; *see*
  also ballads
out-relief *see* New Poor Law

Palmer, B.: on the linguistic approach to
  historiography 36–7
parish relief *see* New Poor Law;
  workhouses
parliamentarians: autobiographies of
  113–19
political aspirations: of the working classes
  18, 20, 46, 50–1, 66–7
political conservatism *see* conservatism
political ideology: of Chartism 35–6,
  37
politicization: of historical interpretation
  see historical interpretation,
  politicization of
Poor Law *see* New Poor Law
poor, the: alienation of 138–49; attitudes
  to 135–6, 138–9, 140, 146, 148, 149;
  exploitation of 131–2, 133–6, 137,
  141; and respectability 148; *see also*
  poverty
popular agency: and historical evidence
  63–8 (*see also* historical evidence, from
  'ordinary' people); and historiography
  60; and social identity 62; *see also*
  autobiographies; social identity
populism: and dialect 88, 95; and
  literature 88; and respectability 67–8;
  and social identity *see* social identity,
  and populism
post-structuralist historiography 51, 54,
  57–8, 90

postmodernism 155–6, 168
poverty: attitudes to 100; in Bolton
121–5, 187–98; and inequality 176;
interpretations of 176–7; *see also* the
poor; social exclusion
power: concepts of 2–4
proletarian consciousness: compared to
working class consciousness 21
proletariat *see* working classes
proof *see* historical evidence

radicalism: changes after Chartism 23,
66–7; and Chartism 14, 15, 36; and
class 55; and class hegemony 21–2; and
consensus values 48–9; decline 30–1;
development of 48–9; language of 30;
in Oldham 28–9, 30–1; and working
class values 46; in the working classes
28–9, 30–1, 48–9, 66–7; *see also*
working classes, empowerment
reform: attitudes of autobiographers
105–6; effects on Chartism 35–6; and
the state 12, 36
reformism: as an object of explanation
163–4, 166–7; and decline of class
consciousness 23
Reid, A.: on populism 66–7
relativism: and historical interpretation
156–8
religion: and the working classes 45–6
representations: of history *see* historical
interpretation
respectability: and acceptance of the social
order 170–1; and class analysis 67–8;
definition 73; and independence 138;
and poor people 148; and populism
67–8; and social identity 67–8, 93–4;
and social stability 44–5; and the
Sunday school movement 45–7, 70–2;
and the working classes 44–51, 70,
72–3
revisionist historiography 34, 47–8, 61,
157–8, 168–70; *see also* Marxist
historiography
revolutionary class consciousness *see*
working class consciousness
rhetorical analysis: of history 160
riots: for Chartism 19–20
Rothstein, T.: on Chartism 18–20, 23
Royle, E.: on Chartism 15

salaries *see* wages
Saville, J.: on Chartism 22–3

Schiller, F. von *see* von Schiller, F.
Schwarzkopf, J.: on Chartist women
64–5
Scott, J.: the evidence of experience 68–9;
on the linguistic approach to
historiography 37–8
Select Committee into Poor Law
administration 137–49
skilled workers *see* labour aristocracy;
working classes
social exclusion: nineteenth century 93–4,
120, 130, 135–7, 143–4, 149;
twentieth century 178–80; *see also*
poverty
social identity: ambiguity in 61, 62, 63,
70, 73, 74, 76, 90, 99, 104, 105,
118–19; and class analysis 35, 60–2,
71, 74–80, 84–5, 111–12, 129, 135;
and discourses 54–7; diversity of 68,
125, 136–7; economic 132–3, 135; and
individuality 62–3, 72–3; and literature
56–7; and oral culture 56–7; and
popular agency 62; and populism 54–7,
61, 66–7, 86, 88, 90, 95, 101, 102–3,
104, 108, 110, 135, 166, 168; and
respectability 67–8, 93–4; and trade
status 27–8, 111–12, 135–7; of women
101, 109–10, 115, 122, 124, 137, 139;
see also class; popular agency
social order: acceptance of 120, 122, 123,
125–36, 140, 147, 149, 167, 170–1
social stability: as an object of explanation
164–6; and capitalism 181; causes 38,
51–2, 53, 54, 61, 73–4; interpretations
of 164–6; as a myth 181; and
respectability 44–5; and socialism 182;
see also consensus values
social structures 50–1
social support *see* community support
socialism: as an agent of hegemony 175–6;
criticisms of 172, 173–4; and the
Labour Party 174–5, 180–1; and social
stability 182; *see also* Christian socialism
songs *see* ballads
stability *see* social stability
state: and reform 12, 36
Stedman Jones, G.: on a labour aristocracy
33; on the linguistic approach to
historiography 34–7
strikes: attitudes to 117–18; Chartist 19;
see also trade unions
structural class analysis 61–2, 70
structural inequity: awareness of 137

subjectivity: of historical evidence 68–71, 74, 77–80, 95–6, 132, 149–50, 177, 178; of historical interpretation 57–8, 65, 70; *see also* experience; objectivity

Sunday school movement: and class hegemony 45; and class identity 96; development of 45; and respectability 45–7, 70–2

technological innovation *see* industrial development

Ten Hour Act 16, 31

textile industry: nineteenth century 29–30, 31–2, 52–3; regulation 130–2, 133–6

textual production: laws of 65

Thatcher, M.: on conservatism 174; on poverty 176; on socialism 172, 173–4; on Victorian values 171–3, 174, 176; *see also* Conservative Government

Thatcherite discourses 171–4, 176, 177–8

Tholfsen, T.: on capitalism 181–2, 183; on liberalism 49–50; on social stability 164–5; on working class values 44, 67, 73–7

Thompson, D.: on Chartism 15–18; and popular agency 63–4

Thompson, E.P.: on class consciousness 9; on religion 45–6

Thompson, F.M.L.: on social structures 50–1; on working class values 67, 70

trade status: and social identity 27–8, 111–12, 135–7

trade unions: development 11, 19, 28–9, 43–4, 56, 114–15, 116–17; recognition 17; *see also* mutualism; strikes

truck system 131, 132

truth: and historical narratives 61, 152–3; and power 3

unemployment: attitudes to 135–7

values: development of 42–3; of the labour aristocracy 39, 40–1, 43, 67; of the working classes *see* working classes, values; *see also* culture; respectability

Victorian values (Thatcherite) 171–3, 174, 176

vocabulary analysis *see* linguistic approach to historiography

von Schiller, F.: on aesthetic in history 161

voting patterns: of the working classes 53, 54

wages: and capitalism 24–5; nineteenth century 24–5, 27, 28, 29; stoppages from 130–2, 133–6

Walvin, J.: on Chartism 15

Ward, J.T.: on Chartism 14–15

Webb: S. and B., on Chartism 10–11, 23

welfare benefits: experiences of 178–80; principles 105, 179–80; *see also* New Poor Law; the poor; poverty; social exclusion; workhouses

West Ham: Poor Law administration in 137–49

White, H.: on historical interpretation 153–63

women: attitudes to workhouse 145, 146–7; community support for 144, 145; discrimination against 123–9; evidence from 51, 53–4, 80; and the New Poor Law 143–8; and popular agency 64–5; social identity 101, 109–10, 115, 122, 124, 137, 139

workhouses: attitudes to 138, 139, 140, 142, 145, 146–7, 148–9

working class consciousness: ambiguities in 14; awareness of 17, 135; and Chartism 8–9, 14, 15, 34, 70; compared to proletarian consciousness 21; decline 13, 23; development 28, 29, 30, 38, 60–1, 182–3; and environment 72–3; false 163, 164, 167–8; and labour aristocracy 23; *see also* trade status

working classes: attitudes to 11, 12, 39, 78, 96–7, 99, 100, 101, 102–4, 106–7, 109–10, 111, 113–17, 118; attitudes to the poor 135–6, 149; and class hegemony 45, 46, 49, 52, 70, 84–5; conservatism 34–5, 36; culture 51–8, 67–8; empowerment 20–1, 32–3 (*see also* Chartism; democracy; radicalism); idealization of 47; and independence 138, 140, 145, 146; and the labour aristocracy 25, 26–7, 28, 39; and liberalism 18, 44, 49–50; lose interest in Chartism 19, 20; and the middle classes 48, 49, 53, 75–7, 82–3; and mutualism 17, 55–6; political aspirations 18, 20, 46, 50–1, 66–7; radicalism in 28–9, 30–1, 48–9, 66–7; and religion 45–6; and trade status 27–8, 111–12, 135–7; values 44–52, 55–6, 67–8, 70–89, 96–102, 110–11,

123, 130, 143–4, 182 (*see also*
respectability; Victorian values); voting
patterns 53, 54; wages 24–5, 28, 29; *see
also* labour aristocracy; the poor
working hours: reduction in 16, 30, 31
working patterns *see* employment patterns